IOWA RAILROADS

MONTEZUMA.
ROCK ISLAND DEPOT
MONTEZUMA, IA

T0346058

EDITED BY H. ROGER GRANT

University of Iowa Press ψ Iowa City

IOWA RAILROADS

The Essays of Frank P. Donovan, Jr.

MONTEZUMA.

University of Iowa Press,
Iowa City 52242
Copyright © 2000 by the
University of Iowa Press
All rights reserved
Printed in the United States of America
Design by Richard Hendel
http://www.uiowa.edu/~uipress

Printed on acid-free paper

Library of Congress
Cataloging-in-Publication Data
Donovan, Frank P. (Frank Pierce), 1909–1970.
Iowa railroads: the essays of Frank P. Donovan, Jr. / edited by H. Roger Grant.
p.   cm.
Includes bibliographical references.
ISBN 0-87745-715-8 (cloth), ISBN 0-87745-723-9 (pbk.)
1. Railroads—Iowa—History.   2. Donovan, Frank P. (Frank Pierce), 1909–1970.
I. Grant, H. Roger, 1943–.   II. Title.
TF24.18 D66   2000
385'.09777—dc21
99-057852

00 01 02 03 04 C 5 4 3 2 1
04 P 5 4 3 2

These essays are reprinted with the gracious permission of the
State Historical Society of Iowa.

TO MILDRED MIDDLETON

A prominent Iowa educator and lifelong friend

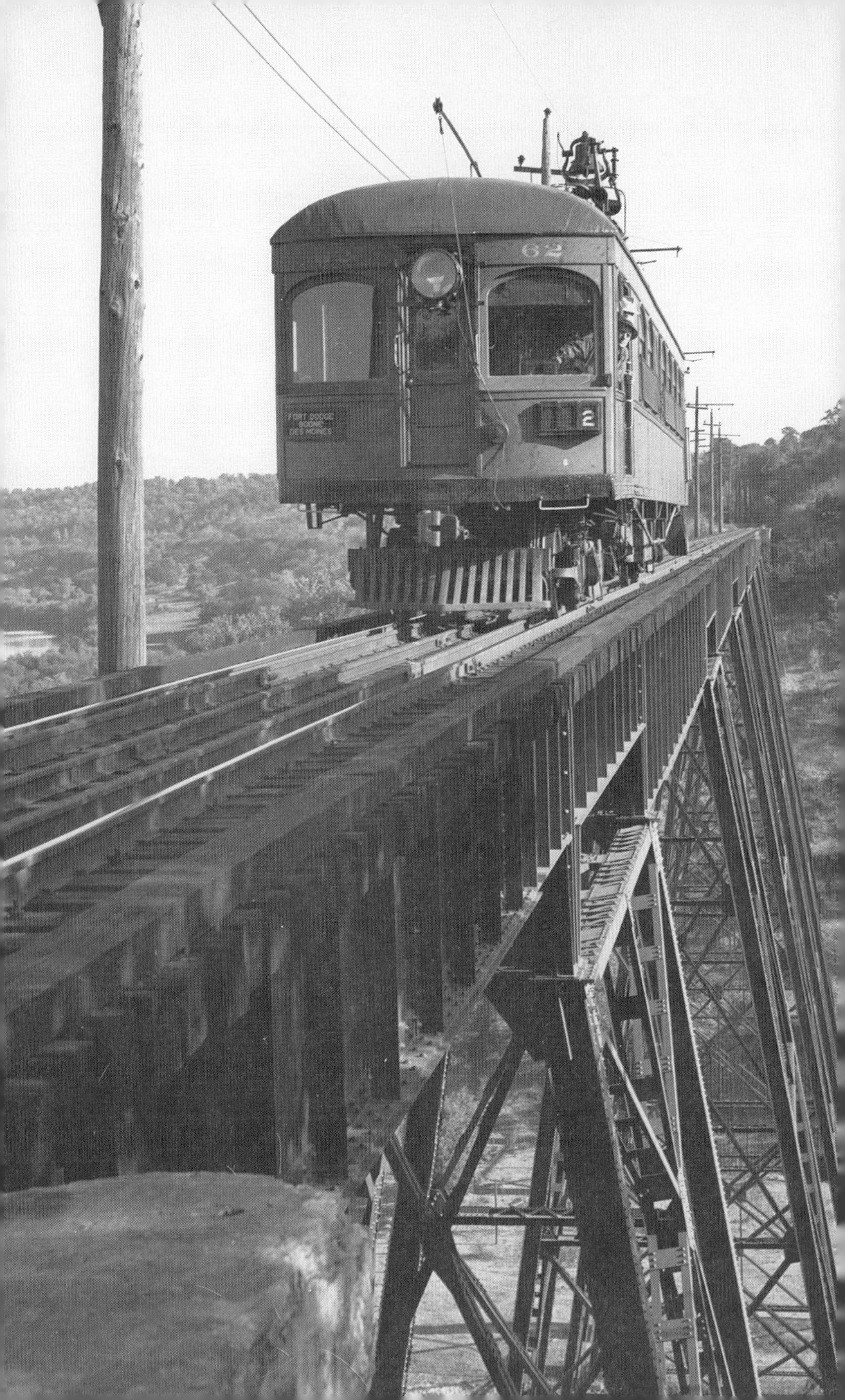
62
FORT DODGE
BOONE
DES MOINES

CONTENTS

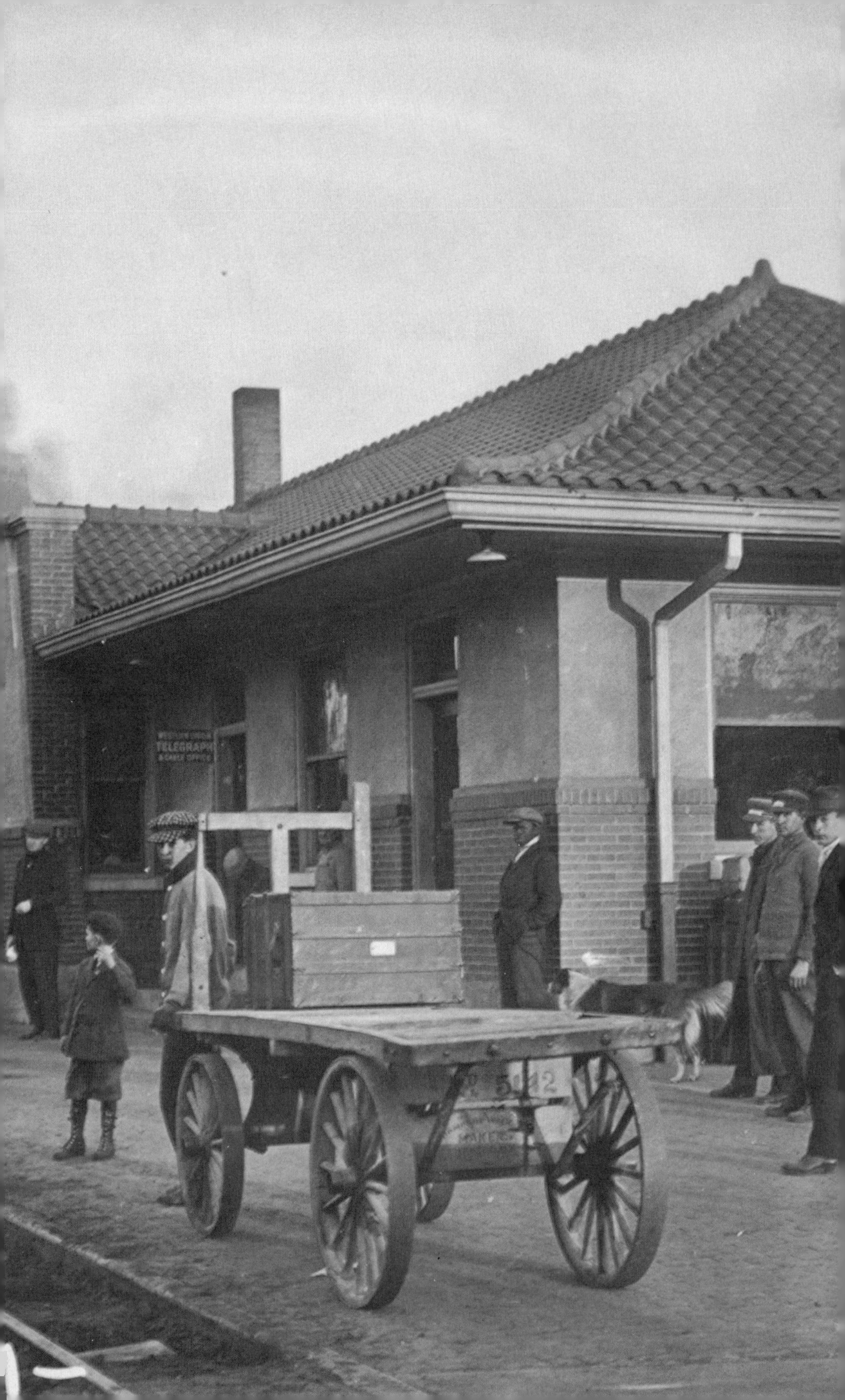
TELEGRAPH

ACKNOWLEDGMENTS

As with earlier book projects, I have received assistance from various individuals and institutions. The notes in my introduction to the Iowa railroad articles in the *Palimpsest* by Frank P. Donovan, Jr., reveal my enormous debt to friend and professional associate Don L. Hofsommer, professor of history and chair of the Department of History at St. Cloud State University in Minnesota. He provided insights into the life and labors of Donovan, critiqued my essay, and supplied rare photographs of Donovan as well as historic images of railroads in Iowa. I received help, too, from the staff of the State Historical Society of Iowa in Iowa City, especially Marvin Bergman, editor of the *Annals of Iowa,* and Ginalie Swaim, editor of *Iowa Heritage Illustrated* (the former *Palimpsest*). A colleague at Clemson University, Suzanne M. Sinke, retrieved the invaluable correspondence between Donovan and William J. Petersen, former State Historical Society of Iowa superintendent and *Palimpsest* editor. Others contributed to the preparation of the manuscript. W. Thomas White, curator of the Hill Papers at the James Jerome Hill Reference Library in St. Paul, Minnesota, located materials about Donovan. A longtime Donovan friend, Donald H. Kota, who lives in Kenosha, Wisconsin, supplied biographical information and correspondence between himself and Donovan. E. Rees Hakanson, who works for the Rail Regulation and Operations of the Iowa Department of Transportation in Ames, brought me up-to-date on Hawkeye State rails, as did Boone resident James L. Rueber, a retired dispatcher for the Chicago & North Western Railway. And the resourceful staff at the Robert M. Cooper Library at Clemson aided my research efforts.

Since illustrations are extremely important to the ten Donovan essays, I wish to thank several individuals who graciously provided photographs. They include John F. Humiston, Olympia Fields, Illinois; the late George Krambles, Oak Park, Illinois; George E. Niles, Des Moines, Iowa; and Don Snoddy, Union Pacific Railroad, Omaha, Nebraska.

Lastly, I thank my wife, Martha Farrington Grant, who reviewed my introduction. As with the previous nineteen books, she's always been my best critic.

IOWA RAILROADS

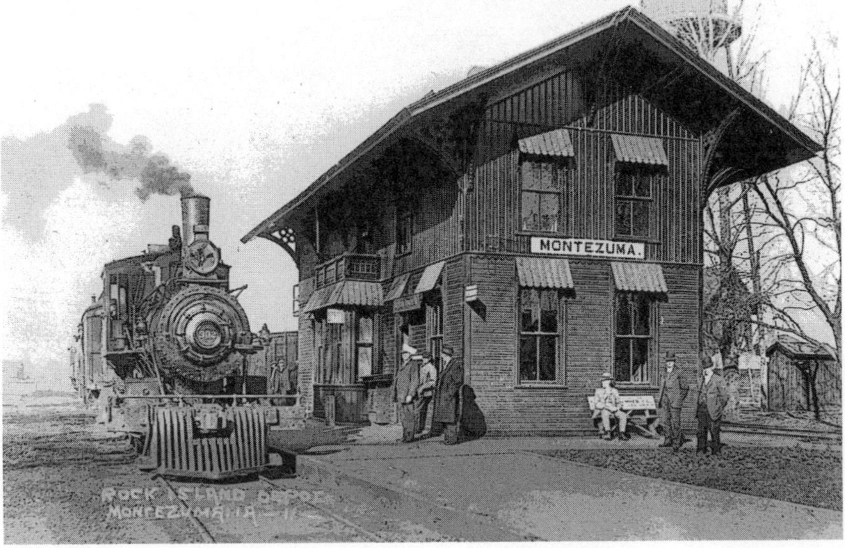
MONTEZUMA.

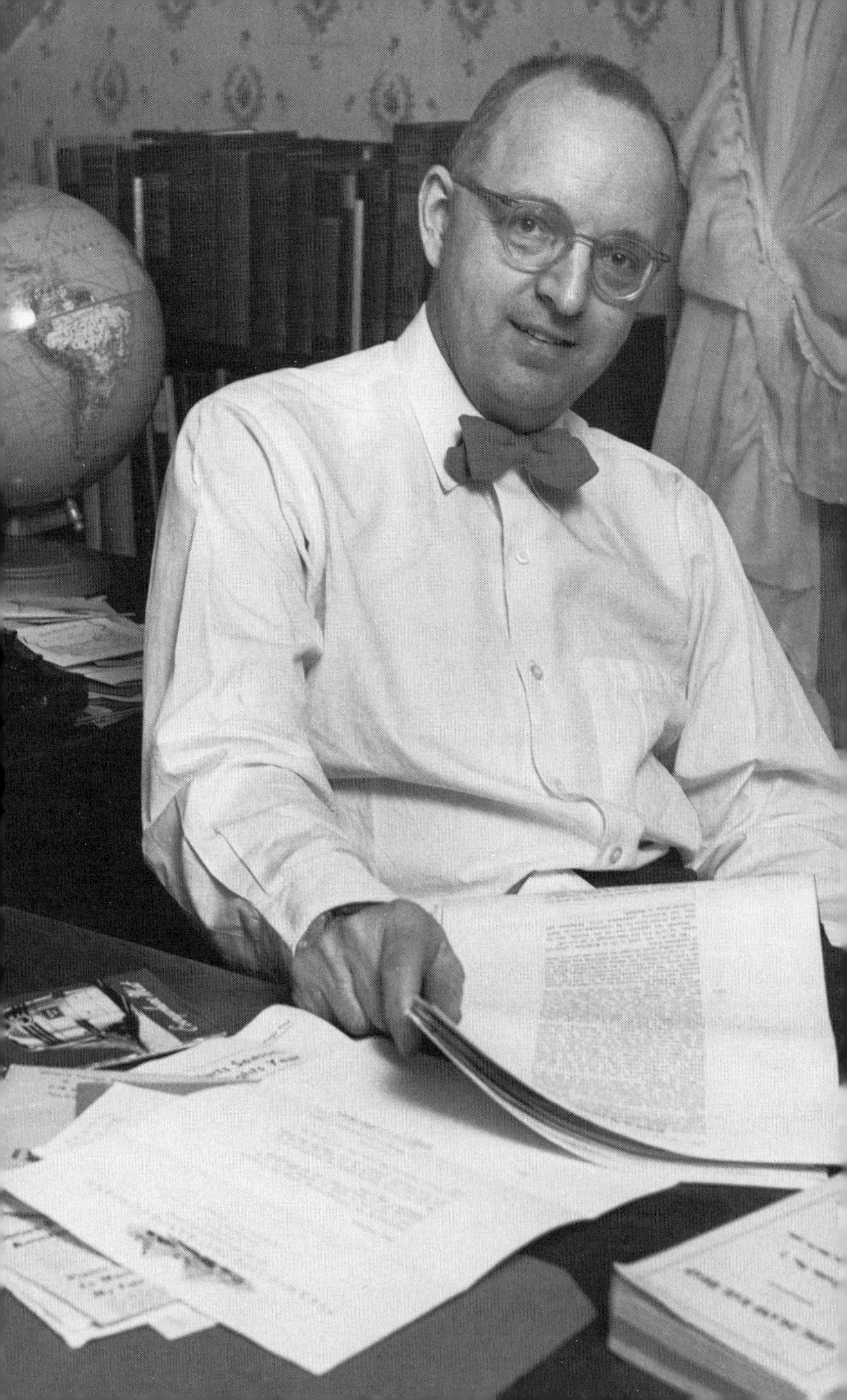

INTRODUCTION

FRANK P. DONOVAN, JR.

A talented, hardworking, and self-trained historian of American railroads was Frank Pierce Donovan, Jr. (1909–1970). During his more than thirty years of research and writing, beginning in December 1937 with publication of "A Thousand Miles by Trolley" in *Railroad Magazine*, he penned scores of transportation articles. Moreover, he was the author, coauthor, editor, or coeditor of nearly a dozen books and booklets, mostly dealing with railroading.[1]

This railroad focus, even passion, for Frank Donovan was understandable. "As a youngster he spent more time down by the freight yards than at his studies," observed an associate in 1950, "and it was said that he'd pass up a textbook any day to thumb through the *Official Guide to the Railways*." Later Donovan himself made these candid remarks about his favorite reference work: "I bought my first *Guide* in 1927. Penny for penny, it gave me deeper pleasure than any other publication I have owned. Adventure? It was more exciting than Sherlock Holmes, more romantic than Stevenson's *Treasure Island* or the classic novels by Dumas. I used to spend hours thumbing through its 1000-odd pages, dreaming of places I would see and the trains I would ride."[2]

Whenever possible, Donovan took to the rails, enjoying trips with organized groups, friends, family, or by himself. In June 1949 he described to a fellow enthusiast a recent all-day outing in Wisconsin. "Wish you could have been with Bob Adams and [me] . . . last Monday. We took the C&NW's [North Western] mixed [from Milwaukee] to Clyman Jct, then the gas-electric car to Jefferson Jct, then the Milwaukee's local to South Wye (about a mile from the Jct.). And finally the train from Mineral Point which we boarded at the Switch. Some fun!"[3]

Although a student of midwestern railroads and a longtime resident of Minneapolis, Frank Donovan moved about the country. He was born on October 4, 1909, in Wayne, Pennsylvania, a suburb of Philadelphia, and at

the age of seven his middle-class family relocated closer to the city in Wyn-
cote. It was in the City of Brotherly Love that Donovan received a largely
private education, graduating from a high school sponsored by the Society
of Friends (Quakers). During the Great Depression he spent much of his
time in college, attending Maryville College in Maryville, Tennessee, the
State University of Iowa in Iowa City, Iowa, and the American University in
Washington, D.C. In 1938 the latter institution awarded him the A.B. degree in English and Speech.[4]

Between undergraduate studies and World War II, the peripatetic Donovan lived on both coasts. In the first venue, California, his main endeavor
was graduate work, probably in English, at the University of Southern California in Los Angeles. But his activities involved more than academic studies. In order to pay tuition and living expenses he performed manual labor for the Railway Express Agency and worked as a clerk for the Pacific
Electric Railway, a giant interurban. By May 1939, however, Donovan, sans
graduate degree, had returned to the nation's capital to accept a research
position with the Public Relations Department of the Association of American Railroads, the industry's principal trade group.[5]

With the outbreak of World War II, Donovan, a devout Quaker and
strong pacifist, registered as a conscientious objector. His decision took
courage because nearly every American considered the conflict to be a
"good war," a life-or-death struggle between democracy and totalitarian-
ism. Although Donovan spent most of the war years working in a mental
health institution in Philadelphia, he apparently participated in an army
medical experiment. "[H]e was put in one of those test programs," recalls
a friend, "and was (I believe) starved to determine how a person would
react." In his spare time Donovan expressed his intense interest in transportation and his commitment to Quakerism by handling domestic travel
arrangements for the American Friends Service Committee.[6]

After peace returned, Donovan joined the staff of *Trains*, a Milwaukee-
based monthly magazine oriented toward railroad enthusiasts. At the time
of his hiring, the six-year-old publication announced that its new research
editor shared readers' interests in things associated with flanged wheels:
"It has been said that a man with a hobby is a happy man and the adage
certainly applies to Frank. His hobby is building up a railroad library and
traveling on the railroads." During his stint at *Trains* Donovan originated
the magazine's "Of Books & Trains" department, and later he edited for
the parent Kalmbach Publishing Company *Railroads of America*, which included his chapter on the Minneapolis & St. Louis Railway (M&StL).[7]

Not long after publication in 1950 of Mileposts on the Prairie, *Frank P. Donovan, Jr., traveled to the Minneapolis & St. Louis Railway station in Lake Mills, Iowa. This photograph, taken by the local Johns Studio, shows Donovan standing with retired M&StL telegrapher Charles H. Macombes at a desk once used by agent Richard Warren Sears, who subsequently founded the mail-order firm of Sears, Roebuck & Company. Don L. Hofsommer Collection.*

In the summer of 1948 Frank Donovan again changed his employment, although he was still involved with railroads. His growing railroad bibliography and his association with railroad-oriented organizations had prompted Lucian C. Sprague, the publicity conscious president of the M&StL, to hire Donovan as a "Special Representative." Donovan left *Trains* on good terms and moved to Minneapolis, home of the M&StL and also the place where during World War II he had married nurse Janice "Jan" Goerner, a native of Eureka, Missouri. His position with the M&StL likely paid much more than his earlier job and provided an opportunity to expand his list of publications. Donovan's principal assignment involved writing a popular history of the company, *Mileposts on the Prairie: The Story of the Minneapolis & St. Louis Railway*, which Simmons-Boardman published in 1950.[8]

A year or so after the appearance of the well-received M&stL history, Frank Donovan became a full-time writer-for-hire. He turned out a raft of articles, mostly on railroad topics, although in 1954 Itasca Press released his coauthored study of a Twin Cities bank, *The First through a Century, 1853–1953: A History of the First National Bank of Saint Paul.* And he repeatedly, albeit unsuccessfully, sought other major contracts, including one with the Great Northern Railway. That carrier ultimately employed Ralph Hidy, then of New York University, and his wife, Muriel, to produce its corporate history.[9]

During this period Donovan hoped that his earlier labors on the M&stL would pay additional dividends. He eagerly anticipated a lucrative sale of movie rights from *Mileposts on the Prairie* and the opportunity to consult on the film script. In July 1952 prospects seemed especially bright when Hedda Hopper, in her popular gossip column, wrote that "'Mileposts on the Prairie' by Frank Donovan, the colorful success story of Lucian C. Sprague and the Minneapolis & St. Louis Railroad, was bought by Nat Holt for a Paramount production." Hopper erred, yet for some time Donovan dreamed of dollars from Hollywood.[10]

Income from writing, whether on railroad topics or other subjects, barely allowed the Donovan family to survive financially. "It's hard at best to making a living free-lancing," he observed in January 1953. His wife, who apparently did not work outside the home, suffered from bouts of illness and their son, Robert ("Bobbie"), born in 1951, was afflicted with mental retardation and poor health. "I find I am going deeper in the hole the more I write so I'm giving it up entirely," Donovan wrote in a moment of despair in June 1954. "As for individual railroad histories [which he longed to do] the field for the independent writer is nil. Thanks to Casey and Douglas with their very poor C&NW book it has cut off the market for just about all independent writers in the company history work. Now unless you have a PhD and are affiliated with a university, especially the business history department, its [*sic*] no go. Reviews don't mean a thing; its [*sic*] all a matter of degree, connections and backing." Donovan decided that the only way to manage mounting debt was to find a job with a steady income. In October 1954 he became a caseworker for the Hennepin County Welfare Board in Minneapolis. "It is a right steady ticket (the job)." This position, moreover, provided him with an outlet for his strong religious commitment to social service.[11]

It was during the freelance years that Donovan began his long involvement with the strong-willed and powerful head of the State Historical Society of Iowa, Dr. William J. "Steamboat Bill" Petersen (1901–1989). Petersen, an expert on river steamboating, had joined the society in 1930 as a research associate after earning his doctorate from the State University of Iowa. Then in 1947 he became society superintendent and the next year editor of its widely circulated popular history magazine, the *Palimpsest*, posts he held until his retirement in 1972.[12]

Frank Donovan and William Petersen's the *Palimpsest* were a good fit. Launched in June 1920, the monthly magazine featured articles for an educated general audience rather than a professional one. Its small-size format contained only a few pieces or a single one per issue, making it unique among publications of state historical societies. The circulation was impressive, reaching about 5,000 members by the 1950s and more than 11,000 a decade later. The kind of railroad works Donovan contributed to the *Palimpsest* were designed for nonacademics; they were carefully researched and written yet unfootnoted, precisely the format that Donovan and Petersen preferred.[13]

Editor Petersen favored articles from authors like Frank Donovan. In the mid-1950s as superintendent he permitted the society's quarterly scholarly publication, the *Iowa Journal of History and Politics*, to die and then devoted much of the society's publication resources to popular history. A skilled bureaucrat and politician, Petersen saw the *Palimpsest* as a means to increase membership; to court board members, lawmakers, and other important individuals; and *always* to promote himself. This strategy worked, and by the 1960s in the minds of most Iowans "Steamboat Bill" *was* the State Historical Society of Iowa.[14]

William Petersen found Frank Donovan to be a cooperative contributor. For that matter, no one disliked Donovan; he was honest, sincere, and agreeable. "A Quaker by faith and a Quaker by practice," remembers railroad historian Don L. Hofsommer. "I never met a nicer human being." Recalls another acquaintance, "Frank's word was always his bond."[15]

Donovan possessed both common and uncommon physical characteristics. He was of average height and build, perhaps five feet, nine inches and 150 pounds and balding. And he possessed an "eager smile." Somewhat unusual for an individual of his background, he was always a "dapper dresser." In fact, during a rail enthusiast trip in 1953 on the Fort Dodge, Des Moines & Southern Railway, he wore his typical summer attire: hat, white shirt with bow tie, and lightweight sports jacket. Wrote an early railfan acquaintance, "He evidently never had enough money to be a really elegant dresser, but he always managed to have a 'touch' about his dress."

Perhaps friends and acquaintances were struck by another feature of his persona rather than dress; he stuttered. The speech abnormality worsened when he became excited, strained, or self-conscious. Fortunately, when relaxed, his speaking problem lessened. Work with speech therapists, dating from as early as 1937, helped to moderate this condition.[16]

It is not clear when Frank Donovan and William Petersen first met. Likely it happened when Donovan conducted research on the M&StL and its merger partner in 1912, the Iowa Central Railway. Petersen surely was aware of *Mileposts on the Prairie*, which the M&StL distributed widely to employees, shippers, and libraries. Still, it might have occurred at a yearly meeting of the Lexington Group, a small, active, and informal association of academics, librarians, and industry personnel interested in railroad and transportation history. Launched in May 1942 by Richard C. Overton, who later became a friend of both Donovan and Petersen, and eight other students of railroading who attended the annual gathering of the Mississippi Valley Historical Association (today's Organization of American Historians) in Lexington, Kentucky, the organization served as a clearinghouse for happenings in the field, namely who was doing what and the location of pertinent research materials.[17]

The earliest letter in the extensive Donovan-Petersen correspondence, preserved in the State Historical Society of Iowa in Iowa City, is from March 1951. In the first missive Donovan used the salutation "Dear Dr. Petersen" rather than the subsequent "Dear Bill." In that initial exchange, Donovan offered the historical society some documents from the Iowa Central that dated from the late nineteenth century and had been found in the St. Anthony, Iowa, depot on the Story City branch of the M&StL.[18]

About a week later Petersen, who greeted Donovan as "Frank," replied with an appreciative statement about "that source material on Iowa history" and added these thoughts: "I'm thinking that sometime you ought to do an issue of *The Palimpsest* for us on the M.& St.L." He suggested that "maybe it shouldn't be an entire issue, and maybe we should have sixteen pages on the M.&St.L. and sixteen on the [Chicago] Great Western." Petersen concluded by asking, "Do you know of anyone on the Great Western who could do this and would you be interested in tackling it for *The Palimpsest?*"[19]

Although Frank Donovan undoubtedly appreciated the offer to become a contributor to the *Palimpsest*, he gave a guarded response. "I must think about the bread-and-butter angle first," he wrote Petersen. "In view of the fact that I'm not sure of my next assignment I'd rather not take on writing commitments just yet. I may do a history of another road or go into some other line of work."[20]

But Petersen persisted. Surely sensing Donovan's precarious financial situation, he offered to pay for the contribution on the M&STL, tendering an inducement of $50. "This will help in no small measure in keeping the wolf from the door and at the same time would provide us with a competent, well balanced account for *The Palimpsest.*"[21]

Donovan relented. The chance of being compensated for a subject that he knew so well and loved so much prompted a quick, positive response and a rough outline of an article on the M&STL in Iowa. And he made a comment that was his hallmark: "I'd like a story or two of human interest."[22]

At the time the *Palimpsest* was unusual for a state historical publication in its willingness to pay some authors. Frank Donovan was about to join a select group who received financial compensation; most contributors received only extra copies of issues in which their articles appeared. In 1958 Petersen told Donovan bluntly: "As you know, there are darned few people who get checks from me." In a subsequent letter Petersen emphasized that "these things [articles] are largely labors of love and a writer never gets what he justly deserves measured in time and effort, when they prepare such a manuscript for a historical society." The first offer by Petersen was hardly a token gesture. Adjusted to 1999 dollars, the $50 amount exceeded $325 in buying power. And when Petersen concluded that he would dedicate the entire thirty-two-page issue to the M&STL, he duly increased payment to $100, making such a contribution even more attractive to the impecunious Donovan.[23]

Frank Donovan received remuneration for each publication in the *Palimpsest.* His span of writing ran for nearly twenty years, from 1951 to 1969, and included the core ten articles on Iowa's railroads: the "Big Four" carriers (Burlington, Milwaukee Road, North Western, and Rock Island) and the "Little Three" (Great Western, Illinois Central, and M&STL), as well as Hawkeye State roads of lesser importance (Wabash, Great Northern–Santa Fe–Union Pacific), and the electric interurbans. Donovan contributed additional railroad articles, ones on the Iowa Railway Historical Museum; on Harry Bedwell (1888–1955), an Iowa-born writer of railroad fiction; and on the Manchester & Oneida Railway (M&O), an eight-mile short line in Delaware County. Donovan also wrote one nonrailroad-related article, a study of Robert J. Burdette (1844–1914), an American humorist and sometime resident of Burlington, Iowa. The rate of payment in the 1950s was customarily $100 for the standard thirty-two printed pages. However, an extremely pleased Petersen authorized a somewhat larger check for Donovan's contribution on the Chicago Great Western. When Donovan wrote sixty-four-page "double" articles, as he did in 1962 on the North Western, compensation reached $200. Petersen, too, occasionally agreed to pay for maps, but this money usually went to individuals whom Donovan engaged for those cartographic assignments. Then in the 1960s, likely as a response to Donovan's good performance and cooperative attitude and the impact of inflation, Donovan received $200 for standard-length pieces and $300 for longer ones. Still, in 1964 Petersen told Donovan that for his work on the Wabash Railroad, "You are getting a check for $200 which is really higher than I normally plan for a 32-page [standard] article."[24]

Donovan received other considerations. Petersen generously provided complimentary copies of the *Palimpsest*. Rather than the usual fifteen or twenty, he customarily supplied thirty-five or fifty, at times even more, and Donovan could always acquire additional ones at cost. Petersen repeatedly provided mailing envelopes and postage stamps so that Donovan could send issues to individuals who helped him with research or loaned illustrations or who might promote his writing career. When Donovan agreed in March 1957 to examine the M&O, Petersen facilitated the research process. The society recently had obtained the road's records, and Petersen permitted Donovan to work in the historical society, located in Schaeffer Hall on the University of Iowa campus, after hours and on weekends. Petersen told Donovan that "I am going to have all of the material [on the M&O] set out methodically so you can begin analyzing it on you [*sic*] arrival. I will have paper and typewriter down there so you need have no delay setting to work." Petersen suggested that Donovan stay in the nearby Burkley Hotel, and Donovan readily agreed, opting for the $1.50 a night room without bath rather than a more expensive one with such amenities. Since Donovan disliked to drive, he planned to travel from Minneapolis to Iowa City by rail, and Petersen agreed to take him to Manchester. Donovan rightly wanted to interview former M&O officials, employees, and "local folk" and to view the remains of this carrier that had ceased operations six years earlier. "In a grass roots railroad history one must get the feel of the country and know something of its folkways." Petersen heartily endorsed the Donovan strategy.[25]

Even though Frank Donovan lacked credentials and training as a professional historian, his research activities resembled those of other academics. When conducting work on Iowa railroads, he examined "standard" primary sources, including *Poor's Manual of Railroads*, trade publications, annual reports, newspapers, timetables, and brochures. Donovan also used the obvious secondary book and article literature, especially corporate histories and individual biographies.[26]

Although some contemporary historians shared his interest in social history, Donovan relished the opportunity to discuss the experiences of common people. At the time he would have been labeled a "pots and pans" historian, a denigrating term that he would have gladly accepted. When Donovan included material that might be judged as colorful or episodic, he usually tried to relate it to the larger story or to illustrate a particular trend or event.

Unlike most professional business or railroad historians, Donovan repeatedly sent carbon copies of his article manuscripts to industry personnel. When he researched the electric interurbans then operating in Iowa, he not only sent a draft of his narrative to an appropriate official for comments, but he enclosed specific questions. In a letter to Sutherland Dows, president and general manager of the Cedar Rapids & Iowa City Railway (Crandic), he posed these queries: "When did the Cedar Rapids–Lisbon branch cease running? How many locomotives were built in your Cedar Rapids shops by John Munson? I know of one; were there more? How heavy are your new rails and in the relaying program have you entirely replaced the joints opposite each other or have you still some stretches of track with this almost-unique feature?"[27]

Frank Donovan discovered that his research strategy of mailing text and queries to industry personnel could be frustrating, although naively he never seemed to question the reliability of their responses. Some railroaders cooperated more than others. In the case of President Dows, after much prodding an underling at the Crandic answered the queries. At the close of the interurban study, Donovan told Petersen, "I am very happy to get this off my chest as it entailed an immense amount of research and I suppose the writing of 100 letters. Most of the difficulty stemmed from no-help from the carriers or slow-help, very slow, indeed. What a job!"[28]

Even if at times Donovan found his assignments for the *Palimpsest* frustrating and exhausting, he established a successful pattern of work. After he became a full-time social worker, his discretionary moments were limited. When he received the green light to prepare studies of the North Western, Rock Island, and Milwaukee, he revealed to Petersen that he expected to complete the projects in a few months. "Barring unforseen circumstances such as sickness, etc., I'll work on the series every night, except Sunday, and all day Saturday." Occasionally, after attending a Quaker meeting, he worked on Sunday.[29]

It would be on Saturdays that Frank Donovan likely left his modest house on West 45th Street in Minneapolis, with its rooms and hallways lined with books and a cluttered, cramped upstairs study, to visit the James Jerome Hill Reference Library in downtown St. Paul. Using public transportation, often including trains, he explored the card catalog and wandered the stacks of this well-endowed business-oriented public library and carried volumes to his upper-floor carrel. In June 1953 Donovan informed Petersen that "I'm hard at work on 'Iowa Interurbans' and have a stack of *Street Railway Journals* and *Electric Railway Journals* eight feet wide on shelves of my room in the Hill Reference Library."[30]

When working at home Donovan utilized his extensive library of books and reference works and continually added to his holdings. He did more than buy new and used books, he frequented shops that offered railroad ephemera, including the well-known Owen Davies Book Store in Chicago. Donovan especially liked public timetables, name-train folders, and promotional brochures and posters. He found them to have an intrinsic beauty and considerable utilitarian value. And he read what he acquired, developing an impressive knowledge of railroads and their impact upon American life.[31]

Frank Donovan worked hard at his writing. He made several drafts of each piece, a process his superb typing skills made somewhat easier. As an interviewer reported shortly before Donovan's death, where Donovan revealed the challenges of this craft, "[It] is very hard work for [Donovan] . . . and every time he writes something he promises himself, 'never again.'" But that was not the case; Donovan derived great satisfaction from a published article or book.[32]

At first glance, the ten major railroad articles that Frank Donovan wrote for the *Palimpsest* between 1951 and 1969 appear to be part of an organized sequence. The opposite, in fact, is the case. Although the first two contributions, ones on the M&STL and Chicago Great Western, were instigated by Superintendent Petersen, the third, the electric interurban piece, was Donovan's suggestion.

A conversation between Frank Donovan and Arthur P. Wheelock, president of the Fort Dodge, Des Moines & Southern Railway, likely inspired the interurban study. Wheelock indicated that he wanted a brief history of his electric road, and this appealed to Donovan. Although Donovan originally contemplated a self-published booklet, he decided that a *Palimpsest* article would be more practical.[33]

Once the interurban issue appeared, Petersen took the initiative. "Here's hoping we can set you to work on something else that will be of interest during the coming year." Donovan happily responded with the suggestion of a study of Iowa native Ralph Budd, well known for his tenure as president of the Burlington Railroad and a highly respected spokesperson for the industry. "Budd is a fine person in every way," Donovan told Petersen, "and I believe he is almost as outstanding an Iowan as Herbert Hoover." But Petersen had other plans. "I'll readily admit that Ralph Budd is one of Iowa's outstanding men, deserving to be ranked with Herbert Hoover. But I believe Dick Overton of Northwestern University should be given an opportunity since he worked so close to Budd for a number of years and would have certain advantages along that line."[34]

Petersen's position on a Budd article disappointed Donovan, yet he understood that Richard Overton, the foremost student of the Burlington and a leading scholar of American railroads, probably should have the privilege of first refusal. Later, however, Donovan suggested that Overton was not necessarily the right person for a *Palimpsest* assignment. "I think Dick Overton favors out-and-out business histories rather than popular works regardless of how well they are done as informal stories."[35]

On June 22, 1954, a more positive letter came from Iowa City. Petersen told Donovan that "I appreciate your three contributions to *The Palimpsest* and if my Illinois Central friend (Corliss) [Carlton Corliss] doesn't get a wiggle on him I had planned to turn that assignment over to you." The superintendent added: "That would take care of our short line railroads and leave only the Big Four."[36]

Still, Donovan and Petersen lacked an agenda for studies on Iowa railroads. Donovan responded to Petersen's thoughts about an Illinois Central piece in this fashion: "Thanks for your toying with the idea of giving me the Illinois Central issue work but I do not think it is feasible. It would mean several weeks in Chicago going over the records and the expense of living in the Windy City would eat up all the profits." And there was deference to author Corliss, the leading authority on the Illinois Central: "Carl Corliss I'm sure will do a wonderful job when he gets the time. His IC book is a fine product."[37]

Superintendent Petersen wanted an Illinois Central study. When he concluded that Carlton Corliss would not be able to make a contribution to the *Palimpsest*, Petersen told Donovan, expecting him to volunteer. But this did not immediately happen. Rather, Donovan asked Petersen to consider a nonrailroad assignment, a history of William Penn College, a struggling Quaker institution of higher education in Oskaloosa, Iowa. "Being a Friend and very familiar with that Quaker school, a talk before its student body, I think the subject would be right down my alley." Petersen did not agree, bluntly responding: "I think a Penn College article would be out of your line. You wouldn't have access to the historical material available for it . . . [and if] you had a Penn background you would be in a much better position so I would urge you to choose some other topic."[38]

That other subject needed to be a railroad one, and for Petersen it remained the Illinois Central. "That certainly is one railroad that ought to be done in our publication." Still, Donovan failed to yield to Petersen's wishes. In time, though, he and Petersen would have a meeting of the minds. But a new topic burst upon the scene. When the superintendent in March 1957 wrote that "we have recently come into possession of all the materials on the old M&O Railroad," it did not take long before Donovan enthusiastically plunged head-first into the study of this recently abandoned Hawkeye short line.[39]

Petersen's promotion of the M&O study, which appeared in the September 1957 *Palimpsest*, however, tested the relationship between editor and author. Although the M&O issue elicited positive reader comments, Donovan badgered Petersen to accept a plan that he believed would result in "a small profit" for both author and society. Donovan requested a printing of five hundred extra copies that he could have bound and then sell. And he wanted a number of things from Petersen: "1. Put title and author on outside front cover leaving off all other material except photos and caption. 2. On contents page take off *Palimpsest* notes but leave general contents with an additional note that book is a reprint of September 1957 *Palimpsest*. 3. Page consecutively and take out "Palimpsest" on first page and each succeeding left-hand page." Peterson agreed, although he told Donovan that "we retain the copyright in the article. We are making no investment in the book beyond the printing of the extra copies with the changed folio lines and pagination." And he added, "Our Society will not be interested in distributing unused surplus at 25 cents. It will not have *Palimpsest* pagination, etc. Hence, this would be your investment; and profit or loss as the case may be."[40]

Once Donovan got the unbound copies of his M&O work, he made a number of additional requests. One was this: "If agreeable to you I will indicate, with all the review copies, that the book may be had from the historical society at $2.00. This will be a permanent, stable address as I suppose the book will be selling for several years." In a later letter he asked that the society have the work copyrighted as a book, "this will . . . give it greater prominence since LC cards will be printed and it will be officially listed in the Library of Congress." Petersen consented and truly hoped that Donovan, always hard-pressed for funds, would make financial gains, but he told him that "one thing is certain, however. I don't want to enter into another—what shall we say—extracurricular type of activity like this again. There's too much nuisance value to it." Eventually, both the society and Donovan made a modest profit from this venture.[41]

Soon after publication of the M&O article, Donovan indicated to Petersen that he planned to write a biographical sketch of Harry Bedwell and expected it to be a future issue of the *Palimpsest*. At first Petersen expressed little enthusiasm. "It's an obscure connection [Bedwell and Iowa] and not too important for our membership." He then told Donovan that "I would be much more interested in a story of a railroad such as the Illinois Central." But Donovan persisted. "And now about the Harry Bedwell theme. Can you let me know one way or the other on this if you want a *Palimpsest* story on Bedwell? When you phoned . . . I understood you to say the theme was acceptable if (a) it had an adequate Iowa background . . . ; (b) article to be held to 32 pp." He added, "I took a week off to get the Iowa background; and will see that the ms. is held to 32 pages of *Palimpsest* copy." Then Donovan explained his feelings in greater detail:

> I may have crowded you on this when your mind was on the M&O proof but it was not intentional. I just wanted to start on the research while Bedwell's kin were living; one close friend of his died about a fortnight before you phoned me. I really feel this is good Americana (and it will have one full chapter on Bedwell's boy- and early manhood in the state) as he was the last "great" railroad fiction writer and marked an end of an era. . . . I've been getting letters from all over the country on him, including photos, as a result of my letter-writing and visit to southern Iowa. . . . I'll try not to bother you about any more books, articles and the like for quite a spell.[42]

Superintendent Petersen relented, quickly responding: "If you got quite a bit done and considerable investment, I'll certainly consider taking it over from you. I don't want you to lose anything and actually the story may surprise us and be even better than the railroad [Illinois Central] story." He concluded with these words of encouragement: "So go ahead on the project, limiting it to 32 pages, and I'll try to do well by you."[43]

Although "Harry Bedwell—Railroad Raconteur" graced the pages of the May 1958 issue of the *Palimpsest*, an Illinois Central article remained missing from the series, and then there was the "Big Four." Donovan, however, had other railroad topics in mind. "It occurred to me you might like an issue on 'The Rise and Fall of the Country Depot,'" he told Petersen on June 26, 1958. "Theme would only cover Iowa and besides bringing in the folkways and life about the rural railroad station it would give some characteristics of depot architecture, trends in design, a back-drop on the station restaurants and lunch counters, etc."[44]

Petersen responded positively but with a warning: "The story of the old depot might make a very interesting yarn and I would be interested in it only if I could have your assurance that you would not propose to have it reprinted in book form." Petersen vividly recalled the aggravation caused by the M&O project. And he had his own thoughts about a noncorporate railroad study. "[O]ne idea I've had, with a little work done on it, has been the story of the caboose in Iowa history. That would make quite a story and of course if you are working around on depots you might have in mind this matter of the caboose itself."[45]

Neither the depot nor the caboose projects progressed beyond the discussion stage. In August 1958 the ever-creative Donovan suggested an issue of the *Palimpsest* on the activities of the Iowa Railway Historical Museum and the affiliated Iowa Chapter of the National Railway Historical Society. Although lukewarm to the topic, Petersen, who always needed popular pieces for his monthly publication, grudgingly agreed, and the article appeared in October 1959.[46]

Donovan once more told Petersen that he wanted to contribute several nonrailroad manuscripts, including one on Wendell Johnson, an Iowa City speech pathologist, and another on Frank Luther Mott, the Iowa-born Pulitzer Prize–winning historian and professor of journalism at the University of Missouri. Petersen rejected these proposals. In the case of Mott, he wrote: "I don't think a sketch of Frank Luther Mott is in your line. He is a close personal friend of mine and eventually if anything is done on *The Palimpsest* on him I certainly would want to do that myself." Again he urged Donovan to focus on railroad pieces, particularly company ones.[47]

In April 1961 Donovan, who finally had convinced Petersen to permit him to prepare a biographical sketch of humorist Robert Burdette, wrote that "I want to assure you I have no intention of giving up railroad assignments for the *Palimpsest*. Indeed I am prepared to gather material on an article concerning the railroad station in Iowa and the part it played in the social, economic and cultural life of the town people." He also shared several thoughts about the Illinois Central: "I'd rather let it go for a time as I am reluctant to cross wires with Corliss. I worked under him in the Association of American Railroads and I'm afraid it could hurt his feelings. He knows the IC history better, perhaps, than any man alive."[48]

Frustrated by the dimming prospects of an article on the Illinois Central, in July 1961 Petersen asked Donovan if he knew of anyone other than Carlton Corliss who could write about the road. At last, for whatever reasons, Donovan volunteered. A delighted and generous Petersen offered to pay $300 for a maximum of forty-eight pages and "also $25 for any art work you may contract for so you won't be out of pocket there."[49]

The green light from Donovan caused Petersen to plan articles on the remaining Iowa railroads. "Dick Overton has promised to do the Burlington . . . and we might get our Rock Island friend [William Edward Hayes?] to do it. I think it would be grand if you would think in terms of the Chicago & North Western as a possible next and the Milwaukee as a third story." Petersen logically suggested that "you could be collecting on both while working on the IC."[50]

The strategy for the three railroad articles pleased Donovan. "I'll continue working on the Illinois Central piece and keep my eyes open for material on the North Western and the Milwaukee Road. In short I'll spend the next twelve months or so thinking about these roads, working on material and generally devoting my spare time to the articles."[51]

Even though the Iowa railroad projects gave Donovan much to do and guarantees for additional income, he kept proposing nonrailroad ones, much to the annoyance of Petersen. In October 1961 he wrote: "Bill, I've got what I think is a corking good theme and a very timely subject for you. It's the filming of the 'The Music Man.' This is a million dollar motion picture which should be almost to Iowa as the musical 'Oklahoma' was to its namesake." And he had given the structure of the essay some thought. "I would have half of the article on the filming of 'The Music Man' and the pains they took to capture the Mason City setting circa 1912. The second half of the piece would concern [Meredith] Willson's boyhood in Mason City and his subsequent fame as a song writer, composer and orchestra leader." Petersen fired back a turgid reply: "The Music Man is old stuff. I don't think that we could compete with newspapers and cover magazines in a project of this kind."[52]

Once again Donovan returned to his knitting. By April 1962 he had completed the manuscript on the Illinois Central, and soon he focused on the North Western. On September 30, 1962, Donovan happily informed Petersen that "my Chicago & North Western article is just about done and it runs to 48 double-spaced, *Palimpsest*-size pages." Petersen responded:

"Get right to work on the Milwaukee and Rock Island—and it would be easier to do the research on both at the same time."[53]

By November 1962 plans for the remaining articles on Hawkeye State rails had mostly fallen into place. Donovan suggested this arrangement:

The Milwaukee In Iowa (64 pages; now being undertaken)

The Rock Island In Iowa (64 pages; now being undertaken)

The Burlington In Iowa (64 pages)

The Wabash In Iowa (32 pages)

Iowa's Railroads: The Santa Fe; the Great Northern; the Union Pacific. (all three combined into a 32-page issue.) [54]

The progression, however, varied somewhat. Donovan finished his study of the Rock Island before the Milwaukee Road, and he did not tackle the Burlington until the end of the series. Donovan wanted Richard Overton, the foremost authority on the "Q," to decide if he would pen the work, and Petersen agreed. Indeed, in March 1965, when Donovan finished the ninth article on Iowa carriers, the piece on the Great Northern, Santa Fe, and Union Pacific, he commented, "Guess this ends up our RR series in Iowa." But Overton declined to produce the Burlington issue, and Donovan gladly assumed the responsibility. On May 11, 1969, Donovan sent Petersen a detailed chapter outline, and with publication in September 1969 of "The Burlington in Iowa" the series finally ended.[55]

The timing of the last railroad article for the *Palimpsest* was fortuitous for Petersen and readers of the *Palimpsest*. Not long thereafter Donovan's health declined rapidly. On September 7, 1970, a malignant brain tumor caused his death at age sixty in a Minneapolis hospital. Consistent with his religious convictions, the body was willed to the University of Minnesota Medical School. Although the Donovan family, including his wife, son, and brother, hosted a brief open house, there was no formal memorial service.[56]

Long before his death Frank Donovan hoped that his essays on Iowa railroads would appear in book form. As early as March 7, 1953, he posed this question to William Petersen: "What about a volume titled *Iowa's Railroads* being articles on the major roads of the state which have appeared or will appear in the *Palimpsest*?" Volunteered Donovan, "I'd like to edit such a collection and I would be willing to write a preface which would integrate all the chapters or selections. It also should have a complete index which I could do too." Petersen expressed receptiveness. "I'm already ahead of you on a volume entitled *Iowa's Railroads*. Indeed this is the very reason why I am having these issues."[57]

Even though Petersen seemingly favored the project, nothing happened, probably because of other interests at the State Historical Society. This inaction prompted Donovan in July 1961 to remark, "I'd very much like to see a book on the railroads of Iowa . . . as I think it would be a valuable reference work and of [*sic*] permanent source of information." Again Donovan wanted to be involved. "If the Society gets out such a volume could I act as editor or co-editor for it would be nice to have my stuff in a permanent form along with others laboring in the same vineyard." Petersen failed to comment, and soon Donovan repeated his wish to edit an Iowa railroad book. Finally, the superintendent responded: "If we could ever get all these railroads together, I'd be tempted to put them in book form under several authors' names. . . . In other words, it could very well be you in the major role, [Richard] Overton, and myself."[58]

No more was mentioned about the Iowa railroad book until November 1962. With Donovan's work on several carriers in progress, Petersen indicated that "once completed . . . we can start thinking in terms of wrapping the whole story up in possible book form." Clearly, he wanted Richard Overton, not Donovan, to write an issue on the Burlington and, considering Petersen's ego, he likely contemplated serving as editor-in-chief of the proposed project. If Donovan, Overton, and Petersen were equal co-authors, the customary listing would be alphabetical, and Petersen's name would be last. And that would be unacceptable to the superintendent.[59]

After January 1963 discussion of the railroad book ended, although Petersen gave lip service to such a volume. "I want to canvass the whole situation of developing a book using this material [*Palimpsest* articles], plus additional data that might be added to the articles themselves." But with Donovan's death and the society's lack of interest in book publications, prospects of a rail title diminished. Also increasing conflict between some members of the academic community and Petersen over access to collections, publication strategies, and personality issues doomed a collection of popular railroad history pieces.[60]

IOWA RAILROADS SINCE 1970

If the collection of *Palimpsest* railroad articles by Frank P. Donovan, Jr., had appeared in book form during his lifetime, an appropriate introduction would surely have been provided. But that portion of the volume would have rapidly become outdated. In the three decades since Donovan's

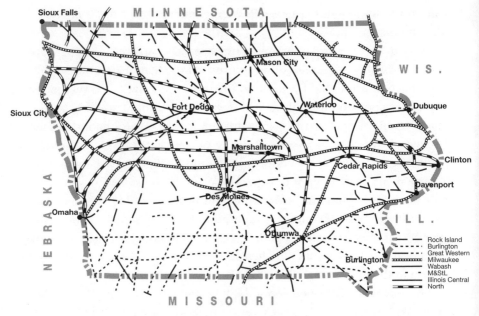

Map 1. Steam Railroads in Iowa, ca. 1930. Courtesy Sam Girton.

death, the Iowa railroad scene has changed enormously. A combination of events, including massive line abandonments, corporate mergers, regulatory reforms, and technological betterments, have reconfigured an industry that Donovan would find difficult to recognize. In the 1950s and 1960s no one correctly predicted the scope of change nationally or in the Hawkeye State by the end of the twentieth century.

If Donovan were to roam the Iowa landscape today, he would be struck by the plethora of stripped railroad grades. Since 1970 an orgy of abandonments has occurred. In 1968 mileage stood at 8,225 miles, but by 1985 it had plunged to 3,646 miles. Since then additional trackage has been retired, making Iowa a state with one of the greatest declines in rail service.[61]

Why has the railroad map of Iowa contracted so dramatically? The reasons are several. For one thing, "merger madness" affected trackage. By the late 1990s *every* railroad serving the state had been involved in at least one corporate union and some in several. The major carriers became the Union Pacific (née North Western and Minneapolis & St. Louis) (1,675 miles) and the Burlington Northern & Santa Fe (673 miles); the former in 1995 acquired the Chicago & North Western and the latter, a product of the 1970 fusion of the Burlington, Great Northern and Northern Pacific (Burlington Northern), in 1997 merged with the Atchison, Topeka & Santa Fe. Thus two, rather than seven, railroads dominate Iowa.[62]

Mergers promoted line cutbacks as hundreds of miles became redundant. Examples abound. When in 1968 the Chicago & North Western acquired the Chicago Great Western, the expanded carrier upgraded some former Great Western trackage but quickly downgraded or abandoned many more miles. Later, in 1983, the North Western acquired the 430-mile Kansas City–Twin Cities "Spine Line" of the bankrupt Rock Island and then proceeded to rip up most of its former connection to the Kansas City gateway, namely the ex-Great Western route between Marshalltown, Iowa, and St. Joseph, Missouri. This abandonment meant the disappearance of the last long segment of the "Great Weedy" in Iowa.[63]

Even if mergers had not swept Iowa railroading, increased modal competition resulted in reduced traffic and earnings on many branch, secondary, and even main lines, making them candidates for abandonment. By the 1980s the network of national interstate highways, launched in 1956, neared completion. Moreover, the state's primary and secondary highway system continued to improve with additional miles of hard-surfaced roads, more routes sporting multiple lanes, and bypasses skirting county seats and other metropolises. These roadways attracted larger and more powerful motor vehicles. Rail lines that served scattered grain elevators, fertilizer distribution centers, and lumberyards faced replacement by trucks that could provide convenient and dependable service.[64]

Since Donovan's time the regulatory milieu, reflecting changes in patterns of transport, has become more conducive to railroad companies that wished to trim trackage, even if they had not recently experienced merger. Although the Transportation Act of 1958 made line abandonments somewhat easier than in earlier years, the process still required considerable effort. Ben W. Heineman, head of the Chicago & North Western, for one, thought it best for his company to retain appendages, dispatching occasional way freights to serve remaining customers. "Mr. Heineman believed that political hassles in the 1960s were still too great to seek the abandonments that the company really needed," observed an associate.[65]

In 1980 a new era dawned for railroads that sought to pursue aggressively "line rationalization." Congress passed and President Jimmy Carter signed the Staggers Act. This landmark measure brought about partial deregulation and also made abandonments easier. Iowa railroads, including the North Western, seized this opportunity to shed hundreds of miles of unwanted trackage.[66]

Immediately prior to the Staggers Act Iowa railroads were rapidly drifting toward disaster. By the late 1970s several dominant carriers were in dire financial straits. In December 1977 the Milwaukee Road entered bank-

ruptcy following three years of heavy losses. Eight years later a greatly truncated Milwaukee joined the Soo Line. The Milwaukee had made an extensive reduction in its Iowa plant; for example, no longer did trains rumble
over the length of its main trans-Iowa line where just a few years earlier
streamliners had traveled. Although the Chicago & North Western managed to avoid bankruptcy, in part because of innovative leadership and
injections of federal funds derived from the Railroad Revitalization and
Regulatory Reform Act (4R Act) of 1976, the Rock Island was not so lucky.
A paucity of capital, deteriorating track and rolling stock, increased modal
competition, lack of a merger partner, and other factors in 1975 pushed
the "Rock" into its final bankruptcy. Chicago industrialist Henry Crown,
who since 1946 had been speculating in Rock Island securities, decided
that the road was worth more dead than alive. His considerable influence led to the railroad's shutdown on March 31, 1980, and to its profitable liquidation.[67]

The long-term impact of the Staggers Act on Iowa has meant a profitable existence for the surviving companies. They can now negotiate rates
with shippers and offer them rebates for guaranteed traffic volume, therefore providing a predictable traffic base. With more money in the till, railroads can afford expensive technological betterments, further strengthening their competitive position. New rolling stock, including more efficient
and powerful diesel-electric locomotives and container or "stack" equipment, have become commonplace on mega-roads Burlington Northern &
Santa Fe Railway (BNSF) and Union Pacific. Computers and satellite communications have also proliferated, making artifacts of older technologies
museum pieces.

The railroad renaissance has occurred, too, because of more favorable
union work rules. The notorious acts of featherbedding, so widespread
among train crews and station personnel during Donovan's time, have
vanished. Two- rather than five-person train crews have become the norm,
and additional employees have been cut because of the closing of country
stations, towers, and most division offices. This sizable contraction of the
workforce has resulted in the virtual disappearance of both the caboose
and the depot.[68]

Another remarkable change has been massive corporate restructuring.
Although mega-mergers grabbed the news headlines, the appearance of
spin-off companies has greatly altered the complexion of railroads in Iowa.

Several relatively large spin-offs have emerged. These are known in industry circles as regionals, or as the Association of American Railroads de-

fines them: "A non-Class I line-haul railroad which operates 350 or more miles of line and/or which earns [annual] revenues of at least $40 million." In the 1980s and 1990s the giants happily sold portions of their lines that generated disappointing earnings or that failed to fit with the rest of their systems. The champion creator of regionals nationally has been the Illinois Central Gulf Railroad (later renamed Illinois Central). In December 1985 the company disposed of its trackage west of Chicago, including the main stems to Omaha, Nebraska, and Sioux City, Iowa. The new regional, the 798-mile Chicago, Central & Pacific Railroad (CC&P) (558 miles in Iowa), selected Waterloo, Iowa, as its headquarters. Although the CC&P experienced both good and bad times, in 1998 the former parent reacquired its "westend," an unusual fate for a new-breed regional. And as the decade ended, the Illinois Central joined the Canadian National Railway in still one more corporate marriage.[69]

At the time the CC&P trackage reentered the Illinois Central, another regional railroad made its debut. In 1997 an investor group that earlier had launched one of America's largest regionals, Montana Rail Link, created I&M Rail Link. This 1,386-mile regional operates trackage that once was part of the Milwaukee's sprawling system, including 655 miles in Iowa. The mileage consists in part of the former Kansas City extension and what was called the Corn Lines, which extend from the Iowa towns of Marquette west through Mason City to Sheldon and from Mason City to the Minnesota communities of Austin and Jackson. In the mid-1980s a smaller Milwaukee (Milwaukee II) offered itself for sale. In the bidding war that followed, the Soo Line won, paying a whopping $570 million for the 3,100-mile property. Although the Iowa lines flew the Soo Line banner, a decade later the parent Canadian Pacific Railway (CP) decided to liquidate, not finding the former Milwaukee in the Hawkeye State to be particularly attractive to its strategic ends. Indeed, the CP moved to dispose of about a quarter of its mileage in the United States and Canada. The newly formed I&M Rail Link, based in Davenport, Iowa, however, retains financial ties with its former owner, having a one-third equity position.[70]

Just as the CP disposed of its Iowa holdings, the Chicago & North Western, before its purchase by Union Pacific, sold unwanted trackage. In 1986 it made a major sale, conveying most of its lines in South Dakota and southern Minnesota to the Dakota, Minnesota & Eastern Railroad Corporation. This 644-mile regional has a presence in the Hawkeye State, dispatching trains over the seventy-mile segment between Waseca, Minnesota, and Mason City.[71]

The "fallen flag" Milwaukee indirectly gave birth to the regional I&M Rail Link, but the "fallen flag" Rock Island directly spawned a regional. In the largest railroad abandonment in American history, in the early 1980s the "Rock" exited the business world; its trackage was either sold to established or newly launched carriers or abandoned. In Iowa, for example, the Twin Cities–Kansas City line and several grain-gathering branches entered the orbit of the Chicago & North Western, but in 1981 the former main east-west line of the "Rock"—which links Davenport, Iowa City, Grinnell, Newton, Des Moines, Atlantic, and Council Bluffs—and several branches became the Iowa Railroad. Several years later that company, with 349 miles in the Hawkeye State, restructured, becoming Iowa Interstate Railroad, Ltd. This Iowa City–based regional works closely with the ex-interurban, the 60-mile Cedar Rapids and Iowa City Railway, which in the 1980s had expanded by acquiring the former Iowa City–Hills branch of the Rock Island and 21 miles of the former Milwaukee branch between Cedar Rapids and Middle Amana.[72]

In recent decades nine other independent railroads, typical short lines, likewise appeared in Iowa. Illustrative of the genre is the Appanoose County Community Railroad (ACCR). In 1982 business interests in Centerville, seat of Appanoose County, became alarmed with the loss of a rail outlet when the Burlington Northern ended service on its Alexandria, Missouri–Centerville branch (earlier the Southern Iowa Railway and the Rock Island had ceased local operations). These public-spirited citizens did more than fret; they started their own short line. On December 19, 1984, the first revenue train on the 11.8-mile ACCR departed Centerville, traveling over a short portion of the old Burlington and then over a longer segment of the former Rock Island "Golden State Route." North of Moulton, the train reached the Des Moines–Moberly, Missouri, line of the Norfolk Southern (NS) (née Norfolk & Western and Wabash). But in 1993 the upstart carrier faced a crisis: NS announced plans to abandon most of this secondary trackage. Although NS would continue to serve the Iowa capital, it would do so by using the Burlington Northern from St. Louis through Burlington and Albia. The choice for the ACCR was either to expand or to die. The road did the former, acquiring 25.9 miles of well-maintained NS trackage from near Moulton through Moravia to Albia. In Albia the greatly lengthened short line now interchanges its cars of grain, plastic pellets, and scrap metal with the Burlington Northern & Santa Fe and the NS, and it can connect with the Union Pacific at Maxon, a short distance to the east.[73]

The extent of railroad restructuring in Iowa surely would have amazed, even troubled Frank Donovan. Yet in 1954 he foresaw some of this change, predicting the end of electric traction. Although Donovan did not anticipate that most of the state's "juice" roads would cease operations, he expected dieselization. But that technology did not fully occur. Amazingly, at the end of the twentieth century, the Hawkeye State claims a bona fide transportation anachronism, an electric-powered common carrier. The Mason City & Clear Lake, reorganized in 1961 as the Iowa Terminal Railroad and reorganized again twenty-six years later as the Iowa Traction Railroad, remains under wire, providing carload freight service on approximately ten miles of line in the Mason City area. Not only is Iowa Traction the country's oldest continuously operating electric railroad, it is also the last true primarily freight interurban.[74]

If Frank Donovan wandered the length and breadth of present-day Iowa, he might not be too surprised to see a Baldwin-Westinghouse steeple cab locomotive with several freight cars rumbling alongside a road in Cerro Gordo County, but he might be astonished to encounter a pair of sleek Genesis P42 locomotives and a consist of bilevel Superliner cars with their distinctive red, white, and blue markings. In less than a year after Donovan's death, most of the nation's remaining passenger carriers gladly surrendered their intercity trains to the National Railroad Passenger Corporation, commonly called Amtrak. Since its debut on May 1, 1971, this quasi-public agency has maintained and at times expanded its long-distance rail passenger operations. Iowa, however, has received only limited Amtrak service. Indeed, there has been little change in Amtrak scheduling from its start until the present. The California Zephyr speeds along the BNSF (Burlington) and the Southwest Chief, initially the Super Chief–El Capitan, also operates over the BNSF (Santa Fe). The former calls daily at Burlington, Mount Pleasant, Ottumwa, Osceola, and Creston and the latter at Fort Madison. But Amtrak may eventually provide additional runs through Iowa, possibly over two historically strategic passenger routes, the Iowa Interstate (Rock Island) and the Union Pacific (North Western).[75]

The "lemon socialism" represented by Amtrak might bother Frank Donovan, but another dimension of the contemporary Iowa railroad story might have pleased him, a creative use for former railroad rights-of-way. When lines were abandoned, leaving nothing but naked grades, some Iowans believed that the public might still benefit from these former transportation arteries. The Hawkeye State became a national leader in the rails-to-trails movement. The concept lacks complexity, namely conversion of

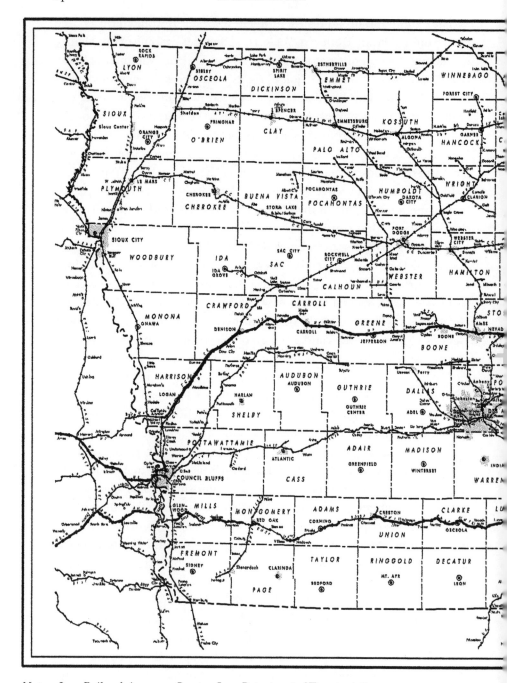

Map 2. Iowa Railroads in 1999. Courtesy Iowa Department of Transportation.

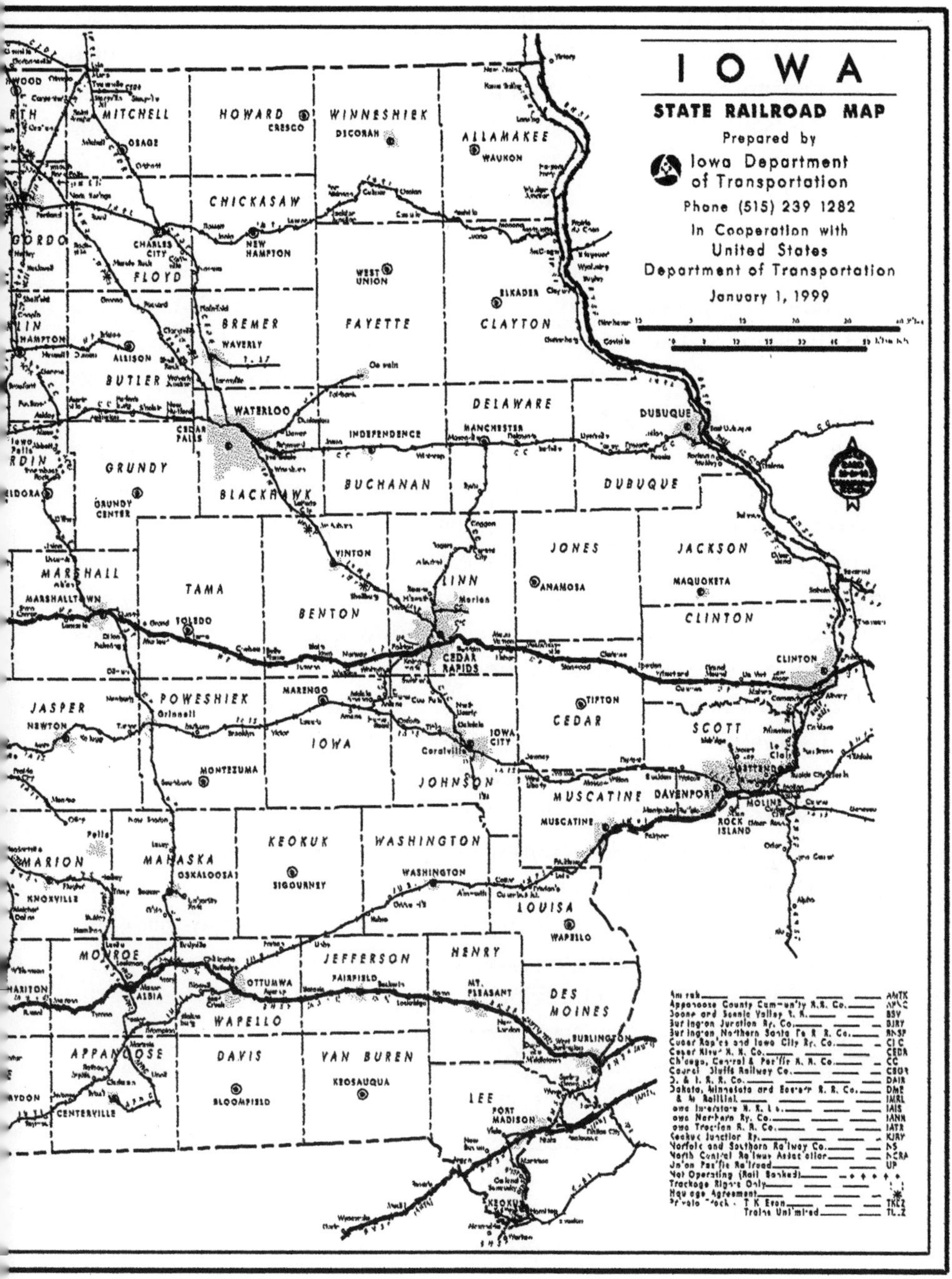
IOWA
STATE RAILROAD MAP
Prepared by
Iowa Department of Transportation
Phone (515) 239 1282
In Cooperation with
United States
Department of Transportation
January 1, 1999
MITCHELL
HOWARD
CRESCO
WINNESHIEK
DECORAH
ALLAMAKEE
WAUKON
CHICKASAW
NEW HAMPTON
CHARLES CITY
FLOYD
WEST UNION
ELKADER
BREMER
WAVERLY
FAYETTE
CLAYTON
ALLISON
BUTLER
WATERLOO
CEDAR FALLS
DELAWARE
DUBUQUE
INDEPENDENCE
MANCHESTER
GRUNDY
GRUNDY CENTER
BLACKHAWK
BUCHANAN
DUBUQUE
VINTON
JONES
JACKSON
MARSHALL
MARSHALLTOWN
TAMA
TOLEDO
BENTON
LINN
ANAMOSA
MAQUOKETA
CLINTON
CEDAR RAPIDS
CLINTON
JASPER
NEWTON
POWESHIEK
Grinnell
MARENGO
IOWA
IOWA CITY
Coralville
TIPTON
CEDAR
SCOTT
MONTEZUMA
JOHNSON
MUSCATINE
DAVENPORT
MOLINE
ROCK ISLAND
MUSCATINE
KEOKUK
SIGOURNEY
WASHINGTON
WASHINGTON
MARION
MAHASKA
OSKALOOSA
KNOXVILLE
LOUISA
WAPELLO
MONROE
ALBIA
OTTUMWA
JEFFERSON
FAIRFIELD
HENRY
MT. PLEASANT
DES MOINES
WAPELLO
BURLINGTON
APPANOOSE
DAVIS
BLOOMFIELD
VAN BUREN
KEOSAUQUA
LEE
FORT MADISON
CENTERVILLE
KEOKUK
AMTK
BSV
CIC
CEDA
CC
DAIR
DME
IMRL
IAIS
IATR
KJRY
UP
Not Operating (Rail Banked)
Trackage Rights Only
TKEZ

abandoned rights-of-way into surfaced trails, often using the original rock or cinder ballast, for hiking, biking, horseback riding, cross-country skiing, and snowmobiling. By the 1980s a national Rails-to-Trails Conservancy and many state affiliates, including one in Iowa, were operational. A decade later the state boasted more than forty rails-to-trails, and more are proposed. They range from units that measure only a few miles in length, like the 1.6-mile McVay Trail in Indianola, which uses a former Burlington branch line, to much longer ones, like the Hoover Nature Trail, planned to extend 115 miles over the old Rock Island line between Cedar Rapids and Burlington. These former paths of the iron horse also have been "banked," available, if necessary, for use again as freight or conceivably high-speed passenger lines.[76]

Similarly, the presence of several railroad operating museums would delight the ardent railfan Donovan. The premier one in Iowa is the Boone & Scenic Valley Railroad, which opened in 1983 and preserves a section of the one-time interurban Fort Dodge, Des Moines & Southern. This project of the Boone Railroad Historical Society offers a fifteen-mile round-trip ride, highlighted by passage over a 156-foot-high bridge above Bass Point Creek. Like other railroad operating museums, the rolling stock is eclectic, including a 2-8-2 steam engine acquired in 1989 from the Chinese Locomotive Works in Datong, China, a Rock Island caboose, and a Charles City Western interurban car.[77]

Except for the burst of construction in the Gilded Age, in no other period in the story of Hawkeye rails has there been so much change. When Frank Donovan wrote about the "Big Four" and the "Little Three," he described what was largely a stable industry, albeit one that always has experienced change. Even though the Iowa railroad scene today sports two giants, the appearance of new regionals and short lines harkens back to the nineteenth century before "system building" had run its course. Donovan would have been intrigued.

Frank P. Donovan, Jr.,'s comprehensive study of Iowa railroad provides material of lasting value. Admittedly, some of it is badly dated, but collectively it remains an excellent historical overview of the state's steam and electric carriers. Even though the inclusion of the colorful and episodic occasionally detracts from the narrative, Donovan places his subjects in the context of change over time. The ten articles that initially appeared in the *Palimpsest* have not been dramatically altered. However, some editing has occurred. Errors of fact have been corrected, and there have been changes in capitalization, punctuation, and the like.

A strength of the Donovan histories is the coverage of personalities, whether John Insley Blair, Charles Perkins, or A. B. Stickney. Most of the railroad builders and leaders are correctly viewed in positive terms. Lucian C. Sprague, who in the 1930s saved the M&STL from dismemberment, nearly walks on water. Yet Donovan distinguishes between the good and the bad. William H. Moore and Daniel G. Reid, who early in the twentieth century seized control of the Rock Island, are rightly criticized for their acts of arrogance and greed. Donovan, however, is overly negative toward Jay Gould, architect of the Wabash system, accepting contemporary accounts that he was the devil incarnate. Unfortunately, the best analysis of Gould, a biography by Maury Klein, who cogently argues that this railroader was more a builder than a wrecker, did not appear until sixteen years after Donovan's death.

The treatment of Iowa railroads by Frank Donovan reveals his biases. Repeatedly, he bemoans the disappearance of passenger trains, for example, castigating the Chicago & North Western, "a dreary freight road today," for ending service in Iowa except for the Kate Shelley 400, which until 1971 connected Clinton with Chicago. Donovan is reluctant to concede that the North Western and other carriers could not afford passenger trains even before the Post Office Department provided the fatal blow in 1967 by canceling nearly all of its Railway Post Office contracts. Similarly, Donovan laments abandonment of branch lines, although at times he admits that highway competition warranted such actions. Understandably, Donovan glorifies railroads in the Hawkeye State during their Golden Age, the several decades before the Great Depression of the 1930s, when "high iron" encountered the iron horse, often in grand style.[78]

What becomes even more evident about the Donovan essays is their readability. His engaging prose style helps to explain why the State Historical Society of Iowa repeatedly received laudatory comments. In one specific testimonial, a station agent in Pleasantville, Iowa, who supplemented his income by performing janitorial chores at the local library, told how he discovered copies of the *Palimpsest* railroad histories and devoured them over and over "because they were so much fun to read." This excitement was hardly unique and in all probability will continue.

NOTES

1. See Frank Donovan, Jr., "A Thousand Miles by Trolley," *Railroad Magazine* (December 1937):116–25. The principal railroad books of Frank P. Donovan, Jr., include: *Destination Topolobampo: The Kansas City, Mexico & Orient Railway* (with John Leeds Kerr) (San Marino, Calif.: Golden West Books, 1968); *Gateway to the Northwest: The Story of the Minne-*

sota Transfer Railway (Minneapolis: privately printed, 1954); *Harry Bedwell: Last of the Great Railroad Storytellers* (Minneapolis: Ross & Haines, 1959); *Headlights and Markers: An Anthology of Railroad Stories* (with Robert Selph Henry) (New York: Creative Age Press, 1946); *Mileposts on the Prairie: The Story of the Minneapolis & St. Louis Railway* (New York: Simmons-Boardman Publishing Corporation, 1950); *Railroads in Literature: A Brief Survey of Railroad Fiction, Poetry, Songs, Biography, Essays, Travel and Drama in the English Language, Particularly Emphasizing Its Place in American Literature* (Boston: Railway & Locomotive Historical Society, 1940); *Railroads of America* (Milwaukee: Kalmbach Publishing Company, 1949).

2. Dust jacket, Frank P. Donovan, Jr., *Mileposts on the Prairie*; Frank P. Donovan, Jr., "One Night on a Southbound Limited," *Railroad* (April 1964):18.

3. Frank P. Donovan, Jr., to Donald H. Kotz, June 2, 1948, in possession of Donald H. Kotz, Racine, Wis., hereafter cited as Kotz Coll.

4. Newspaper clipping, Frank P. Donovan, Jr., Collection, James J. Hill Reference Library, St. Paul, Minn., hereafter cited as Donovan Coll.; Donovan, "One Night on a Southbound Limited," pp. 16–17.

5. Clipping, Donovan Coll.; "Donovan Rides Trains, Writes," *Country Family* (February 1969):2.

6. Clipping, Donovan Coll.; Donald H. Kotz to author, January 7, 1999.

7. Clipping, Donovan Coll.; *Trains* 31 (January 1971):56.

8. Frank P. Donovan, Jr., to Donald H. Kotz, October 6, 1948, Kotz Coll.; author interview with Wallace W. Abbey, Chicago, October 9, 1998; author interview with Don L. Hofsommer, Chicago, October 19, 1998.

9. See Frank P. Donovan, Jr., and Cushing F. Wright, *The First through a Century, 1853–1953: A History of the First National Bank of Saint Paul* (St. Paul, Minn.: Itasca Press, 1954); Hofsommer, interview.

10. *Los Angeles Times*, July 21, 1952; Frank P. Donovan, Jr., to James W. Zarbook, June 2, 1952, in possession of Don L. Hofsommer, St. Cloud, Minn.; Hofsommer, interview.

11. Frank P. Donovan, Jr., to William J. Petersen, January 28, 1953, June 20, 1954, October 16, 1954, March 3, 1955, in William J. Petersen Collection, State Historical Society of Iowa, Iowa City, Iowa, hereafter cited as Peterson Coll.; Hofsommer, interview; author telephone interview with Don L. Hofsommer, St. Cloud, Minn., July 9, 1998; clipping, Donovan Coll. Donovan refers to a company-sponsored history, *Pioneer Railroad: The Story of the Chicago and North Western System*, by Robert J. Casey and W. A. S. Douglas, which Whittlesay House in New York published in 1948. The book received mostly negative reviews from professional historians.

12. *Iowa City Press-Citizen*, February 3, 1989; *Cedar Rapids Gazette*, February 2, 1989.

13. William J. Petersen, "The *Palimpsest*: 1920–1965," *Palimpsest* 46 (June 1965):273–305; Peter T. Harstad and L. Edward Purcell, "The *Palimpsest*: Old Friend with a New Face," *Palimpsest* 53 (December 1972):501–506.

14. Walter Rundell, Jr., *The State Historical Society of Iowa: An Analysis* (Ames, Iowa: privately printed, 1971).

15. Hofsommer, telephone interview; Abbey, interview; *St. Paul Dispatch*, June 7, 1973.

16. Hofsommer, telephone interview; Donald H. Kotz to author, February 17, 1999.

17. Hofsommer, interview; H. Roger Grant, ed., *Richard C. Overton: Railroad Historian* (St. Cloud, Minn.: Lexington Group, 1998), pp. 11–12, 22–26.

18. Frank P. Donovan, Jr., to William J. Petersen, March 15, 1951, Petersen Coll.

19. William J. Petersen to Frank P. Donovan, Jr., March 26, 1951, Petersen Coll.

20. Frank P. Donovan, Jr., to William J. Petersen, March 27, 1951, Petersen Coll.

21. William J. Petersen to Frank P. Donovan, Jr., March 31, 1951, Petersen Coll.

22. Frank P. Donovan, Jr., to William J. Petersen, April 12, 1951, Petersen Coll.

23. William J. Petersen to Frank P. Donovan, Jr., May 14, 1958, August 27, 1958, April 16, 1951, Petersen Coll.

24. William J. Petersen to Frank P. Donovan, Jr., March 5, 1953, October 27, 1964, Petersen Coll.

25. William J. Petersen to Frank P. Donovan, Jr., March 11, 1957, March 21, 1957; Frank P. Donovan, Jr., to William J. Petersen, March 17, 1957, March 26, 1957, Petersen Coll.

26. Hofsommer, interview.

27. Frank P. Donovan, Jr., to S. C. Dows, December 5, 1953, Petersen Coll.

28. Frank P. Donovan, Jr., to William J. Petersen, February 20, 1954, Petersen Coll.

29. Frank P. Donovan, Jr., to William J. Petersen, April 17, 1962, Petersen Coll.

30. Hofsommer, interview; Frank P. Donovan, Jr., to William J. Petersen, June 23, 1953, Petersen Coll. When Frank and Jan Donovan arrived in Minneapolis in 1948, they rented a room in a residence near Lake Harriet; later they took care of the home of a nearby Quaker minister; next they took an apartment; finally they purchased a house on West 45th Street. See Frank P. Donovan, Jr., to Donald Kotz, October 6, 1948, May 13, 1949, May 29, 1949, Kotz Coll.

31. Hofsommer, interview.

32. Ibid.; "Donovan Rides Trains, Writes," p. 2.

33. Frank P. Donovan, Jr., to William J. Petersen, March 7, 1953, July 14, 1953, Peterson Coll.

34. William J. Petersen to Frank P. Donovan, Jr., March 22, 1954, April 20, 1954; Frank P. Donovan, Jr., to William J. Petersen, April 17, 1954, Petersen Coll.

35. Frank P. Donovan, Jr., to William J. Petersen, July 9, 1954, Petersen Coll.

36. William J. Petersen to Frank P. Donovan, Jr., June 22, 1954, Petersen Coll.

37. Frank P. Donovan, Jr., to William J. Petersen, July 9, 1954, Petersen Coll.

38. William J. Petersen to Frank P. Donovan, Jr., n.d., 1955, July 12, 1956; Frank P. Donovan, Jr., to William J. Petersen, July 7, 1956, Petersen Coll.

39. William J. Petersen to Frank P. Donovan, Jr., July 12, 1956, March 11, 1957; Frank P. Donovan, Jr., to William J. Petersen, March 17, 1957, Petersen Coll.

40. Frank P. Donovan, Jr., to William J. Petersen, August 18, 1957, August 25, 1957; William J. Petersen to Frank P. Donovan, Jr., August 27, 1957, Petersen Coll.

41. Frank P. Donovan, Jr., to William J. Petersen, September 25, 1957, September 28, 1957; William J. Petersen to Frank P. Donovan, Jr., October 11, 1957, Petersen Coll.

42. Frank P. Donovan, Jr., to William J. Petersen, April 15, 1957, October 19, 1957, November 22, 1957; William J. Petersen to Frank P. Donovan, Jr., October 25, 1957, Petersen Coll.

43. William J. Petersen to Frank P. Donovan, Jr., November 27, 1957, Petersen Coll.

44. Frank P. Donovan, Jr., to William J. Petersen, June 26, 1958, Petersen Coll.

45. William J. Petersen to Frank P. Donovan, Jr., July 1, 1958, July 15, 1958, Petersen Coll.

46. Frank P. Donovan, Jr., to William J. Petersen, August 26, 1958; William J. Petersen to Frank P. Donovan, Jr., August 27, 1958, October 17, 1958, Petersen Coll.

47. Frank P. Donovan, Jr., to William J. Petersen, June 19, 1959, August 23, 1959; William J. Petersen to Frank P. Donovan, Jr., June 25, 1959, August 24, 1959, December 13, 1960, Petersen Coll.

48. Frank P. Donovan, Jr., to William J. Petersen, December 6, 1960, April 9, 1961, Petersen Coll.

49. William J. Petersen to Frank P. Donovan, Jr., July 13, 1961, August 14, 1961; Frank P. Donovan, Jr., to William J. Petersen, July 31, 1961, Petersen Coll.

50. William P. Petersen to Frank P. Donovan, Jr., March 23, 1962, April 23, 1962, Petersen Coll.

51. Frank P. Donovan, Jr., to William J. Petersen, August 13, 1961, Petersen Coll.

52. Frank P. Donovan, Jr., to William J. Petersen, October 4, 1961; William J. Petersen to Frank P. Donovan, Jr., October 9, 1961, Petersen Coll.

53. Frank P. Donovan, Jr., to William J. Petersen, September 30, 1962; William J. Petersen to Frank P. Donovan, Jr., October 3, 1962, Petersen Coll.

54. Frank P. Donovan, Jr., to William J. Petersen, November 13, 1962, Petersen Coll.

55. Frank P. Donovan, Jr., to William J. Petersen, March 14, 1965, May 11, 1969, Petersen Coll.

56. *St. Paul Pioneer Press*, September 9, 1970; *Minneapolis Tribune*, September 9, 1970.

57. Frank P. Donovan, Jr., to William J. Petersen, March 7, 1953; William J. Petersen to Frank P. Donovan, Jr., March 11, 1953, Petersen Coll.

58. Frank P. Donovan, Jr., to William J. Petersen, July 16, 1961, July 31, 1961; William J. Petersen to Frank P. Donovan, Jr., August 4, 1961, Petersen Coll.

59. William J. Petersen to Frank P. Donovan, Jr., November 15, 1962, Petersen Coll.

60. William J. Petersen to Frank P. Donovan, Jr., January 10, 1963, Petersen Coll.; Rundell, *The State Historical Society of Iowa*.

61. *Yearbook of Railroad Facts* (Washington, D.C.: Association of American Railroads, 1970), p. 61; *Railroad Facts* (Washington, D.C.: Association of American Railroads, 1986), p. 43; E. Rees Hakanson, Ames, Iowa, to author, October 5, 1998.

62. See Richard L. Saunders, *Railroad Mergers and the Coming of Conrail* (Westport, Conn.: Greenwood Press, 1978), and Frank N. Wilner, *Railroad Mergers: Mergers, Analysis, Insight* (Omaha, Nebr.: Simmons Boardman Books, 1997); Hakanson, letter.

63. H. Roger Grant, *The North Western: A History of the Chicago & North Western Railway System* (DeKalb: Northern Illinois University Press, 1996), pp. 210, 232–234. As of 1999, only short pieces of the former Chicago Great Western in Iowa remained in service: Belmond to Somers, Bondurant to Des Moines, Coulter to Allison, Manly to Meservey, and Oelwein to Waterloo.

64. William H. Thompson, *Transportation in Iowa: A Historical Summary* (Ames: Iowa Department of Transportation, 1989), pp. 259–312.

65. See George W. Hilton, *The Transportation Act of 1958: A Decade of Experience* (Bloomington: Indiana University Press, 1969); "The Branch Line Problem: 'Is Anyone Listening?'" address by Larry S. Provo, president, Chicago & North Western Transportation Company, before the Grain Transportation Workshop, Iowa State University, Ames, May 14, 1974; author interview with James A. Zito, St. Charles, Ill., May 4, 1994.

66. Author interview with Charles C. Shannon, Arlington Heights, Ill., October 1, 1988.

67. Thomas H. Ploss, *The Nation Pays Again: The Demise of the Milwaukee Road, 1928–1986* (Chicago: privately printed, 1986); Dan Rottenberg, "The Last Run of the Rock Island Line," *Chicago Magazine* (September 1984):197–201, 234–237.

68. Grant, *The North Western*, pp. 241–242.

69. Edward A. Lewis, *American Shortline Railway Guide*, 5th ed. (Waukesha, Wis.: Kalmbach Publishing Company, 1996), pp. 4–5, 80; Hakanson, letter; Mark W. Bailey, "IC's Iowa Division Rebounds," *Trains* 57 (July 1997):24–25.

70. Hakanson, letter; *Trains* 57 (February 1997):17; *Trains* 58 (December 1998):25; Grant, *The North Western*, pp. 234–236; John Gruber, "I&M Rail Link Celebrates One Year," *RailNews* 417 (August 1998):39.

71. Lewis, *American Shortline Railway Guide*, p. 94; Grant, *The North Western*, p. 244.

72. Lewis, *American Shortline Railway Guide*, pp. 65, 161.

73. Ibid., p. 26; Dana L. Grefe, *The Iowa Railfan Guide* (Grimes, Iowa: privately printed, 1997), p. 116.

74. Grefe, *The Iowa Railfan Guide*, p. 162; Karl Zimmerman, "Roadside Electrics in Corn Country," *Trains* 57 (August 1997):65–69.

75. H. Roger Grant, *We Took the Train* (DeKalb: Northern Illinois University Press, 1990), p. xi; Amtrak public timetable, May 1, 1971, October 25, 1998.

76. Greg Smith and Karen-Lee Ryan, eds., *700 Great Rail-Trails: A National Directory* (Washington, D.C.: Rails-to-Trails Conservancy, 1995), pp. 31–37.

77. *Steam Passenger Service Directory* (Richmond, Vt.: Locomotive & Railway Preservation, 1991), pp. 101–104; Charles Roberts and Paul Swanson, "The Best Little Railroad in Iowa," *Iowan* 33 (Summer 1985):18–22.

78. Frank P. Donovan, Jr., to William J. Petersen, July 31, 1961, Petersen Coll.

THE IOWA CENTRAL

Iowa had long dreamed of a north-and-south main line. Back in pre–Civil War days that prince of pioneers, Josiah B. Grinnell, headed a company to fulfill that mission. But the war came and the project was dropped. Later an energetic twosome composed of David Morgan, a New Sharon school-teacher, and Peter Melendy, a Cedar Falls newspaper editor, gave much zeal and some capital to the enterprise. Considerable grading was done between Albia and Oskaloosa, between Cedar Falls and Toledo, and also in the vicinity of Tama, and then, because the money ran out, the under-taking languished. What was termed the "Grandest Railroad Project of the Age" turned out to be a fiasco. It looked as if the longitudinal rail line was an empty dream. Such, however, was not the case. Today the main stem of the Minneapolis & St. Louis Railway cuts right through the midriff of Iowa from the Minnesota border to within a few miles of the northern rim of Missouri.

The story of the Iowa Central Railway, which eventually became the M&StL's main line in Iowa, is the old dream with new twists: a different group of backers, an altered route, and an exceedingly humble beginning. And for some forty years this section of the road was independent of the M&StL. Here's how it started.

When coal was discovered in the vicinity of Eldora, the problem of cheap transportation became of paramount importance. This led to the formation of the Eldora Railroad and Coal Company on February 7, 1866, to build a railway to Ackley, sixteen miles north. At Ackley the Eldora road would connect with the east-west road which is now the Illinois Central. By July 1868, the new road was completed, but its connection with the outside world was not entirely satisfactory. It was finally decided to build twenty-eight miles south from Eldora to tie in with the east-west line of the Chicago & North Western at Marshalltown. A new company, the Iowa River Railway, headed by Charles C. Gilman (who was also president of the older road), took over the Eldora line on September 1, 1868. Just before completion, on September 30, 1869, to be exact, the River Railway became the Central Railroad Company of Iowa. Now it threw away its mantle as a purely local road to carry on the tradition of Morgan and Melendy and become an important north-and-south route.

Marshalltown welcomed the formal opening of the new road by a gala celebration on January 7, 1870. Indeed, the shops and general offices were to be removed later from Eldora to Marshalltown, and the latter town had reason to be proud. The road athwart central Iowa would be operated from *central* Iowa at Marshalltown. Great things were expected of the new company, for the cross-state vertical line was to become—and finally did become—a reality.

Physically, the north-and-south route from Mason City to Albia was completed in 1872, but it was many years before it came into its own economically, financially, and strategically. For the next three decades the road was to remain in precarious financial condition, with a round of receiverships, shifts in management, and constant name-changing. During the mid-seventies Isaac M. Cate succeeded Gilman to the presidency, and shortly afterward Josiah B. Grinnell was appointed receiver. Grinnell's hectic trusteeship lasted only about two years, when he was superseded by H. L. Morrill. Finally, on May 5, 1879, the road emerged from the court's hands as the Central Iowa Railway.

The Iowa road was dubbed the "Hook and Eye" because in the early timetables the initial "C" was placed on its back across the top of the "I" so that the former initial resembled a hook and the latter an eye. The railway continued to expand during periods of solvency. Apparently the charter forbade building branches, for all the offshoots from the main stem were constructed by separate companies and then sold to the Central Iowa. Most important of these additions was the New Sharon Coal Valley and Eastern, incorporated January 29, 1880. By January 7 of '82 the name was changed to the high-sounding Chicago, Burlington and Pacific, and on April 1 of the same year the road was sold to the Central Iowa. Eighteen eighty-two also saw the completion of the road from Oskaloosa to the west bank of the Mississippi opposite Keithsburg, Illinois.

Meantime dirt was flying in Illinois. The old Peoria & Farmington Railway (chartered March 27, 1869) was purchased by the Central Iowa Railway (of Illinois), and it was pushing westward to the Father of Waters. In 1883 the Central Iowa of Illinois line started operating from Peoria to Keithsburg, eighty-eight miles.

To cross the Mississippi a small paddle-wheel steamer, the *William Osborn*, churned its way from shore to shore with its quota of four freight cars. When the river was frozen—well, passengers either walked across or they, together with freight, rode on sleighs. At least one winter, however, when navigation ceased, the pioneer railroaders constructed a temporary wooden trestle. When the ice melted in the spring, the jerry-built trestle was removed so that river traffic could be resumed. The first permanent bridge was completed at Oakville in 1886. It had eight spans of through-truss design and a 362-foot swing draw.

Here, then, was the Central Iowa's route very much as it is today: from Mason City through Marshalltown and Oskaloosa to Keithsburg and Peoria in Illinois. The northern terminus, as we have said, was at Mason City, but this was later extended northward to Manly in Worth County. The gap between the latter town and Albert Lea, Minnesota, was closed in 1877 when the M&StL and the Burlington, Cedar Rapids & Northern (now the Rock Island) finished a joint line linking the two communities.

By the mideighties all the branches had sprouted and grown and were duly absorbed by the Central Iowa. They included the twenty-two-mile Belmond line veering off the main stem at Hampton; the thirty-four-mile Story City branch running westward from Minerva Junction (near Marshalltown); the twenty-six-mile State Center feeder from Newburg; the fourteen-mile stub out of the old Grinnell & Montezuma to Montezuma; and finally the twenty-eight-mile branch to Newton running north-northwest from New Sharon. All and all, the Central Iowa had a system of nearly five hundred miles, less than a hundred of them outside the Hawkeye State.

Such a railroad patrimony purchased and absorbed throughout the years needed a coat of arms or a trademark to lend prestige and distinction. So thought H. P. Nourse, the general passenger agent. Action followed inspiration, and the road's official emblem made its debut in the May 1887 timetable. Like Mark Twain's map, it was truly the only one of its kind.

Under a hodgepodge of arms, hands, circles, and bands came this descriptive gobbledygook: "An escutcheon, inverted, or PER PALY BENDY, AZURE, Nebuly on an annulet sable, between four hands gules, One hand rampant gardant, three hands grabant, and all hands around. Our motto will be, 'The Handy Line'—(Battle cry Hi! Hi! Hi!, the last syllable prolonged)."

It took the foreclosure of 1888 to get rid of this nonsense; and the Iowa Central Railway, the new company, henceforth operated without a coat of arms or a battle cry. Incidentally, this was the last name-change the road had as an independent company.

To recapitulate, the lineage of the Iowa Central begins with the Eldora Railroad and Coal Company, which in succession became the Iowa River Railway, Central Railroad Company of Iowa, Central Iowa Railway, and finally the Iowa Central. Another Iowa road, the Chicago, Burlington and Pacific, came into the fold in 1882. About the same time the Peoria & Farmington (an Illinois road) came under Iowa Central interests and was soon completed from Peoria to the Mississippi at Keithsburg.

In common with most roads near the end of the nineteenth century, the Iowa Central was quick to make traffic alliances at terminals. These alliances depended on the road's presidents who came and went with the ups and downs of management. When Cate ruled at Marshalltown—and he held office for about a dozen years—the Milwaukee Road was the favored route from Mason City to the Twin Cities. Cate's short-term successors, Alfred Sully and Elijah Smith, made little change, but when A. B. Stickney gained control he promptly made the northern connection his own Minnesota & Northwestern, now the Chicago Great Western.

The Iowa Central had long pioneered in through passenger trains, and its Twin City–St. Louis service, in connection with the Milwaukee on the north and the Wabash on the south, achieved considerable popularity. But Stickney did more. Being an audacious and independent thinker, and above all an individualist, he had his own ideas. They were, to say the least, far ahead of his time. Today we think of through sleepers from the east to points west of the Mississippi as being the brainchild of Robert R. Young of the Chesapeake & Ohio. Not so. In the mideighties Alpheus Beede Stickney inaugurated cross-country "Woodruff Chair and Sleeping cars" from the capital of Minnesota to the capital of Ohio.

Before me I have a yellowing timetable dated November 7, 1886. It shows Train No. 4 leaving Minneapolis at 6:30 P.M. (St. Paul at 7:05) and arriving at Columbus, Ohio, at 4:10 A.M. two days later. The routing: Minnesota & Northwestern and the Central Iowa to Peoria, Illinois, thence the Indiana, Bloomington & Western (now the New York Central) to destination. Returning on No. 1, passengers left the Buckeye capital at 9:00 A.M., and at 8:30 on the evening of the second day they arrived in Mill City.

When Russell Sage, the New York financier, replaced Stickney in 1890, the northern connection reverted to the Milwaukee. Sage and General Francis M. Drake, onetime governor of Iowa, were active in the management of the Centerville, Moravia & Albia Railroad, which the Iowa Central operated until 1910. This road, which linked all the towns in its title, was subsequently electrified and is now an interurban freight line controlled by the Iowa Southern Utilities.

The Sage regime, although not outstanding in itself, produced some very able railroaders. General Manager C. H. Ackert in later years left the old Hook and Eye to head the Southern Railway, and Master Mechanic John Player went from Marshalltown to a similar position on the far-flung Santa Fe system. Although with "home guards," the Iowa Central always had a large quota of "boomers." Indeed, it is said with a measure of truth that one "never saw the same crew twice." Itinerant railroaders from coast to coast often took a hitch on the Hook and then settled elsewhere. Never a wealthy road and at times run-down, it did the best it could with the equipment at hand. If a man passed muster on the Iowa Central he was trained for the exigencies of railroading almost anywhere.

When Sage relinquished the presidency in 1897, he was followed by Horace J. Morse and then a year or so later by Robert J. Kimball. In the coming era of big business and consolidations, the Iowa Central would have to buy or be bought. Clearly the former was out of the question. That was the status of the "Marshalltown Route," as Iowans affectionately called their home road, as the new century dawned.

ENTER THE M&StL

When Edwin Hawley became president of the Minneapolis & St. Louis in 1896, that road was little more than a local enterprise. When Hawley died sixteen years later, the M&StL had become an important midwestern carrier, serving four states, and had quadrupled in mileage. The very backbone of the enlarged M&StL was, and is today, the mileage in the Hawkeye State, more than half of which was the Iowa Central.

Hawley was quick to sense the importance of the Iowa Central as a complement to the "Louie," as the M&StL was nicknamed. Both roads as separate units were relatively weak. United they would have considerable economic and strategic value. By 1900 fifty-year-old Edwin Hawley, a New Yorker, had acquired control of the Hook and Eye, and not long afterward key M&StL executives held similar positions on the Iowa Central. Incidentally, up until the turn of the century Hawley was unheard-of as a railroad officer and financier. After heading the Minnesota and Iowa roads, however, he became known in business circles and on the street as a shrewd, practical railroader. And well he might, for in a dozen years Hawley and Hawley men controlled the Alton, the Toledo, St. Louis & Western, the St. Louis–San Francisco, the Missouri-Kansas-Texas, and the Chesapeake & Ohio. Indeed, at the time of his death he is said to have amassed a fortune of $30 million. But the fact remains: it was the Louie and the Hook which gave him his start to fame and fortune.

Unlike Russell Sage, Hawley was a builder, for every property under his control was improved. The Iowa Central was no exception. One of the first major improvement jobs of the new management was the grade relocation on School House Hill. Today one can still see remains of the old right-of-way between Searsboro and Oak Grove just east of the present track. Again modern (at that time) motive power was purchased and the passenger service speeded up. Hawley sensed the importance of Peoria as a gateway to bypass the congested Chicago terminal area.

During Hawley's administration the second (and present) Mississippi River bridge was built. The old structure was far too light for the increased traffic and heavier equipment. Furthermore, it required the tedious business of spacing engines several cars apart in a train rather than coupled together when double-heading. In this way the weight was more evenly distributed and the pioneer bridge given a reprieve. But the old span had to go, and it, along with a nearby bridge across Blackhawk Chute, was replaced during 1909–1910. The structure across the main channel of the Mississippi, extending from Blackhawk Island to the Illinois shore, is 2,304 feet in length. A lift-span, on the Keithsburg side, permits passage of boats and barges. The smaller bridge from Blackhawk Island to the Iowa mainland measures 1,506 feet. Total cost of the entire project was $725,000. Some piers of the old bridge may still be seen about 60 feet downstream from the present Mississippi structure.

Even though the actual merger of the Iowa Central with the M&STL did not take place until 1912, the two roads were operated very much as if they were one system. Hawley, a laconic, aloof individual, had his equally terse and down-to-business lieutenant, L Ferman Day, boss the Iowa Central. (Day, whose first name was just plain "L," always insisted that it be unadorned by a period.) He for many years was vice president and general manager of both the M&STL and the Iowa Central. "LFD" became to all intents and purposes chief of the combined roads, since Hawley spent most of his time in New York looking after other properties.

A word, now, about the other M&STL lines in Iowa. Back on July 22, 1876, some farmers and other local folk incorporated the Fort Dodge and Fort Ridgeley Railroad and Telegraph Company to lay rails from Fort Dodge to the northern boundary of Webster County. Meantime, an M&STL-sponsored road, called the Minnesota and Iowa Southern, was building south from Albert Lea, Minnesota, to meet the Fort Ridgeley line. Finally, on April 20, 1881, both companies were merged into the M&STL, making a through line linking Albert Lea with Fort Dodge. The next year the Louie built what was jocosely called the Old Mud Line from Fort Dodge to Angus. It was so named because the track was built right on the prairie with God's brown earth as ballast. Unfortunately, the once-thriving mining operations in Angus had already started to decline when the Louie made its southern terminus there. A miners' strike in 1884, followed by the panic of '93, just about decimated the population. At the present time Angus is very nearly a ghost town, and all mining operations have long since been abandoned.

At Angus the M&STL connected with the Des Moines and Fort Dodge Railroad and had trackage rights over it to the state capital. The DM&FTD, by the way, was a successor to one of the earliest roads in Iowa: the Keokuk, Fort Des Moines & Minnesota Rail Road, incorporated in 1854 and later known as the Des Moines Valley Rail Road.

At the beginning of the century the M&STL's line, Winthrop to New Ulm, Minnesota, was extended southward to Estherville, Spencer, and Storm Lake. Known as the Southwestern Extension, the line was projected to Omaha, but it never reached that goal. At this juncture Hawley and Day cast a covetous eye on the Des Moines and Fort Dodge, a ward of the Rock Island. The DM&FTD operated from Des Moines through Tara to Ruthven. From Tara to Fort Dodge, six miles, the road had trackage rights over the Illinois Central.

Through a clever stock-buying coup the Hawley interests wrested control of the Des Moines road from the Rock Island. The M&STL leased it in 1905 and ten years later took title. Since Ruthven is only thirteen miles from Spencer, it was a simple matter to get running rights over the Milwaukee Road between these two points; by so doing it linked the Southwestern Extension with the so-called Central Division serving Fort Dodge and Des Moines.

Summing up: The M&STL in Iowa began as the Fort Dodge and Fort Ridgeley Railroad and Telegraph Company, which was taken over by the Louie in 1881. That same year the Minnesota and Iowa Southern was also merged into the M&STL. By 1900 M&STL interests controlled the Iowa Central (but did not own it), and in 1905 the Louie leased the Des Moines and Fort Dodge. In 1912 the M&STL purchased the Iowa Central, and in 1915 the Des Moines and Fort Dodge was also bought.

To most people in Iowa this railroad strategy was an academic subject; they were interested in train service and events directly concerning their community. Circuses and state fairs, then as now, were stellar attractions. And the Des Moines line was a favorite routing for circus trains on their circuits from the Iowa capital to Minneapolis, or vice versa. Occasionally, their unorthodox cargo posed some problems. Such was the case in the late nineties when a northbound circus special came to an unscheduled stop between Humboldt and Luverne. The Sellars injector on the engine would not pump water, and the gauge showed the boiler nearly empty. The enginemen were at a loss to explain the deficiency of water. Something was amiss. At this point Fireman George Nelson glanced back over the train. There he espied the trunk of an elephant extending out of the end door of a stock car and down into the tank of the tender. Getting a trunkful, the large pachyderm then playfully proceeded to squirt water along the right-of-way. Mr. Nelson, I may add, is still living and can vouch for the authenticity of this story.

Several years later, being hard-pressed for motive power, the M&STL leased a few "compound" freight locomotives, that is, engines having both high- and low-pressure cylinders, from the Soo Line. They were more complex and, to the uninitiated, harder to "steam" than the normal or "simple" engines heretofore used on the Louie. As a result, many freights had to double the Iowa and Minnesota hills. Finally, a dispatcher demanded to know why the compounds could not pull their tonnage ratings. The answer promptly came back from one conductor, stating he had:

> Forty cars of coal,
> Twenty cars of beer,
> A compound engine, and—
> A simple engineer.

It is hard to realize that the M&STL once did a spanking short-haul passenger business. Most of the local riders on the Louie, as on nearly every other American railroad, now have their own automobiles. But in the horse-and-buggy era such locales as Albia, Oskaloosa, Marshalltown, and Fort Dodge had busy depots with lunch counters. Now only Albia and Fort Dodge sport eating facilities. In addition, lunches could be had at Livermore and Hampton. All the passengers had to do was tell the conductor in advance. He would wire ahead and have basket lunches waiting at the depot. One could have country fried chicken, a generous cut of roast beef, or hot pork with vegetables, a salad, rolls, and steaming coffee. The price: fifty cents.

On the Iowa Central, trains were chartered at the drop of a hat. Many a ball team, lodge, or church group had its special for a big game, a trip down the Mississippi from Keithsburg, Illinois, or just an outing to some choice picnic ground. Once every year, too, the Hook ran special trains and extra cars to Oskaloosa, where the Quakers had their annual gathering. At the beginning of the century it was quite common for Friends to inquire as to their mode of travel to Yearly Meeting. The question was put: "Did thee come Woolman or Pullman?" As a word of explanation it may be added that "Woolman" referred to one John Woolman, a revered Quaker preacher who practiced and expounded the virtues of thrift and plain living. Therefore if the reply was "Woolman," it meant day coach with the inference of Spartan simplicity and minimum of comfort—a state of affairs which is said to have characterized the old Iowa Central.

Another facet of the Iowa scene in yesteryear were the "crummy" or miners' trains. The Iowa Central (and later the M&stL) had extensive mines in the vicinity of Albia through ownership of the Hocking Coal Company. Early in the morning and late in the afternoon these "crummies," composed of a train of boxcars with potbellied stoves and wooden benches, shuttled between Albia and the mine shafts. The Iowa Central served many diggings, probably the most noted of which were the Excelsior mines near Oskaloosa. Whole trainloads of coal went from Excelsior for distribution to many points within and without the state.

THE PEORIA GATEWAY LINE

Until the eve of the First World War, the M&stL was called the Albert Lea Route, but thereafter it became known as the Peoria Gateway Line. The reason is obvious. More emphasis was placed on freight, and Peoria is an important gateway for east-and-west tonnage. Albert Lea, on the contrary, was chiefly regarded as a passenger junction point. The new slogan was indicative of the coming importance of freight.

All, however, was not well on the M&stL. The drubbing the road took under government operation during World War I was a big factor in bringing on the receivership of 1923. A long siege of crop failures, unfavorable business conditions, and finally the Great Depression prolonged the court's control. In an effort to pare expenses, all passenger trains except the North

Star Limited were motorized. Many locals which did not earn their keep were withdrawn and segments of branch lines abandoned. During this trying period the road was piloted by William H. Bremner, a native of Marshalltown. "Billy" Bremner started on the Iowa Central as a baggage clerk. He later was graduated from the State University of Iowa at Iowa City and came to the M&stL as general attorney in 1909. At the outbreak of America's entry into World War I he became president, then federal manager, and subsequently receiver.

When Bremner died at the end of 1934, Lucian C. Sprague was appointed a receiver and president. Mr. Sprague began his railroad career on the Burlington. Then came a spell as machinist helper, a few years firing a locomotive, and finally advancement to the right-hand side of the cab. But that was just a start. From the "Q" Lou Sprague went into engineering and supervisory positions with the Great Northern, Baltimore & Ohio, and Denver & Rio Grande Western. In 1923 he was made vice president and general manager of the Uintah Railway, a Utah ore road.

When Mr. Sprague first arrived in Minneapolis to run the M&stL, the day was stormy and bitter cold. The job before him seemed even bleaker. "The day I took the receiver's job," he recalls, "$524,000 in unpaid vouchers for current bills were dumped on my desk with the warning, 'You'll never get another dollar's worth of material!'"

Meeting the payroll with nearly an empty till was his No. 1 job. Many expressed the opinion that the road was "of little worth as a railroad but of considerable junk value." That was Lou Sprague's cue. He could not go along with the first part of the phrase, but the latter he knew to be true. A thousand obsolete freight cars rotting in the yards gave him an idea. By long-distance telephone he contacted a friend in the wrecking business. A day or two later a certified check came for $60,000 in part payment for the superannuated cars, sight unseen.

From that time on the M&stL started on the long road to complete rehabilitation. Just prior to the Sprague administration the Burlington had abandoned most of its Tracy-Winfield branch; the remainder it sold to the M&stL. The Louie purchased the Martinsburg-Coppock section and another stretch between Tracy and Oskaloosa. The former segment had fewer curves, fewer bridges, and more moderate grades than the M&stL's route between the same points. Under Sprague's direction the ex-Burlington road was rebuilt to conform with the new main line standards on the Peoria Gateway Line. The old M&stL track going through Richland and Ollie was then dismantled.

All along the line a general face-lifting became noticeable. One hundred–pound (to the yard) rails took the place of lighter steel on the main line, and crushed rock ballast replaced slag and cinders. The steam engine which heretofore had been the only type of locomotive on the road shared a place with the diesel. Marshalltown and Oskaloosa saw diesel switchers ranging from 600-, 660-, 900-, to 1,000-h.p. jobs shunting cars in the yards. During the late war the rebuilt Mikados (2-8-2), known as Mac-Arthurs on the M&STL, did valiant service; but the days of the steam engine were numbered.

The advent of "road" diesels, that is, engines for service from one division point to another and beyond, meant faster and more economic freight operation. Big two-unit 3,000-h.p. diesel-electrics cut out the water and coal stops of yesterday. Still larger three-unit 4,050-h.p. monsters meant no more doubling on hills. Indeed, when Mr. Sprague came to the road, the fastest freight took thirty-two and a half hours to make the 476-mile run from Minneapolis to Peoria. Today the "three units" barrel from terminal to terminal in seventeen hours and fifty-five minutes. With the acceleration of time freights and a modernized plant, Iowans no longer joke about the Louie. Such nicknames as the "Midnight and Still Later," the "Maimed and Still Limping," and "Misery and Short Life" just don't fit.

In December 1943 the M&STL emerged from a twenty-year receivership with the same name except that "Railway" replaced "Railroad" in the title. This receivership was the longest of any Class I railroad (a road having operating revenue of over $1 million a year) still running in America. The Minneapolis & St. Louis Railway now pays substantial dividends and is one of the few railroads in the nation with no bonded indebtedness. Apart from virtually complete diesel operation, the road is proud of the fact that better than 80 percent of its freight cars have been acquired new since 1940.

Time was when Iowa folk used to check the reins of Old Dobbin and watch the North Star Limited steam by. That once-famous train symbolized the M&STL thirty years ago. Today a lad in a convertible on U.S. Highway 65 paces Time Freight 20. That fast freight between Minneapolis and Peoria, with its trim green-and-yellow diesel, now typifies the road. The Louie is still vital to Iowa and the Midwest, and more tonnage is shipped over its rails than ever before. But the North Star Limited was discontinued in 1935, for the automobile had taken away most of the passenger traffic. Some local service, however, is still provided by rail motor cars pulling comfortable stainless-steel air-conditioned coaches.

Other changes are noticeable. Certain nonprofitable branches have ceased to operate, namely: the Old Mud Line, branches to Montezuma and State Center, and part of the Belmond branch from Corwith to Algona. Because of light traffic and the high cost of extensive bridge maintenance, the Spencer–Storm Lake section of the Southwestern Extension was lopped off in 1936. Subsequently, that part of the branch from Rembrandt south was acquired by the Milwaukee and operation retained.

When the Tracy branch was ripped up west of Fosterdale on account of serious washouts, it marked the end of the second oldest railroad bridge in the country. This was a four-hundred-foot through-truss span crossing the Des Moines River. Prior to its Iowa location it carried the Burlington's tracks over the waters of the Missouri at Plattsmouth, Nebraska.

To this day you will find old-timers on the Eastern Division—that is, from Albert Lea to Peoria—who started railroading on the old Iowa Central. At the Oskaloosa station one can still discern "IC" on the cornice stones, and some of the older depots have potbellied stoves with "Iowa Central Railway" on their fire doors. Long diesel-operated fast freights roll over a modern railroad, but much of the right-of-way, some of the buildings, and a great deal of the tradition go back to the days of the Iowa Central. Such is the heritage of the Minneapolis & St. Louis.

IOWANS OF THE M&stL

Of all Iowa towns Oskaloosa is probably more of an "M&stL community" than any other within the state. Being an important junction point and division center, Oskaloosa is vital to the Minneapolis & St. Louis: the railway is one of the largest employers in town. Moreover, this thriving seat of Mahaska County has provided its full share of the road's officials.

Back in 1925 a tall, lanky lad just out of high school handed a letter to the Railway Post Office clerk on the North Star Limited as it halted at Oskaloosa's station. The writer was Charles LeRoy Fuller; the letter was a query about a job. Two days later a telegram came to him from Dexter Denison, freight traffic manager of the M&stL. It was a notice to report to work as a stenographer in Minneapolis; a "wire pass" for transportation accompanied the note. "Skeet" Fuller took the job. He has been with the road ever since.

Roy Fuller (born in Oskaloosa, March 24, 1905) liked railroading and subsequently became traffic agent in Des Moines, then traveling agent working out of Cincinnati, and in 1935 general agent in Indianapolis. A year later he came in from off-line territory to the general agency in Minneapolis. Promotions followed: general freight agent, assistant traffic manager, and, in 1950, freight traffic manager. One of the tallest men on the railroad (he is, in his own words, "five feet, seventeen and a half inches"), Roy Fuller is also outstanding because of his pleasing personality and sunny disposition. He likes to play pocket and three-cushion billiards, in which he is proficient. He married Susan Dale Riley; the Fullers have a boy and a girl. Mr. Fuller asserts he is "nonpartisan in politics"; he is a Congregationalist and holds membership in the Traffic Club of Minneapolis, Army Transportation Association, and the Minneapolis Athletic, Optimist, and Toastmasters Clubs.

Another Oskaloosan—and a veteran on the Louie—is Purchasing Agent Fred B. Matthews. Born in "Osky" May 19, 1890, young Fred looked to the Iowa Central for employment after finishing high school and the Oskaloosa Business College. His rail career began as receiving clerk in the hometown freight depot. That was, he recalls, "back on December 15, 1908." He subsequently became assistant timekeeper, then chief timekeeper. In 1916 he left Oskaloosa for a stint at chief clerking: first in the OS&D (Over, Short and Damaged) Department at Minneapolis, then a like position with E. E. Kerwin, superintendent at Watertown, South Dakota. When the Watertown superintendency was abolished late in 1917, Matthews was made assistant chief clerk to C. P. Stembel and shortly afterward chief clerk to Robert E. Ryan (both superintendents) back in Minneapolis. On April 15, 1935, he was appointed purchasing agent.

Mr. Matthews married Nancy Jane Klepper of Oskaloosa; they have one living son, their other boy lost his life in the late war. Fred Matthews is fond of hunting and fishing, although he finds little time to do either. When in Iowa he had quite a reputation as second tenor in the Knights of Pythias Glee Club and sang at many social engagements.

Up until 1910 Centerville was an Iowa Central point, for the Albia & Centerville Railway was operated by the former road. Around train-time at the Centerville depot, townsfolk of all ages came to see the trains depart. Among these was a youngster, one of the Sandahl kids, called Oscar. He was, however, more fascinated by the sound of the telegraph key than the commotion of a departing train. Oscar, in short, decided he'd be a telegrapher. Moreover, he backed up his decision with well-directed training.

In town the Methodist minister's boy had the same idea—and a new telegraph set. Oscar managed to get some old battery jars and a key; a friendly lineman helped string secondhand telephone wires between the parsonage and the Sandahl residence, and both boys started pounding the keys. Whatever additional aid was needed Oscar's brother, Carl, who was then an "op" for the Iowa Central, gladly proffered. Came the day when Carl was transferred from Centerville to Moravia, and brother Oscar promptly applied for his old job. On November 1, 1904, when only fifteen (he was born January 11, 1889, in Centerville), Oscar Sandahl started railroading on the local road at $25 a month.

After some two years on the Hook he switched to the Kansas City Division of the Milwaukee—the pay was better. By midsummer of 1909 he was back on an Iowa road—the Des Moines Union—at the state capital, as operator. Sensing greater advancement in traffic work, he went with the New York Central as stenographer and solicitor in Des Moines. After a stint in the army during World War I, Oscar Sandahl returned to railroading, this time with the M&stL as clerk and solicitor at Des Moines. Advancement to traveling agent soon followed, along with better jobs at the off-line points of Chicago, Detroit, and Boston. On May 1, 1937, Mr. Sandahl was summoned to Minneapolis as assistant general freight agent. Other promotions came, and by the end of 1943 he was appointed freight traffic manager.

Mr. Sandahl married Ruth Tilton of Des Moines; they have a son and a daughter. He likes to sing and remembers the day when the brothers Sandahl (Carl, Paul, Fred, and Oscar) had an amateur quartet which had engagements in Iowa and in the East. Mr. Sandahl is a Republican and a member of the Traffic Club of Minneapolis and the Minneapolis Athletic and Golf Clubs.

In the Executive Department of the M&stL, Iowa is represented by Merle E. Eaton, assistant to the president. Born in Chester, May 4, 1892, Eaton was educated at Cresco High School and the Minnesota School of Business, Minneapolis. He came to the M&stL in 1923 as secretary to William H. Bremner, then president and receiver. Mr. Eaton was subsequently made chief clerk in the receiver's office. When L. C. Sprague succeeded Bremner as head of the road in 1935, Merle Eaton was made assistant secretary of the company; three years later he became secretary. In 1943 he was appointed assistant to the president and assistant secretary.

Methodical and businesslike, he has a quiet sense of humor and enjoys nothing better than to harmonize with a group of singers at the piano. When a schoolboy he excelled in basketball—he still likes the game—but now enjoys the less arduous sport of billiards. He was married to the late Helen Hayes; his daughter lives near Minneapolis; his son died in World War II. Mr. Eaton married Luella Hauser in 1950. He is a Shriner and a Republican and holds membership in the Traffic Club of Minneapolis and the Minneapolis Athletic and Golden Valley Golf Clubs.

The youngest Iowan in the official brackets is William J. Powell, general attorney for the railway. Although born in Floris, November 22, 1914, he spent his boyhood at Ottumwa where his father, William H. Powell, and his uncle, James F. Powell, had both edited the *Ottumwa Courier*. Educated at Carleton College, Bill Powell chose the law as a career and received an LL.B. from the University of Minnesota in 1938. He practiced in Spring Valley, Minnesota, where at the age of twenty-eight he was elected president of the Tenth Judicial District Bar Association. He came with the M&stL in 1947 as general attorney.

In spite of the fact that he went to the University of Minnesota, Bill Powell stoutly avers he always cheers for the Hawkeye team whenever Minnesota plays the State University of Iowa. His fondness for Iowa and his dry wit are two noticeable characteristics. His avocations include "gardening in the summer; snow shoveling in winter." He married Meredith Burnap; the Powells have a son and a daughter, in that order. Mr. Powell is a Republican, an Episcopalian, and a member of the Minnesota Bar Association and the Minneapolis Athletic Club.

It is an odd coincidence that in reviewing the former executives of the M&stL one finds the longest and the shortest terms were held by Iowa men. William H. Bremner, mentioned elsewhere in this article, was president of the road from 1917 to 1934 except for a year and a half during World War I when he was federal manager. Born in Marshalltown, October 24, 1869, Bremner, after passing his bar examination, hung up his shingle in the state capital. Before entering the M&stL's law department he had been city solicitor for Des Moines.

In contrast to Bremner's long tenure, Edward L. Brown held the presidency for less than half a year. Serious illness forced his untimely resignation, but after a period of convalescence at the Mayo Clinic his health improved; he later headed the Denver & Rio Grande Western Railroad. Brown was born in Iowa, January 3, 1864; he began his rail career as a messenger boy on the Rock Island. After rising to become train dispatcher on that road, he went with the St. Paul & Duluth (now the Northern Pacific), becoming superintendent in 1896. Six years afterward he changed to the Great Northern. He relinquished a superintendency on the GN to head the M&stL late in 1916. Brown died in 1921, and his body was taken by special car to his old home in Pella for burial.

Probably the most distinguished ex-M&stL official is Judge Matthew M. Joyce. Judge Joyce was born in Emmetsburg, April 29, 1877; he took his law degree from the University of Michigan in 1900 and practiced in Missoula, Montana, and in Fort Dodge. Coming with the M&stL as general solicitor in 1917, he was subsequently made general counsel. In 1932 he left the railroad when appointed judge of the United States District Court in Minneapolis, which office he still holds.

Another Iowan held in high esteem on the M&StL was the late John H. Reinholdt. Born at Manning, November 23, 1883, and educated a Lafayette College, Easton, Pennsylvania, Reinholdt had a long and varied engineering career. Beginning as rodman on the Chicago Great Western in 1901, he later held responsible engineering positions on the New York Central Railroad, Easton Transit Company, and the Lehigh Valley Railroad. Reinholdt left the latter road to become the M&StL's assistant engineer in 1909. He went with the Kansas City Terminal Railway as general roadmaster early in 1917 but returned to the Louie by summer to become chief engineer. In 1920 he was made superintendent at Fort Dodge. Three years afterward Reinholt left the M&StL to go into the contracting business for himself. He died in 1935.

Iowa's role in the M&StL looms large. Why? Because the M&StL has more mileage in the Hawkeye State than in Minnesota, South Dakota, and Illinois combined. Operating as it does 1,400 miles from Leola, South Dakota, to Peoria, Illinois, the bulk of the "north-and-south main line" is still in Iowa. Since the seventies the Marshalltown shops have been in continuous operation; they are now and have been for many years the repair headquarters for freight cars on the entire Minneapolis & St. Louis system. The shops' payroll provides a livelihood for 135 employees. Marshalltown also has a new diesel service building, the most modern on the railroad. Finally, in the just-completed $1 million M&StL office building in Minneapolis, there are many officials who are proud of the fact that they were born and raised in Iowa.

Palimpsest 32 (July 1951)

A pioneer piece of motive power on Minneapolis & St. Louis rails was No. 61, a stately American (4-4-0) locomotive. During the nineteenth century this popular engine type was used in both freight and passenger service. H. Roger Grant Collection.

Around the turn of the century the Iowa Central erected in Oskaloosa one of Iowa's most imposing county seat depots. For decades the second floor contained offices for both the Iowa Central and its successor, the Minneapolis & St. Louis. H. Roger Grant Collection.

*Typical of small-town depots that dotted the Iowa landscape along the Minneapolis &
St. Louis was the one at Ogden, a station on the road's Mud Line. This forty-eight-mile
appendage linked Angus and Fort Dodge; it was abandoned early on.
Don L. Hofsommer Collection.*

*Early in the century it was train-time at the Minneapolis & St. Louis station at Spencer.
The bustling Clay County seat was on the Winthrop, Minnesota–Fort Dodge line.
Don L. Hofsommer Collection.*

Until dieselization, a common freight locomotive found on the Minneapolis & St. Louis featured a 2-8-2 wheel arrangement. For decades the company embraced an unusual system of numbering its motive power, using the month and year of purchase. Number 632 arrived in June 1932. H. Roger Grant Collection.

Number 348, acquired in March 1948, was a first-generation Minneapolis & St. Louis diesel freight road unit. H. Roger Grant Collection.

*The end was near for passenger service on the Twin Cities–Mason City–Marshalltown–
Oskaloosa–Albia route. In October 1956 a motor train including one of the Minneapolis
& St. Louis's $100,000 stainless-steel air-conditioned coaches, waits at the Albia station
for a 4:15 A.M. departure. H. Roger Grant Collection.*

THE CHICAGO GREAT WESTERN RAILWAY

STICKNEY'S RAILROAD

"An institution," said Emerson, "is the lengthened shadow of one man." If Emerson had lived in the Midwest around the turn of the century, he might have had the Chicago Great Western Railway in mind as the institution and A. B. Stickney as the man. It was Stickney who founded, built, and headed that 1,500-mile railroad serving Iowa, Minnesota, Illinois, Missouri, and, to a very limited extent, Kansas and Nebraska. Practically no mileage has been added since Stickney's death, nor have there been abandonments of any consequence. Other men have since taken over, and they have done —and are doing—a good job. If it had not been for the courage, resourcefulness, and determination of a New England schoolteacher, lawyer, and entrepreneur, however, there would not have been any jobs for them—at least not on the CGW. The story of the Great Western then is largely the story of Alpheus Beede Stickney.

Born in Wilton, Maine, June 27, 1840, Stickney remained in New England long enough to get an education and to spend his late teens in studying law and teaching school. Later admitted to the bar, he found his legal training of considerable aid in subsequent railroad work. In 1861 he came west to Stillwater, Minnesota, where he taught school and later hung out his shingle. At the end of the sixties, sensing greater opportunities in the state capital, he moved to St. Paul, gave up his law practice, and became actively engaged in promoting, constructing, and operating railways. He served as vice president, general manager, and chief counsel of the St. Paul, Stillwater & Taylors Falls Railroad (now the Omaha Road) and also as superintendent of construction of the St. Paul, Minneapolis & Manitoba, which later became the Great Northern. In 1880 he served with the

Canadian Pacific, supervising several hundred miles of line. The following year he returned to railroad building in the United States.

With this varied background, Stickney decided to build his own railroad. He acquired the charter of the Minnesota & Northwestern Railroad. Associated with Stickney in this enterprise were Maurice Auerbach, W. R. Merriam, Wm. Dawson, R. A. Smith, Crawford Livingston, W. R. Marshall, and Ansel Oppenheim of St. Paul; Wm. L. Boyle of Winnipeg, Canada; and C. W. Benson, K. D. Dunlop, and C. F. Benson of Sibley, Iowa. The company, which had been chartered on March 4, 1854, had never laid a yard of track. The energetic Stickney was quick to change this. Construction started in September 1884, and by October of the following year the road was in operation from St. Paul southward to Lyle, on the Minnesota-Iowa border, 109 miles. Late in 1885 he extended the road to Manly Junction in Worth County, Iowa, on the Iowa Central. Meanwhile the ex-schoolteacher had his sights set on Chicago.

From Hayfield, Minnesota, a few miles north of Lyle, a prong of the road pushed southeast to Dubuque, Iowa, which it reached on December 1, 1886. The Iowa section completed, the company went forward with construction in Illinois. This particular segment, however, was built from east to west because of hilly terrain in the vicinity of Winston, Illinois, twenty miles east of Dubuque. At that point a long tunnel had to be bored. The line from Forest Park (just outside of Chicago) to South Freeport was railed in 1887. Trains, however, did not run from the latter point westward through the 2,493-foot Winston Tunnel to Aiken, Illinois, until the following year. Between Aiken and Dubuque running rights were had over the Burlington and the Illinois Central railroads; from Forest Park to Grand Central Station in downtown Chicago, Stickney ran his trains over what is now the Baltimore & Ohio Chicago Terminal Railroad. Thus the dream of a new Twin Cities–Chicago route became an actuality.

Obviously the name Minnesota & Northwestern was misleading to many people. Stickney was fully aware of this, so he and his associates incorporated the Chicago, St. Paul & Kansas City Railway in Iowa on June 1, 1886, to further his expansion program. The new company purchased the old Wisconsin, Iowa & Nebraska Railway, extending from Waterloo to Des Moines with a branch from Cedar Falls Junction to Cedar Falls. Because of its catercornered route in Iowa the WI&N was known as "The Old Diagonal"; it was incorporated under the laws of Iowa on March 17, 1882. The Chicago, St. Paul & Kansas City bought all the properties of the Minnesota & Northwestern in 1887.

Now the Stickney-envisioned system struck out for Kansas City. It spanned the gap between Waterloo and Oelwein, Iowa (the latter town being on the Minnesota & Northwestern), in 1887. It built from Des Moines to St. Joseph, Missouri, reaching "St. Joe" by the end of 1888. As a final step, it leased the Leavenworth & St. Joseph Railway in 1891. With certain trackage rights over other roads in Missouri, it ran into the heart of Kansas City, thus serving all the places in its name: Chicago, St. Paul, and Kansas City.

From the time that its rails first extended south from St. Paul, the Stickney road did a brisk cattle business. It was A. B. Stickney and his associates who in 1882 started what is now the famous St. Paul Union Stockyards. As the cattle and packing center grew, the railroad operated many stock trains from South St. Paul to Chicago. Contemporary accounts say that cowboy attendants on these trains sat atop the cars and whiled away the time shooting at the glass insulators on telegraph poles. They kept linemen busy repairing the damage.

During Stickney's regime the railroad always had its headquarters in St. Paul; until 1899 its shops were located at South Park, near the capital city. Among the executives of the road were Ansel Oppenheim and Arnold Kalman, well-known St. Paul businessmen and financiers. Later other prominent St. Paulites, such as Frank B. Kellogg and C. O. Kalman, were active in the affairs of the company. Samuel C. Stickney, son of President Stickney, was for many years general manager and subsequently became vice president.

Never a wealthy road, the Stickney enterprise needed all the managerial ingenuity its officers could muster to keep it on the black side of the ledger. Beset on all sides by well-entrenched trunk lines linking the Twin Cities with Chicago, the newcomer in this territory met intense and often cutthroat competition. Stickney had to be ever on the alert to capture and hold traffic. For a time in the late eighties he headed the Iowa Central Railway as a means to shunt more traffic to his road at Manly, Iowa. He even put on through sleeping car service between the Twin Cities and Columbus, Ohio—a bizarre route over the roads he headed to Peoria, Illinois, and thence on the Big Four to the Buckeye capital.

When it came to courage, audacity, and original thinking, it was hard to beat A. B. Stickney. The redheaded and red-bearded railroader was a nonconformist of the first water. He dared to sympathize with the Grangers when all other railroad presidents were dead set against restrictive legislation affecting rates.

Not content with running his railroad—a job in itself—Stickney found time to write a book called *The Railway Problem* (1891) in which he sharply criticized railroad management. Stickney foresaw the Hepburn Act and state and federal legislation which would prohibit all forms of discrimination. Time has vindicated his judgment. It may be added that Stickney was not necessarily for lower rates, but he was more ardently for *one rate for all shippers for a specific commodity between two given points*. He felt the Granger legislation was enacted because of rate cutting, rebating, and other forms of discrimination.

Stickney cut rates along with his competitors. He had to, as long as other carriers posted one tariff and then found ways to lower the rates for favored shippers. Today this is an academic subject, but in the nineties it was very real. Nor was it entirely the railroad managers' fault. They were frequently dominated by large shippers, and they had to grant a rebate. Sometimes it meant a special rate or a special master in receivership. And the specter of receivership on the Stickney system was always imminent.

In fact, the Chicago, St. Paul & Kansas City became virtually insolvent. Stickney, however, avoided receivership by reorganizing the road in 1892 as the Chicago Great Western Railway—a new company with no mortgage indebtedness. He prevailed upon the shareholders to exchange bonds of the old road for stock of the new. A novel feature of the reorganization was the issuance of debenture stock along with three other kinds of stock. Since most of the shareholders were English, they agreed to the proposition of having debenture stock in lieu of bonds. Thus the Chicago Great Western was the only American trunk line at the time without mortgage indebtedness. When the panic of 1893 came, the CGW rode the storm.

A few years earlier the railroad offered a prize for the best emblem in a contest open to ticket agents in the United States. R. G. Thompson, a Wabash employee at Fort Wayne, Indiana, won the award by designing a maple leaf on which the veins showed the lines of the railway. During the remainder of Stickney's tenure the CGW's timetables and advertising literature featured the maple leaf as the road's colophon.

In 1899 the CGW purchased stock control of the Wisconsin, Minnesota & Pacific, a road which never operated in the Badger State and fell short of the Pacific by over 1,500 miles. It had a curious history, being operated in two parts: one from Red Wing on the Mississippi westward to Mankato on the Minnesota River; the other, or western end, from Morton, Minnesota, to Watertown, South Dakota. It was the eastern segment, which crossed Stickney's north-south line at Randolph, of which the CGW had control and, curiously enough, which A. B. Stickney helped build in the early eighties. Prior to CGW interest the road had been controlled by the Rock Island and operated by the Minneapolis & St. Louis. In 1900 an up-and-coming young lawyer by the name of Frank B. Kellogg was elected president of the eastern part of the WM&P. He later became world famous as author of the Kellogg Pact to outlaw war. The Great Western subsequently operated the WM&P as part of its system.

No sooner had the Great Western controlled the WM&P than the latter company acquired other roads. The Duluth, Red Wing & Southern, extending from Red Wing south to Zumbrota, Minnesota, 25 miles, was purchased on July 3, 1901; on September 10 of the same year the Winona & Western came into the fold. The W&W road operated a 113-mile line from Winona, Minnesota, to Osage in Mitchell County, Iowa. It also had a 7-mile branch from Simpson to Rochester, Minnesota. In 1903 the 26-mile gap between Rochester and Zumbrota was spanned, giving the Great Western access to Rochester from both the north and south over its own rails.

All this time it was the driving force of Stickney which brought about these consolidations. He remained president of the Great Western and its predecessor companies except for the period from 1890 to 1894, when he was chairman of the board. During the interim John M. Egan, formerly general manager of the Stickney system, was president. Egan, onetime general superintendent of the Canadian Pacific's Western Division and a civil engineer for several roads in America, had almost as varied a career as Stickney. In later years Egan headed the Central of Georgia.

This, roughly, is the history of the Chicago Great Western up to the twentieth century. It subsequent expansion was chiefly in Iowa.

THE GREAT WESTERN IN IOWA

Slightly over one-half of the Chicago Great Western mileage is in Iowa today. Because the Hawkeye State has played an important role in the road's growth, a review of the antecedent companies in Iowa may be in order. One company's history, at least, goes back to 1870. It is that half-mythical, half-real Iowa Pacific, which palimpsest-like shows traces of cuts and fills and old rights-of-way here and there on the prairies. Many of the vestigial remains are hardly decipherable even to the student of railroad history. Until some patient antiquarian with a stout pair of legs and a liberal endowment can disclose the whole story of the ill-fated road, we will have to be content with fragments of its history.

The Iowa Pacific was graded from a point in Fayette County, called Fayette Junction, westward through Sumner, Waverly, and Hampton to Bel-mond in Wright County. Another section veered southwest from Belmond to Fort Dodge. The records seem to indicate that the company had laid only about a dozen miles of track in the vicinity of Waverly. A company titled the Dubuque & Dakota—nicknamed the Damned Doubtful—ac-quired some ninety-five miles of the old Iowa Pacific right-of-way and laid tracks from Sumner to Hampton in 1879 and 1880.

Enter now the Stickney-controlled railroads. The Minnesota & North-western (a predecessor of the Chicago Great Western) purchased the Du-buque & Dakota's line from Sumner to Hampton in 1887. The Mason City & Fort Dodge (incorporated in Iowa June 10, 1881) had built from Mason City to Fort Dodge in 1886, utilizing part of the abandoned Iowa Pacific grade. At this time the MC&FtD was controlled by Stickney interests, and in 1901 it was leased to the Chicago Great Western for one hundred years.

Stickney now extended the Mason City & Fort Dodge to fulfill his last major objective for the Maple Leaf System: a direct line between the Twin Cities and Omaha. The short Mason City–Manly Junction gap was spanned in 1901. The longest uncompleted section, the 133 miles from Fort Dodge to Council Bluffs, was finished in 1903. It featured a lofty bridge nearly a half-mile long over the Des Moines River at Fort Dodge. The 2,588-foot structure, reputed to be the second largest railway bridge in Iowa, entailed no loss of life in its building, the most serious accident being a smashed finger of one workman! From Council Bluffs the CGW had trackage rights into Omaha.

This completes the present Great Western except for the Clarion-Oelwein side of the triangle near the center of the system so conspicu-ous on the map. As previously mentioned, the rails had already been laid from Sumner to Hampton—a part of that triangle. The western gap from Hampton to Clarion, twenty-six miles, was closed in 1902; on the east-ern end, the twenty-nine-mile segment from Waverly to Oelwein was com-pleted in 1904.

As was the case with many roads in the nineteenth century, the build-ing of the Great Western was often done by construction companies affili-ated with the railway. For example, on the Twin Cities–Chicago line, that portion of the road between Dubuque and Thorpe, Iowa, was built by the Stickney-controlled Dubuque & Northwestern and on completion was promptly sold to the Minnesota & Northwestern. Again, land companies were formed to purchase rights-of-way and sites for depots and shops. The Iowa Development and the Iowa Townsite companies, which Stickney formed to acquire land, are still in existence. Their book value, however, is now listed at $1 each!

The turn of the century witnessed the moving of the Great Western's shops from South Park, Minnesota, to Oelwein. The new shop headquarters were officially dedicated on September 28, 1899, but it was not until about four years afterward that they were fully equipped for repair work of all kinds.

It was intended that Oelwein should have the shops in the early '90s, but the panic of 1893 and the business depression which followed postponed the road's plans. A. B. Stickney, however, was fully aware that the Iowa community was the logical place for the company's major repair base. The practice of bringing bad-order cars and faulty locomotives all the way to the St. Paul area from Chicago and Kansas City entailed much wasteful mileage. After many premature announcements, Stickney declared on February 21, 1898, at the opening of Oelwein's Hotel Mealey, that the shops would be built that year. The news caused much rejoicing and moved a local bard, Mary H. Millard, to write an eighteen-stanza poem on "Oelwein's Glory." Her verses ended with a stirring

> Long live the noble president
> Of western railroad fame!
> And well may Oelwein's sterling men
> Pay honor to his name,
>
> For in the years that are to come,
> Oft we'll tell the story:
> How A. B. Stickney laid the road
> That led to Oelwein's glory.

In 1890 Oelwein had about 800 people; a half century later the population had risen to 7,801. A large part of this increase may be attributed to the removal of the shops to Oelwein and the subsequent enlargements of the repair facilities. Contemporary accounts describe the main shop quarters as two large buildings separated by a transfer pit and table. The one structure housed the general storehouse, the machine and erecting shop, the boiler shop, and the coach shop. The other building embraced the freight car shop, the blacksmith shop, and the paint shop. Some idea of the size of the layout may be learned from the fact that fifteen tracks were to go into the machine and erecting shop, six into the coach shop, and five into the boiler shop.

A novel feature in one of the smaller buildings was a recreation room called "Liberty Hall," where employees could spend their leisure time. The "club room" with reading matter is said to have been personally paid for by Stickney.

When Walter P. Chrysler came to supervise the shops from the Colorado & Southern in 1907, he found them among the most modern in the country. In his autobiography, *Life of an American Workman*, he describes them in glowing terms:

> They were the biggest shops I had ever seen. Sixteen or eighteen locomotives could be hauled inside them. In the winter darkness they were brilliantly illuminated with sputtering bluish arc lamps. There were great cranes aloft that could lift a locomotive in their chains. Everything was marvelous, and when I saw the transfer tables I felt like applauding. Best of all, everything in those shops was to be in my charge. . . .

Chrysler rose to become superintendent of motive power for the Great Western but left the road after a tiff with Stickney's successor, Sam Felton. From the Maple Leaf System he went to the Pittsburgh plant of the American Locomotive Company as works manager. He subsequently quit "Alco" to try his hand at automobile manufacturing and later founded and built the huge Chrysler Corporation. It is significant that Oelwein remembers him as the owner of the town's first automobile—a Locomobile.

During Stickney's reign the locomotives were almost as individualistic as he, for their stacks were painted a bright red; the Great Western itself was frequently referred to as "The Red Stack." In a day when there was great rivalry between steam roads and electric interurbans, Stickney had his company operate in close harmony with the Waterloo, Cedar Falls & Northern. The interurban operated over CGW tracks from Waverly to Sumner, whereas Stickney's road had running rights over the "juice" line from Denver Junction to Waterloo. This rapprochement was further strengthened when L. S. Cass, head of the interurban, was made a vice president of the Great Western.

Stickney vigorously fought to get legislation enacted prohibiting discrimination in rates. He dared to say what he thought anywhere and at any time. At one important traffic meeting in the East he complimented the railroad presidents on their honesty, integrity, and fine character, saying he would trust any one of them with his entire personal fortune. Then, according to the recollection of a former Great Western official, he added: "But, gentlemen, as railroad presidents I would not trust any one of you with my watch!" Stickney knew that once the presidents left the meeting, the rate agreements which they had just made would promptly be broken. In a booklet entitled *Railway Rates* (1909), Stickney also advocated tariff simplification and devised his own system which, he asserted, would reduce the rate sheets from an estimated four thousand volumes to just thirty-one.

Rumors of an impending financial crisis at the Great Western offices drifted through Wall Street during the first days of 1907. The year had opened propitiously for businessmen and investors, but the unconfirmed reports of low earnings and unpaid obligations were a harbinger of the famous panic of 1907. Despite a floating debt of $10,653,000, on January 7 Samuel C. Stickney denied a report from New York "that a receiver had been or was about to be asked for the Chicago Great Western Railway." However, cabled news from London which came in the next morning confirmed the rumor. The British noteholders had met with A. B. Stickney and reached a decision on the company's financial plight. Out of their conference came a plan to place the railroad into bankruptcy "to maintain the status quo during the time necessary to prepare a first mortgage bond covering all the indebtedness of the road, and to obtain a vote of the stockholders on this measure." At this London meeting the elder Stickney declared that the financial climate in the United States was so unhealthy that the 7 percent note obligations could not be met. Bankruptcy seemed to be the only answer. Wall Street reacted to the news with a wave of selling, and before the ticker closed on January 8, 1908, Chicago Great Western stock was selling for four and three-quarters.

Stickney and C. H. F. Smith of St. Paul were appointed coreceivers of the railroad by the court, but within a year's time Stickney severed all his connections with the Great Western and for the remainder of his life lived in retirement at St. Paul.

In 1909 the road was sold and its properties conveyed to the Chicago Great Western *Railroad*, a newly formed company. That year Samuel M. Felton became president, an office he held until 1925, after which he served as chairman of the board until his death in 1930. Sam Felton had started his career as rodman for the Chester Creek Railroad (now part of the Pennsylvania Railroad) in 1868. For the next twenty years he served in various capacities, such as engineer, chief engineer, general superintendent, or general manager, on a dozen roads. He headed the East Tennessee, Virginia & Georgia (now Southern) in 1890, and up to the time of his CGW appointment he had been successively president or receiver of another dozen roads, including the Mexican Central and the Chicago & Alton.

With the Felton management came fresh capital, an item sorely needed to rehabilitate the Great Western. Indeed, an almost complete physical regeneration characterized his incumbency. Even the maple leaf was discarded and a "Corn Belt Route" emblem used in its stead. Much of the motive power was run-down and obsolete. The most popular type locomotive, used in both freight and passenger service, was the Prairie (2-6-2). (The designation "2-6-2" indicates a locomotive with a two-wheel leading truck, six driving wheels, and two wheels following the driver.) In the motive power reformation, the Prairies used on passenger runs were rebuilt into faster and easier riding Pacifics (4-6-2). The Prairies in freight operation were changed from compound to simple cylinders and provided with superheaters. Forty new Consolidations (2-8-0) were in service or on order by the second year of Felton's administration. Finally, ten Mallet Compounds were placed in operation to expedite tonnage on the 1 percent grades between Stockton, Illinois, and Oelwein. They were of the 2-6-6-2 wheel arrangement, with a tractive force of 81,175 pounds each. Later the Mikado (2-8-2) type made its appearance; these were followed by diesels.

The millions poured into the system also accounted for grade reductions, a new bridge across the Mississippi at St. Paul, block signals between Chicago and Oelwein, and rail motor cars to cut down the cost of passenger operation. The Great Western pioneered in utilizing self-propelled vehicles in local service. The annual report of June 30, 1911, shows three 200-h.p. McKeen gasoline motor cars on the roster. At this writing one of the McKeens is still in service shunting cars in Winona, Minnesota, having been converted to a switcher several years ago. In 1924 the road took delivery of its first gasoline-electric car, which, incidentally, was Electro-Motive's first rail motor vehicle, too. Known as the M-300, it hauled General Manager C. L. Hinkle's eighty-five-ton business car on a trial run from Chicago to Oelwein, much to the surprise of all concerned. As a final tribute to Felton's presidency, the CGW's Western Division won the coveted Harriman safety award in 1924.

When Sam Felton became board chairman in 1925, Nathaniel L. Howard, an Iowan, succeeded him as president. Born in Fairfield, March 9, 1884, Howard was educated at Parsons College in his hometown and at the United States Military Academy at West Point. He started railroading as a civil engineer for the Burlington and subsequently became division superintendent at Hannibal, Missouri. With the outbreak of the First World War he went into the army and was commissioned a colonel in 1918. After the conflict he returned to the "Q" as assistant to the federal manager, and following government operation he rose to be superintendent of transportation of that road. In 1924 he was made general manager of the Chicago Union Station Company and the following year took his Great Western appointment.

Tall, slim, and white-haired, Howard had a West Point bearing, but at the same time he was democratic and friendly. In contrast, Felton was somewhat austere, being brought up in the old school of railroading, which was rough and autocratic. It was during the administration of these totally different men that amazing developments in passenger service took place.

After a trip abroad Sam Felton became greatly impressed with the trim, clean appearance of British locomotives. Perhaps he saw the immaculate-looking coaching stock of England's Great Western Railway; at any rate he came back with some new ideas for his Great Western. He had Oelwein streamline a conventional Pacific-type locomotive so that all outside pipes were concealed. The driving rods and cylinder heads were polished, the wheels painted red, the spokes golden. Engine No. 916, in short, had everything but a coat of arms! It, along with four cars, one of which was a baggage-mail unit, was painted Venetian red with gold lettering. The train was named the Red Bird and put on a nonstop run between the Twin Cities and Rochester, Minnesota, via Dodge Center. The CGW had trackage rights from Dodge Center to Rochester over the North Western.

Six years after the Red Bird appeared, Oelwein came out with another "bird" which fluttered even more in the limelight. Convention was tossed to the winds when the road's draftsmen designed a deluxe, three-car, gasoline-electric train for companion service with the Red Bird. The resourceful Oelwein craftsmen took the original underframes of the old McKeen cars and then built anew. One car had a six-cylinder, 300-h.p. Electro-Motive engine at the head-end followed by a Railway Post Office and baggage compartment. The next unit was a passenger coach seating seventy-four. It had deep seats, spacious windows, and wide aisles covered with soundproof linoleum. But the crowning achievement was the last unit: a parlor-observation-club car with a rounded end, anticipating today's streamlining. Its low-backed reed chairs, upholstered in soft old rose and shimmering blue mohair, were the last word in travel elegance. A deep-yielding Wilton carpet of blue-gray and some artistic wall-bracket lamps added to the smart decor. The car also had two complete Pullman sections in which the seats could be quickly converted to lower berths. The latter were very much appreciated by sick folks going to the Mayo Clinic for treatment.

The motor-train was painted blue, with striping and lettering in gold leaf. Called the Blue Bird, the novel little "streamliner" was put into service in the ominous year of 1929. It operated between the Twin Cities and Rochester via Red Wing. Unfortunately, the Blue Bird had a short life, for the depression curtailed travel, and the increased use of automobiles took many of the short-haul riders.

While the mighty "Pennsy" and the equally powerful Santa Fe made headlines by inaugurating air-rail service from coast to coast in conjunction with the Transcontinental Air Transport ("The Lindbergh Line"), the Great Western officials launched their own plane-train operation. This, too, began in 1929. Through-ticketing arrangements were made with Universal Air Lines, and bus service was provided between Chicago's Grand Central Station and the municipal airport. One went by Great Western train to Chicago, thence by UAL plane to St. Louis or Cleveland. Leaving Des Moines (for example) at 9:00 P.M. on a sleeper, one's train steamed into Grand Central at 7:35 next morning; and by 9:45 one's tri-motor plane left the airport for St. Louis, arriving at the latter city by 1:00 P.M. The flight to Cleveland, however, required a layover in the Windy City until 4:00 P.M.; arrival time in Cleveland was 7:45 P.M. This, too, was an interesting, although short-lived experiment.

From the days of Stickney until the Great Depression, the CGW showed great ingenuity in providing extensive passenger service on main lines and branches. It featured daily through sleeping cars from the Twin Cities to Los Angeles in conjunction with the Santa Fe at Kansas City. Through Pullmans were also provided from Minneapolis–St. Paul via "KC" to Dallas and Houston on the Missouri-Kansas-Texas Railroad. Such Chicago–Twin City trains as the Great Western Limited, later the Legionnaire and still later the Minnesotan, were bywords in the Midwest. The Nebraska Limited (Twin Cities–Omaha) was also a favorite, but the Mill Cities Limited (Twin Cities–Kansas City) was usually the most popular on the system. In its heyday it was a common sight to see from three to five Pullmans on the Mill Cities Limited.

Iowans were particularly fond of their Chicago Special, a through train which highballed from Des Moines to the Windy City, making only a limited number of stops. Advertised as "an inviting train to enter—a comfortable train to ride on," "Des Moines' Own Train to Chicago" is now only a memory.

For many traveling men the Iowa communities of Oelwein and McIntire had a very special significance. It was at these stations that sleepers were set out or added. True, some trains managed to get by McIntire without shuffling equipment, but at Oelwein, never! On some runs the night train from Chicago set out a couple of cars at Oelwein for Kansas City; another car or two was shed at McIntire for Rochester, Minnesota. The balance of the train continued to the Twin Cities. On the eastbound trip, sleepers were added. The arrangement varied with the year, the season, and the routing. The point is that any evening train going through Oelwein was generally shunted around midnight or very early in the morning. The test of an experienced traveler was to sleep through Oelwein. If he succeeded he was regarded as a thirty-two-degree veteran by seasoned drummers.

Occasionally, switching cars at Oelwein caused complications. The late Sigmund Greve recalled a classic incident of this kind. On the day in question a porter took the shoes from his Twin Cities car into one of the other sleepers, where he could have the companionship of a fellow porter. After polishing the shoes, he started back to his Pullman but became confused and ended up in a Kansas City sleeper. Well, Oelwein came and went and so did the shoes—to Kansas City. Consternation reigned after the error was detected, but it was too late. When the train arrived in St. Paul, the passengers were obliged to walk in their stocking feet about a block and a half to the nearest hotel. Here they were met by a passenger representative who took their measurements and provided them with new pairs of shoes, compliments of the Chicago Great Western!

The automobile and streamlined service on other competitive roads better equipped to run fast trains caused gradual retrenchment in CGW passenger service. But the plucky Great Western continued to fight a losing battle. As late as 1935 it tried a new plan: that of providing tourist-sleeper operation on the Twin Cities–Chicago run at coach rates. Instead of paying first-class fare, the passenger merely bought a coach ticket and paid for his berth.

The depression years were trying to all railroads, and the Great Western was no exception. A high standard of maintenance had reached its peak about the time of World War I. After that it perceptively declined. Government operation during the war was responsible for diverting traffic to other rival lines. The Great Western's high joint-facility costs hung like a millstone around its neck. A relatively high percentage of freight cars on its rails made the per diem charges soar.

In 1929 Victor V. Boatner, formerly head of the Peoria & Pekin Union, succeeded Howard to the presidency. Boatner in turn was followed in 1931 by Patrick H. Joyce, who continued as president for fifteen years. Before coming to the Great Western, Joyce had been a prominent railway supply manufacturer. He aided in founding the Liberty Car & Equipment Company and in 1918 became its president. The following year he headed the Liberty Car Wheel Company, and when it merged with the Illinois Car & Manufacturing Company in 1921, he was elected president of the combined firms. The latter organization became the Standard Steel Car Company in 1928, and it in turn was sold to Pullman-Standard Car & Manufacturing Company in 1930. Joyce was successively vice president of the "Standard" firms.

During the early thirties a fleet of modern Texas-type (2-10-4) engines appeared on the motive power roster. In 1936 the seemingly dormant Great Western ingenuity recrudesced with the inauguration of trailer-on-flatcar operation over the 425-mile route between Chicago and St. Paul. Here, again, the road pioneered in a new type of service. While the CGW did not originate the idea of truck trailers by rail, it did operate the first service of this kind over *comparatively long distances on a permanent basis.* In 1939 trailers were also rolling on flatcars between Chicago and Council Bluffs.

No amount of ingenuity, however, could stem the decline in car loadings as a result of the Great Depression. The plight of the road was so serious that it went bankrupt in 1935. Joyce was appointed a cotrustee by the court; at the same time he continued as president of the corporation. Reorganization was effected in 1941, and the Chicago Great Western *Railroad* became the Chicago Great Western *Railway.* The successor company is generally referred to as the second Great Western *Railway,* since Stickney's road as far back as 1892 had the identical name.

During World War II the Great Western hauled a record tonnage, due in no small measure to the admirable performance of the Texas-type locomotives. These Baldwin- and Lima-built engines were equipped with boosters, giving them a maximum starting tractive force of 97,900 pounds. In the late thirties Oelwein modernized them still more with lightweight rods and disk wheels. With the advent of diesels, modernization was on the other foot; the internal-combustion engine modernized the Oelwein shops rather than the shops modernizing the locomotives. Today Oelwein's shop facilities are strictly up-to-date, being completely revamped for all-diesel repair.

THE CHICAGO GREAT WESTERN TODAY

The current rehabilitation of the Chicago Great Western may be said to have started soon after World War II; it has continued with renewed vigor ever since. In 1946 Harold W. Burtness succeeded Pat Joyce as president. Mr. Burtness started railroading at the age of seventeen as a clerk on the Burlington and shortly thereafter switched to the Pennsylvania, where he became secretary to the traffic manager. In 1922 he went with the Great Western as secretary to President Sam Felton and twenty-four years afterward found himself in his former boss's chair.

During Burtness's administration the Corn Belt Route bought its first diesels: three 1,000-h.p. switchers, which were put to work marshaling cars at Oelwein in 1947. Later that year six 4,500-h.p. diesels began replacing the faithful Texas steamers in road service. During the next two years there was a wide variety of diesels, running the gamut from 660-h.p. switchers to ponderous four-unit 6,000-h.p. road freighters.

On October 19, 1948, Grant Stauffer, representing a group of investors who had purchased control of the road, succeeded Burtness as president. Stauffer headed the Sinclair Coal Company and was also a director and chairman of the executive committee of the Kansas City Southern. His untimely death on March 31, 1949, resulted in the assistant to the president, William N. Deramus III, being elected to his place.

When Mr. Deramus took office at the age of thirty-three, he is said to have been the youngest Class I railroad president in America. He is a railroader by heritage and choice. His father is chairman of the board of the Kansas City Southern; an uncle, Louis S. Deramus, was trustee and chief executive officer on the Monon. Educated at the University of Michigan and at Harvard Law School, Deramus entered railroading after receiving his LL.B. His first job was as transportation apprentice on the Wabash. He left that road as assistant trainmaster of the St. Louis Division in 1943 to enter Military Railway Service. Mustered out in 1946 as a major, Deramus became assistant to the general manager of the Kansas City Southern. In November 1948 he was appointed assistant to the president of the Great Western.

Under Deramus's presidency complete dieselization was brought about in 1950. Within the past three years the main lines have been extensively reballasted and many miles of heavier rail laid. Radio communication has been installed, making it possible for train crews to contact dispatchers and yardmasters while their trains are in motion. It also permits men in the cab to talk with crewmen in the caboose. Modern brick stations have recently been erected at Des Moines, Marshalltown, and Fort Dodge. In addition to shop improvements and more office buildings at Oelwein, a new icing plant and dock have been constructed in that community.

Time freights have accelerated to meet or to better competitive schedules of other roads in Great Western territory. Trailer-on-flatcar service is now available at Des Moines. The pioneer Chicago–St. Paul and later Chicago–Council Bluffs service of truck trailer haulage on rails has been extended to include Chicago–Kansas City, St. Paul–Kansas City, and St. Paul–Council Bluffs operation.

On the other hand, the unprofitable dining and sleeping car service has been discontinued, and all branch-line passenger service has been withdrawn. Local air-conditioned coach operation, however, continues on all the main lines.

The Chicago Great Western still serves virtually the same communities over the identical routes it did in the days of A. B. Stickney. In a few instances, noticeably on the Winona branch from Planks to Winona, Minnesota, forty-one miles, the CGW scrapped its own line and now operates over the North Western. A series of spindling trestles, along with a 3.3 percent grade plus a winding horseshoe curve, made that line uneconomical to operate. More recently the five-mile Sycamore-DeKalb branch in Illinois was pulled up, and CGW trains now use the parallel route of the North Western.

In several minor cases branches have been scrapped and service discontinued. As this is being written the road has received authorization to abandon the five-mile Bellechester Junction–Bellechester, Minnesota, spur. An earlier casualty in the same state was the Eden-Mantorville stub, six miles long, which had a daily milk train to St. Paul. For years the local was dubbed "The Milk Shake."

In 1951 the six-mile segment of the Waverly-Sumner branch between Waverly and Bremer, Iowa, ceased operation. The other abandonments in Iowa occurred many years ago as a result of mining operations being worked out or rendered unprofitable. In this category were the long-forgotten three-mile stub from Valeria to the Oswald coal mines and the so-called Coalville branch, which left the Fort Dodge–Lehigh branch at Gypsum for mines three miles away. The thirties saw the Lehigh branch cut back to Gypsum and the tracks ripped up east of that point.

With the removal of most of the general offices from Chicago to Oelwein in 1952, Iowa's role in the Great Western will be increasingly important. Having over half of its system in the state, it is a logical corollary for the Chicago Great Western to have its management also within the state. Oelwein, Iowa, more or less the geographical center of the railway, is now the managerial hub as well.

Railroads have been called the "key to the prairies" because of their contribution to the settlement and growth of the Midwest. The history of railroading in Iowa is largely the story of the "Big Four" and the "Little Three." The "Big Four" is comprised of the Rock Island, the Burlington, the Chicago & North Western, and the Chicago, Milwaukee, St. Paul & Pacific— with almost 7,000 miles of track in Iowa. The "Little Three" includes the Minneapolis & St. Louis, the Illinois Central, and the CGW, with a combined trackage of over 2,200 miles in Iowa. Even in a jet-powered era, the Iowan still looks to the steel rails for much of his transportation needs. In 1953 there is every indication that the Chicago Great Western and her sister railways will keep pace with scientific achievements. The changes had been from wood, to coal, to electricity and fuel oil. The only question seems to be: When will atomic-powered locomotives haul their cargoes over Iowa's prairies?

Palimpsest 34 (June 1953)

About 1920 a long freight stands at the station in Peru, thirty-five miles south of Des Moines, an important location on the Chicago Great Western's Southern Division. H. Roger Grant Collection.

Although the Chicago Great Western possessed a wide range of steam locomotives, including the ubiquitous American Standards (4-4-0), it also operated some unusual ones. Most notably, in 1910 the company purchased ten giant 505,000-pound 2-6-6-2s from Baldwin. These Mallets ("Snakes," as Great Western employees called them) could pull heavy loads, but they were slow, prone to derail, damaged the track, and were expensive to maintain. Within a few years the road wisely sold its fleet, including No. 608, which is seen at the roundhouse in Oelwein. H. Roger Grant Collection.

While the claim that Clear Lake was "The Saratoga of the West" might be challenged, hundreds of Iowans annually flocked to its shores. The Great Western, in conjunction with the Mason City & Clear Lake electric interurban, offered attractive rates to this popular vacation destination. H. Roger Grant Collection.

Several midwestern railroads, including the Chicago Great Western, briefly offered joint connections with commercial air carriers. Starting in February 1929, the Great Western coordinated service with Universal Air Line, but the stock market crash later in the year did much to kill this land-air relationship. H. Roger Grant Collection.

Never a rich road, the Chicago Great Western made do with equipment that most other carriers had long retired. On April 18, 1949, a McKeen motor car, No. 1003, and trailer operating as Train No. 35, "burns the ballast" near Oelwein. W. L. Heitter photograph, H. Roger Grant Collection.

In the twilight of steam operations on the Great Western, locomotive No. 721 pulls a long train of mostly meat cars near Oelwein. H. Roger Grant Collection.

In the early 1950s a Great Western freight train with a string of piggyback trailers, a company innovation, moves across the Iowa countryside. H. Roger Grant Collection.

On August 31, 1963, the distinguished photographer of Iowa rails, W. S. Kuba of Cedar Rapids, caught a Great Western freight north of Oelwein. The Deramus administration, which assumed control in the late 1940s, made the carrier famous for its long freight trains, powered by multiple diesel units. W. S. Kuba photograph, H. Roger Grant Collection.

In the spring of 1966, two years before the Chicago & North Western took control, Great Western Train No. 192, consisting of four modern GP-30s and 167 cars, winds through the hills and dales west of Dubuque. Mark Nelson photograph, H. Roger Grant Collection.

INTERURBANS IN IOWA

FORT DODGE, DES MOINES & SOUTHERN

Iowa's biggest interurban—the Fort Dodge, Des Moines & Southern Railway—began as a small coal carrier running from mine to connecting railroad. Later it expanded and became a common carrier hauling freight, passengers, mail, and express. A subsequent metamorphosis changed it from steam to electric operation with greatly increased mileage. It has operated streetcars and buses in the past. In one way history repeats itself: the road began its existence almost exclusively as a freight line; it evolved to a point where passenger revenue exceeded that from tonnage; today it is again primarily a carrier of freight, with gypsum products its chief revenue producer. But it has grown from a 3-mile line to approximately 150 miles. Operating revenues exceed a million dollars a year, making it a Class I carrier.

In the eighties one of the largest coal operators in Boone County was the Clyde Coal Company. That firm sank its first shaft mine at Incline, west of Moingona, in 1885. The manager was Hamilton Browne, an energetic and experienced operator, who later became as active in railroading as he was in mining. He and his associates formed the Boone Valley Coal & Railway Company, chartered February 23, 1893, to run from Fraser to a point on the Minneapolis & St. Louis Railway called Fraser Junction. Fraser was named after Norman D. Fraser, vice president of the company. The road was built to haul coal from mines in Fraser to the M&STL connection. The directors were Hamilton Browne and O. M. Carpenter of Boone; Norman D. Fraser and David R. Fraser of Chicago; and S. T. Meservey of Fort Dodge. Browne headed the company.

The Boone Valley Coal & Railway Company opened late in 1893 with about three miles of track. It commenced operation with a "40-ton locomotive." For the year ended June 30, 1897, the road hauled—with the help of another engine—122,838 tons of coal. Two years afterward a company called the Marshalltown & Dakota Railway purchased the property of the bvc&ry. The new road, headed by Hamilton Browne, was chartered "to build . . . from Story City . . . via Fraser, Gowrie, Manson, Pocahontas, Laurens and Hartley to Sibley, Ia., 145 miles, and thence northwest into southeastern South Dakota." It completed its line westward from Fraser Junction to Gowrie in 1899.

In 1901 the name was again changed, this time to the Boone, Rockwell City & Northwestern Railway, with Browne again serving as president. The next year a new company took over the road under the banner of the Newton & Northwestern Railroad, with Browne as chief executive. The n&nw, to quote *Poor's Manual of Railroads* for 1903, owned "two large bituminous coal properties, which have been profitable producers for years. . . . The output from the mines at present is about 400 tons a day, but this will be increased upwards of 1,500 tons a day during the current year."

Extensions were pushed from Fraser to Newton on the east and from Gowrie to Rockwell City on the west. The biggest engineering feat, however, was bridging a tributary of the Des Moines River near Fraser. To span this valley a lofty wooden bridge 156 feet high and 784 feet long was erected. A million feet of lumber went into the long trestle. The entire line, Newton to Rockwell City, was completed in 1904.

One of the new towns along the line, Napier, took the maiden name of Hamilton Browne's wife, Mary L. Napier. Browne was not to remain president much longer, for a group of New Englanders secured control. In 1905 a Bostonian named Homer Loring headed the company. Among the new directors was Henry W. Poor, a well-known private banker who, with his father, Henry V. Poor, inaugurated *Poor's Manual of Railroads*. A branch was built from Goddard to Colfax in 1905, serving mines in the Colfax community. The Newton & Northwestern was now a line over a hundred miles long. But it went from a comparatively small community on the east to a still smaller town on the west. Its principal source of income was coal, yet several mines were already becoming unprofitable. The road needed new industries, bigger and better terminals, and, most of all, fresh capital.

Enter now another company—the Fort Dodge, Des Moines & Southern Railroad, incorporated in Iowa on February 16, 1906. New Englanders furnished the needed capital, and Homer Loring of Boston was made the road's president. Further east-and-west expansion stopped, and instead the new managers looked to the gypsum area of Fort Dodge on the north and to the industries of Des Moines on the south. The FtDDM&s acquired control of the Newton & Northwestern, along with the Fort Dodge Street Railway (a local trolley line) and the Ames & College Railway. The latter company, a two-mile steam "dummy line" organized on September 9, 1890, operated from Ames to the Iowa State College. To connect with the "dummy line" a seven-mile extension from Kelley to Ames was built.

The main feature of the improvement program was the electrification of new lines: Fort Dodge to Hope and Des Moines to Midvale. Overhead wires were also strung on the N&NW between Midvale and Hope. The Ames-Kelley branch was likewise electrified. This meant high-speed, frequent interurban service from the capital to Fort Dodge. The remainder of the system continued to be operated by steam, as did freight service on the entire railroad. Company coal furnished fuel for the new turbine-driven power plant at Fraser.

The $2,500,000 improvement project featured large, fifty-three-foot interurban cars built by Niles Car Company. With interiors furnished in mahogany, leather upholstery, and clerestory windows, they were the pride of central Iowa. Fast through service on the eighty-five-mile run between Des Moines and Fort Dodge commenced late in 1907. Entry into Des Moines was over the tracks of the local street railway.

The expense of electrification proved too much for the company, and it became bankrupt. In 1910 Homer Loring and Parley Sheldon of Ames were appointed receivers. To expedite the handling of heavy freight by electric locomotives, the receivers converted the line from 600-volt to 1,200-volt operation. About that time the road extended a branch from Niles to Ogden with running rights over the M&stL for two miles to nearby mines. Later the FtDDM&s had an interest in the Ogden mines, but labor troubles and floods made the operation impracticable. The Ogden branch was eventually abandoned.

Troubles continued to beset the management. The mines at Colfax were worked out, and the Colfax-Goddard branch was ripped out. Indeed, the whole line from Midvale to Newton proved to be a mistake, and abandonment by the receivers was authorized in 1912. Meanwhile, the road west of Hope, hitherto operated by steam, was electrified. This meant all-electric operation of the entire system.

In the spring of 1912 a disastrous flood washed out the center span of the high bridge near Fraser. It took a dozen men seventy days to replace the old structure with a modern steel span costing $110,000. To this day it provides the road's passengers one of the best scenic views in the state.

The road was sold under foreclosure in 1913 to the bondholders, Old Colony Trust Company of Boston, for $3,900,500. The name remained the same, and Homer Loring continued as president. It is significant that "The Fort Dodge Line," as it was called, differed from many contemporary interurbans in that it aggressively solicited carload freight business. It followed steam-road practices in operating rules, and it interchanged with trunk lines. When the government took over the railroads during World War I, the FtDDM&S was taken over also. It was one of the few interurbans operated by the United States Railroad Administration.

Some idea of the fast-growing freight business is attested by the fact that the road had 2,500 freight cars in 1918. It was said to have more cars for its size than any other road in America! Apart from freight the road once boasted of two parlor-observation cars with wicker seats, smoking compartments, and high-quality Brussels carpets. An excess fare of twenty-five cents was charged between Des Moines and Fort Dodge, and porter service was provided.

In line with the road's policy to serve more industries, it purchased the Crooked Creek Railroad in 1916. This pioneer carrier was chartered on November 8, 1875, and began operating a year later. It started as a three-foot gauge, eight-mile extension from Judd, on the Illinois Central Railroad, to coal mines at Lehigh. President and general manager was Walter C. Willson of Webster City. Willson was the first coal mine operator of importance in the Lehigh district.

In the middle eighties the Crooked Creek was widened to standard gauge and operated in conjunction with the Webster City & Southwestern Railroad, which had a fourteen-mile line from Border Plain Junction (on the Crooked Creek) to Webster City. A. K. Hamilton of Milwaukee, Wisconsin, who headed the Webster City line, was also a director of the CCRR. In 1892 the Crooked Creek bought the WC&SW, and around 1900 the road from Judd to Border Plain was scrapped.

When the FtDDM&S purchased the historic little road, it constructed its own line to Border Plain from Fort Dodge. That portion of the Crooked Creek from Border Plain running northeast to Brushy was taken up. A shortcut between Evanston and Brushy was built, providing a direct route from Fort Dodge to Webster City. The entire line was electrified. The Crooked Creek's roundhouse was still standing in Webster City in 1954.

Changing conditions led to the forming of the Fort Dodge, Des Moines & Southern Transportation Company in 1924. Bus service was inaugurated between Boone and Ames, also to Des Moines. The bus subsidiary, however, was later sold. In the twenties, with the exception of Des Moines–Fort Dodge service, all passenger rail operation was discontinued. Local street-car operation in Fort Dodge and Ames also ceased.

The road suffered from financial reverses in the late twenties, and in 1930 Clyde H. Crooks, who succeeded Homer Loring as president in 1920, was made receiver. In 1942 the company was reorganized as the Fort Dodge, Des Moines & Southern Railway, with Crooks as president. Upon his death four years afterward, Vice President and General Counsel Walter R. Dyer headed the road.

The boom in construction following World War II saw an increased use of gypsum and greater business for the road. To handle longer trains, three sixteen-wheel "steeple cab" locomotives were purchased from the Oregon Electric Railway in 1947. These husky four-truck jobs greatly expedite freights up the 2-1/2 percent grade west of Fraser.

Recent improvements include modernizing the power plant at Fraser. This means cheaper power for the railway and more kilowatt hours for communities to which the company sells electricity. Under the steward-ship of Arthur P. Wheelock, who succeeded the late Walter Dyer as president in 1953, continued progress is assured. Delivery of two hundred new steel boxcars is part of the present rehabilitation program. Dieselization of some of the road is in the offing. At any rate, the Fort Dodge–Des Moines Line, as it is now called, will continue to be an important factor in providing the heart of Iowa with modern and efficient freight service.

WATERLOO, CEDAR FALLS & NORTHERN

No Iowa interurban is better built than the Waterloo, Cedar Falls & Northern Railroad. This line has been called "a steam railroad with trolley wire over it" because of the substantial manner of its construction. When Westinghouse wanted an outstanding example of electric freight haulage in the heyday of the interurban, it chose the WCF&N. As a result the manufacturing concern published an attractive eighty-four-page book titled *The Story of the Cedar Valley Road* to show what could be done to build up a lucrative freight business. Later *Electric Traction* conducted speed contests to stimulate faster running. A score of electric roads were listed each year, but only one appeared from Iowa. That was the "Cedar Valley Road." It ranked ninth in 1929 and in 1930. The average speed for both years was 45.9 m.p.h. on the sixty-four-mile Cedar Rapids–Waterloo run.

In the vital matter of keeping on the black side of the ledger, the WCF&N has paid modest dividends each year since its reorganization in 1944. In the ten-year period the railroad has paid out $551,884.02 in dividends and has reduced its bonded indebtedness from $2,273,200 to $827,700, a reduction of $1,445,500, or about 64 percent. Because of its strategic location and good management, the ninety-nine-mile road takes in enough revenue to rank as a Class I carrier.

The story of the railroad is largely that of three brothers: Louis S. Cass, Claude D. Cass, and Joseph F. Cass. Louis and Joseph Cass formed the Waterloo & Cedar Falls Rapid Transit Company, the forerunner of the present system. The Rapid Transit was incorporated in 1895 to connect the two cities in its name. Louis S. Cass, or "L. S." as he was called, for railroaders habitually use initials, headed the newly formed road. In 1896 he bought the Waterloo Street Railway, a horse-car line with two miles of track. This was electrified, and four miles were added. The next year the Rapid Transit reached Cedar Falls but could not get a franchise to operate downtown. To overcome this obstacle the "interurban" ran a short distance over the tracks of the friendly Chicago Great Western Railway. Through the purchase of the Cedar Falls street railway in 1898, access was had to the heart of the city, and operation over the CGW was given up. Meanwhile, the local line was converted to electricity, having formerly been operated with Patton gasoline cars.

Constructed with fifty-six-pound rails on private right-of-way, the intercity line was more or less an interurban. As the century drew to a close, it even hauled some freight. This consisted of bricks shipped from a plant near Cedar Falls to Waterloo by a regular interurban unit pulling a flatcar. The operation was conducted between midnight and early morning, and delivery was made in the city streets. In 1900 the first electric locomotive was purchased, and the following year another was added. The pioneer engines had the task of taking coal cars up a 2 percent grade to the normal school—now Iowa State Teachers College in Cedar Falls.

In 1901 the road was extended thirteen miles north to Denver, Iowa. At the same time a 22,000-volt transmission line was built along the route to supply power to the new railroad. It is reputed to be the first high-tension line in Iowa. A year later the road reached Denver Junction, where it connected with the Chicago Great Western. From the Junction the interurban secured trackage rights over the CGW to Sumner via Waverly, thirty-one miles. In fact, the trolley company operated the Waverly-Sumner branch of the Great Western with steam trains in both freight and passenger service. In 1904 the name was changed to the Waterloo, Cedar Falls & Northern Railway.

What may seem a bizarre alliance between electric and steam roads is not so strange when analyzed in detail. The farsighted A. B. Stickney, head of the CGW, saw the interurban as a shortcut for cars going from Waterloo to points on his Omaha line, instead of by the roundabout route via Oelwein. Moreover the "juice" road tapped some busy industries in Waterloo which the Great Western did not.

Two of the Cass brothers learned to "railroad" on Stickney's system. The Casses liked Stickney personally, and he liked them.

A few biographical notes on the Cass family might be in order. Louis S. Cass was in between his brothers in age, but he always headed the interurban. Born in Wisconsin in 1865, he received his higher education at Iowa State Teachers College. "L. S." entered railroading as freight brakeman on the Minnesota & Northwestern, earliest predecessor of the Great Western. Later he switched to "braking" on the Milwaukee Road, then went as telegraph operator for the Burlington, Cedar Rapids & Northern (now Rock Island) and finally with the Dubuque & Dakota (CGW) as conductor. His association with the "Maple Leaf" was renewed when he combined his stewardship of the WCF&N with the vice presidency of the Great Western from 1905 to 1908, and he became chief executive for the receivers, 1908–1909. He also served for many years as vice president of the American Short Line Railroad Association under the strong leadership of Bird M. Robinson. A man of varied interests, "L. S." had other irons in the fire, including banking, real estate, and lumbering.

Claude D. Cass, youngest of the trio, was born in Sumner in 1879. He likewise went to Iowa State Teachers College and later to the Iowa College of Law at Drake University. He "conductored" on his brothers' trolley line during vacations and then became permanently identified with the traction company. He became superintendent, general passenger agent, and, in 1905, general manager. In later years he served as vice president.

The third brother, Joseph F. Cass, like "L. S.," was born in Wisconsin and was two years his senior. After a public school education he went with the Dubuque & Dakota Railroad. Biographical material on him is scant, but he served for many years as vice president of the WCF&N. He differed from his brothers in physical makeup, being rather tall, whereas Louis was stocky and Claude portly.

The Cedar Valley Road had an amazing variety of rolling stock, from open-bench, single-truck streetcars to four-wheel "convertibles"—a type of trolley in which the panels could be removed for summer operation; they bore little if any resemblance to the streamlined "convertibles" of today's automobiles. Closed city cars were featured along with large monitor-roof interurbans. For a time a motor bus on flanged wheels was operated on the Sumner branch.

Shortly after the Great Western went into receivership the Cedar Valley Road ceased operating over it from Denver Junction to Sumner. The interurban thereafter built its own all-electric line from the Junction to Waverly. It subsequently built south from Waterloo to Cedar Rapids. This extension had catenary construction of overhead wires, eighty-five-pound rails, easy curves, and no grades over 1 percent. Originally of 650-volt current, it changed to 1,300-volt in 1915.

The southern extension (completed in 1914) boasted of all-steel passenger cars, three of which were parlor-observation units. The parlor facilities had such niceties as buffet service operated from a Tom Thumb kitchenette, six feet by three feet, two inches, and built-in writing desks with stationery bearing the Cedar Valley Road emblem. Finally, in the grand tradition, they had the company's herald on the brass railing at the observation end. The observation cars are still in service.

The railroad was poorly maintained during government operation in World War I. This condition, combined with a recession, put the company in precarious financial shape after its return to private ownership. In 1923 Cass retired from his long term as president and was succeeded by C. M. Cheney, who ran the railroad for a protective committee of first mortgage bondholders, since the company was unable to pay its first mortgage bonds. In 1940, as the first step in reorganization, Cheney was made receiver. Four years later the reorganization was completed and the name changed to Waterloo, Cedar Falls & Northern Railroad, with Cheney as president and general manager. Thus, in its whole lifetime, the Cedar Valley Road has had only two presidents.

Like his predecessor, Cheney began his railroad career on the Great Western, where he had worked as station agent and telegrapher from December 1892 to October 1904, leaving the Great Western at that time to become general freight and passenger agent for the Waterloo, Cedar Falls & Northern Railway, in which position he remained until September 1920, when he severed his connections with the Waterloo road to become vice president and general manager of the Des Moines & Central Iowa Railroad. He remained in this position until October 1923, when he returned to the wcf&n as president and general manager.

Mr. Cheney was born in Illinois but came to Iowa as a small boy, spending his childhood in Marshalltown. The little hamlet of Cheney, on the Cedar Rapids line, is named after him.

Today the Cedar Valley Road is a heavy-duty carrier with three daily time freights between Cedar Rapids and Waterloo. Fifty-car trains are common, and seventy-car doubleheaders are not unusual. For passengers the road valiantly runs a daily train each way between Cedar Rapids and Waterloo, with an additional run "Dly. Ex. Mon. Tue. Wed. Thur.," as the working timetable quaintly puts it. Cars no longer go into downtown Cedar Rapids over the local streetcar lines (discontinued in 1940), but they do terminate at the road's smart Tudor-type depot on the north side of town. Daily round-trip service is also provided between Waterloo and Waverly.

Some types of operation, like that on the Waterloo Belt Line serving the John Deere plant and the Rath Packing Company, have been profitable. Local streetcar service in Waterloo and Cedar Falls ceased over a decade ago. In 1952 the railroad sold the bus line that supplemented interurban cars in the Cedar Rapids–Waterloo service and relinquished its local bus rights in Waterloo and Cedar Falls the following year. On the other hand, service continues between the two cities with lightweight trolleys formerly operated by Knoxville Transit. The low-level vehicles still have the United States mail slots peculiar to the Tennessee system. They are the last streetcars (as distinguished from interurbans) in Iowa.

Some dozen electric locomotives busily pulling road freights and yard cuts are indicative of the type of service for which the road is best fitted. More changes may be in order. And yet, barring a depression, the Cedar Valley Road will probably continue to pay modest dividends in the future.

CEDAR RAPIDS & IOWA CITY

From the start the Crandic was designed as a high-speed electric line primarily concerned with hauling passengers. Its foresighted management, however, perceived the value of carload freight, and by 1907 it printed tariffs in conjunction with the steam roads. In the process of growing up it shed the "& Light Company" from its title. From its inception to the present day, however, the road was operated in conjunction with the electric firm—now called the Iowa Electric Light & Power Company. With the exception of the road's third president, a Dows has always headed the company. S. L. Dows and Colonel W. G. Dows were the first two presidents, and Sutherland C. Dows is the present head.

In 1914 an extension was built to Mount Vernon, fifteen miles east of Cedar Rapids. According to the *Electric Railway Journal*, a special four-car excursion was run on March 11 of that year. The *Journal* of May 16, 1914, reported that "the line eventually will connect Cedar Rapids with Davenport." The student traffic on the Crandic was heavy, for the road served both the State University of Iowa at Iowa City and Cornell College at Mount Vernon. The Mount Vernon branch was subsequently extended another two miles to Lisbon.

In addition to its "interurbans," the power company ran streetcar lines in Cedar Rapids, Boone, and Marshalltown and operated trolleys on the three-and-a-half-mile Tama & Toledo Railroad connecting the towns from which it took its name. All are now abandoned. After the Cedar Rapids–Lisbon line was scrapped in 1928, the company's local streetcars in Cedar Rapids continued to run over its tracks in the city until the late thirties.

Another interesting phase of development was that of a subsidiary, Crandic Stages, Inc., which in the early thirties boasted of buses running from Chicago to Denver via Cedar Rapids. The railway's versatile master mechanic, John Munson, doubled in brass by supervising repairs on some sixty buses as well as on interurban cars and locomotives. Incidentally, the buses had the same Iowa-shaped heraldic symbol as the cars. The buses were later sold to the Interstate Bus Lines.

Munson's ingenuity was responsible for many distinct features of the Crandic which were peculiar to that road. Among these were movable frogs on the overhead wires. When a trainman threw a track switch, he automatically moved the overhead frog, thereby guiding the trolley shoe in backup movements. Formerly crewmen had to pull down the trolley pole and re-set it for the wire on a siding. Munson also invented controllers on switch engines operated from both sides of the cab, so that the motorman could observe signals on either side. Munson even had a locomotive constructed in the road's Cedar Rapids shops.

To observant passengers and especially to students making high scores on their Seashore music tests, the clickety-clack of the Crandic is offbeat. And it is! The rail joints are opposite each other instead of being staggered like other railroads. With the recent program of laying heavier rail, however, orthodox rhythm will prevail!

In 1939 the Crandic took on a new look when six lightweight, high-speed cars were purchased from the defunct Cincinnati & Lake Erie Railroad. Capable of obtaining 80 m.p.h. on the C&LE, these low-slung, semi-streamlined vehicles replaced heavier wooden cars. Painted yellow with brown-and-red trim, they virtually lapped up the hills and cut from ten to fifteen minutes from the running time. Later another "lightweight" was bought, this time from the Indiana Railroad, a once mighty system now abandoned.

More recently the Crandic augmented its motive power with "boomer" electric locomotives from the dieselized Washington & Old Dominion Railway in Virginia and the late Union Electric Railway in Kansas and Oklahoma. Rebuilt cabooses, painted all-yellow, also enlivened the picture. Heavy double-headed freight trains became common. Meanwhile, in spite of new equipment, revenue passengers declined from over 500,000 in several of the World War II years to 188,317 in 1952.

The last day of passenger service, however, looked like a familiar football special of yesteryears. About three hundred people made the final run, including United States Senator Bourke B. Hickenlooper, who had ridden the line as a young lawyer. At least one passenger, Alfred N. Scales of Iowa City, had the distinction of having ridden the first passenger run in 1904. Railfans came from many sections of the country to ride the farewell trip. It took six cars to haul the throng, all of whom were issued souvenir tickets. At the Iowa City station a band played "Auld Lang Syne."

DES MOINES & CENTRAL IOWA

The Des Moines & Central Iowa Railway was incorporated on November 28, 1899, as the Inter-Urban Railway. Its first road was a twenty-four-mile electric line from Des Moines to Colfax opened early in 1903. H. H. Polk of Des Moines was president and general manager; A. W. Harris of Chicago was vice president; and two Des Moines men, G. B. Hippee and W. I. Haskit, filled the offices of treasurer and secretary, respectively.

Coal mines along the route provided considerable freight, while Colfax, then a popular health resort, accounted for a relatively heavy passenger business. Freight came into the north side of Des Moines on the interurban's own rails, but passenger cars used the local street railway's Douglas Avenue line passing the State Fair Grounds. Later, when the road built its new passenger terminal, all cars entered from the north side.

The Inter-Urban Railway did not become important until it built the so-called Beaver Valley Division. This thirty-four-mile road, opened in 1906, veered northwest upon leaving Des Moines, running through Herrold and Granger to Perry. About the same time a three-mile branch was built from Moran to Woodward.

When eight interurban cars with arched windows and heavy pilots came on their own wheels from the American Car Company in St. Louis, they presaged a new era in transportation. Several units of the big wooden vehicles operated in trains carrying passengers, baggage, United States mail, and Wells Fargo express. The road also had electric locomotives. In its heyday the Inter-Urban built up a flourishing freight business. A. B. Stickney, the farsighted head of the Chicago Great Western, encouraged freight in-terchange and saw to it that cattle cars originating on the Inter-Urban were highballed over his road to the Chicago stockyards. There were also ship-ments of bituminous coal and of ice and milk, the milk being shipped in cans from way stations.

For a time the Inter-Urban served what was locally called "the third largest 'city' in Iowa"—Camp Dodge—which was said to have had a popu-lation of from 40,000 to 50,000 during World War I. Camp Dodge served as the cantonment for the 13th Division of the United States conscript army. Many a graying father in Iowa and adjacent states recalls being shipped to Camp Dodge over the interurban line upon being mustered into service. It is said the road once moved 3,500 men and their bag-gage from a connecting railroad to camp, twenty-five miles distant, in five hours. Whole trains of a dozen Pullmans or more were shunted by the Inter-Urban's electric locomotives from interchange points to the busy army post.

Camp Dodge reopened for inductees during World War II but on a smaller scale. Even so, the Inter-Urban had to borrow cars from the Cedar Rapids & Iowa City Railway to handle the extra movements. Like most Iowa interurbans, the carrier had "boomer" equipment: that is, cars purchased from other railroads.

When this writer rode the line in 1944, its steel passenger cars had a familiar look—like that of an old friend. Having ridden the now-defunct Lake Shore Electric Railway between Cleveland and Toledo almost a de-cade earlier, he quickly recognized these sixty-foot cars as having come from that Ohio interurban. The same feeling was experienced on the Ce-dar Rapids–Iowa City road. It was a peculiar quirk of fate to be a passen-ger bowling along "The Crandic Route" on cars of the abandoned Cincin-nati & Lake Erie's Daniel Boone from Toledo to the Queen City and the old Indiana Railroad. Iowa, in short, is a haven for interurban cars and lo-comotives from all over the nation!

Getting back to "the Perry and Colfax interurban," its days as an elec-tric road were numbered. In 1922 it was renamed the Des Moines & Cen-tral Iowa Railway. Unfortunately, declining revenues continued between the two world wars, and in 1946 the Colfax line was scrapped. Five years earlier the short Moran-Woodward stub had ceased operations. In Novem-ber 1946 the Des Moines & Central Iowa Railway went bankrupt. Three years later it was purchased by Murray M. Salzberg, a New York scrap-iron dealer, who continued operations under the old name. Salzberg managed to make both ends meet by dieselizing the property in 1949 and discontinuing passenger service. The little-used section from Perry to Granger was abandoned in 1953. Previous to 1952, freight service to Fort Des Moines and to Urbandale, operated in conjunction with the Des Moines Railway, was withdrawn.

For many years the DM&CI was affiliated with the Des Moines Railway, but when the latter converted to buses it cut off all rail service to the suburban points of Fort Des Moines and Urbandale. There are still some valuable industries along the road between Des Moines and Granger and on the three-mile segment of the "Colfax Division" to Highland Transfer. By pruning unprofitable branches the remainder of the system may operate indefinitely.

THE SOUTHERN IOWA RAILWAY

The Southern Iowa Railway started as a steam road and was later electrified. At various times it was operated independently or by larger systems, and again there were months when it did not operate at all. Much of the road's earlier records are hard to come by, but there is enough evidence to indicate that its history was both colorful and hectic.

The original company, according to L. L. Taylor's *Past and Present of Appanoose County*, was chartered May 6, 1879, as the Centerville, Moravia & Albia Railroad. It was built in 1880 as a branch of the Missouri, Iowa & Nebraska Railroad (then part of the Wabash system) and leased by the latter road. Francis M. Drake of Centerville and Russell Sage of New York were the leading promoters and for many years served as officials of the road.

For a time the Wabash operated its St. Louis–Des Moines trains in conjunction with the MI&N from Glenwood Junction, Missouri, to Centerville and the CM&A from Centerville to Albia. Upon the disintegration of the Wabash system in 1885 the lease was canceled, and the Centerville, Moravia & Albia was turned over to the bondholders. Operation thereafter was sporadic, and the road remained idle for a time.

At the close of the eighties the CM&A was leased to the Iowa Central, headed by Russell Sage. It was reorganized in 1890 as the Albia & Centerville Railway. The Iowa Central, which subsequently became part of the Minneapolis & St. Louis, continued to operate it until 1910. A new company, headed by W. A. Boland of New York, with J. L. Sawyers of Centerville as vice president, reorganized the Albia & Centerville in February 1910, changing its name to the Southern Iowa Traction Company. Apparently no change in management was made until late in 1910. Meanwhile, the road was being run by the Iowa Central (M&STL), much to the dissatisfaction of the new owners. How they overthrew the M&STL's operation is graphically related in the following letter by the late J. P. Boyle, formerly traffic manager of the little road.

President Boland and Vice President Sawyers figured that it would do no good to ask the M. & St. L. to hand the property over because there was a deficit then of about $40,000.00 against it of expenses above income, so it was secretly decided to take the road by force. November 26, 1910, at 8:00 A.M. was the date and hour we were to go over the top. We borrowed a coach, engine, train and engine crew from the C.B. & Q. here [Centerville] and followed the regular M. & St. L. train out of here (after fixing the telegraph wire so it would not work) without their knowledge, without a train order or any rights whatever and arrived at Albia in due time after stopping wherever we found an employee discharging him as an A. & C. employee and hiring him as an employee of the S.I.T. Company. The M. & St. L. in some way heard we were coming and arranged that we would be allowed to go [to] their depot and then block the track so we could not get out and in that way compel us to sue for peace, but we anticipated that and stayed on our own track at Albia during the several days it took to fix matters up.

After that dramatic episode the Traction Company operated the road. Despite the name "Traction," the line continued to be run by steam. In June 1914 the name was changed to the Centerville, Albia & Southern Railway after Frank S. Payne and D. C. Bradley of Centerville purchased the line. These men owned a majority of stock of the Centerville Light & Traction Company, which operated the street railway in Centerville and which had built a short interurban to Mystic in 1910. The new management electrified the Albia line in the summer of 1914. In 1916 the name of the Centerville Light & Traction was changed to the Iowa Southern Utilities Company, and the CA&S was conveyed to the utilities firm.

By operating over local streetcar tracks at both terminals the Albia-Centerville interurban went direct to the railway stations. It made connections with the Wabash, M&STL, and Burlington trains at Albia and the Rock Island and Burlington in Centerville. Agents also made Pullman reservations for passengers using connecting steam lines.

Two center-entrance cars with baggage, smoking, and a "ladies" compartment handled passengers, and two "box motors" (baggage-type locomotives) handled carload freight. The "ladies" compartment provided privacy for female passengers, as the road hauled many miners who sometimes became quite boisterous, particularly on paydays.

Coal from the mines along the route provided a very substantial amount of freight. The interurban interchanged with all connecting steam railroads. For years, too, through package cars were run in conjunction with the Wabash to St. Louis and via the Milwaukee to Chicago.

During the early years of the depression passenger service became unprofitable, and it was withdrawn on the entire railroad in 1933. Eleven years later the two-and-a-half-mile segment on the "Mystic Division" between Appanoose and Mystic was abandoned; in March 1948 the ten-and-a-quarter-mile section of the historic main line north of Moravia was scrapped. Today, however, the remaining sixteen miles of the road continue to handle freight, the bulk of which is coal from on-line mines to the large Iowa Southern Utilities electric plant in Centerville. The line is still run by Iowa Southern Utilities, although corporately known as the Southern Iowa Railway since 1941. Its president is Edward L. Shutts, who also heads the ISU.

SHORT LINE INTERURBANS

The Mason City & Clear Lake Railroad

Shortest of all Iowa interurbans is the ten-mile Mason City & Clear Lake Railroad, yet mile for mile, it has been among the most profitable. During the depression, when all five steam roads serving Mason City were in receivership, the MC&CL alone remained solvent. It vies with the Waterloo, Cedar Falls & Northern for the distinction of being the oldest *electric interurban railway* in Iowa, both roads having begun intercity service in 1897. The MC&CL is said to have been the first electric railway in the United States to have joint freight tariffs with steam railroads.

In 1896 W. E. Brice, Lew H. Ong, and others formed the Mason City & Clear Lake Traction Company. C. T. Dike, a young engineering graduate from Cornell who lived in Mason City and who later became vice president of the Chicago & North Western, was selected as the road's engineer. Brice was president and general manager of the new firm, and Ong served as vice president, secretary, and superintendent. The road commenced operation with an excursion on July 4, 1897, in which Mr. and Mrs. Brice, with their dog, Sanko, occupied the front seat of an open car. At Emery Sanko took out after birds and delayed the train.

Brice continued as head of the Mason City & Clear Lake Railroad until it was taken over by the United Light and Railways Company in 1913. Besides constructing the interurban, he built the Chicago & North Western's branch from Belle Plaine through Mason City to Blue Earth, Minnesota. This road was originally called the Iowa, Minnesota & Northwestern Railway and was sold to the C&NW in December 1900.

The equipment of the old MC&CL was unusual. A large combination passenger and baggage car, equipped with four 75-h.p. motors, pulled double-truck open trailers, each seating fifty-six people. The road was busiest during the summer, hauling excursionists to Clear Lake. In winter ice harvested from Clear Lake proved an important source of revenue. Before the days of mechanical refrigeration hundreds of boxcars of natural ice were shipped to many points in Iowa and neighboring states.

In the early days through coaches from connecting steam roads often went direct to Clear Lake, making it unnecessary to change cars at Mason City. Many prominent railroad executives had their business cars hauled to the lake to enjoy the sensation of being drawn by electric power on this pioneer line.

Around the turn of the century the road dropped the name "Traction" in favor of the more interurban-sounding "Railway." In 1910 the company was reorganized under its present title—the Mason City & Clear Lake Railroad. The road also operated local streetcars in Mason City until they were superseded by buses in 1936. During that decade company-owned buses supplanted electric cars on the interurban, although freight service continued by rail.

The MC&CL is now owned by a local group headed by Charles E. Strickland. While red wooden interurban passenger cars no longer shuttle between Mason City and Clear Lake, the road's four electric locomotives do a brisk business in freight. Hauling ice is a thing of the past, but there are still elevators, coal and lumber yards, tank farms, and cement plants which furnish the road with lucrative traffic.

The Charles City Western

The Charles City Western Railway is a grassroots interurban with headquarters in Charles City, about thirty miles east of Mason City. This twenty-one-mile road started life as a steam and gasoline-operated carrier. It was chartered on February 3, 1910, and the following year began operating between Charles City and Marble Rock, a distance of thirteen miles. Passengers rode a fifty-five-foot-long pointed-front, gasoline-operated McKeen car that had porthole-type windows, a center entrance, and a large pilot, or "cowcatcher." Steam locomotives handled the freight traffic. C. W. Hart of Charles City headed the road; and he and C. H. Parr, E. M. Sherman, C. D. Ellis, A. E. Ellis, N. Frudden, and F. W. Fisher, all of Charles City, served on the directorate.

In 1915 the CCW was electrified and an extension was built to Colwell, eight miles northeast of Charles City. The road also operated the Charles City street railway. The interurban sported a fascinating variety of rolling stock: new steel cars; an odd off-center-door car from the defunct Shore Line Electric Railway in Connecticut; a sturdy deck-roof car from the Twin City Rapid Transit; and other quaint but serviceable equipment. In more recent years diesels have been added along with a heavy-duty electric freight engine hailing from the abandoned Texas Electric Railway. Because of its variegated equipment and rural setting, the CCW has long been regarded as a paradise by traction historians and railroad fans.

Now and then, when the power failed on the eastern end of the line, the motorman would coast down to the bridge crossing Little Cedar River, reach for his bamboo pole, and get in some fishing. The crews were paid by the month; like the skipper of the famous Toonerville trolley, they could afford to indulge in this pleasant pastime.

The Charles City Western serves important industries in its home community, including the large Oliver Plow Works, and smaller firms along the way. It interchanges with the Milwaukee and the Illinois Central railroads at Charles City and with the Rock Island at Marble Rock. Some idea of its importance to the agricultural populace is suggested by the sign "Interurban View Farm" located about midway between Charles City and Marble Rock. Indeed, the road has been something of a family affair, locally operated and controlled, with Ellis and Frudden names invariably appearing on the directorate as presidents or as other officials. M. W. Ellis was formerly president, and at this writing (1954) H. O. Frudden heads the carrier.

During World War I the Charles City Western received considerable publicity as the first electric railway in Iowa to have a "motorwoman"—Miss Marjorie Dodd, a college girl and the daughter of the mayor of Charles City. During 1918 all the "one-man" streetcars in Charles City were operated by women. For a brief period, too, the interurban had an all-women section crew. Due to high cost of operation and automobile competition in the postwar era, city service was discontinued in 1921.

In spite of extremely light patronage the interurban routes continued to feature two round-trips, daily except Sunday, over the entire road. In the summer of 1952, however, this luxury was dropped; and the interurban, like an ever-increasing number of its fellows, is operated for "Freight Service Only."

This completes the story of all Iowa interurbans now operating. With the exception of the defunct Clinton, Davenport & Muscatine Railway, it includes every interurban line run in the state. The CD&M started as the Iowa & Illinois Railway in 1904, connecting Clinton with Davenport. In 1912 the Davenport & Muscatine Railway linked the two towns in its name. Four years later the two lines consolidated, forming the Clinton, Davenport & Muscatine. Unlike the interurbans still running, the CD&M never had a freight business sufficiently lucrative to enable it to continue operating as a tonnage carrier. This proved a major factor in its demise in 1940.

From the foregoing trend it is safe to make two predications. One is that the so-called interurbans will all go out of the passenger business, at least by rail. The other is that dieselization will replace electric operation on most if not all Iowa interurbans in the near future. Indeed, the very name interurban will become archaic; and, except in a historical sense, it will have little meaning. Most of Iowa's "interurbans" will continue to be more or less economically important as dieselized, short-line railroads handling freight exclusively. But as passenger-carrying, high-speed electric, inter-city roads, one regretfully concludes their day is over.

Palimpsest 35 (May 1954)

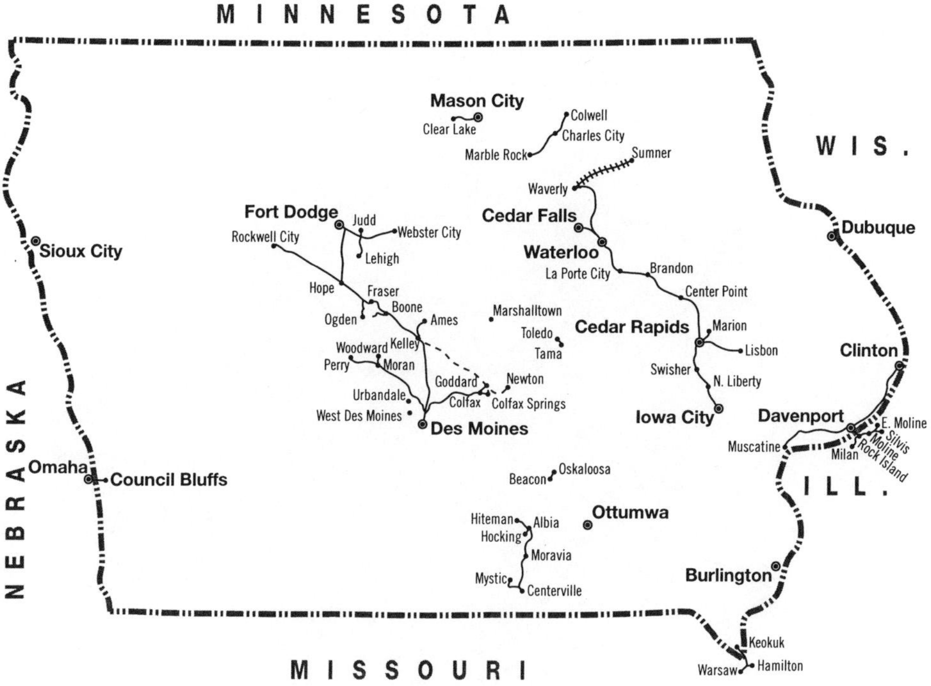

MINNESOTA
WIS.
ILL.
NEBRASKA
MISSOURI
Mason City
Clear Lake
Colwell
Charles City
Marble Rock
Sumner
Waverly
Cedar Falls
Waterloo
La Porte City
Brandon
Center Point
Fort Dodge
Judd
Webster City
Lehigh
Rockwell City
Hope
Fraser
Boone
Ogden
Ames
Marshalltown
Toledo
Tama
Cedar Rapids
Marion
Lisbon
Swisher
N. Liberty
Iowa City
Woodward
Kelley
Perry
Moran
Goddard
Newton
Urbandale
Colfax
Colfax Springs
West Des Moines
Des Moines
Sioux City
Dubuque
Clinton
Davenport
E. Moline
Silvis
Moline
Rock Island
Milan
Muscatine
Omaha
Council Bluffs
Beacon
Oskaloosa
Ottumwa
Hiteman
Albia
Hocking
Moravia
Mystic
Centerville
Burlington
Keokuk
Warsaw
Hamilton

Map 3. Electric Interurban Railways of Iowa. Courtesy Sam Girton.

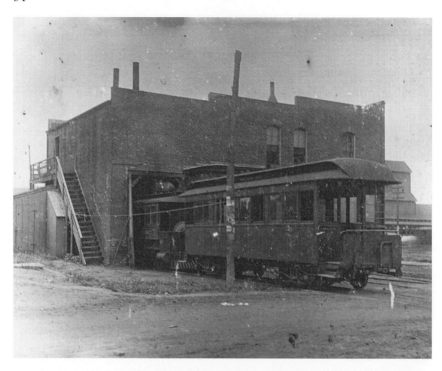

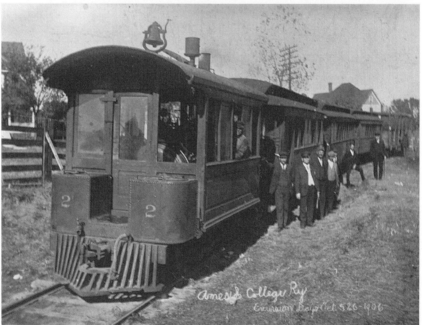

The electric Fort Dodge, Des Moines & Southern evolved out of several independent short lines, including the Ames & College Railway (1893–1908). In October 1906 an excursion train on this steam "dummy" road is seen near Ames. H. Roger Grant Collection.

On September 24, 1939, Fort Dodge, Des Moines & Southern Train No. 2, Car No. 62,
ambles across the high bridge north of Boone. John F. Humiston photograph.

On May 13, 1939, Waterloo, Cedar Falls & Northern Train No. 1, Car No. 102, is about to cross the tracks of the North Western and Rock Island on Fifth Avenue S.E. in Cedar Rapids. John F. Humiston photograph.

In the late 1940s, Car No. 102 travels down a city street in Waterloo. A popular feature of this heavy-weight steel interurban car was its open platform. George Niles photograph.

The last streetcars in Iowa operated in an interurban fashion between Cedar Falls and Waterloo. This lightweight trolley, pictured in the early 1950s, had formerly served transit riders of Knoxville, Tennessee. George Niles photograph.

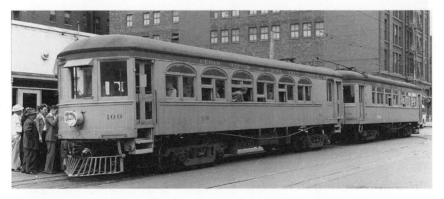

Riders eagerly enter Crandic Cars Nos. 109 and 102 in Cedar Rapids. On May 31, 1948, this extra shuttle train is destined for Hawkeye Downs. Krambles Archive.

About 1910 two wooden interurban cars of the Inter-Urban Railway (later Des Moines &
Central Iowa) creep along a Des Moines street. One interurban is headed for Woodward and
Perry and the other for Colfax. A. O. Harpel photograph, Krambles Archive.

On June 8, 1935, photographer Robert V. Mehlenbeck caught Des Moines & Central Iowa
wooden Car No. 1701 at the Des Moines station. Robert V. Mehlenbeck photograph,
Krambles Archive.

*In 1939 Des Moines & Central Iowa Car No. 1712, which the company had purchased
from the abandoned Lake Shore Electric Railway of Ohio, is about to enter Des Moines.
Robert B. Mehlenbeck photograph, Krambles Archive.*

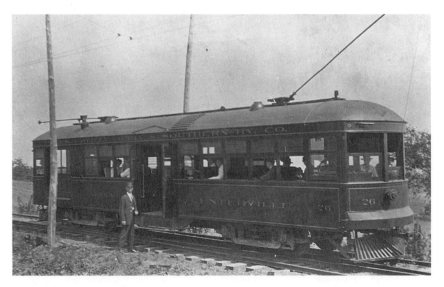

*The year is 1916, and the location is near Selection, a coal camp between Albia and
Moravia. Conductor John L. Johnson stands by one of the two center-entrance steel passenger
cars of the Centerville, Albia & Southern Railway. H. Roger Grant Collection.*

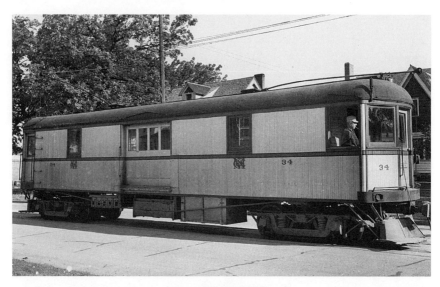

Box Motor Car No. 34 of the Mason City & Clear Lake is "running light" on a public street. Nominally an express car, it was in reality a freight locomotive. Robert V. Mehlenbeck photograph, Krambles Archive.

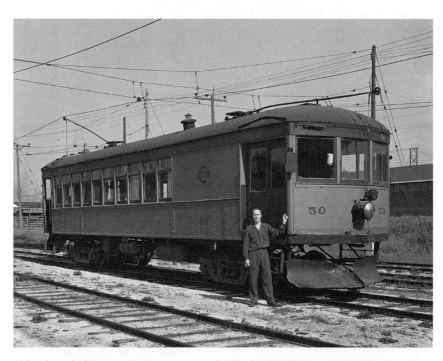

After the end of passenger service in 1952, the Charles City Western retained Car No. 50 for special excursions. This piece of equipment served the company well, having been purchased in 1915 as an arched-roof semisteel car from McGuire-Cummings. For decades Car No. 50 performed the bulk of the road's passenger service. Krambles Archive.

On August 26, 1952, Charles City Western Freight Motor No. 300 pulls a two-car train through its namesake city. Thomas H. Desnoyers photograph, Krambles Archive.

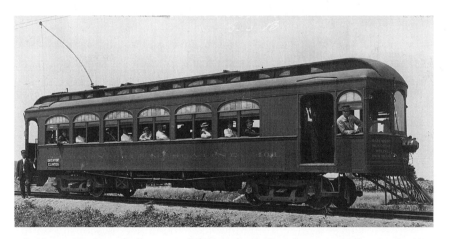

On August 1, 1912, the Davenport & Muscatine Railway began service between the cities in its corporate name. Arched-window wooden Car No. 404, with its two-person crew, epitomizes the era's early interurban rolling stock. In 1926 the Davenport & Muscatine joined the Iowa & Illinois Railway to become the Clinton, Davenport & Muscatine Railway. Krambles Archive.

DUBUQUE'S FIRST RAILROAD

In the middle of the nineteenth century the largest towns in Iowa were along the Mississippi River. They were Burlington, Dubuque, Muscatine, and Keokuk, in that order. Iowa City, then the capital of the state, had only 1,250 inhabitants; whereas Burlington had 4,082, Dubuque 3,108, Muscatine 2,540, and Keokuk 2,478. It was clearly evident that the Father of Waters was responsible for most of the population of the Hawkeye State.

By 1850, however, farsighted men in the river towns saw the railroad as a means of fostering travel westward from the Mississippi across the state. Even before this time, the citizens of Dubuque were exhorted not only to span Iowa by rail but to continue it on to the Pacific Ocean. What is believed to be the first public meeting to promote a railroad to the Pacific was held in Dubuque in 1838. The spokesman was John Plumbe, Jr., who had migrated to Dubuque from the East, where he had worked under the famous civil engineer Moncure Robinson in surveying the Allegheny Portage Railroad in Pennsylvania. Plumbe subsequently was a superintendent of a pioneer Virginia railroad. Later he turned to photography, in which he achieved considerable success.

Plumbe envisioned a railroad from Milwaukee to Dubuque, thence westward to the Pacific Coast. He seems to have enlisted very little support, and his name is scarcely remembered today. But in 1838 he did get $2,000 from Congress to survey a route from Milwaukee to Sinipee, Wisconsin, on the Mississippi above Dubuque. The grant was largely through the efforts of Territorial Delegate George Wallace Jones, later United States senator from Iowa. Furthermore, Plumbe made a trip to California on his own, which convinced him even more that a transcontinental railroad was feasible.

While John Plumbe was ahead of his time, and was for the most part regarded as an impractical visionary, he planted the germ which culminated in Dubuque's "railroad fever" of the 1850s. Once the germ was planted, others nurtured it. Foremost among these were George Wallace Jones and his colleague Augustus Caesar Dodge, the first two United States senators from Iowa, who insisted that the rapidly building Illinois Central Railroad terminate on the Mississippi River opposite Dubuque. Heretofore the Illinois Central had planned to end its tracks at Galena, Illinois, seventeen miles east of the Mississippi on the Fever River.

Once assured that the Illinois Central would come to Dunleith (known today as East Dubuque), it was up to Dubuquers to build their own railroad. Already plans were hatching for railroads into the hinterlands from Davenport, Burlington, Keokuk, and the Clinton-Lyons area. Iowa newspapers were full of "railroad talk," and Dubuque must not be caught napping.

One by one the businessmen and leading citizens in Dubuque rallied to the cause. Preliminary meetings were held in which Lucius H. Langworthy, pioneer Dubuque lead miner, acted as spokesman. Hardly less important was Jesse P. Farley, merchant, ex-mayor, and pioneer steamboat builder and operator. These meetings led to the chartering of the Dubuque & Pacific Railroad Company on April 28, 1853.

From the start, several of the Illinois Central's key men were active in promoting Dubuque's first railroad. Farley was elected president, and Colonel Roswell B. Mason, chief engineer of the Illinois Central, was made engineer-in-chief. Other officers included Platt Smith, a prominent Dubuque lawyer, who became solicitor of the road, and Frederick S. Jesup, a local banker, who was made treasurer. Among the original incorporators were Robert Schuyler, president of the Illinois Central, and General C. H. Booth, first mayor of Dubuque and owner of the city's earliest sawmill and its pioneer flour mill. Senator George Wallace Jones, who did so much to foster railroads in Iowa, was elected chairman of the board of the Dubuque & Pacific.

Despite the impressive list of important Dubuquers associated with the project, the new company encountered many difficulties. While the people of Dubuque County subscribed to approximately $250,000 worth of stock, bonds sold as low as fifty cents on the dollar, and land and other collateral were accepted in lieu of cash. By the summer of 1855 there was little to show for its existence except a surveyed route a few miles westward from Dubuque.

On July 31, 1855, Colonel Mason resigned as chief engineer, and B. B. Provost, a division engineer on the Illinois Central, succeeded him. At this juncture the "paper" railroad made a contract with the firm of Mason, Bishop & Company, which Colonel Mason headed, to construct the line to

Dyersville. Meanwhile, the Illinois Central had reached Dunleith, so that railroad was more interested than ever in backing a friendly connection west of the Mississippi.

On October 1, 1855, George Wallace Jones dug the first shovel of earth for the Dubuque & Pacific. The following spring construction went on apace through the rocky, hilly Dubuque County terrain. On September 10, 1856, the first locomotive, the Dubuque, was ferried across the Mississippi from Dunleith, marking the occasion when the first steam engine turned a wheel in northern Iowa. The crude wood-burner was outshopped by the historic firm of Rogers, Ketchum & Grosvenor of Patterson, New Jersey. Not long afterward a second locomotive, the Jesse P. Farley, named in honor of the road's president, arrived on the scene.

It was on May 11, 1857, that the first train made the twenty-nine-mile run from Dubuque to Dyersville. The Jesse P. Farley pulled an assorted consist of passenger coaches and freight cars filled with joyful celebrants. In traveling the unballasted line, the engine jumped the track three times before completing the historic run. James S. Northrup was the conductor, while Thomas W. Place pulled the throttle. Place later became chief mechanical officer of the road. When he retired in 1901, the Waterloo roundhouse shopmen presented him with a trim horse-and-carriage as a tribute to his leadership.

The panic of 1857 halted construction, and for two years the Dubuque & Pacific had its end-of-track at Earlville, "a crossroads which boasted two houses," eight miles west of Dyersville. Even the road's extensive land grant of 1,162,373 acres (thanks to the efforts of George Wallace Jones) was of little use since it did not become available until the road reached the respective areas stipulated in the grant. Not until a very substantial part of the road was completed would the struggling Dubuque & Pacific realize much from its land sales. Furthermore, what little land there was available along the constructed line brought low prices due to the business depression.

As a result of unfavorable economic conditions, poor credit, and lack of a significant western terminal, the Dubuque & Pacific defaulted on its bonds and underwent reorganization. But it was still in business, although feeble and halting in operation. In short, it was marking time. Its future was uncertain . . . if, indeed, it had a future.

DUBUQUE & SIOUX CITY RAILROAD

How and why John Edgar Thomson became president of the Dubuque & Pacific in 1859 would provide an interesting chapter in a biography of that great railroad executive. Thomson had built the Pennsylvania Railroad by sound expansion and through such uncanny foresight that for many decades it was known as "The Standard Railroad of the World." And, while Thomson headed the lucrative Pennsylvania, his almost boundless energy spilled over to the weak, ailing, thirty-seven-mile-long prairie road that was the Dubuque & Pacific.

Perhaps Thomson was put on the Dubuque & Pacific to attract eastern capital. He may have viewed the potentialities of the Iowa line as a feeder to the Pennsylvania—along with having designs on the Illinois Central. At any rate, his incumbency on the Dubuque & Pacific was short, but it marked the turning point in that road's future. Construction was resumed in the summer of 1859. By the end of the year track was extended through the thriving town of Manchester to Independence. In the spring of 1860 its rails reached the western border of Buchanan County, where a station was erected called "Jesup," named after Morris K. Jesup, brother of Frederick Jesup.

Morris Jesup held many of the Dubuque & Pacific's defaulted bonds and wished to reorganize the road and put it on a sound financial basis. To do this he forced the road into receivership. It was reorganized as the Dubuque & Sioux City Railroad Company and incorporated August 1, 1860. Although Herman Gelpcke was elected president (and he was to be followed by Edward Stimson), it was really Jesup who dominated the company. Jesup was active in its management for twenty-seven years. He held the presidency from 1866 to 1887.

Morris Ketchum Jesup was a God-fearing Connecticut Yankee who, after a meager education in New York City, entered the employ of Rogers, Ketchum & Grosvenor locomotive builders. After rising to become manager of their New York office, he went into partnership in forming a small business dealing with railroad supplies on a commission. Later he switched to banking and with John S. Kennedy formed the house of Jesup, Kennedy & Company. This firm, specializing in railroad "paper," became very prosperous.

A person of varied talents and wide interests, Jesup was active in Protestant church work, in the study of natural science, and in numerous philanthropic organizations. He also helped finance Robert Peary's Arctic expeditions but died before Admiral Peary discovered the North Pole. Cape Morris Jesup in Greenland was named for him.

Jesup saw to it that the Dubuque & Sioux City had funds to push westward. Waterloo soon rejoiced to the sound of the engine whistle. By the end of March 1861 the railhead was established at Cedar Falls, six miles beyond Waterloo.

Cedar Falls had patiently waited for the railroad for seven years. Its 1,600 inhabitants were alternately elated or dejected by its progress or lack of progress. A cheerful note in the *Cedar Falls Gazette* brought joy to the people in the Cedar River valley. Periods of inactivity and scant news of railroad construction elicited doubts and depression. In July 1860 the *Dubuque Herald* made the prediction that trains could be expected in Cedar Falls in ninety days. The news was relayed with enthusiasm. Later the *Gazette* set the date at December 1st. But there were delays—winter came and went—and still no trains.

The spring of 1861, however, found crews grading the line, laying rails, and building the Cedar Falls station. With this tangible assurance of a railroad the whole town prepared to greet the Dubuque & Sioux City with the most elaborate preparations ever planned in that community. A preliminary ovation would welcome the first train at five o'clock in the afternoon on Easter Monday, April 1, 1861. But the wonderful citywide celebration proclaiming a new era for Cedar Falls was slated for April 11th.

The first train arrived on schedule, with Engineer Cawley at the throttle and Conductor Northrup punching tickets in the coaches. Amid incessant whistling and continuous bell ringing, the locomotive steamed into town. When the train stopped, Chief Marshal John Milton Overman gave the signal for the bugler to sound reveille. Then the train crew was escorted uptown to the strain of patriotic airs befitting visiting nobility. At the American House the railroaders were toasted and dined.

Virtually every able-bodied citizen had a hand in the grand celebration. Men and boys ranged the riverbanks for cedar boughs. Women and girls wove these evergreens into elaborate festoons. The festoons lined the streets and also served as a triumphal arch spanning the railroad tracks under which the engine would go to receive a giant cedar crown to be placed around its smokestack.

To this crown were attached pennants eulogizing the men who built the line and extolling the virtues of the railroad. On the pennants were such inscriptions as "Herman Gelpcke, the Fuel and Steam of the D. and S.C.R.R."; "Edward Stimson, Esq., the Tender of the D. and S.C.R.R."; "Platt Smith, the Driving Wheels of the D. and S.C.R.R."; "The Iron Horse, the Best Blue Blood of Modern Stock"; "Ladies of Dubuque and Cedar Falls, the True Moral Conductors on the Great Railroad of Life"; "Iowa, the Granary of the West"; and "Cedar Falls, the Paradise of the West."

The reception committee was composed of 128 representative citizens headed by Chief Marshal Overman. It also included Mayor J. F. Jaquith and Master of Ceremonies Sheldon Fox. In spite of inclement weather the celebration was staged with railroadlike reliability. When the locomotive came to a slow stop, the big cedar lei was lowered so it encircled the puffing smokestack. Through the mud and rain a cavalcade of carriages and wagons met the train and took the honored guests to the Overman Block. Here they listened to welcoming speeches, to which Platt Smith responded on behalf of the railroad. In the evening they repaired to the American House for dinner accompanied by the Germania orchestra from Dubuque.

At ten o'clock the celebrants danced in Overman Hall, dimly lit by candles and swaying kerosene lamps and redolent of the ever-present cedars. The party is said to have lasted until sunup. Among those who could not stay to the end was Editor George D. Perkins of the *Gazette*. He left early to go down to the editorial office on the first floor, light a tallow candle, and write as follows:

> The Railroad is completed, the cars running regularly into Cedar Falls, the event so long expected, yet so long deferred, the advent of "the Iron Horse" into our city is at length realized, and the "Metropolis of the Great Cedar Valley and its Tributaries" is bound with iron bands to the great commercial marts of the world.

The Civil War ended further construction except for a feeder line called the Cedar Falls & Minnesota Railroad Company, incorporated April 16, 1858. It was controlled by Platt Smith, Roswell B. Mason, and others largely associated with the Dubuque & Sioux City. Most of the stock was held locally. Peter Melendy of Cedar Falls, an avid railroad enthusiast, and William McCoy were given the contract "to grade and tie" the first ten miles of line. This was between Cedar Falls and Janesville. They also subcontracted the remainder of the road to Waverly. Messrs. Melendy and McCoy fulfilled their terms of the contract for the grading, but the company failed. In his autobiography Melendy tersely relates:

> McCoy and I took contract on the Cedar Falls and Minnesota Railroad, from Cedar Falls to Waverly to Grade, Bridge, Culvert and Pile— on the 29th day of September, 1860. Company failed and we lost $300.

Later the road was reorganized. After many delays it was completed to Waverly the latter part of 1864.

Construction crews and tracklayers advanced rapidly west from Cedar Falls following the close of the Civil War. By June 1865 rails were spiked to ties in Boyd; by October trains were running to Ackley. On June 1, 1866, through service was inaugurated from Dubuque to Iowa Falls, 143 miles from the Mississippi. The fledgling railroad now was almost halfway across the state.

On each train came an influx of hearty immigrants: settlers from New England and the eastern states, homesteaders from the central states, sturdy foreigners from the Scandinavian countries, and a heterogeneous mixture of newcomers from England, Ireland, and Scotland.

While the Dubuque & Sioux City was plodding slowly westward, other roads were racing across Iowa to Council Bluffs and Omaha. The first transcontinental railroad was nearing completion, with Council Bluffs as its eastern terminus. The road which won the race across Iowa to meet the Union Pacific would more than likely get most of the traffic and be a favored connection. At different periods during the spectacular contest to reach Council Bluffs first, the Burlington, the North Western, and the Rock Island forged steadily westward in their effort to win the prize.

Back in Chicago a railroad president sat in his office greatly disturbed by this turn of events. He was John M. Douglas, the new head of the Illinois Central. The year 1867 was a trying one, for the Illinois Central had come through the Civil War badly battered and almost bankrupt. Moreover, the road's line west was a big disappointment to him. Three great railroads were rushing to Council Bluffs, and his own Illinois Central was marking time at the Mississippi. Its Iowa connection was accessible only by ferry; and the Dubuque & Sioux City's rails petered out on the prairie scarcely halfway across the state. To be sure, there were some friendly men on the Dubuque & Sioux City board, but the Illinois Central had only a nominal interest in the property. What if a competing line gained control of the Iowa road? The Illinois Central's route from Freeport to Dunleith would wither and die. The predicament is summed up by Carlton J. Corliss in his *Main Line of Mid-America—The Story of the Illinois Central*:

> . . . it was learned on good authority that Jesup and associates had lost interest in completing the road to Sioux City and were flirting with the idea of disposing of their holdings to a rival railroad company. It seemed almost certain that if the Illinois Central did not take steps to gain control of the Iowa lines another Chicago railroad would do so, thus depriving the Company of its most logical and profitable western connection and practically shutting it out of northern Iowa.

After carefully studying the problem and conferring with associates, John Douglas determined it was time for the Illinois Central to step in and complete the Dubuque & Sioux City to the Missouri River.

THE ILLINOIS CENTRAL TAKES HOLD

The first step in the Illinois Central's western program was to lease the Dubuque & Sioux City. It would then be able to control its policies and could expedite construction to Sioux City. Accordingly, on October 1, 1867, the Dubuque & Sioux City (including the Waverly branch) was leased to the Illinois Central for twenty years. The agreement stipulated the IC was to pay 35 percent of the Dubuque & Sioux City's gross earnings for the first ten years of the contract and 36 percent for the remainder of the lease.

Working closely with the Illinois Central management was Platt Smith, vice president of the Iowa road. He was also instrumental in forming a subsidiary, the Iowa Falls & Sioux City Railroad Company, at the time the IC lease became effective, acquiring with it the franchise, right-of-way, and land grants of the Dubuque & Sioux City west of Iowa Falls to Sioux City.

To insure speedy completion of the road across Iowa, the energetic John I. Blair of Blairstown, New Jersey, was made head of the new company. Blair was characterized as "a human dynamo let loose in railway-mad Iowa." He built the Chicago & North Western to Council Bluffs months ahead of schedule and was by common consent just the man for the job.

Meanwhile, concerted efforts were made to resurrect plans for a bridge across the Mississippi at Dubuque. Back in 1857 the Illinois legislature had granted a charter to the Dunleith & Dubuque Bridge Company for the purpose. But the panic of 1857, the Civil War, and lack of funds left the project dormant. On April 8, 1867, however, the bridge company was reincorporated under the direction of William Boyd Allison, the able United States senator from Iowa, who resided in Dubuque. Others associated with the enterprise were Platt Smith, Colonel R. B. Mason, and Joseph F. Tucker, general freight agent of the Illinois Central.

Andrew Carnegie, noted steelman and formerly a Pennsylvania Railroad division superintendent, was awarded the contract to build a new span. He, as head of the Keystone Bridge Company, while not the lowest bidder, had agreed to meet the minimum bid. It came about in this manner: the lowest bidder specified cast iron in the structure, whereas Carnegie's firm advocated wrought iron. To clinch the contract, Carnegie used all the arguments he could muster. He pointed out that if the bridge was hit by a boat, the cast iron would break, whereas the wrought iron in all probability would just bend. In his autobiography Andrew Carnegie writes:

> One of the directors, the well-known Perry [Platt] Smith, was fortunately able to enforce my argument by stating to the board that what I said was undoubtedly the case about cast iron. The other night he had

run his buggy in the dark against a lamp-post which was of cast iron, and the lamp-post had broken to pieces. Am I to be censured if I had little difficulty here in recognizing something akin to the hand of Providence, with Perry [Platt] Smith the manifest agent? "Ah, gentlemen," I said, "there is the point. A little more money and you could have had the indestructible wrought iron and your bridge would stand against any steamboat. We never have built and we never will build a cheap bridge. Ours don't fail."

The contract went to Carnegie.

Work began on the structure in January 1868, and it was completed by December. The original bridge was 1,760 feet long, 16 feet wide, and consisted of seven spans, including a 360-foot drawspan. Curiously enough, the cost of the steel bridge as constructed was $570,900, or slightly less than half of the estimated $1,200,000, which the bridge officials had first anticipated. Total cost, however, including tracklaying, approaches, and betterments, is carried in the valuation records as $1,050,643.49.

The Illinois Central originally had about one-quarter interest in the bridge firm, but in 1888 stock control was effected. It was not until 1946, however, that the Illinois Central purchased all the stock and bonds. The bridge was rebuilt at the turn of the century. During this time one span was eliminated by a "fill" on the Dubuque side near the city's historic shot tower. This shortened the length of the structure by 225 feet.

With the spanning of the Mississippi, rails and supplies were more readily moved to extend the track toward Sioux City. On August 16, 1869, regular train service was established between Chicago and Fort Dodge. While work was progressing westward, construction crews were pushing the rails eastward from Sioux City.

Although John I. Blair was always the dominant factor in building the line, he was aided by J. E. Ainsworth, who had charge of construction. Blair not only built railroads, he also named numerous towns along the line. What is more, he formed townsite companies to encourage the sale of lots and foster development of new communities. In naming towns, Blair drew on his family, his friends, and his business associates. Aurelia in Cherokee County is named for his pretty daughter, Aurelia Ann; and Marcus in the same county derives its name from his son, Marcus L., who died in 1873.

Blair is also credited with naming Remsen and Le Mars, both in Plymouth County. The former gets its name from Dr. William Remsen Smith, a pioneer Sioux City physician and a friend of Blair's. On the other hand,

Le Mars is so named because an excursion party could not agree on what to call an end-of-track locale. Blair had arranged a trip to the westernmost part of the unfinished line and offered to let the ladies on the train name the settlement. Finally, one lady suggested the place be spelled out by using the initial of each woman's Christian name. This resulted in a variety of spellings, including "Selmar" and "Le Mars." The majority favored "Le Mars," and Blair readily consented to that name.

It is fitting that the two Iowa railroads on which John Blair built the most track should each have a town named in his honor. They are Blairsburg in Hamilton County on the Illinois Central and Blairstown in Benton County on the Chicago & North Western. Both are on the main lines of the respective railroads crossing the state.

Returning to the Iowa Falls & Sioux City project, the two construction crews met on July 8, 1870, at a point known as the "Sag" (milepost 431.5), about 3 miles west of the Storm Lake depot. A "golden spike" was driven to signify completion of the 184-mile Iowa Falls–Sioux City line. Blair and his crews had built more miles in two years than his predecessors had done in the entire previous history of the trans-Iowa undertaking.

Why, it may be asked, had Sioux City been selected as the terminus when Council Bluffs was the loadstone to so many railroads running out of Chicago? Part of the answer lies in the Act of 1862, which empowered the Union Pacific to build a road to Sioux City. It was to run from a point on the Union Pacific main line near Fort Kearney, 249 miles west of Omaha in Nebraska Territory. But a subsequent act in 1864 amended the original provision and released the Union Pacific from its obligation to build the road.

That same year the Sioux City & Pacific Rail Road was organized in Dubuque to link Sioux City with the Union Pacific. Among its directors were such Dubuque men as Platt Smith and William B. Allison. The dynamic John I. Blair was president. Early in 1868 a line was built along the east bank of the Missouri River from Sioux City to a point called Missouri Valley Junction, near Council Bluffs, on the main stem of the Chicago & North Western. The Sioux City & Pacific was subsequently taken over by North Western interests, and it is part of that system today.

Many thought that Sioux City ultimately would rival Council Bluffs and Omaha as a transcontinental gateway. For this reason the Illinois Central aggressively fostered construction of its affiliated lines in Iowa. Naturally, too, Platt Smith, John I. Blair, and others were also interested in promoting Sioux City as a gateway. While it was an important western town,

Sioux City never seriously vied with Omaha as a significant transcontinental route. Thanks to the coming of the railroads, however, it grew from a frontier outfitting post for Dakota and Montana to a busy industrial center.

During the same time its main line was being extended across Iowa, the Illinois Central had resumed construction on the Waverly branch. The Cedar Falls & Minnesota reached Charles City on October 18, 1868, and St. Ansgar on December 12, 1869. It reached the Minnesota state line at Mona on May 1, 1870.

By the end of 1870 the Illinois Central was operating 1,107 miles of railroad—705 in Illinois and 402 in Iowa. No matter how one viewed it, Iowa was an important part of the two-state railroad. Furthermore, it was a little over 500 miles from Chicago to Sioux City, whereas the southernmost part of the system from Chicago to Cairo, Illinois, was only about 360 miles. Thus the Illinois Central went farther west than it did south.

Meanwhile, the Illinois Central had not yet built its own line between Chicago and Freeport, Illinois. True, it had through service from Chicago to Iowa, but its trains ran over the track of what is now the Chicago & North Western to span the gap. If one had insisted on using only Illinois Central rails from Iowa points to Chicago, he would have been obliged to go south all the way to Centralia, thence north again to the metropolis on Lake Michigan. This would have involved a detour of 525 miles! It was not until 1888 that the Illinois Central had completed its own line between Chicago and Freeport.

For the next seventeen years there was no further expansion of Iowa lines under lease by the Illinois Central. One reason was the intense competition of rival lines rapidly building in the state. This in turn reduced the revenue of the Illinois Central, and in 1884 it is said to have actually lost money on its Iowa properties. Another reason was that if the IC wanted to extend its leased lines it would have to do so largely to the benefit of the lessors, who would get 36 percent of the increased earnings without an outlay on their part.

The problem was finally resolved in the Illinois Central's front office. In 1883 a thirty-four-year-old broker by the name of Edward H. Harriman was elected a director of the railroad. That same year James C. Clarke, vice president of the Chicago, St. Louis & New Orleans, a subsidiary of the Illinois Central, became president of the latter road. Clarke soon embarked on a bold program of expansion and branch line expansion. In this policy he was supported by Harriman, who became a potent force with the Illinois Central.

When it came to reviewing the Dubuque & Sioux City lease, Clarke,

Harriman, and Stuyvesant Fish (a vice president, three years younger than Harriman) unanimously agreed the Iowa road must be purchased. But how? It was known that several of the large stockholders of the Hawkeye line would try to force the Illinois Central to buy them out at par—or, failing in this, insist upon a new lease at terms onerous to the lessee. Inasmuch as shares were currently quoted at greatly below par, either alternative would be untenable to the Illinois Central. It fell to Harriman to acquire the Iowa road for the IC.

Meanwhile, Drexel, Morgan & Company, acting as trustees for the Dubuque & Sioux City stockholders, were garnering proxies for the annual meeting of the road to be held in Dubuque on February 14, 1887. Harriman likewise had bought all available stock he could get on the open market. But it was quite clear the Morgan-Jesup-Roosevelt interests held the majority.

When a showdown came at the spirited stockholders' meeting, however, the Illinois Central forces controlled a majority of *all those present*. They forthwith organized the meeting and nominated five directors (a majority of the board) friendly to the Illinois Central. Then they proceeded to disqualify the stock held in trust by Drexel, Morgan & Company. Quoting the *Commercial and Financial Chronicle* of February 19:

> During the call of the roll of stockholders, a large number of proxies, representing about 5000 shares of stock, were presented and rejected by the parties in control of the meeting, on the ground that proxy voting in Iowa is not legal. The whole block of stock held by Drexel, Morgan & Co. as trustees was rejected also, on account of the vote having been signed by Drexel, Morgan & Co., personally, and not as trustees. The only shares which could be voted were those held by Harriman & Co. who voted them personally. At the close of the meeting, the following were declared elected: Edward Harriman, Albert Wilcox, and William D. Guthrie, of New York; and Edward C. Woodruff, of New Jersey. To fill the unexpired term of George H. Warner, resigned, W. J. Knight, of Dubuque, was declared elected. During the noon recess, the persons interested with Drexel, Morgan & Co. held a meeting and elected the former directors: James A. Roosevelt, Abram S. Hewitt, J. Pierpont Morgan and Lorenzo Blackstone for the full term, and William G. Hunt for the unexpired term . . . the final adjudication of the matter will be made by the courts.

As the *Chronicle* predicted, litigation ensued for several months. The Morgan brokers held out for purchase of their shares at par. The Illinois

Central declined to buy at that inflated figure. In the end Harriman made a final offer of $80 a share, an offer that was reluctantly accepted.

This was Harriman's first battle with Morgan. Harriman had outgeneraled the powerful Morgan forces even when the latter clearly held the majority of stock in the struggle for control waged in the little river town of Dubuque. Few people, then or now, have heard of the fight. But at the turn of the century all the world was aware of the Homeric struggle between James J. Hill, backed by Morgan, and E. H. Harriman, financed by Kuhn, Loeb & Company, for control of the highly prosperous Chicago, Burlington & Quincy Railroad. After the "battle of Dubuque" the Dubuque & Sioux City became Illinois Central property.

ROUNDING OUT THE SYSTEM

With the Iowa leased lines now owned lock, stock, and barrel by the Illinois Central, the expansion program in the Hawkeye State was pushed with vigor. The railroad endeavored to strengthen its position by building feeder lines. In 1887 the Cherokee & Dakota Railroad Company was organized to build a ninety-six-mile line from Cherokee to the rapidly growing city of Sioux Falls, South Dakota. Included in the project was another branch running southwest from Cherokee to Onawa, sixty-one miles long.

Tracklaying on the Sioux Falls branch commenced in Cherokee, September 26, 1887, and by October 30 the rails had been spiked down at Primghar, twenty-five miles to the north. This was at the rate of better than a mile a day, excluding Sundays. Carlton Corliss, in his well-researched history of the Illinois Central, describes the exuberance of the crowd in the county seat of O'Brien County as seen by J. L. Peck, an eyewitness:

> The crowd waited patiently, and at last the whistle of the engine was heard below the town. . . . The crowd gave a mighty shout. The construction train, loaded with iron rails, came near. The inimitable F. M. (Pomp) McCormack, founder of the *O'Brien County Bell*, had gone down to meet the train, two miles below. He had mounted the high top of the engine, and, waving the Stars and Stripes and hollering and yelling at the top of his voice . . . he came in . . . patriotically breaking the Sabbath . . . Primghar was on the map!

Spurred to even greater efforts, construction forces of five hundred men determined to reach Sioux Falls, seventy-two miles distant, by Christmas day. That would mean laying more than one and one-half miles of track each working day. So great was the progress that the last rail was hammered down in Sioux Falls at 11:30 P.M. on December 18, a week before Christmas. Mayor John F. Norton drove the last spike by lantern light. The "tarriers" had averaged one and two-thirds miles of tracklaying a day from Primghar. So grateful were the citizens, they refused to let the construction men sleep in their East Sioux Falls camp that frigid night. They hastily corralled a fleet of sleighs and took the tired men to comfortable beds in the Cataract House in Sioux Falls.

Regular train service between Sioux Falls and Chicago was inaugurated early in February 1888, thereby linking the Windy City with the westernmost point reached by the Illinois Central. The Onawa branch was also put in operation in June of that year. At Onawa it connected with what is now the North Western's line running south to Council Bluffs.

The year 1888 likewise saw entry of the Illinois Central to the thriving city of Cedar Rapids with the completion of the forty-two-mile branch from Manchester. Organized in 1886 as the Cedar Rapids & Chicago Railroad Company, the firm was sold to the Illinois Central shortly after it was completed.

JOHN F. MERRY

At this point it is appropriate to mention one of the best-liked Iowans ever to hold an important office on the Illinois Central. He was Captain John F. Merry of Manchester. Born in Ohio, brought up on a farm north of Manchester, Merry served in the Civil War and later turned to railroading, working for the Illinois Central from 1880 to 1911. Starting as an excursion agent, he rose to be assistant general passenger agent of the system. To Iowans and many people elsewhere he was "Mr. Illinois Central."

Of a warm, jolly disposition, John F. Merry was gregarious, popular, and, above all, friendly. If ever a railroad had a goodwill ambassador, it was Captain Merry. Nor was his work limited by his title. Actually, he was an agricultural agent, industrial agent, immigration agent, publicity representative, frequently writing promotional booklets and homeseekers' guides. In reviewing his *Where to Locate New Factories* (1892), the *Ottumwa Daily Courier* said:

> Captain J. F. Merry . . . is a versatile man. He can sing like a Sankey in a Methodist camp meeting or at a Loyal Legion love feast. He can plead like a lawyer! He used to see more goods than any man who ever called himself a competitor. He can recite an anecdote like an actor . . . Captain Merry . . . now a railroad official . . . has found time to write a 160-page book, "Where to Locate New Factories," . . . Two years ago he issued a pamphlet on the Northwest, dwelling especially upon agricultural resources of the new counties in northern Iowa, along the Illinois Central

Railroad. . . . He gathered the data for his book by driving all over the new counties, interviewing farmers and reproducing much of their conversations. . . . Everything he argued therefore was backed by voluminous proof from the farmers themselves.

Up to the time of his retirement Captain Merry had compiled, with one exception, every pamphlet, leaflet, and circular concerning immigration issued by the Illinois Central since he started working for the road. His literature concerning the South had been so conservative and his facts so accurate that bankers, trust companies, and lawyers, as well as homeseekers, constantly relied on his pamphlets.

Returning to the expansion program, there was the linking of Albert Lea, Minnesota, with the main stem in Iowa by way of the Cedar Falls branch at Mona on the Iowa-Minnesota state line. The road was extended to Grenville, Minnesota, in 1900. A right-of-way was purchased from that town to Albert Lea, but this section of the line was never built. Instead, trackage rights were acquired over the Rock Island between Glenville and Albert Lea. Now the Illinois Central had a direct connection via the Albert Lea gateway to the Twin Cities over the Minneapolis & St. Louis Railway. To round out the Albert Lea district trackage, mention should be made of the eight-mile Stacyville branch, opened late in 1897.

During this period by far and away the most significant undertaking was building to Council Bluffs. Heretofore the Illinois Central had trackage rights over the Chicago, St. Paul, Minneapolis & Omaha (Chicago & North Western) to Council Bluffs. But this agreement did not prove satisfactory, and it was later terminated.

Omaha, key city of the Missouri Valley and one of the greatest growing cattle markets in the Midwest, was still a long way from Illinois Central rails. Such a situation became intolerable. All the other railroads crossing the length of Iowa had made Omaha their goal—the North Western, the Rock Island, the Burlington, and the Milwaukee. Even the Wabash had built up to Omaha from Missouri, cutting across southwestern Iowa to reach its coveted goal. And it was a known fact that the Great Western was coming south to Omaha. What was the trouble with the Illinois Central?

Stuyvesant Fish, at that time president of the Illinois Central, determined to see his far-flung railroad tap the Omaha gateway. Under his authority preliminary surveys were made to ascertain the best route. The proposed line would diverge at Tara, west of Fort Dodge, the engineers agreed, and run in a general southwestern course to Council Bluffs, a distance of 131 miles. A new company called the Fort Dodge & Omaha Railroad was chartered September 14, 1898, to build the last and longest branch of the Illinois Central in Iowa.

Chief Engineer John F. Wallace was in general charge of the project. Wallace later gained worldwide fame as chief engineer of the construction of the Panama Canal. A novel feature of the undertaking was that the "golden spike" would be driven first instead of last. As it turned out, the initial spike was driven by a woman, although Superintendent Charles K. Dixon had been slated to do the honors. When the time for the ceremony came, Dixon, finding it impossible to keep the engagement, sent his wife in his stead. So it was that Kitty Dixon performed what heretofore had always been considered a man's prerogative. With more zeal than skill she finally drove the gold-plated spike home. The unorthodox event occurred May 25, 1899. Just 208 days later the last spike, without any fanfare, was driven by a man. The Illinois Central had at long last fulfilled its western destiny.

MAIN LINE — WEST

The Illinois Central is generally thought of as a north-and-south railroad, with its main stem running from Chicago to New Orleans. However, with the completion of the branch to Omaha (it has trackage rights from Council Bluffs to Omaha) the Iowa Division earned the distinction of being a vital east-and-west main line. Through passenger service was provided between Chicago and Omaha. More important still was the increasing role the road played in funneling transcontinental freight through the Omaha gateway.

The Illinois Central competes on substantially equal terms with most of the six other Chicago–Council Bluffs–Omaha roads. True, it has the longest route, except for the circuitous Wabash, although it is only a scant five miles longer than the Chicago Great Western, which reached Council Bluffs in 1904. On the other hand, the "Omaha branch" was built to the highest standards of its time, and it has been constantly modernized up to this day.

Having sketched the growth of the Illinois Central in Iowa, it is fitting that we discuss the part it played in social history and economic advancement. In other years there was no phase of railroading so intimately associated with the region it served as its passenger service. And the Illinois Central had passenger trains on all its lines in Iowa. It provided a cheap, convenient way to travel from village and town to the metropolitan centers, particularly Chicago.

A glance at the 1913 timetable gives a representative picture of the golden age of passenger service in the state. There were five daily round-trips from Chicago to Waterloo, two daily trains each way from Chicago to Omaha, and three daily round-trips between Fort Dodge and Sioux City. Sleepers were standard equipment on trains running from the Windy City to Omaha, Sioux City, and Sioux Falls. The remaining branch lines had daily-except-Sunday coach service.

Being a later comer to Omaha, the road did not feature passenger service through that gateway without change to connecting lines. But in conjunction with the Minneapolis & St. Louis Railway, it exploited the Albert Lea gateway. Its Chicago and Minneapolis and St. Paul Limited boasted of an "Electric-Lighted Steel Sleeping Car, Buffet-Club Car, Free Reclining Chair Car and Coach, Chicago to Minneapolis and St. Paul; Dining Car Chicago to Freeport." On the return trip a diner was coupled on at Dubuque for Chicago.

Up to about the time of World War I the Albert Lea Route was an important, although secondary, line between Chicago and the Twin Cities. It had to compete with the Burlington, the Milwaukee (then known as the St. Paul Road), the North Western, the Great Western, the Rock Island and the Soo . . . all having limited through trains between these destinations. The traveler in the early part of the twentieth century had an incredible amount of diverse routings available to him!

Mr. E. L. Holmes, passenger traffic manager of the Illinois Central, remembers the colorful pre–World War I days, when local ticket agents frequently had a supply of choice cigars. The stogies were left by traveling passenger agents from other lines trying to solicit business for their respective roads. Traffic, like kissing, often went by favor.

Holmes, who was born in Alta, Iowa, also recalls the resourcefulness of Illinois Central men in "getting" the business, capturing a major share of the Omaha-Chicago excursion traffic. The road featured $8 weekend fares, leaving Omaha, Sioux City, and Sioux Falls Saturday afternoon and returning the following day. In almost every instance the excursions were crowded. Why? It happened that the Illinois Central passenger agent in Omaha, A. J. Lightfoot, had his own orchestra. The road obligingly provided a baggage car for his band with sufficient room for dancing. It is said some of the excursionists danced all the way to Chicago. That was competition hard to beat.

This was an era when "drummers," as commercial travelers were called, covered their territory almost exclusively by rail. The Illinois Central sold two-thousand-mile mileage tickets at $50—"refund of $10 if used within one year." A smaller "book" of a thousand miles sold for only $20. They were very popular with traveling salesmen, lecturers, and businessmen.

All along the road were station restaurants, most of which were operated by the Van Noy news concession. Dubuque, Fort Dodge, Albert Lea, Cherokee, Sioux City, and Omaha had (and some still have) lunch counters or restaurants to "feed the trains." Indeed, employees were given the option of taking part of their wages in lunch tickets, or "pie cards" as they were dubbed.

Mr. Holmes, who started working on the Illinois Central as a station helper at Alta for $25 a month, remembers how his pie card "practically saved" him from slow starvation. He used his pass to go east, traveling on the proverbial shoestring. Like other young men in quest of adventure, the Iowa railroader ran short of funds. Too proud to write home for money, he faced the prospect of riding all day without eating. Then he remembered his pie card. It was good all along the Illinois Central.

Understandably, too, the pleasantest sound in his early days of railroading was the whistle of the little engine pulling the pay car. The pay train "made" the division once a month. In those days men were paid in hard money, often silver and gold. Checks were unknown. Holmes considered Paymaster H. D. Warner "the most important man on the railroad."

The morale of the Iowa Division has always been high. Come flood or blizzard, when duty calls, the Iowa railroader is first to respond. A story is told by Otto H. Zimmerman, vice president of operations, who at the time of the incident was superintendent at Waterloo. It concerned an unexpected blizzard which struck Fort Dodge, filling the cuts with drifting snow and stalling trains. The wind blew so fiercely across the prairie it blinded the eyes of trainmen and made life miserable for anyone out on the line.

On that particular day there were twenty-seven men on the roster who were due to get their day off. But did they take it? No, not they. As the storm increased in violence the phone began to ring in the division office. One after another of the trainmen and enginemen announced they were coming in to fight the storm. Several had bad colds, but they came anyway. Two were in bed sick, one with pneumonia. Their spouses called in, very apologetic that the men were not able to help out in the emergency.

Another railroader, chairman of the Local Order of Railroad Conductors, phoned to say that his wife was in the hospital awaiting a serious operation. "I can't go out on a run, because they are going to operate on her soon," he explained, "but I'll come down to the roundhouse and help any way I can." And he did. He was in the roundhouse from midnight to five in the morning, helping to get engines in shape to keep the line open. Indeed, the conductor worked right up until the time the hospital phoned him.

Not a single man of the twenty-seven had to be called. They knew when they were needed and they came.

The Illinois Central prided itself on up-to-date equipment and on-time operation of its principal trains. Often the humble local was an institution to the communities it served. Ruth Suckow, in her homespun Iowa novel *Country People*, brings out this fact in describing her fictitious town of "Richland."

"For one thing," she writes, "there was a railroad, the main line of the Illinois Central which connected Richland directly with Chicago." And the institution? It was "the morning 'Clippers,' the Chicago train, by which clocks were set and risings timed. . . ."

The "Clipper" was No. 28 eastbound and No. 27 westbound. In 1913 it left Waterloo at 7:10 A.M., arriving in Dubuque at 10:30 A.M. Returning, the through train departed from Dubuque at 3:45 in the afternoon and rolled into Waterloo at 7:15.

The day of the branch line local has long since gone, but the Illinois Central's handsome brown-and-gold main line passenger trains still speed across Iowa. The Hawkeye, an overnight express, runs the entire length of the state on its way from Chicago to Sioux City. It has coaches and sleepers with a set-out Pullman for Waterloo.

In addition, the Land O'Corn provides fast daytime service between Chicago and Waterloo. It carries an attractive diner, featuring tasty southern-style meals. A novel item in the consist are specially designed flatcars, on which ride Flexivans, or truck trailers. These containers, carrying United States mail, are quickly transferred from flatcar to truck at several major points on the line. By this method distant off-line communities receive the benefit of fast rail shipment to the nearest station where, without breaking bulk, mail is taken by truck to its ultimate highway destination.

In the more leisurely era before World War I nearly every station boasted of cattle pens, and freight trains picked up stock along the line. Cattlemen rode drovers' cabooses, furnished with mattresses for sleeping, to market and returned in comfort on regular passenger trains. Stock pickups were often scheduled to move trainloads of cattle from the West in the spring for fattening and out to market in the fall.

Cattle on the hoofs is still a significant item in today's tonnage, but dressed meat predominates. The Illinois Central claims to move more meat and meat products in Iowa than all other railroads in the state combined. This is not to say the road neglects wheat and corn, manufactured goods, lumber and millwork, coal and gypsum. Tractors made in Iowa and clay products from the Fort Dodge area are standard items found on many through freights. But more than anything else the Iowa Division is the "Main Line of Meat."

To expedite meat and other perishables and general freight, the Illinois Central operates a fleet of "symbol" trains. There is the "cc-6," for example, a manifest freight operating at near-passenger-train-speed between Omaha and Chicago. (One "c" in the name stands for Council Bluffs, the other "c" for Chicago.)

An Illinois Central switch crew picks up meat and livestock cars in the transfer yard of the South Omaha Terminal Railroad and transfers them to Council Bluffs. At the latter point the cc-6, or "hotshot" as railroaders call it, is made up for Chicago. The manifest runs nonstop the 135 miles to Fort Dodge. Here another crew takes over for the 100-mile trip to Waterloo. This is along beautiful high-speed track, equipped with automatic train stops. cc-6 fights the grade out of the Des Moines River valley and is soon wheeling along at 60 m.p.h. At Waterloo, headquarters of the Iowa Division, cars are set out while others are added. A fresh crew takes the train the rest of the way across the state. Nearing the Mississippi, the long freight weaves between limestone bluffs in the hilly country on the way to Dubuque. At Dubuque the cc-6 parallels the Mississippi, then veers to the right through silvery lattice steel girders to cross the Father of Waters. Ahead in Illinois is a tunnel, some sharp curves, and then more or less straight track all the way to the great city of Chicago.

Today the Illinois Central has substantially the same mileage in Iowa that it had at the beginning of the twentieth century. With the exception of the retirement of a thirty-mile segment of the Cherokee-Onawa branch between Onawa and Anthon, there have been no abandonments. As a matter of fact, in 1955 the Illinois Central purchased jointly, with the Rock Island, the Waterloo Railroad connecting Waterloo and Cedar Rapids. Formerly an electric interurban line, the sixty-four-mile dieselized property gives the Illinois Central an additional freight route to Cedar Rapids together with a valuable belt railway in Waterloo.

From a two-state railroad with a third of its mileage in Iowa, the Illinois Central later built south and to a limited extent east. It now serves fourteen states, going east to Indianapolis and Louisville and south to the Gulf of Mexico. It also goes to Birmingham and nearly reaches Texas on the branch to Shreveport. It has 6,500 miles of line in all three districts—Eastern, Southern, and Western—by which the Interstate Commerce Commission classified the carriers geographically.

Once a crude prairie railroad with 60-pound rail on unballasted roadway, the main line of the Illinois Central in Iowa now is basically in 112- and 115-pound rail on crushed rock ballast with the remaining "old standard" 90-pound rail steadily being replaced. It is largely protected by block signals and automatic train control. In the days of steam, well-kept Pacific-, Mikado-, and Mountain-type locomotives characterized its fast passenger and time freights. The more economical diesels have taken over. Like all the Illinois Central's rolling stock, they are kept up to a high state of efficiency.

In the future as in the past, the modern Iowa Division (the second biggest of all the Illinois Central's nine divisions) and its terminals will continue to be the strong east-and-west line of the strategic Chicago-to-Gulf railroad. Time will only increase its importance to Iowa and to the nation.

Palimpsest 43 (June 1962)

About 1910 a group of freight handlers take a break from their chores at the Illinois Central freight house in Council Bluffs. H. Roger Grant Collection.

It is April 1954, and Illinois Central passenger Train No. 11, the Hawkeye, leaves Fort Dodge for Sioux City. Don L. Hofsommer photograph.

In September 1969 No. 12, the Hawkeye, rumbles along the main line east of Storm Lake on its way to Fort Dodge, Waterloo, Dubuque, and Chicago. The end of Illinois Central passenger service is near; on May 1, 1971, Amtrak will make its debut, but not on the rails of the Illinois Central in Iowa. Don L. Hofsommer photograph.

On a September night in 1969 at the Illinois Central's Fort Dodge station, Train No. 12 waits to leave for Chicago. Railway Post Office car No. 102 claimed the distinction of being the last of its breed to operate in Iowa; three months later it would disappear. Don L. Hofsommer photograph.

In August 1976 a mostly meat train passes the Illinois Central station at Archer on the Sioux Falls, South Dakota, line. This trackage would be subsequently abandoned. Don L. Hofsommer photograph.

THE
NORTH WESTERN
IN IOWA

THE RACE TO COUNCIL BLUFFS

The Chicago & North Western has more miles of track in Iowa than any other railroad. It was first to cross the state and first to feature through passenger service in conjunction with the newly formed Union Pacific–Central Pacific transcontinental route in 1869.

The North Western–Union Pacific–Southern Pacific's strategic middle line was the standard way to travel between Chicago and San Francisco. Other transcontinentals came: the Northern Pacific, Great Northern and Milwaukee on the north; the Santa Fe, the Rock Island–Southern Pacific's Golden State Limited, and the Southern Pacific's Sunset Route on the south; and the newer Burlington–Rio Grande–Western Pacific line, which closely paralleled the first transcontinental. Yet for some eighty-six years the strategic middle route, with the Chicago & North Western at the eastern end, dominated transcontinental rail travel.

Today, alas, the North Western no longer participates in through cross-country passenger service. On the other hand, it is still a mighty factor in handling transcontinental tonnage. Great long freights still barrel through Iowa, but the glory of its named limiteds and plush streamliners is now only a nostalgic memory.

The story of the North Western in Iowa begins with the race to Council Bluffs. It concerns three trunk lines, all struggling to reach the coveted Council Bluffs–Omaha gateway first. Associated with the enterprise was a New Jersey railroad builder who rose to great heights and a grandiose railroad scheme which fell to abysmal depths. Leaving out western mountains and Indians, the drama in building across Iowa has much of the heroic qualities which characterized construction of the storied Union Pacific.

The byways which led to the North Western in Iowa go back to the ill-fated Iowa Central Air Line Rail Road Company—organized in 1853. Also known as the Lyons and Iowa Central Railroad, the Iowa Central was to run in more or less a straight line from the little Mississippi River town of Lyons via Iowa City to Council Bluffs. At Lyons a lofty bridge was to carry the Air Line across the Mississippi.

The Air Line lost no time in dispatching surveyors and charting the road. It also did considerable grading between Lyons and Anamosa. At other points there is evidence of work done, and it is said an old grade can still be seen east of Iowa City. The Air Line received extensive local aid, mostly in the form of bonds issued by counties along its route in exchange for stock of the road.

Meanwhile, what was to be Iowa's first operating railroad, the Mississippi & Missouri, was being surveyed westward from Davenport in 1853. It likewise had planned to go through Iowa City on its way to Council Bluffs. Crews of the two rival lines often met; and competing promoters vied with each other in soliciting funds for their respective enterprises. All along the routes surveyors were greeted with enthusiasm.

Council Bluffs, for example, welcomed Grenville M. Dodge of the Mississippi & Missouri with a lavish reception and ball. A few days later equal elation was shown rival surveyors of the Air Line. Agents of the two railroads exhorted towns and villages to support their companies and get on the "great through route" across Iowa. Public meetings were held, and each party spoke in glowing terms of his projected line.

The Air Line is said to have had about two thousand Irish immigrants, including their families, camped in Lyons to expedite construction of the road. But the visionary project was doomed from the start. Its principal backer, H. P. Adams of Syracuse, New York, absconded with the bonds and left the counties with taxes to pay and Irish laborers to feed. Many of these workers were forced to settle for groceries and dry goods in place of wages. Because of the latter item, the defunct line was dubbed "The Calico Road." It was subsequently discovered that Adams was a fugitive from justice with a criminal record. While the Air Line was permanently grounded, certain aspects of its corporate existence appeared later to play a very significant role in the North Western's history.

No sooner had one contestant dropped out of the race for Council Bluffs than another took its place. The newcomer was the Chicago, Iowa & Nebraska Rail Road, organized January 26, 1856. It had the backing of several upstate New Yorkers, including Lucius B. Crocker of Oswego and Thomas T. Davis and Austin Meyers, both of Syracuse. Others lending financial help were John Bertram, a sea captain of Salem, Massachusetts, Oakes Ames of North Easton, Massachusetts, and Alfred W. Johnson of Belfast, Maine. Milo Smith was the chief engineer.

Construction began at Clinton in 1856. By June 1859 the road had reached Cedar Rapids, eighty-one miles distant. This was farther west than the Mississippi & Missouri, which had completed its line from Davenport to Iowa City by January 1, 1856, and halted there for several years. But down the Mississippi River a third railroad was pushing its rails across the prairie. Called the Burlington & Missouri River, later known as the Burlington, it proudly reached Ottumwa in August 1859.

That was the railroad picture in Iowa when a tall, well-built, fifty-eight-year-old businessman, John Insley Blair of Blairstown in the Kittatinny Mountains of northern New Jersey, left his tiny community to attend the Republican Party national convention in Chicago, May 16, 1860. He was one of about five hundred delegates to the great political rally, at which there were over ten thousand spectators.

When the convention ended, with Abraham Lincoln duly nominated for the presidency, the delegates were invited on a free trip to Iowa. John Blair eagerly accepted the invitation. He went with a party of three hundred by rail to Dunleith (opposite Dubuque), thence by boat from Dubuque to Clinton. At the latter town they boarded "the cars" on the newly completed Chicago, Iowa & Nebraska Rail Road for Cedar Rapids. The visitors were dined and entertained at the end-of-track community and told of the wonders of the West. On returning, Blair wrote in his diary: "I Consider this Road [the Chicago, Iowa & Nebraska] Considering its extension with the land grant on the 200 Miles West of Cedar Rappids, one of the Most desirable and if Rightly Managed out to pay."

Spelling and grammar were not subjects in which John I. Blair excelled. But when it came to vision, business foresight, and making money, he had few peers. Blair was destined to return to Iowa in 1862 and build railroads faster and more extensively in that state than anyone else—before or since.

Blair never went to high school. At ten he is said to have declared: "I have seven brothers and three sisters. That's enough in the family to be educated. I am going to get rich."

At eleven he went to work in a country store at Hope, New Jersey, not far from Belvidere, where he was born in 1802. When eighteen, he owned a store at Gravel Hill. Nine years later he had a chain of five general stores in northern New Jersey, and he operated four "flouring-mills."

Always alert to new business opportunities, Blair branched out into mining, manufacturing, and railroading. Modest success in mining at Oxford Furnace, New Jersey, led to an active part in founding the Lackawanna Coal & Iron Company in 1846. Later, with his son, DeWitt Clinton Blair, and Oakes Ames as partners, he established the Lackawanna Steel Company to make rails. Heretofore nearly all steel rails had been imported from England. Blair was also one of the original directors of the Delaware, Lackawanna & Western Railroad and soon became its biggest stockholder.

At sixty, when most men are thinking about retirement, John I. Blair began his remarkable career as a builder of western railroads. When he came to do business in Iowa in 1862, the Hawkeye State was ready to do business with him. The Cedar Rapids and Missouri River Railroad had been organized on June 14, 1860, to extend westward from Cedar Rapids to the Big Muddy. More important, from the investors' standpoint, was the fact that the road persuaded the Iowa General Assembly to turn over the land grant of the defunct Iowa Central Air Line to the very much alive Cedar Rapids and Missouri River Railroad.

The new railroad had capital provided mostly by eastern financiers, among whom were John Bertram, Lucius B. Crocker, and Oakes Ames. These men, it will be recalled, were also instrumental in building the Chicago, Iowa & Nebraska Rail Road. In addition, the Cedar Rapids and Missouri River Railroad had the backing of John Weare and John F. Ely of Cedar Rapids and G. M. Woodbury of Marshalltown. Crocker became first president and W. W. Walker secretary. With capital and a bountiful land grant, the road built westward from Cedar Rapids. But it lacked the drive, soon to be provided by John Blair, the "human dynamo let loose in railway-mad Iowa."

Blair appears to have first taken a hand in the road's management in 1861. After that, dirt began to fly. By the end of that year the track reached Otto Creek Station (now Chelsea), forty-one miles west of Cedar Rapids. In 1862 the road was completed to Marshalltown. Two years later (1864) it reached Nevada and in 1865, Boone. Now it was over halfway across the state.

In the meantime, the Mississippi River had been bridged, replacing a slow, cumbersome ferry. The bridge was started in 1858; and the following year a seven-span McCallum truss, built of wood, connected Fulton, Illinois, with Little Rock Island, 1,400 feet from shore. It was not until 1864, however, that the deeper western channel of the Mississippi, from the island to Clinton, was bridged by Howe truss spans. The drawspan was of the Bollman pattern. Subsequently, the whole structure proved to be too light, and it was replaced over the years by heavier and stronger pin-connected Pratt trusses.

While Blair was blazing his own trail across Iowa, his two competitors were not idle. Far to the south the aggressive Burlington had reached Albia in 1866. But the Mississippi & Missouri (soon to become the Chicago, Rock Island & Pacific Railroad), which formerly set the pace in Iowa railroad building, was marking time in Grinnell.

Thanks to additional land grants made available by Congress and the energetic leadership of Blair, the Cedar Rapids and Missouri River Railroad went all-out in construction. The railroad builder from New Jersey along with his young assistant, W. W. Walker, made a splendid team. Together they visited towns and villages along the projected route. Both were shrewd traders. They often pitted one town against another in seeking donations, station lands, and bonds. They matched their wits against promoters of the Burlington and the Rock Island in enlisting public support and in seeking both public and private aid.

In Council Bluffs, where "railroad fever" was so pervasive, an enthusiastic crowd greeted Blair and Walker on July 9, 1886. The two spoke in Burhop's Hall on a stage flanked by "first citizens" amid a backdrop of American flags. At the other end of the hall a band aroused the audience to religious fervor. The following resolution was passed:

> Resolved, That we feel under obligations to Messrs. Blair and Walker, the gentlemanly officers of said company, for their visit to our place, and for the interest manifested by them in the early completion of their road to our city, and for the free, full and frank expressions given by them of the prospects for the speedy completion of their road, and of the future prospect of our city.

John I. Blair must have beamed with the results of the meeting. Heading the subscription list was Major M. Turley with a gift of eighty acres of land in Council Bluffs for a depot and other railroad buildings. One business house donated $2,000; eleven subscribers pledged $1,000 each, and 106 other signatures brought the total up to $36,000.

The popular demand for a railroad is evinced in the zealous words of Editor William S. Burke of the *Council Bluffs Nonpareil*. Said he:

> It would be better for every lot owner in the city to donate one half of his possessions—be they much or little—if, thereby, these railroad connections could be secured, than to own twice what he now has and allow them to go elsewhere. Without her railroads, we would scarcely

give a baubee for the best vacant lot in Council Bluffs; with them, we will see how rapidly every stagnant impulse will be stirred into life, and the flush of a radiant but permanent prosperity mantle all the future.

Shortly after the Council Bluffs meeting Walker advertised in the *Chicago Times* for five thousand laborers to expedite construction to the Missouri River. The last lap of the race was on!

Meanwhile, the Chicago, Iowa & Nebraska Rail Road, it may be added, was leased on July 3, 1862, to the Galena and Chicago Union Rail Road Company and by modified lease on December 10, 1869, to the Chicago & North Western Railway Company.

The Cedar Rapids and Missouri River Railroad was leased on July 8, 1862, to the Galena and Chicago Union Rail Road Company and by modified lease December 1, 1865, to the Chicago & North Western Railway Company.

We have seen that the race across Iowa began when the Rock Island (Mississippi & Missouri) first built westward from Davenport, thereby getting a head start. Next came the Burlington (Burlington & Missouri River), which soon forged ahead of its pioneer competitor. Lastly, the North Western (Chicago, Iowa & Nebraska and the Cedar Rapids and Missouri River railroads) appeared as a latecomer. All three were in a close and exciting race at various stages of their mad rush across Iowa.

The Rock Island had such distinguished engineers as Peter A. Dey and General Grenville M. Dodge. But bankruptcy and management dissension retarded its progress. The Burlington had President James F. Joy and an able young superintendent by the name of Charles E. Perkins. Moreover, it was financed by the "Boston Group." Finally, there was the North Western. And in Iowa Blair was the North Western, and the North Western was Blair.

The race ended differently from the way it started. The first road came in second, the last first, and the Burlington at the tag end. In other words, the race ended with the North Western first; the Rock Island second; and the Burlington last.

The Burlington had, perhaps, man for man the ablest management, to say nothing of the solid support of conservative Boston bankers. But the North Western had Blair. It was as simple as that. Blair was absolute boss.

In the case of the Rock Island, very competent engineers were hamstrung by management difficulties. As for the Burlington, the management was of the best, but the Bostonians were cautious. Not so with John Insley Blair. He had the power, the money, and engineering talent. He dominated the Cedar Rapids and Missouri River Railroad. He was owner, manager, and financier. While others waited for the necessary funds or for a nod from the front office, Blair was in the field—building, building, building.

West of Boone, construction started in December 1865. By the following spring the railhead was within fifteen miles of Denison. A few months later the husky Chicago gandy dancers were hammering spikes and surfacing track down the valley of the Boyer River. On September 15, 1866, ground was broken for the Council Bluffs depot with an elaborate ceremony accompanied by the Council Bluffs Brass Band. On Tuesday, January 22, 1867, the last rail was laid in front of the new station, marking the completion of the first railroad into town.

Ironically, General Grenville M. Dodge, who helped survey the Rock Island across Iowa, was the principal speaker to celebrate the North Western's arrival. By this time, however, he was chief engineer of the rapidly building Union Pacific, and he welcomed the railroad from the East with genuine enthusiasm. He looked for the day when "five great trunk railroads" would serve Council Bluffs and when it would become "a railroad centre . . . second to none in the State of Iowa."

ONE OF THE "BIG THREE"

It is almost impossible to trace the early development of the North Western in Iowa without continual references to the Burlington and the Rock Island. Iowa was (and still is) a battleground where each road fought for tonnage. Unlike the heavily populated, highly industrialized states, Iowa's local business, while important, is far overshadowed by its through traffic. Nor are the major cities of Iowa strongholds of any one railroad such as San Francisco is of the Southern Pacific or Philadelphia of the Pennsylvania.

After the Union Pacific–Central Pacific Omaha-to-the-West-Coast line had been completed on May 10, 1869, there was a lively jockeying for position by the three trans-Iowa connecting links. Having reached Council Bluffs first, the North Western had the advantage of priority. According to the *Omaha Herald*, the Union Pacific in the late 1860s was to build "two hundred and fifty cars for the transportation of their own material over the Chicago and North Western." It goes without saying the North Western hauled much of the Union Pacific's supplies. Furthermore, the North Western's first president, William Butler Ogden, was also the first incumbent to that office on the Union Pacific. In addition, Oakes Ames, who was so active in the Union Pacific's management, was likewise prominent in the early affairs of the Cedar Rapids and Missouri River Railroad. Not content with building the North Western across Iowa, John I. Blair found another outlet for his tremendous drive in constructing the first hundred miles of the Union Pacific in Nebraska.

But fully as important in the transcontinental railroad strategy was the Rock Island. It very adroitly claimed a major share of the Union Pacific's traffic, for had not Thomas C. Durant, Henry Farnam, and John A. Dix, representing the Union Pacific's management, also been active in promoting the Mississippi & Missouri road?

On the other hand, there was little community interest between the Chicago, Burlington & Quincy and the Union Pacific. But the Burlington was a skillful bargainer; it had the soundest financing of the Big Three and, like its Iowa-Missouri satellites, was dominated by the able James F. Joy.

There was also a dark horse in the picture to further complicate matters. This was the Kansas City, St. Joseph & Council Bluffs Railroad, which entered Council Bluffs more or less by the back door, coming in from St. Joseph, Missouri, on the south. A Joy property, it connected with other Joy-controlled roads, forming a roundabout route from Council Bluffs to Chicago via northern Missouri and southwestern Illinois.

All in all, the complex situation would seem to equate a knock-down-and-drag-out battle of rate wars, rival construction, and unbridled competition. Such direct action often characterized the turbulent era of early railroad expansion. But nothing of the kind happened in Iowa, at least for fifteen years. Instead, the Big Three formed the Iowa Pool, which Dr. Julius Grodinsky has described as "the envy of the railroad world."

The initiative came from President John F. Tracy of the Rock Island after conferring with the North Western's executive committee. Both roads were fearful of the Burlington's expansion program. As an alternative to cut-throat competition, they suggested pooling the earnings of all three trans-Iowa roads serving the Omaha gateway. Joy, who headed the Burlington, was amenable. Although not adverse to extending the Burlington where it seemed expedient, he nonetheless favored restricting competition and considered rate wars disastrous to all parties concerned.

A series of conferences between the Big Three, with the tacit approval of the Union Pacific, led to the formation of the very real, yet scarcely tangible institution known as the Iowa Pool. For authority, effectiveness, and informality, it is unique in the annals of American railroading. Based only "upon confidence between man and man," it lasted from 1870 to 1884. In his *The Iowa Pool,* Julius Grodinsky writes:

> While the competitive forces swirled in all directions, the Pool roads continued to function as members of an organization which, in its in-

formality, flexibility, and tentative—almost experimental—nature, was unprecedented in American business history. The roads carried traffic and distributed earnings without the help of any written contract. Neither was there any formal organization set up to administer the operations of this co-operative enterprise.

The three pool roads made a verbal agreement in which each line retained 45 percent of the passenger revenues and 50 percent of the freight to meet the cost of doing business. The balance of the revenues was equally divided among the members of the pool.

Until the wily and unpredictable Jay Gould got control of the Union Pacific about 1875, the Iowa Pool operated with surprising harmony. But when Gould began exerting undue pressure in Union Pacific affairs, discord immediately developed. For one thing, he felt the Union Pacific should have a greater share of the "division" of the Chicago–Pacific Coast freight receipts. To this idea the pool members were obdurate.

By one manner or another the crafty Gould sought to break up the pool. He tried to get control of the Kansas City, St. Joseph & Council Bluffs road and thereby divert traffic from the pool. He had himself elected a director of both the North Western and the Rock Island. By so doing he hoped to align these two against the Burlington. In none of these undertakings was he successful. Probably he dealt his most telling blow when he brought the Wabash into Council Bluffs and for a time shunted a major part of Union Pacific freight routed via Omaha to and from the far-flung Wabash system.

The Iowa Pool valiantly withstood the assaults of Gould. Other economic factors, however, led to its inevitable downfall. The railroad picture had changed. Early in the 1880s the Wabash was admitted to the pool and subsequently the Missouri Pacific (which came up from the south through eastern Nebraska to Omaha) and the Chicago, Milwaukee & St. Paul. By this time the North Western had considerable mileage in northeastern Nebraska; the Burlington had a line to Denver; and the Rock Island was expanding in the Southwest. The Omaha gateway could easily be bypassed so that poor members were no longer constrained to share their revenue as they had formerly done. The pool triumphed over Gould-made traffic changes, but it could not hold out against changes made by an expanding railroad economy. In 1884 the Iowa Pool quietly expired.

What effect did the pool have on the North Western? It stabilized rates, kept other railroads from encroaching on its territory, and aided in its weathering the panic of 1873. But the great system which William B. Ogden envisioned was neither very great in the 1870s nor was it entirely independent. For about a year it wore the collar of the St. Paul (now known as the Milwaukee Road) when Alexander Mitchell, president of the St. Paul, also headed the North Western. On June 3, 1870, John F. Tracy, head of the Rock Island, doubled in brass by starting his three-year term as the North Western's president. He was followed by Albert Keep, who restored the North Western to a measure of independence.

The North Western did not come into its own, however, until a young man by the name of Marvin Hughitt rose from general superintendent to top executive in 1877. Hughitt came to the North Western from the Pullman Company in 1872. As he rose in position and power, so rose the North Western in public esteem and financial stature.

While the Iowa Pool flourished, the North Western's expansion in the state was mostly confined to its own immediate bailiwick—beginning at the eastern edge of Iowa at Lyons, where it had acquired the land grant of the ill-fated Iowa Central Air Line Rail Road and transferred it to the Cedar Rapids and Missouri River Railroad. With the transfer there was a curious stipulation: the new land-grant recipient had to build a line from Lyons to connect with the Chicago, Iowa & Nebraska Rail Road. Thus, the Cedar Rapids company, whose nearest rails were 82 miles away, was required to build a 2.6-mile stub line from Clinton to Lyons in 1870.

The same year, the Iowa Midland Railway Company was chartered to build over the partly graded Air Line from Lyons to Anamosa via Maquoketa. The entire seventy-one-mile line was completed in December 1870. It was subsequently leased to the North Western. Farther west the Stanwood & Tipton Railway Company was organized (and completed) in 1872 to connect the main line with Tipton, eight miles to the south.

To tap coal banks in Boone, a spur line (called the Iowa Railway, Coal and Manufacturing Company) was organized in 1873. Three miles of track were laid the following year.

The longest affiliate in Iowa, however, was the Toledo and Northwestern Railway, organized in 1869. Before outright purchase by the Chicago & North Western some twenty years later, it grew to almost four hundred miles. Starting on the main line at Tama, it ran in a northwesterly direction to Jewell, thence north through Webster City and Eagle Grove to Elmore on the Minnesota border. Another line veered west from Eagle Grove to Hawarden on the western boundary of the state. Still a third branch struck off from Jewell to Lake City, fifty-eight miles west. The road got off to a quick start with an eighty-three-mile route connecting Tama with Webster

City in 1880. Two years afterward, all the above-mentioned sections were completed.

The North Western was careful not to go far south and thereby encroach upon Rock Island and Burlington preserves. It did, however, organize the Iowa South Western Railway Company in 1880 to build from Carroll to Kirkman. The thirty-four-mile extension was finished in 1881. The next year Manning and Audubon were linked.

Another ganglion of lines sprang up out of Maple River, appropriately called the Maple River Rail Road Company. Chartered under North Western auspices in 1876, the affiliate had a sixty-mile crescent-shaped road to Mapleton in 1877. By 1883 a branch headed for Sioux City linked Wall Lake with Kingsley, about twenty-five miles short of its planned destination. The ubiquitous John Blair had a hand in building the road, and his associate, Horace Williams, headed the company. Like other Blair roads, the Maple River had its headquarters in Cedar Rapids.

Blair comes into the picture even stronger with his Sioux City & Pacific. This company came into being after the failure of the Union Pacific to build to Sioux City under the provisions of the Act of 1862. The original Union Pacific act was amended on July 2, 1864, releasing that company from its obligation and permitting another road to link the Union Pacific with Sioux City. The Sioux City & Pacific Rail Road Company was organized at Dubuque, September 10, 1864, for that purpose. The incorporators and first directors were William Boyd Allison, John I. Blair, L. B. Crocker, A. W. Hubbard, Morris K. Jesup, Charles A. Lambard, Frederick Schuchardt, Platt Smith, and James F. Wilson. Blair became first president and W. W. Hamilton secretary.

With a congressional grant of 42,500 acres of land, financial help from the North Western and its principal Iowa leased lines, along with aid from Illinois Central affiliates and the Union Pacific, the new road set out to make Sioux City a transcontinental gateway. Its six-mile segment from Missouri Valley Junction to California Junction was built by the Cedar Rapids and Missouri River Railroad in 1867. The rest of the line from California Junction to Sioux City was in operation by February 1868.

Meanwhile, a branch was built from California Junction across the Missouri River to Fremont, Nebraska, where it connected with the Union Pacific. Cars were ferried across the river during the summer, and in winter they went on a temporary bridge. A permanent all-year bridge was built in 1883 by the Missouri Valley and Blair Railway and Bridge Company, organized in 1882.

Blair seems to have had a particular fondness for the Sioux City & Pacific Rail Road Company. Usually he had only about 15 percent interest in most so-called Blair roads, but the Sioux City he dominated almost up to his death. For many years his son, D. C. Blair, was vice president and his brother, James, a longtime director. Then, too, it served as a bridge route from his Iowa properties to those in Nebraska.

Foremost of the latter was the Fremont, Elkhorn and Missouri Valley Railroad Company, forming a complex of lines out of Fremont. Organized in 1869, the "Missouri Valley" had a 100-mile system a dozen years later. When purchased by the North Western in 1903, this swelled to 1,372 miles.

Freight and passengers seemingly went from one railroad to another between the Mississippi River and Missouri Valley points. Actually, they went from one Blair property to another. Like the famous baseball double play from Tinker to Evers to Chance, so traffic went from the Cedar Rapids and Missouri River *to* the Sioux City & Pacific Rail Road Company *to* the Fremont, Elkhorn and Missouri Valley Railroad Company. They were all different roads, yet they all worked together on the same Blair team.

Thanks largely to Blair's industry, the North Western, through owned, leased, and controlled lines, became one of the Big Three in Iowa. In the early eighties its finances had improved. It had well-entrenched lines in eastern Wisconsin extending up into the Michigan peninsula. It had a line from Chicago through southern Minnesota to halfway across Dakota. And its Chicago–Council Bluffs route was proving to be a valuable trunk line that was no longer dominated by the St. Paul. The latter, however, did give it stiff competition when it built to Council Bluffs in 1882.

ENTER THE OMAHA

A very important factor in strengthening the North Western's position in the Midwest was its purchase of control of the Chicago, St. Paul, Minneapolis & Omaha Railway Company in 1882. At one stroke it obtained a bow-shaped line, 1,147 miles long (including branches), from Elroy, Wisconsin, through the Twin Cities to Sioux City and Omaha. It also had a nearly completed branch from Hudson to Bayfield, Wisconsin, on Lake Superior.

This railroad gave the North Western a direct line to the Twin Cities from both Chicago and Omaha. It likewise gave the controlling road an outlet to the Ashland area on Lake Superior. In every way it was an asset in rounding out the North Western.

The Omaha Road, as the CStPM&O was called, evolved from the consolidation of the Chicago, St. Paul and Minneapolis and the North Wisconsin railways in 1880, under the name of the Chicago, St. Paul, Minneapolis & Omaha Railway, and the purchase of the St. Paul and Sioux City Railroad

Company in 1881. These lines brought with them other companies which they had garnered before the merger. The man who tied the assorted railroads together was Henry H. Porter.

Porter came west from Machias, Maine, to seek his fortune. Bound for California at seventeen, he stopped off in Chicago for temporary work. He found a job as a junior clerk in the office of the Galena and Chicago Union Rail Road, predecessor of the North Western. He soon rose to be general ticket agent and is said to have issued the first coupon ticket west of Chicago. During the cholera epidemic of 1854 he took a turn at braking and sometimes served as conductor when regular trainmen were ill.

Employment on other railroads, a partnership in the lumber business, and associated activities made Porter forget about the Golden West. Chicago became Henry Porter's home port. In 1869 he was made a director of the Rock Island, which soon controlled the North Western. In this roundabout way he again became interested in his first Chicago employer.

The panic of 1873 gave Porter the opportunity to buy and reorganize bankrupt railroads. First it was the West Wisconsin, linking Elroy and Hudson. He offered it to the North Western at cost. The offer was refused. The latter's directors felt they already had "too much railroad." Porter bided his time. If they wouldn't buy his modest little package at bargain rates, he would get a big bundle of roads, tie them up neatly, and command a good figure. And that is precisely what he did.

The West Wisconsin Railway Company was reorganized and acquired by the Chicago, St. Paul and Minneapolis Railway Company, which the Porter syndicate controlled. The latter was afterward consolidated with other roads, forming what was popularly called the "Omaha." When tied together, the assortment presented an attractive package custom-made for the North Western and was promptly bought at a price. Having made the desired sale, Porter, who headed the Omaha, then relinquished the presidency. His place was taken by the young and energetic Marvin Hughitt, by this time vice president of the North Western.

Let us roll back the years again and trace the Omaha's antecedents on their trek to Iowa. To do this we must begin with the Sioux City and St. Paul Railroad Company. It was the southern counterpart of the St. Paul and Sioux City Railroad Company and was later sold to that company. The first road built *up* from Sioux City; the second *down* from St. Paul. The point of junction was St. James, Minnesota.

Surveying parties started work from St. James in a southwesterly direction in March 1871. General Judson W. Bishop, the chief engineer, relates in the *Minnesota Historical Society Collections* how he "with team and driver, covered spring wagon, and his old army 'mess kit' with six days' rations and forage, a large pocket compass, and the best maps then obtainable, started to find and mark by his wagon wheels, an approximate line across the uninhabited country from St. James to Sioux City."

Although "the wagon was steered by compass over the desolate prairie as a vessel would be guided across the ocean," the line of the present Omaha Railroad between St. James and Le Mars, Iowa, is not at any point "more than eighty rods distant from that wagon trail of . . . 1871."

In September of 1872 the line was completed to Le Mars, and from that point trackage rights to Sioux City were obtained over what is now the Illinois Central. This agreement with the Illinois Central is still in effect.

Two hazards of early-day operation were drifting snow and hordes of grasshoppers in summer. The first was rectified by widening the cuts, erecting double lines of snow fences, and planting trees to stem drifts. The 'hoppers posed more of a problem. They not only slowed trains by making it difficult for the locomotive drive-wheels to get traction but also ruined the farms, thereby reducing the freight revenue. To combat this situation, Bishop and his associates formed what was dubbed "The Grasshopper Syndicate."

They purchased acres of the road's land-grant holdings in the heart of the grasshopper districts. One of these areas was near Sheldon. Here they broke the sod and planted wheat. But the "little hoppers outnumbered the wheat plants five to one." This time, however, Bishop and his men were ready. They had an armada of "land boats." That is, plates of sheet iron eight feet long by four feet wide turned up at each end. In these panlike boats was liquid coal tar. The boats were pulled in unison across the field by a fleet of horses in front and to the sides of the iron rigs, to which they were attached by wires. As the phalanx advanced across the field from north to south, the grasshoppers jumped from under the horses' feet. Another jump or two and they landed in the sticky tar. A few weeks later the process was repeated.

Expansion was continued by an affiliated Minnesota corporation called the Worthington and Sioux Falls Railroad Company, linking the two communities in its name by 1878. The next year the company built a branch south from Luverne, Minnesota, to Doon, Iowa.

Another branch to the Iowa border left the main stem at Lake Crystal (south of Mankato) and ran in a southeasterly direction to Elmore, all in Minnesota. It was completed by the St. Paul and Sioux City Railroad Company in 1880.

Entry into Omaha was effected by a series of affiliated roads on the west side of the Missouri River in Nebraska. By 1881 a through route was opened between Sioux City and Omaha.

EXPANSION

The 1880s saw a period of aggressive railroad expansion in Iowa and in the Midwest. With minor exceptions, this decade witnessed the completion of practically all of the North Western's Iowa lines. Much of the expansion took the form of extensions of lines previously constructed in the late seventies and early eighties by roads associated with the North Western. The Omaha Road, as has been pointed out, was an exception in that it was built mostly by independent interests.

Another independent line was the Des Moines and Minnesota Rail-Road Company, organized in 1870. Its three-foot-wide track was running from Des Moines to Ames by 1874. Under the banner of the Des Moines and Minneapolis Rail Road, the little railroad reached Callahan (now Jewell) four years later. The latter community was named after the road's president, James Callahan, a prominent Des Moines banker and real-estate operator. During this period the North Western purchased control and changed the gauge to standard. The short line proved to be valuable in routing freight between Des Moines and the Twin Cities in conjunction with the Toledo and Northwestern–Omaha Road via Elmore, Minnesota.

The Toledo and Northwestern was further strengthened by a twenty-six-mile branch from Eldora Junction to Alden. Organized in 1882 as the high-sounding Chicago, Iowa & Dakota Railway Company, it was completed in two years. The line picked up most of its traffic from a large lime quarry in Alden. Incidentally, some of its original fifty-four-pound rails are still in service. In 1886 the Toledo and Northwestern built a fifteen-mile extension from Lake City to Wall Lake Junction, thereby connecting that line with the Maple River Rail Road Company.

In 1886 a twenty-mile line from Mapleton to Onawa, on the Missouri River, was built by the Maple Valley Railway Company. Farther to the north the Sioux City branch was heading toward completion when the nine-mile Kingsley-Moville section was finished in 1887 by the Sioux Valley Railway Company. The twenty-mile gap between Moville and Sioux City (Sergeant Bluff) was finally spanned in 1901 by the Moville Extension Railway Company.

The Boyer Valley Railway Company, organized on October 17, 1898, constructed the sixty-one-mile branch line from Boyer to Mondamin on the Missouri River and the twenty-five-mile Wall Lake–Denison branch line in 1899. This gave the Wall Lake area three lines to the Missouri River, two to the North Western's main stem on the south and an easterly connection via Wall Lake Junction to Jewell, Tama, and other eastern points. In its heyday as a railroad junction, Wall Lake (population 766) had twelve passenger trains going in six directions! Two of these carried sleepers.

The biggest Johnny-come-lately in the North Western's Iowa domain was the 195-mile Iowa, Minnesota and Northwestern Railway Company. Organized in 1898, completed and sold to the North Western in 1900, the road was built with Blair-like rapidity. In 1899 the 59 miles from Blue Earth, Minnesota, to Mason City, Iowa, were in operation. By the end of the following year the railroad had spiked down rails from Mason City to Belle Plaine and from Blue Earth to Fox Lake in Minnesota. As its name suggests, the line runs in a northwesterly direction more than halfway across Iowa and catercornered into a large section of southwestern Minnesota.

Another interstate line built during this period was the Minnesota and Iowa Railway Company, incorporated in 1898. It built from Burt, Iowa, on the Elmore–Des Moines line, through Fox Lake and Sanborn to Vesta, all Minnesota towns. When acquired by the North Western in 1900, it had a 118-mile line.

The North Western's boldest incursion into the territory south of its Clinton–Council Bluffs "high iron" began with the line from Belle Plaine to the mining town of Muchakinock. The sixty-mile coal road, organized in 1883 as the Ottumwa, Cedar Falls and St. Paul Railway Company, was completed the next year. In 1901 a twenty-one-mile extension built by the Southern Iowa Railway Company gave it access to the Negro colliery of Buxton. At one time the mines along this railroad are said to have furnished the North Western with enough coal for nearly the entire system.

To round out the lower Iowa railroads, mention should be made of the six-mile addition to the Carroll-Kirkman branch. Built by the Harlan and Kirkman Railway Company in 1899, it served the Shelby County towns from which it was named.

From time to time the North Western sought to purchase its many controlled and affiliated lines and thereby simplify its corporate structure. The first big purchase came in 1884 and included the following Iowa companies:

> Cedar Rapids and Missouri River Railroad
> Chicago, Iowa & Nebraska Rail Road
> Des Moines and Minnesota Rail Road Company
> Iowa Midland Railway Company
> Iowa South Western Railway Company

Maple River Rail Road Company
Ottumwa, Cedar Falls and St. Paul Railway Company
Stanwood & Tipton Railway Company

In 1887 four more were acquired:

Iowa Railway, Coal and Manufacturing Company
Linn County Railway Company (Cedar Rapids bypass)
Maple Valley Railway Company
Sioux Valley Railway Company

In 1890 the 385-mile Toledo and Northwestern Railway was purchased. At the turn of the century the following were purchased:

Boone County Railway Company (line revision)
Boyer Valley Railway Company
Harlan and Kirkman Railway Company
Iowa, Minnesota and Northwestern Railway Company

By 1901 the North Western had corralled the Southern Iowa Railway Company along with the Sioux City & Pacific Rail Road Company. In 1903 the little Chicago, Iowa and Dakota Railway and the big Fremont, Elkhorn and Missouri Valley Railroad were purchased.

With the purchase of the "Missouri Valley," the last of the major Blair roads was taken over by the North Western. It is here that we should say a few more words about this railroad builder who meant so much to Iowa. Blair, while retaining his beloved Blairstown, New Jersey, residence until his death, always had one foot in Iowa from the time of his first visit to Cedar Rapids. Indeed, the headquarters of his far-flung railroad empire was in the three-story brick structure known as the Blair Building in that city. The imposing $60,000 building was financed by his two principal Iowa railroads, by his land company, and by the First National Bank, which he helped organize in 1864. Also housed therein were the Iowa Rail Road Land Company and similar organizations he formed to promote new towns.

Blair is said to have laid out more than eighty townsites. He is known to have personally named at least twenty communities in Iowa. Among these are Ames, Belle Plaine, and Ogden. The first is named after his friend, backer, and Union Pacific official, Oakes Ames; the second is believed to be in honor of his granddaughter, Isabelle Scribner, whose father was Charles Scribner, the publisher; and the last is a tribute to Chicago's first mayor and first president of the North Western, William B. Ogden.

Others include Scranton (Greene County), probably named after his two early New Jersey business associates, George W. and Selden T. Scranton; Whiting (Monona County), named for Judge Charles E. Whiting, a local farmer; and Colo (Story County), so-called from a child's pronunciation of Carlo, the favorite dog of a person who owned land on which the station was built. All are on the North Western.

Blair was a man of simple tastes. A teetotaler, he inserted clauses in deeds of lots he sold prohibiting the vending or manufacture of liquor. A staunch Presbyterian, Blair, by donating land and money, helped build more than one hundred churches of all communions on his townsites. He is estimated to have given $5 million to charitable and educational institutions. When Iowa College (now Grinnell) was demolished by the tornado of 1882, Blair contributed to its restoration.

At one time Blair headed sixteen railroads. His western holdings were scattered in Wisconsin, Missouri, Kansas, Nebraska, Dakota, and Texas, to say nothing of Iowa. In spite of being a millionaire, the poverty of his youth made him frugal and almost parsimonious. A story is told of Blair's having had a meal at a restaurant on one of his Iowa lines leased to the North Western. The owner of the eating house told him the price was fifty cents. Blair brought out a quarter instead. After some altercation, the vendor admitted the charge to railroad men was twenty-five cents. "I am a railroad man," snapped Blair. "I own this road!" and he walked out angrily.

A person of remarkable vitality, he is reputed to have taken "two steps at a time" when going upstairs. Attired in a Prince Albert coat, a white waistcoat, and a beaver hat, under which he sometimes carried his papers, Blair made many trips to personally supervise his railroad holdings. When in his sixties he used to travel up to forty thousand miles a year. At eighty-five, however, he was obliged to reduce this to twenty thousand. Never afraid of work, Blair, at ninety-two, was often at his desk at 5:30 A.M. He died in 1899 at ninety-seven.

Blairstown, in Benton County, one of the smallest Iowa towns on the railroad having the largest mileage in the state, honors a man who had come from a tiny village to build one of the biggest midwestern railroad systems!

PROSPEROUS YEARS

From 1887, when Marvin Hughitt became president, until his death in January 1928, the North Western was regarded as a Hughitt road. Hughitt's ability and his prodigious capacity for work had been demonstrated while on the Illinois Central. As a youthful superintendent on that road, he had sat for thirty-six continuous hours at the telegraph key dispatching troop trains southward through Cairo to reinforce hard-pressed Union forces at Corinth. Then, after a few hours sleep, he took the key for *another* thirty-six grueling hours to move the same troops to a different battlefield.

Marvin Hughitt began railroading on the St. Louis, Alton & Chicago Railroad (Chicago & Alton). Later he went with the Illinois Central. Then he switched to the Chicago, Milwaukee & St. Paul Railroad, and just before coming to the North Western he was for a short time superintendent of the Pullman Palace Car Company. As we have seen, Hughitt rose rapidly on the North Western. Under his firm guiding hand the railroad prospered. Hughitt had two dominating interests in life—his family and his railroad. For twenty-three years he shaped the policies of the North Western as its president. When made board chairman in 1910 he, as elder statesman, still ran the railroad. Even as chairman of the finance committee from 1925 to his death at nearly ninety-one, his consuming interest was the Chicago & North Western.

During his tenure as president, and later as board chairman, the North Western's mileage was virtually doubled. Under his direction the main line across Iowa had been double-tracked by 1902. Like the main stem in Illinois, trains operated on the left-hand track as is customary in Great Britain. Contrary to popular belief, it was a matter of economy and not the influence of English investors which led to "southpaw" operation. Most of the stations being on the north side of the original single-track line, it was cheaper to add another track to the south. By reversing the normal direction of traffic the depots could remain intact and passengers could buy tickets without crossing the track before boarding trains for Chicago.

The most spectacular improvement in this period was building "the longest, highest double-track railroad bridge in the world" over the Des Moines River near Boone. Opened in 1901, the 2,685-foot structure, known as the Kate Shelley Viaduct, rose 184 feet above the beautiful valley. Completion of the bridge marked the use of the 7.25-mile cutoff built by the Boone County Railway Company. This eliminated the longer single-track line through Moingona, with its steeper grade and greater curvature. It also did away with "pusher" operation. The older line, on which the immortal Kate Shelley's signal saved victims from a washed-out railroad bridge, was later abandoned.

This brings us to the legend of Kate Shelley. What Casey Jones is to folksong and John Henry is to Negro folkways, Kate Shelley is to American railroad heroines. All three were railroaders, and their stories are founded on fact. But their exploits have transcended actual happenings to emerge into ballad and folklore, adding luster and shedding fact. Here, however, are the known facts of Iowa's famous woman and the nation's most popular railroad heroine.

Kate Shelley, daughter of a North Western section foreman, was born on a farm near Moingona, September 25, 1865. After the death of her father, Kate and her two sisters and brother remained at home helping her mother run the farm and support the family. On July 6, 1881, a violent storm swept the Des Moines Valley, and fifteen-year-old Kate was obliged to get the livestock out of the stable, which was partly flooded by the waters of Honey Creek. As the rain increased in fury, Kate became very apprehensive. She feared driftwood in the creek and in the nearby Des Moines River would back up against the railroad bridges and undermine them.

Just before midnight the frightened girl heard a "pusher" engine going east. As it neared the Shelley farm, she noted an eerie tolling of the bell, a crash, and a hissing of steam. Kate sensed at once the locomotive must have plunged from the Honey Creek bridge. If so, who would flag No. 4, the Atlantic Express, due shortly from the west? It was up to her!

She hurriedly put on a hat and coat, grabbed a lantern, and ran to the bridge. Part of the structure remained, but the engine was in the creek. Clinging to driftwood was Ed Wood, the engineer, and Adam Egar, a brakeman. Others in the crew had perished in the raging creek. Seeing she could not help them, Kate went to seek aid—and to flag the express. To do so she had to cross the Des Moines River on the railroad bridge above the rushing water. Her lantern had since gone out, and she groped along the ties on her hands and knees in the dark. The wind almost blew her from the structure; and she was afraid lest any minute the express would bear down on her. But courageous Kate finally made it. She then sped down the track to the depot at Moingona.

Nearly exhausted and half-coherent from fright, Kate told her story to the operator. Summoning all her energy, she later went back with willing railroaders on another engine to help rescue Wood and Egar from the swirling currents of Honey Creek. Kate subsequently became ill from her terrible ordeal, and it was three months before she fully recuperated. By this time all America knew of her heroic deed.

Not content with her truly remarkable feat, legend has it she reached Moingona just in time to have the operator snatch a red lantern and flag the express. Some accounts say she stopped the midnight flyer herself. But careful research by Edward H. Meyers of Boone explodes this myth. In "The True Story of Kate Shelley" in October 1957 *Trains*, Meyers points out there was a "hold order" set up as a precautionary measure. Eastward trains were held at Scranton, some forty miles west of Moingona, and westward trains at Marshalltown, about sixty miles from where Kate contacted the telegraph operator. Furthermore, a bridge at Coal Valley, just west of Moingona, was also washed out.

At any rate, Kate Shelley's name has gone down for posterity. The Iowa State legislature awarded her a gold medal and $200; the Order of Railway Conductors gave her a gold watch; and the *Chicago Tribune* raised a fund to help the Shelley family. In Dubuque a statue was erected in her memory, and the schoolchildren of that community presented her with a medal. The grateful railroad made her the agent at Moingona in 1903, and she continued working there almost up to her death on January 21, 1912. Her name is currently being perpetuated by the Kate Shelley Award given yearly by *Modern Railroads* to individual women and groups of women for outstanding achievement in American railroading.

Many poems have been written about this brave Iowan. One of the best was penned by the well-known Iowa writer MacKinlay Kantor. Titled "The Ballad of Kate Shelley" and first published in the *Chicago Daily News*, the poem ends as follows:

> But if you go to Honey Creek in some dark summer storm,
> Be sure to take a lantern flame to keep your spirit warm.
> For there will be a phantom train, and foggy whistle cries—
> And in the lightning flare you'll see Kate Shelley on the ties.

Along with double-tracking of the main line, considerable track relocation took place, resulting in more favorable grades and reduced curvature. The remains of the old lines may still be seen in several places by sharp-eyed observers even today.

Another major improvement was replacing the old single-track Mississippi River bridge with a two-track structure. The new span was built between 1907 and 1909. It consisted of eight lattice truss spans and one Pratt truss, across the east channel of the river. The narrower west channel is crossed by three spans: one of through riveted lattice, another of through Pratt truss, and a third being a through 460-foot pin-connected swing span. The sturdy modern structure is a few feet south of the original bridge.

In 1886 the Linn County Railway Company was organized to bypass the congested Cedar Rapids area. It resulted in rebuilding a six-mile cutoff between Otis and Beverly, thereby speeding up freight operation.

Apart from line relocation and cutoffs, there were scarcely any new lines built after 1901. An exception was the Sioux City, Dakota and North Western Railway Company, organized in 1909 to build from Hinton Junction to Hawarden Junction. Completed in 1910, the twenty-eight-mile line provided a shorter route between Sioux City and points west of Hawarden.

Another exception was the twelve-mile extension of the Southern Iowa Railway Company to tap coal mines between Consol and Miami in 1915. The line proved to be the last North Western branch built in Iowa (except for a seven-mile power-plant spur built in 1962, near Sioux City) and one of the first to be retired after the mines petered out in the late 1920s.

The financial picture of the North Western appeared never brighter than it did under the presidency of Hughitt. But World War I and its aftermath changed the situation, as did economic conditions over which the railroad had little control.

HEYDAY OF THE NORTH WESTERN

Here and there along the main line of the North Western in Iowa one sees faded, weather-beaten signs warning enginemen to "R.S. 70," that is, reduce speed to 70 m.p.h. They are unheeded today, for the top speed is 60 m.p.h., and if a freight exceeds that limit, the automatic train control will bring it to a stop. At the same time, these signs are a reminder of the long, colorful era when the North Western was the great speedway between East and West.

Presidents and visiting nobility, immigrants and millionaires, tourists and businessmen—indeed, people from every corner of the globe sped across Iowa on their way to and from the fabled West. Fast mail trains kept the rails hot. Solid consists of express, chartered trains of the rich, extra sections and extra trains with rattan seats for homesteaders or the most luxurious appointments for those of means, shuttled across Iowa. It was a grand cavalcade, a spectacular cross section of America and a fair sampling of visitors from every civilized nation. It is safe to say that, while it lasted, more people from more places rode the North Western across Iowa than any other transcontinental rail route in North America.

From the start the North Western fought aggressively for United States mail contracts. Its races across Iowa in competition with the Burlington were classic. While the Burlington is credited with having the first railroad car for sorting mail in transit, it was the North Western which had the original Railway Post Office unit as we know it today. The specially designed car made its initial run between Chicago and Clinton in 1864.

There was magic in the very name "Fast Mail." It called for the swiftest engines, the most skilled "throttle artists," and a clear track all the way. Everything "went in the hole" for the mail. So spectacular was the flight of the mail that in 1899, when the North Western cut nearly two hours from its Chicago-Omaha run, the popular *McClure's Magazine* ran a lead feature about it. Written by Cleveland Moffett, with W. D. Stevens detailed to make on-the-spot drawings, the story related the struggle between the North Western and the Burlington for the "million dollar mail contract." The run across Illinois and Iowa was characterized as

> the hottest, maddest part of its sweep between the oceans . . . where level ground and keenest competition offer such a spectacle of flying mail service as has [never] been seen before since letters and engines came upon the earth.

The article was appropriately called "At Ninety Miles an Hour." At that time the North Western's Fast Mail left Chicago at 10 P.M. and arrived at Omaha at 8:15 the next morning.

To further speed the mail the North Western took delivery of six American-type locomotives, outshopped by Schenectady in 1899. They had eighty-inch drivers and wagon-top boilers with 2,353 square feet of heating surface. Another half dozen 4-4-0s with seventy-five-inch drivers and 2,508 square feet of heating surface were part of the same order for heavy passenger train use. The *Railway Gazette* described them as having "the largest boiler ever used with an eight-wheel locomotive" and having "practically the same heating surface as the new Atlantic type locomotives of the Burlington."

The Burlington's answer to its rival was two 4-4-2s, alluded to above. Built by Baldwin, they had high eighty-four-and-a-quarter-inch drivers and a total heating surface of 2,500 square feet. The *Gazette* characterized them as "the largest engines of this type so far built." These Vauclain compounds, with curious English-style six-wheel tenders, proved a marked contrast to the more orthodox American Standards on the North Western. The new motive power served to intensify the keen competition between the two railroads, and items on the "fast mail" often made newspaper headlines.

In 1869, when the "Overland Route" to California was first opened, the North Western, in conjunction with the Union Pacific and the Central Pacific, was the first to send a train from Chicago to the Pacific Coast. It was also the first to operate dining cars over the route.

For variety of food, few restaurants anywhere came near offering the bountiful selection featured on the Pullman Hotel Cars. In June 1877, for example, there were six kinds of steak on the menu, including venison. Besides such prosaic meats as chicken, chops, and cutlets, one could get pheasant, snipe, quail, plover, and duck. Seven varieties of oysters were offered and four of clams. There were in addition several kinds of fish, along with cold plates of turkey, lobster, and potted game. Nearly a dozen vegetables were included, and the relishes numbered sixteen. Some twenty desserts were listed, including pastries, cakes, and fruits.

For over a half century one train became a distinguished symbol of the North Western–Union Pacific, Southern Pacific route to the coast. It was the Overland Limited. Even the name has a distinct historical connotation. It stood for the land route across the nation, in contrast to the sea voyage around the horn or by way of the Isthmus of Panama. The Overland started in December 1887 and faded out in 1955. But even through the Great Depression of the 1930s the comfortable Overland ran serenely on, seemingly impervious to time and change.

Countless authors and newspaper writers have left the memory of their trips on the "Overland Route" in books and periodicals. Undoubtedly the most detailed account of a journey on the North Western is in the late J. P. Pearson's four-volume *Railways and Scenery*. Pearson, Great Britain's counterpart of the *New Yorker*'s Roger Whitaker, painstakingly recorded minute details. Of the Chicago-Omaha limited he noted:

> Side and end walls were in brown wood, with fine panels, while the clerestory roof and the curve up to it . . . were in a brownish-yellow material with a gilt scroll inside the border of silver colour. . . . A beveled mirror was furnished between every other side window. . . .

In between noting the gradients and "clocking" (he quoted arrivals and departures in seconds), the alert Pearson found time to admire scenery. He was fascinated by the view near Council Bluffs where the Boyer River valley

> fringed with trees—with sunlight on leaves and water—took its way among a park-like expanse of meadows. A marsh and a lake, with the bold outline of bluffs standing out picturesquely on the south-eastern side of the valley, against the soft blue of the sky, followed, and made one of the finest pictures I have ever seen.

In the parade of extra trains racing across Iowa over the years, probably none had more glamour than the Warner Brothers Special of 1940. Operated from Chicago to Nevada, it took motion picture stars, movie magnates, press agents, and others to attend the opening of *Virginia City*. No money was spared to make the premiere a success, and everyone praised the glorious North Western.

RETRENCHMENTS AND ABANDONMENTS

Three presidents followed Hughitt, and then came Iowa's own Fred W. Sargent. Sargent was born on May 26, 1876, in Akron on the Big Sioux River, about twenty-five miles north of Sioux City. The son of a farmer and miller, young Sargent learned hard work and discipline while plowing fields and getting up early to feed cattle. His father, Wesley Sargent, while a strict disciplinarian, was a man of unimpeachable integrity, well thought of by everyone. Indeed, Fred Sargent attributed much of his success to his dad's wise guidance.

After finishing Akron high school, Sargent entered the University of South Dakota in nearby Vermillion. Later he transferred to the State University of Iowa, where he received his LL.B. in 1901. After graduating from the university he opened a law office in Sioux City. In 1905 he became attorney for the Omaha Road and later the North Western. Success in handling railroad cases led to his being appointed general solicitor for the Rock Island in Iowa with headquarters in Des Moines. In 1921 he returned to the North Western as general solicitor in Chicago. Two years later he was made vice president and general counsel, and in 1925 he became president.

When Sargent was a young attorney for the North Western, the road wanted to build a cutoff between Sioux City and Hawarden. Right-of-way was readily purchased, with the exception of one farm through which the track had to cross. Its owner absolutely refused to sell, nor would he enter into negotiation with the railroad. Sargent was about to institute legal proceedings and condemn the property when he decided to pay the farmer a visit. Arriving at the farmhouse, he stated his business. The farmer, however, was not in the least impressed until learning the visitor's name.

"Sargent, huh," the husbandman repeated when he heard the name. "Did you ever happen to know 'Wes' Sargent?"

The attorney replied, "'Wes' was my father."

"Your father!" the man exclaimed. He quickly called into the house, "Mother, come right away, this is 'Wes' Sargent's boy!"

"Wes" Sargent's boy was made to stay for dinner. After a friendly meal the host explained why he had such a high regard for the elder Sargent. He said that he once lived in Calliope, a tiny community near Hawarden, when they had an epidemic of diphtheria. Many people fell sick, and some died. The crops had been bad that year, and the people were poor. Then one day a car of flour arrived on a siding for "The People of Calliope." It was from "Wes." Everyone helped himself, and it tided them over that trying winter.

After the farmer had finished talking, Sargent again brought up the subject of right-of-way through the farm.

"You can have anything you want," he told Sargent. "Just set your own price. Whatever you say is fair will be right with me."

In concluding the story Fred Sargent added, "You may be sure I didn't take advantage of him."

Unfortunately, the stock market crash of 1929 and the ensuing prolonged depression made Sargent's administration a critical period in the road's history. The possession of a high percentage of marginal branch lines together with hundreds of passenger trains operating at a loss aggravated the North Western's position. In 1935 Sargent had no alternative but to seek protection from the courts, and the road went into receivership. Five years later Sargent died.

The North Western was reorganized in 1944, and for a time its earnings were modest. But the basic problems of relatively short hauls and unremunerative branches along with intensive truck, bus, and plane competition left their toll. The income of the 1940s turned into several years of alarming deficits in the 1950s. In 1960 the net loss from railway operations was $7,180,145, largely due to the steel strike and poor grain movements. After additions of special credits, however, the net income was $255,450. The next year, thanks to better business conditions and more economical operation, the road showed a net income from railway operations of $3,075,776. After additions of special credits, the net was $7,384,027.

The road's retrenchment program was forcefully brought to the attention of Iowans by the scrapping of over a hundred miles of branch lines. The bulk of the abandonments came during the depression years. The Omaha Road started with the retirement of its curious branch from Luverne, Minnesota, to Doon, Iowa, in 1934. True, the old Moingona line had been abandoned in 1933, but this was the result of the relocation of the main line by a cutoff via the Kate Shelley Viaduct.

Closing the coal mines at Buxton, Muchakinock, and other points on the Consol–What Cheer branch led to its scrapping in 1935. The remainder of the branch from What Cheer to Belle Plaine, however, continued on a marginal basis until it was likewise abandoned in 1958.

Costly washouts on the Manning-Harlan section of the branch running south from Carroll brought about abandonment of that part of the line in 1937. Service, nevertheless, was continued by trackage rights over the parallel route of the Great Western. In 1940 running rights were secured over the Great Western between Manning and Carroll, and the North Western's line between these points was subsequently removed. In 1953 the short branch running southwest from Manning to Audubon ceased operating due to insufficient earnings.

Probably the most pathetic abandonment was that of the pioneer Lyons-Anamosa branch, formerly known as the Iowa Midland Railway. In 1944 a flash flood washed out the right-of-way between Maquoketa and Anamosa. Conductor James Ryan and his train were stranded at Anamosa. He had to return by a roundabout route over the Milwaukee to Cedar Rapids, thence on "home" rails to Clinton. Since the flood did a great deal of damage, many feared the little-used line would never reopen.

Grass grew up between the rails as the line lay dormant for two years. But with the assurance that shippers would do all they could to patronize the branch, the North Western rebuilt the road. Operation was resumed some twenty-eight months later. A special train of freight cars, a lounge car, and a caboose celebrated the reopening. Conductor Ryan again piloted the train over the line. About forty businessmen and farmers rode the club car and toasted to the success of the railroad. Amid cheers and felicitations one passenger solemnly rose and said: "Gentlemen, your hats. . . . We are on the Midland!"

But with the advent of better all-weather roads, the rebuilt "Midland" failed to prosper. The losses became so great that the North Western had no alternative but to abandon the seventy-nine-year-old line in 1950. Thus the successor to the ill-fated Iowa Central Air Line Rail Road Company, and the only railroad operated on the right-of-way of that grandiose project, passed into history.

The plight of the North Western and its poor financial showing resulted in a change of management in which Ben W. Heineman and his associates acquired control in 1956. Heineman became board chairman, with Clyde J. Fitzpatrick, formerly vice president of operations of the Illinois Central, elected to the presidency. The new management embarked upon a thorough modernization program to improve operating efficiency and increase employee productivity.

To consolidate the railroad's car repair facilities, a $6 million plant was built in Clinton. Opened in 1958, the new car shop eliminated fourteen smaller repair yards all over the system. When operating to capacity, it can build one thousand new cars annually and make some seven thousand old cars look "like new." The largest building in the centralized facility is the thousand-foot-long fabricating and erecting shop. About 250 men are normally employed. During peak operation, however, this may rise to nearly 500.

EXIT THE PASSENGER TRAIN

In this era of the motor car and airplane it is easy to forget the once-important role the railroad played in many hundreds of Iowa communities. The passenger train was often the only link with the outside world. Dakota City, for example, is a little way station, the second one west of Eagle Grove, where shops and offices of the former Northern Iowa Division were located. In the 1920s it had four daily passenger trains, including Nos. 24 and 25, the "Flyer." The Flyer not only covered the 145-mile branch from Eagle Grove to Hawarden, it went east to Chicago and west to Huron, South Dakota.

For a branch line, the Flyer was quite a train. Pulled by a high-stepping Atlantic-type engine with a United States mail car behind the tender, it usually had a brace of express cars, a baggage car, a smoker, and two chair cars, followed by one or two Pullmans. That was the first train west. Basil W. Koob, who started railroading as a clerk at Dakota City station, recalls the hard work required at train time.

> There was often a traveling salesman or two, and when I saw them I knew there would be a lot of excess baggage on that train. They always had big, heavy trunks carrying their wares, which were drayed to local hotels. Every hotel of any consequence had a "sample room," where drummers displayed their merchandise. It was up to me to check all the baggage for excess weight (over the 150-pound maximum) and load it back on the train again when the "traveling men" left town.

More arduous labor followed when the way freight clanked into town between 9 and 10 A.M. It first halted for water, Dakota City being the only water stop between there and Eagle Grove. When the train finally pulled up to the depot, the conductor swung down from the caboose with a fist full of waybills. As Koob relates:

> The usual routine was to begin from the rear car, just in front of the "crummy," and work toward the engine. We unloaded every conceivable size and description of merchandise and foodstuffs, including fruits, vegetables, fresh meats, canned goods . . . even machinery. That took from a half to three quarters of an hour. Then the "peddler" whistled a

reply to the conductor's "highball" and the cars rumbled by, leaving a pile of assorted merchandise on the platform.

Afternoon brought the locals, one east, the other west. This meant issuing tickets, mostly to way points, and checking baggage. Later in the day the erratic eastbound "peddler" showed up. Along between eight and nine o'clock in the evening, tickets would be sold and space confirmed for the Chicago-bound Flyer. That popular train operated over three branches via Eagle Grove, Jewell, and Tama, thence on the main line for its early-morning arrival in the Windy City. Saturday was "stock day," and livestock trains kept the rails polished through early Sunday morning.

The decline of passenger business started with the short-haul rider. Most Iowans felt that the main line's streamliners on the North Western were an institution here to stay. It was a glamorous era that would never end.

One could stand in Clinton and watch the parade of yellow cars go by, starting at 7:02 in the evening and continuing until almost midnight. There were seven trains, beginning with the streamlined City of Denver and ending with the quite orthodox steam-operated Gold Coast. The streamliners had new roomettes along with open sections, drawing rooms, and other customary sleeping accommodations. All West Coast–bound "City" trains were streamliners usually featuring valet service, barbers, and radios. Most of them also had baths.

Even secondary trains had unusual attractions. The Los Angeles Limited and the San Francisco Overland boasted of through sleepers from New York City to the Pacific Coast, in conjunction with the Pennsylvania and the New York Central. The former also had through Pullmans from Washington, D.C., via the Pennsylvania. Apart from this there were other through-car routings of long standing from the Twin Cities to the West, in collaboration with the Omaha Road. Indeed, the Nightingale and the North American were both crack "Omaha" trains with sleepers to and from Los Angeles. They were popular with retired Minnesotans, who fled from zero climes to spend the winter in balmy southern California.

By 1955 trans-Iowa service was trimmed to five Chicago-to-the-West through trains in each direction. The airplane had taken its toll, as had stiff competition from the luxurious California Zephyr on the Burlington–Rio Grande–Western Pacific route and accelerated schedules of the Santa Fe's smart streamliners. Moreover, dissension between the Union Pacific and the North Western did not help matters. The former was not satisfied with the service given east of Omaha; and the latter wanted a bigger division of revenue to help underwrite high Chicago terminal expenses. The outcome of the quarrel made headlines in the Midwest and rated columns in *Time* and *Newsweek* when the Union Pacific announced that on October 30, 1955, it would switch its through trains between Omaha and Chicago to the Milwaukee Road.

The North Western countered by advertising three new streamliners, two of which would cross the state, to substitute for the withdrawn trains. One was the Corn King, an overnight train having coaches, sections, roomettes, and bedrooms, together with a diner-lounge. The other, called the Omahan, consisted of coaches, a parlor car with drawing rooms, and a dining car on its daylight run. A third train, running between Chicago and Boone, was appropriately named the Kate Shelley. It featured modern coaches, a parlor car, and a diner-lounge on a fast afternoon and evening schedule.

The new trains were not profitable, and service soon deteriorated. The Kate Shelley was cut back to Marshalltown, then to Clinton. Pullmans were shed from the night train and the parlor car and diner withdrawn from the Omaha day run. On May 15, 1960, passenger trains between Clinton and Council Bluffs made their final runs. Meanwhile, the Omaha Road had already ceased carrying passengers between the Twin Cities and Council Bluffs as of October 25, 1959.

Today the North Western does not have a single passenger train in Iowa save for a few hundred feet where the Kate Shelley comes into Clinton from the east. Moreover, North Western mail and express service in Iowa is a thing of the past; and what little less-than-carload shipments remain is only of an interstate nature.

M&StL PURCHASE

On November 1, 1960, the North Western purchased the 1,500-mile Minneapolis & St. Louis Railway for $3,488,320. In addition, the purchaser agreed to assume the Minneapolis & St. Louis's liabilities, including $17,441,600 First Mortgage 6 percent bonds issued in connection with the transaction. Heretofore the Minneapolis & St. Louis had had no bonded indebtedness.

It is interesting to reflect that the only other comparable size merger of two major Iowa railroads occurred in 1903. That year the 1,300-mile Burlington, Cedar Rapids & Northern Railway was deeded to the Rock Island, which had previously controlled it. The former road had its headquarters in Cedar Rapids.

That part of the Minneapolis & St. Louis (known as the Iowa Central) was based in Marshalltown. Even today the Minneapolis & St. Louis Division of the North Western still has its car shops and locomotive repair facilities in Marshalltown.

The most notable Iowan associated with the old Iowa Central was Josiah B. Grinnell, who once served as its receiver. Indeed, one of the choice bits of Hawkeye folklore concerns Grinnell when he headed the Grinnell & Montezuma Railway, operated by the Iowa Central. In those primitive days of railroading passes were informal and often written in longhand by the president. It so happened that an employee of the little line was discharged in writing by J. B. Grinnell himself. For many years, it is said, the dismissed employee rode happily over the Grinnell & Montezuma using his letter of dismissal as a pass. Nobody could read anything but the signature!

The Iowa Central came under control of the Minneapolis & St. Louis in 1900, and it was later purchased. The combined roads established a well-publicized freight route from the Twin Cities via Marshalltown and Oskaloosa to Peoria, Illinois. Known as the Peoria Gateway, the routing avoided congested Chicago terminals in expediting shipments between east and west. In addition, the Minneapolis & St. Louis had a line westward from Minneapolis to Watertown and Leola, South Dakota. It had two routes to Des Moines: one from Albert Lea, Minnesota, via Fort Dodge; another from Oskaloosa south to Albia, thence by trackage rights over the Burlington-Wabash to the Iowa capital. There was also an additional line to Fort Dodge coming down from Winthrop, Minnesota, along with several minor branches.

The Minneapolis & St. Louis's greatest value to the North Western is financial. It had been a profitable railroad ever since emerging from receivership in 1942. In the preceding five years before its acquisition, the Peoria Gateway Line had an average yearly income before taxes of $2,754,000. Geographically the Minneapolis & St. Louis's role is less important, for its lines are largely paralleled or bisected by the North Western. This would suggest some sharp cutting to eliminate duplicate mileage in the near future.

Integrating the two railroads has already resulted in many changes. The current Minneapolis & St. Louis Division of the North Western includes all of the former railroad, with the exception of the Western Division from Hopkins, Minnesota, to Leola, South Dakota, 329 miles; the 88-mile Fort Dodge–Des Moines branch; and the M&STL-operated Minneapolis Industrial Railway, running from Minneapolis to Wesota, 115 miles.

The Western Division of the Minneapolis & St. Louis was transferred to the North Western's Dakota Division, the Fort Dodge–Des Moines branch to the Iowa Division, and the Minneapolis Industrial Railway to the Twin Cities Division. To compensate for its greatly reduced mileage, the North Western's 240-mile Belle Plaine to Sanborn Junction, Minnesota, branch was allocated to the Minneapolis & St. Louis Division.

To have more centralized headquarters, the Minneapolis & St. Louis Division offices were moved from Minneapolis to the North Western's old passenger station in Mason City. The depot has been completely modernized for its current functions. With the removal of personnel from the comparatively new million-dollar Minneapolis & St. Louis Building in Minneapolis, the last traces of the Peoria Gateway line as a separate entity have disappeared.

Trafficwise, too, there has been revamping. Twin Cities–Des Moines freight now goes on a more direct and logical route. Formerly it went south to Albia, thence in a northwesterly direction to Des Moines. Present operation is on what was the Minneapolis & St. Louis's main line to Marshalltown, thence over the double-track North Western to Ames, and south on the latter's branch to Des Moines. The new line is seventy-nine miles shorter than the Minneapolis & St. Louis's circuitous routing. It also eliminates sixty-eight miles of trackage rights at an appreciable savings.

The current trend is to route more freight between the Twin Cities and the East via Marshalltown and the North Western's main line to Chicago. This means less emphasis on the Peoria Gateway, which had been the hallmark of the Minneapolis & St. Louis and its principal reason for existence. Be this as it may, consolidations are inevitable and are the pattern of railroad development in Iowa as they are elsewhere in the nation.

MODERN FREIGHT RAILROAD

The North Western's double-track "high iron" across Iowa is ideal for freight. It is mostly straight track, with a few easy curves. It is virtually flat, the steepest grade being only .72 percent. It is protected by continuous automatic train control throughout. High and wide clearances make it an admirable route for piggybacks and oversize shipments. Time freights race across Iowa on schedules operated with passenger-train punctuality. Modern adjuncts, such as International Business Machines, process data on shipments well in advance of their arrival. And radio communication, with walkie-talkies for trainmen, speed up over-the-road operation regardless of the weather.

All through freights are "highball jobs," which is to say they move with dispatch. Operated by the best railroaders and the most modern equipment, the North Western is surpassed by none in expediting transcontinental rail tonnage. Even in the days of heavy passenger traffic, the division headquarters at Boone, and men all along the "left-handed" railroad, had a jealous pride in highballing freight. It is a North Western tradition.

Locomotive Engineer Wallace Hammond recalls how in other years each superintendent had his favorite train. For instance, there was Henry A. Parish. "Hank" Parish's favorite was the "Vegetable." He would invariably leave his office in the two-story brick building to greet the crew upon arrival about 2:00 P.M. One could spot him by a white carnation in his lapel. If they made a good run, he was all smiles. If they were unnecessarily late, someone would be called on the carpet.

Later came Superintendent "Monty" Williams. The apple of his eye, so to speak, was the Calumet, which, incidentally, often had cars of big red apples. It usually came in around 11:00 P.M. No matter how late it arrived, Williams seldom went to bed until it had steamed into Boone.

To expedite its time freights, the North Western had its famous Class H, or 4-8-4-type engines, built by Baldwin in 1929. These beautiful machines were designed for dual service; and, until the coming of diesels, they were the last word in handling the fastest freight and passenger trains. So popular were these versatile locomotives that when they were put on exhibit in Boone, schoolchildren were let out of class to see them.

Thanks to the diesel, however, along with other adjuncts of modern railroading, the North Western's time freights are better than ever. Every day, five through trains speed across Iowa from Chicago via Clinton with tonnage for the gateways of Council Bluffs and Fremont, Nebraska. Much of this is freight for West Coast points. It is highly competitive cargo obtained only by reliable service and on-time performance.

Each day, starting with No. 255 leaving Clinton's West Yard at 1:15 A.M., the long freights roll with goods from east to west. The 255 is dubbed "The Piggyback" because it is largely composed of trailer-trucks on flatcars. At 5:00 A.M. there's No. 261 (Dispatch), a hotshot of mixed freight. But the pride of the road is No. 249, due at 1:45 P.M. and out five minutes later. Unlike the other through freights, it goes to Fremont, Nebraska, instead of Council Bluffs. Leaving the main line at Missouri Valley, the "manifest" goes across the Missouri River to Fremont via the Blair Bridge, bypassing the congested Omaha yards on a route twenty-four miles shorter than going through the Council Bluffs–Omaha gateway. At Fremont, a Union Pacific locomotive replaces the North Western engine, and the train is on its way west. Even the caboose goes through without change.

There's a respite in the West Yard until "The Local" whistles out at 5:45 P.M. This in No. 253, which picks up and sets out cars at the larger towns on its way to Council Bluffs. Finally, at ten at night comes the bright headlight of No. 251. After an all-night run across Iowa it will pull into Council Bluffs in time for an early breakfast.

Such is the modern North Western, a specialist in handling freight and a mighty link in expediting transcontinental tonnage.

Palimpsest 43 (December 1962)

A genuine Iowa heroine was Kate Shelley, who in July 1881 helped to save the lives of two North Western crewmen during a raging rainstorm. About 1904 she stands on the platform of the Moingona station near Boone, shortly after her appointment as North Western agent. H. Roger Grant Collection.

The year is 1911, and the place is four miles west of Stratford on the North Western's Jewell–Wall Lake branch. A threshing crew crosses over the line, and in the distance this local passenger train, powered by an American Standard locomotive, will pass a section gang. H. Roger Grant Collection.

In 1907 a main line passenger train waits at the North Western depot in Tama. This station also served the former Toledo & Northwestern, which linked Tama, Jewell, and other communities in northwestern Iowa. H. Roger Grant Collection.

Jewell was one of the busiest branch-line junctions in Iowa. Two North Western secondary lines crossed at this point, one running north and south between Des Moines, Ames, and Eagle Grove, and the other east and west between Tama, Wall Lake, and Sioux City. H. Roger Grant Collection.

Iowans and other Americans were shocked when they learned of the sudden death of President Warren G. Harding. The Harding funeral train en route from California to Washington, D.C., and then to Marion, Ohio, the late president's home, on August 6, 1923, paused at the North Western station in Boone. A large, sad crowd gathered at trackside. H. Roger Grant Collection.

The depot agent often rivaled the preacher or physician as a community's most respected individual. In the 1920s agent J. C. Stearns is captured on film in his office at the North Western depot in Rutland, a North Western station near Dakota City (Humboldt) on the Eagle Grove–Alton line. H. Roger Grant Collection.

An early locomotive of the Omaha Road (Chicago, St. Paul, Minneapolis & Omaha) is No. 73, a classic American Standard 4-4-0. Between 1882 and 1957 the North Western held stock control of the Omaha, and then in 1957 it leased this approximately 1,700-mile property. Fifteen years later the North Western officially merged the Omaha into its system. H. Roger Grant Collection.

For generations residents of Clinton depended heavily on the payroll coming from employees of the North Western. This view, taken in the 1930s, shows a sprawling C&NW complex. H. Roger Grant Collection.

On May 30, 1948, a westbound North Western freight, running on the leased Linn County Railway between Otis and Beaverly, races through Hawkeye Downs. John F. Humiston photograph.

In the 1920s the North Western and other midwestern carriers acquired a fleet of gasoline-electric (later replaced by diesel engines) motor cars. These pieces of rolling stock, which could pull passenger coaches and even freight cars, reduced costs of branch-line and local passenger operations. Shortly after World War II, a motor train rests in the yards at Sioux City.
H. Roger Grant Collection.

On May 1, 1948, the old and new stand side-by-side in Ames. On the left is a shiny diesel set of E7s and on the right is a streamlined Class E-4 4-6-4 steam locomotive. Don Christensen photograph, H. Roger Grant Collection.

On June 27, 1954, the Iowa Chapter of the National Railway Historical Society sponsored an excursion over the freight-only branch between Gifford and Alden. The train is caught east of Alden and then at the Eldora station. W. H. Armstrong photographs, H. Roger Grant Collection.

THE
ROCK ISLAND
IN IOWA

IOWA'S FIRST RAILROAD

The Rock Island was the first railroad to reach Iowa, the first to lay track in Iowa, and the first to bridge the Mississippi River. It was the second road to cross the state and now operates more miles of railroad than any other railroad in the Hawkeye State—2,075 miles compared with 1,053 miles for the North Western. Currently it is the only road in the state featuring passenger service both east-and-west and north-and-south.

Few, if any, American railroads had such a galaxy of engineers as had the pioneer Rock Island. It served as a training school for several young men who later became distinguished engineers and national figures. Two of these engineers who surveyed and built the line westward from the Mississippi came back to make their homes in Iowa.

Under the direction of Chief Engineer Henry Farnam of the newly formed Mississippi & Missouri Rail Road, Peter A. Dey and his assistant, Grenville M. Dodge, were sent to blaze the trail of what is now the Rock Island across Iowa. Specifically, they were to survey the most feasible route for the M&M from Davenport to the Missouri River. This was in 1853, before there was a foot of railroad in the state. Their subsequent report pleased Farnam and led to further surveys and ultimately to the completion of the line to Council Bluffs years later.

The two men made an admirable team. Peter A. Dey, born in the beautiful Finger Lakes country of central New York and educated at Geneva College, entered railroading as a surveyor for the Erie. From the Erie Railroad he went to the Erie Canal, gaining valuable engineering experience all the while. Sensing greater opportunity farther west, he joined Joseph E. Sheffield and Henry Farnam, who had teamed up to build railroads in Michigan, Indiana, and Illinois. Not content with reaching Chicago, Sheffield and Farnam set their sights farther west. And Dey went with them.

It was while constructing the Chicago & Rock Island Rail Road in the prairie country beyond Chicago that Dey met and hired young Grenville M. Dodge, a twenty-one-year-old New Englander who had studied engineering at Norwich University in Vermont. Fired with the "railroad fever" so prevalent at that time, Dodge had come west, where Dey first encountered him as a surveyor for the Illinois Central Railroad. Dodge soon became Dey's right-hand man, his "wonderful energy" causing Dey to remark that "if I told him to do anything he did it under any and all circumstances."

Later Dey and Dodge went their separate ways, but their paths crossed many times. When they retired after gaining distinction in their respective spheres, they both came back to live along the Rock Island: Dey in Iowa City and Dodge in Council Bluffs.

It was the Chicago & Rock Island Rail Road and affiliated interests which backed the Mississippi & Missouri Rail Road, incorporated in Iowa on February 5, 1853. The M&M was essentially the western extension of the former road, which linked the two cities of its name in 1854. First president of the Mississippi & Missouri was John A. Dix, a prominent New York politician. William B. Ogden, who later gained fame as the builder of the early North Western, was vice president. Equally outstanding was Consulting Engineer John B. Jervis, well on the way to being reckoned as one of the nation's great engineers and railway contractors. The directors included Dix, Ogden, Farnam, and Sheffield plus a newcomer, Thomas C. Durant. Dr. Durant, as he was called, hailed from the Berkshires, had studied medicine in Albany, New York, and had come west about ten years later. Brilliant, unpredictable, and daring, he gave up medicine for the more adventurous role of a railroad promoter and builder.

The Mississippi & Missouri was intended to go in three directions from Davenport. One line would go west through Iowa City; another would run southwest; and a third northwest. As it turned out, the Iowa City line and the southwestern extension to Muscatine were built first. There was considerable discussion as to which side of the river the road would take after leaving Rock Island. Muscatine, Washington, and Oskaloosa wanted the road to run on the east side to a point opposite Muscatine, where it would cross to Iowa. Iowa City and Davenport wanted the road to go directly west through their communities. The latter faction won, and Davenport became the eastern terminus.

Ground was broken in Davenport on September 1, 1853, with an elaborate ceremony witnessed by two thousand. The first shovelful was dug by Antoine Le Claire, proprietor of the popular Le Claire House, which Emerson visited in 1856. Le Claire, a three-hundred-pound Indian and

French Canadian, at first opposed the railroad but later relented and sold part of his property for the right-of-way. He also purchased $25,000 in stock in the new road, and his residence became the first passenger station. Other heavy stockholders included the town of Davenport, which subscribed to the extent of $75,000; Scott County with $50,000; and individuals totaling $100,000.

On July 19, 1855, the first locomotive in Iowa arrived at Davenport, being ferried across the Mississippi. It was an American-type (4-4-0) named Antoine Le Claire, with bronze statues of its corpulent namesake on two sides of the sand dome. By the end of August excursionists were riding to Walcott, a distance of twelve miles.

Construction, however, slowed down because of the retirement of Joseph Sheffield from his partnership with Henry Farnam in railroad contracting. Farnam subsequently formed a new partnership with Thomas Durant, and building went on. But the alliance was not a happy one, for Durant proved to be harder to work with than Sheffield. Construction to Iowa City was under the immediate supervision of John E. Henry.

Tracklaying not only continued on the Iowa City road but also on the Muscatine route, which left the main line at Wilton Junction. The branch to Muscatine was completed first, with a fitting ceremony in that community on November 20, 1855. The weather and the mud militated against much of a celebration, yet nearly the entire population braved the rain to witness the event.

Far more dramatic, nevertheless, was the hectic construction westward to qualify for a $50,000 subscription from Iowa City, provided the first train reached there by January 1, 1856. Christmas day saw the rails still about two and a half miles from Iowa City. As the temperature dropped, machinery froze and numbed hands and feet greatly retarded the work. It looked for a time as if the deadline would not be met. But the citizens of Iowa City turned out to help the tracklayers under the personal supervision of Henry Farnam.

Within two hundred yards of the station the engine "froze up" to harass construction. Not to be deterred, willing hands laid temporary rails to close the gap. Others, armed with pinch bars, coaxed the "dead" locomotive, inch by inch, to the final goal. Amid cheers from railroaders, townsmen, and visitors, end-of-track was reached as church bells pealed the coming of the new year. Upon completion, Charles Stickles, the locomotive engineer, dropped unconscious beside his engine and had to be carried to the depot.

On January 3, the day of the big celebration, the temperature dropped to eighteen degrees below zero. In spite of the frigid weather, a rousing welcome greeted the special train from Davenport. Crowds followed the train as it gingerly edged into Iowa City over makeshift track. A cannon boomed. After the engine stopped, a procession of warmly clad celebrants marched to the "Old Capitol" accompanied by three bands.

Little did the crowd know that the festivities marked the end of steady construction for many years. The panic of 1857 along with management difficulties resulted in sporadic process determined by conditions to meet federal and state land-grant bills.

BRIDGING THE MISSISSIPPI

The same year Dey and Dodge set out to find the best route across Iowa to Omaha, Henry Farnam sponsored an unusual bill through the Illinois legislature. The bill incorporated the Railroad Bridge Company on January 17, 1853, and permitted the company to cross the Mississippi River within the state of Illinois at or near Rock Island. Farnam was president and chief engineer of the new company. Bonds of the bridge firm were guaranteed by the Chicago & Rock Island and the Mississippi & Missouri railroads.

An agreement was made by the M&M whereby it would cooperate in building the Iowa portion of the bridge. The colorful Antoine Le Claire deeded the necessary land on the west side of the river. All in all, the project involved three parts: a span across the narrow section of the river between the Illinois shore and "Rock Island," a right-of-way across the island, and a long bridge between the island and the Iowa shore. The boundary between the two states ran roughly down the middle of the channel, which was west of the island.

To complicate matters, the island was owned by the federal government. When it is realized no bridge had heretofore been constructed across the navigable Mississippi from St. Paul to the Gulf of Mexico, the significance of the project is apparent. To the railroads it meant a new era of rapid and relatively inexpensive shipment of goods and passengers across the nation's largest river. By contrast, ferries were cumbersome, slow, and expensive. To steamboat interests it speeded the end of their supremacy on the Mississippi, which was their stronghold. Besides, a bridge was regarded as a nuisance that hampered navigation. It took little foresight to envision these "nuisances" all along the Mississippi River as railroads spread westward.

It is not surprising that river interests did not wait for the bridge to be

constructed before marshaling their forces. Pressure was brought upon
the secretary of war to prevent construction on the government's island
and construction of the bridges over the river. This led the United States
attorney for the Southern District of Illinois to secure an injunction against
the bridge firm.

The case of the *United States v. Railroad Bridge Company et al.* came before
the United States Circuit Court in July 1855. John McLean, assistant justice of the Supreme Court, presided. The issue was primarily the right to
cross the island, although the matter of obstruction to navigation was also
involved. Judge McLean decided in favor of the Bridge Company, and the
injunction was overruled. Thus round one went to the railroad.

In the interim, work continued on the wooden Howe truss bridge across
the Father of Waters. The structure to span the main body of the river
would have stone piers, plus a larger stone foundation for the drawspan,
to be located on the Illinois side west of the third pier. Small boats and
rafts could easily navigate the 250 feet between the piers. But steamboats,
with their tall smokestacks, would be obliged to go through a narrower
opening, provided by a drawspan when opened for river traffic. The entire
structure was completed late in April 1856, affording a unique gateway
to Iowa.

All went well until the fateful day of May 6, when the steamboat *Effie Afton* was wrecked against the piers in attempting to pass through the bridge.
The boat caught fire and was destroyed, as was part of the wooden span
east of the draw, along with the draw, which likewise went up in flames. It
was over four months before the bridge was sufficiently repaired to admit
trains.

The owners of the *Effie Afton* lost no time in bringing suit against the
Bridge Company. Notwithstanding that there was some evidence to indicate the boat might have been purposely wrecked, the rivermen hoped to
recoup heavy damages by proving the span a menace to navigation. Each
side had much at stake and buttressed their forces for the decisive showdown. The case of *Hurd et al. v. Railroad Bridge Company* came up in the
United States Circuit Court in September 1857. Once again Justice McLean
presided. A young lawyer, Abraham Lincoln, who had previously won an
important case for the Illinois Central Railroad, was retained by the bridge
firm. Although Lincoln and others as counsel for the defense ably acquitted themselves, the jury failed to agree and was discharged. The second
round ended in a draw.

Both sides, however, knew that it was an uneasy truce, as feeling between rivermen and railroaders ran high. The United States House of Representatives appointed a committee to inquire into the whole affair. The committee conceded that the Rock Island bridge did pose a hazard to navigation but felt "that the courts have full and ample power to remedy any evil that may exist in that regard."

Court action was soon forthcoming when James Ward, a St. Louis steamboat operator, filed a bill in the United States Circuit Court of the Southern District of Iowa asking that the bridge be removed. When the final hearing was held before Judge John M. Love in November 1859, the judge upheld the complainant and declared the bridge "a common and public nuisance." Furthermore, the court ordered that the three piers and their superstructure, on the Iowa side of the bridge, be removed.

In view of this adverse decision, the Bridge Company had only one recourse before razing their bridge—at least the Iowa side of it. That was to appeal to the United States Supreme Court. The case was accordingly heard before that august body in December 1862. In this instance the decision of the lower court was reversed, and the bridge was allowed to remain. In somewhat different words the Supreme Court reiterated the statement of Lincoln, who said: "But there is a travel from east to west, whose demands are not less important than that of the river. . . . This current of travel has its rights, as well as that north and south. . . . the statement of its business during a little less than a year shows this importance. It is in evidence that from September 8, 1856, to August 8, 1857, 12,586 freight cars and 74,179 passengers passed over this bridge. . . . This shows that this bridge must be treated with respect in this court and is not to be kicked about with contempt."

The Rock Island, which built the bridge across the Mississippi, not only won the right to keep its own bridge but in doing so opened the way for other railroads to cross that river with impunity.

ON TO COUNCIL BLUFFS

If it had not been for the congressional Land Grant Act of 1856, there is no telling when the Mississippi & Missouri Rail Road would have reached Council Bluffs. The act called for alternate sections designated by odd numbers, six sections in width on each side of the track, to be owned by the railroad and developed for settlement. As it was, progress in building was so slow there was grave danger the road would have to forfeit its claim to these lands. It took the M&M over six years to build the thirty miles from Iowa City to Marengo, which it reached in 1862. The following year trains ran into Brooklyn and in 1864 into Kellogg. By this time the company was so heavily in debt foreclosure was inevitable.

To safeguard the federal land grants assigned by Iowa, a new company was incorporated in the Hawkeye State called the Chicago, Rock Island & Pacific Railroad. Known as Pacific No. 1, the new firm purchased the bankrupt M&M on July 9, 1866. It was empowered to build from Kellogg to Des Moines. Now having a clear title, which included the valuable land grants, the next step was to amalgamate the line in Illinois with that in Iowa. This was effected on August 20, 1866, by the consolidation of the Chicago & Rock Island Rail Road of Illinois with the Chicago, Rock Island & Pacific Railroad, referred to as Pacific No. 2, to designate it from the previous road with the same name. Incidentally, Pacific No. 2 was chartered to construct the railroad from Des Moines to Council Bluffs. Inasmuch as this was a legal matter to insure full title to land grants, no differentiation will hereafter be made between the two companies with identical names.

When the Rock Island finally ran its first passenger train into Des Moines on September 9, 1867, it was given only a modest welcome. The city had posted a $10,000 bonus for an early arrival, but the railroad never made it in time to collect the money. Furthermore, another line, which will be discussed later, had reached Des Moines first and had been given a lavish ovation.

In Council Bluffs, too, the Rock Island came out second best. The North Western had reached that Missouri River town two and a half years earlier and consequently had hauled much of the material for building the Union Pacific. But the Rock Island hammered down its final rail in Council Bluffs on May 11, 1869, the day after the last spike was driven at Promontory Summit, Utah, on the nation's first transcontinental railroad.

To celebrate the Rock Island's arrival, John F. Tracy, who became president of the railroad after the consolidation of 1866, selected a burnished German silver engine to lead the procession. This was the locomotive America, outshopped by the Grant Works of Paterson, New Jersey, for the Paris Exposition in 1867. It had attracted so much attention the Rock Island purchased it for its new road to the West. So, when the official opening of the Council Bluffs line occurred on May 12, the resplendent America was out in front. It, coupled to four other locomotives, pulled a train of crowded coaches and once again became the center of attraction.

While the Council Bluffs line was being built, the branch to the southwest was being extended beyond Muscatine. On September 1, 1858, the first train reached Washington, thirty-six miles from Muscatine. Washington accorded the thirteen-car special, carrying over seven hundred people, one of the best-organized receptions in Iowa's railroad history. For over a dozen years thereafter that thriving community was end-of-track.

When the strong hand of Tracy took over the guidance of the Rock Island, its decade of indecision, mismanagement, and divided control was over. He looked afar to Fort Leavenworth, Kansas, a military post of considerable importance and a gateway to the great Southwest. He foresaw another main line, second only to the Council Bluffs route, as the backbone of the Rock Island system. With the formation of the Chicago & South Western Railway in 1869, Tracy and his associates determined to extend the Rock Island rails to Leavenworth.

Construction in both Iowa and Missouri was pushed with such speed as to rival Farnam's record in driving the pioneer Rock Island across Illinois. The new road veered through southeastern Iowa to Lineville, whence it crossed the border to Missouri and thence to Stillings Junction, opposite Leavenworth. It took only two years to build the line, which commenced regular operation in October 1871. With the completion of the bridge across the Missouri River in 1872, train service to Leavenworth was inaugurated. The Rock Island not only vigorously competed for business through the Omaha gateway, it also had what was to become a strategic and powerful line to the Southwest as well.

THE K&D

The line which reached Des Moines first and received all the glory was the Des Moines Valley Rail Road, better known in after years as the Keokuk & Des Moines. Later to become a part of the Rock Island system, the K&D captured the imagination of the citizens of the new capital probably more than any other ever before or since.

In the words of a contemporary paper, the people of Des Moines "waited for its coming! They prayed for its coming! They talked of its coming until their tongues grew eloquent with the theme!" And when the road did come they madly proclaimed: "All doubts have fled! The great triumph has been achieved! The promised train is here today! The sun shines in a clear firmament! The day, yea, the hour of final victory has come!"

Such was the exuberance which greeted the Des Moines Valley Rail Road on August 29, 1866. The irony of the matter was that the K&D was a secondary line, and it played only a relatively minor role in the development of the city. Why, then, all the excitement?

Part of it may be ascribed to the "railroad fever" of the day. It must be remembered that the line was to connect Keokuk with Des Moines. Keokuk at that time was the "Gate City" for supplies and commerce to Des Moines. Before the arrival of the railroad, boats on the Des Moines River linked these two communities when navigation was feasible; or wagons were driven over the wild prairie.

Then, too, Des Moines was growing rapidly. It sought to have the state capital moved from Iowa City to Des Moines. To do so, however, it would have to be assured of enough votes throughout the state to adopt the Constitution of 1857, which transferred the capital from Iowa City to Des Moines. So Polk County, in which Des Moines is located, made an agreement with Lee County, where Keokuk is situated. If Lee voters would back the new constitution, Polk in turn would materially aid the Des Moines Valley Rail Road. On the strength of this agreement Polk County subscribed to the extent of $100,000 in the railroad, and the voters of Lee County swung the election so the capital could be moved. The result was the people of Keokuk saw their railroad off to a good start; and Des Moines not only rejoiced in getting the state capital but also in seeing its first train.

The line started its corporate existence as the Keokuk, Fort Des Moines & Minnesota Rail Road, organized September 1, 1853. Grading began in 1855. When four thousand tons of rail arrived by boat from New Orleans the following year, tracklaying commenced. Under the supervision of Engineer Colonel J. W. Otley, an Englishman, whose father, Richard Otley, held a similar post on the historic Stockton & Darlington Railway, the line made moderate progress.

In 1857 Bentonsport heard the whistle of the locomotive, and by 1861 trains were running through Ottumwa to Eddyville. The Civil War halted construction at the latter town until 1864, when the road's name was changed to the Des Moines Valley Rail Road and tracklaying continued. In 1866, as we have seen, it reached Des Moines, where it was accorded one of the most elaborate and enthusiastic receptions of any railroad in Iowa.

Apparently the Des Moines Valley exhausted its resources after reaching Iowa's capital. At any rate, nothing was done to extend the road to the Minnesota border, as outlined in the charter. Fort Dodge was particularly incensed at the inaction, for it was anxious to secure a direct line to Des Moines. Land was promised, a tax was voted to aid the road, and still the Des Moines Valley refused to build. As a last resort, the people of Fort Dodge backed rival roads, which failed to materialize, and also sought to have the Des Moines Valley land grant invalidated, to no avail.

When the road finally came to Fort Dodge, it took a circuitous course through Perry, Grand Junction, Gowrie, and Tara instead of the more direct route along the Des Moines River valley. Perhaps it was thought construction costs would be less through "frog ponds, sloughs, muskrat houses, etc.," as the Fort Dodge contingent put it, rather than along the hilly terrain adjacent to the river. But the road did come into Fort Dodge over its own rails by December 1870.

In 1873 the road became bankrupt, and it was split in two at Des Moines and sold in parcels. The southern section went to John E. Henry of New York City, and it was soon reorganized under the name of the Keokuk & Des Moines Railway. The northern part was sold to Colonel C. H. Perry to emerge as the Des Moines & Fort Dodge Railroad.

The K&D, as it was called, proved to be the more valuable of the two, for it served as a shortcut from central Iowa to Keokuk with direct connections to St. Louis. The expanding Rock Island was very much aware of its role, as was the Burlington. Rather than see it fall into the hands of its aggressive competitor, the Rock Island leased the road in 1878. As an independent line the K&D was at the mercy of its connections, but when integrated into the Rock Island its future was secure.

BRANCHING OUT

Under Tracy's administration the Rock Island pursued a policy of conservative growth. It was in better financial health than the competing North Western and nearly on a par with the energetic but stable Burlington. Indeed, from June 1870 to June 1873 John Tracy also headed the North Western and dictated its policies. He likewise was a strong factor in keeping the Iowa Pool intact, thereby prorating revenue between the three roads on traffic through the Omaha gateway. For over a dozen years the pool stabilized rates and discouraged competition in Iowa.

Expansion continued all the while Tracy held office. In southern Iowa a branch was constructed from Washington, on the Leavenworth line, due west through Sigourney and Oskaloosa to Knoxville, reaching these communities in 1872, 1875, and 1876, respectively. To serve prosperous towns in the rich farm country in the vicinity of the state capital, a branch was run from Des Moines to Indianola, passing through Carlisle. It was constructed by the Des Moines, Indianola & Missouri Railroad in 1871. By the fall of 1872 the line had been extended along the Middle River valley from Summerset to Winterset. The twenty-six-mile addition was under the charter of the Des Moines, Winterset & South Western Railway.

The only other branch built in Iowa during Tracy's regime was the fifteen-mile Newton & Monroe Railroad, linking the two towns in its name by 1877. Primarily a coal road, it was a reorganization of the Iowa, Minnesota & North Pacific Railway, chartered to build to the Minnesota boundary.

It was during Tracy's presidency that Iowa had its first train robbery. The date was July 21, 1873; the place, on a remote spot on the main line in the hilly uplands near Adair. On that day No. 2, the eastward night express, was expected to carry a $75,000 shipment of gold. Anticipating the valuable bullion, Jesse James lay hidden in a bank near the right-of-way. Jesse and his confederates had previously loosened a rail, and as the train labored up-grade they pulled the track out of line with a stout rope.

Upon seeking the gap in the track, Engineer John Rafferty whistled for brakes with one hand and reversed the engine with the other. But it was before the widespread use of air brakes, and the train could not be stopped in time. The locomotive derailed and turned over, killing Rafferty and seriously injuring his fireman. Meanwhile, two robbers rifled the express car while others in the gang relieved passengers of their money and jewelry. After the bandits galloped away with the loot, it was estimated that they had collected about $3,000 from the head-end cars and almost as much from the two hundred frightened passengers. In the words of the popular ballad:

> Jesse James all alone in the rain
> Stopped an' stuck up the Eas'-boun' train;
> Swayed through the coaches with horns an' a tail,
> Lit out with the bullion and the registered mail.

The bounty was small because the prized gold shipment had been held over for another train. It was the Rock Island's first train holdup; and, if not especially lucrative for Jesse James, it was successful as far as the desperadoes were concerned. Although a special train of armed guards was quickly dispatched from Council Bluffs to round up the criminals and the posses soon combed the state, no trace of the bandits was found.

With the coming of Hugh Riddle to the presidency in 1877, construction of feeder lines continued at an accelerated pace. Up to the First World War branch lines were considered a source of strength on any railroad. Branches made the haul by horse-and-wagon shorter; and, generally speaking, the road which blanketed its territory with lateral lines got most of the local traffic. For this reason the Rock Island embarked on a policy of throwing out laterals along its main line to Council Bluffs. These were short and confined to the road's legitimate corridor across Iowa. In every case the railroad was careful not to encroach upon the Burlington's territory in the south and the North Western's to the north.

The first lateral west of Des Moines was from Menlo to Guthrie Center, fifteen miles. It was completed by the Guthrie & Northwestern Railroad in 1880. Next came the line intersecting the main stem at Atlantic, running north to Audubon and south to Griswold. The northern lateral, built by the Atlantic & Audubon in 1878, measured twenty-five miles. Its southern counterpart, the Atlantic Southern, finished its fifteen-mile line two years afterward. The two little roads closely followed the East Nishnabotna River.

In the same pattern another lateral extended in both directions from Avoca, following the West Nishnabotna River upstream to Harlan and downstream to Carson. The upper road was completed in 1878 under the charter of the Avoca, Harlan & Northern Railroad and the lower in 1880 by the Avoca, Macedonia & South Western Railroad.

During this period an alternative route between Davenport and Muscatine was built along the west bank of the Mississippi River. It was shorter and better constructed than the original line via Wilton and soon commanded most of the traffic. The old road between Wilton and Muscatine was relegated to local service until abandoned in 1934.

Meanwhile, the Keokuk & Des Moines continued to be leased, a rather dilapidated property 162 miles long with wheezy locomotives operating over light iron rails. In a day when steel rails were rapidly coming into use, the K&D had only a score of miles so equipped. Thanks to the Rock Island, money from the lessee was forthcoming to build a 4-mile branch from Mount Zion to the Indian-named town of Keosauqua, nestled within the horseshoe bend of the Des Moines River. Constructed by the Keosauqua & Southwestern Railroad in 1880, the stub line, like the river, abounded in curves.

It will be recalled that the Des Moines & Fort Dodge was once part of the through line from Keokuk to Fort Dodge, formerly known as the Des Moines Valley Rail Road. When the Des Moines Valley was split in two, the southern part became the K&D, and, as we have seen, it was leased by the Rock Island. But the northern segment continued an independent and orphanlike existence. Somehow it managed to finance an extension from Tara to Ruthven, passing through Rolfe and Gilmore City. The fifty-five-mile line also served the new towns of Plover, Mallard, and Curlew, named by the road's president, Charles W. Whitehead. It appears he was an avid hunter, and the names of stations reflected his choice of game, which was plentiful in that part of Iowa.

When the Rock Island later planned to run a line to the northwest corner of Iowa, the town of Gowrie on the Des Moines & Fort Dodge looked like a favorable starting place. So the DM&FtD was leased in 1887. Hardly

had the road come under Rock Island control when a court battle began to shape up between the Board of Railroad Commissioners and the
DM&FtD. The trouble arose over the abandoning of a six-mile segment of
the latter road between Tara and Fort Dodge in 1878. The railroad subsequently had running rights over the Illinois Central between those two
points. But passengers complained of poor connecting service and demanded the old line be reinstated. The commission thereupon ordered
the derelict line rebuilt. The railroad appealed the decision before the
Iowa Supreme Court and won.

Nor did the trials of the Rock Island in leasing the DM&FtD end here.
In good faith the lessee speedily constructed the Gowrie & Northwestern
Railway, extending from Gowrie to Sibley, 110 miles. The entire line was
in operation by November 1900, it being built in a little more than a year.
While the Rock Island officials were being congratulated on a job well done,
other interests began buying into the Des Moines & Fort Dodge. What was
thought to be a routine extension of the lease, when the contract expired
in 1904, turned out to be a bitter struggle for control. Edwin Hawley, the
New York financier who headed the Minneapolis & St. Louis Railroad, had
his associates quietly buying stock in the line. By 1905 they had control, and
the M&StL forthwith leased the Des Moines & Fort Dodge. A decade later
it was purchased. Thus the Rock Island ended by paying substantial trackage rights from Des Moines to Gowrie on a railroad it formerly operated!

To integrate many of the separate but controlled railroads into the expanding Rock Island, a major consolidation took place on June 2, 1880.
The new consolidated company was called the Chicago, Rock Island & Pacific Railway. It took over most of the associated roads which heretofore
made up the Rock Island system. In Iowa all the separate companies were
absorbed with the exception of the Guthrie & Northwestern, the tiny Keosauqua & Southwestern, the Avoca, Harlan & Northern, and the K&D. The
first two were subsequently purchased in 1890, the Avoca road in 1899,
and the K&D not until 1924.

Up to this time the Rock Island had halted its westward building at the
Missouri River. With the election of the dynamic Ransom R. Cable to the
presidency in 1883, a vigorous policy of expansion beyond the Big Muddy
took place. It soon saw the Rock Island running into Denver and Colorado
Springs in the West and to Oklahoma and Texas in the Southwest.

There was one plum, nevertheless, which was yet unplucked right in
Iowa. That was the profitable Burlington, Cedar Rapids & Northern Railway, in which the Rock Island already had an interest. But Cable, never sat-

isfied with halfway measures, wanted absolute control and got it, with Ransome Cable as chairman of the board.

JUDGE GREENE'S RAILROAD

In all of Iowa there was no railroad quite like the Burlington, Cedar Rapids & Northern. Other lines might be bigger, more powerful, and better known throughout the country, but in the Hawkeye State no road was held in higher esteem than the old BCR&N. To begin with, it was an Iowa enterprise, run by Iowans and having headquarters within the state. Save for the Iowa Central, no local road came anywhere near it in size. Apart from being similar in mileage, the Iowa Central was poorer in service, vastly inferior in earning power, and of far less strategic importance. There was just no comparison. The Burlington, Cedar Rapids & Northern was in a class by itself.

The first president and leading spirit of this big "little" railroad, originally called the Burlington, Cedar Rapids & Minnesota, was George Greene, sometimes called the Benjamin Franklin of Cedar Rapids, if not of Iowa. George Greene had many talents, and he was master of every one of them. As Cyrenus Cole put it: "During his [Greene's] time there was no good thing done in Cedar Rapids of which he was not a part, and often he was all of it." With this as an introduction, let us turn to the railroad Greene did so much to foster.

It will be recalled that when the Mississippi & Missouri was organized, it had planned to construct a line to the northwest, going through Cedar Rapids and up the Cedar Valley to the Minnesota border. In the turmoil to build west and southwest, the road to Cedar Rapids had been forgotten. Other interests broached plans to run a north-and-south line through the city. On October 2, 1865, the Cedar Rapids & St. Paul Railway was incorporated to link the two cities in its title. Two years and five days later another group of promoters formed the Cedar Rapids & Burlington Railroad to build a road from Cedar Rapids through Iowa City to Burlington. Neither of these roads ever ran a train, but their backers pooled their resources and united the two companies to form the Burlington, Cedar Rapids & Minnesota Railway on June 30, 1868. Instead of going through Iowa City, however, the new road elected to go farther east, through West Liberty, crossing the main line of the Rock Island at that point.

Judge George Greene, Cedar Rapids' leading citizen and among the most ardent advocates of a north-and-south artery of commerce, was the road's first president. Charles Mason of Burlington, former chief justice of

the Supreme Court of the Territory of Iowa, became vice president and
J. D. Cameron of Burlington the chief engineer.

Thanks to Greene, who had valuable legal and financial connections in
New York, funds were easily raised in the East. In 1869 construction started
in earnest, and in five years Greene had a compact 368-mile railroad with
headquarters in Cedar Rapids. Building had gone on rapidly. Columbus
Junction (where it crossed the Rock Island's Leavenworth line) was reached
in 1871; and the 119 miles through Cedar Rapids and Cedar Falls to Plymouth Junction was spiked down in 1872. The same year also saw a 94-
mile branch from Cedar Rapids to Independence, Oelwein, and Postville
in the northeast and the 31-mile Muscatine-Riverside branch in the south.
The latter line bisected the main stem at Nichols, below West Liberty.
Before the panic of 1873 halted further construction, a feeder line was
opened between Vinton and Traer—24 miles.

The dream of a north-south road through Iowa with Cedar Rapids as
its hub was a reality. A connecting link from Burlington down the river
to St. Louis was already in operation; and on the north another connection was made at Plymouth Junction with the present-day Milwaukee Road,
thereby forming a through line to St. Paul.

To say that Greene was railroad-minded, Cedar Rapids–minded, and
Iowa-minded is not enough. George Greene was a wonderful person. Born
on April 15, 1817, in Alton, Staffordshire, England, Greene's parents had
moved to Buffalo, New York, when he was two years old. Orphaned at ten,
Greene supported himself and helped his two younger brothers. He gained
a relatively good schooling for his day, reading law in Buffalo and meeting
his expenses by working in a physician's office. Shortly after his marriage
in 1838 Greene came west to the Territory of Iowa.

It was in Iowa that Greene's versatility quickly became evident. First, as-
sisting in David Dale Owens's geological survey, then becoming one of the
earliest schoolteachers in Linn County, Greene continued to study law as
time permitted. Upon being admitted to the bar in 1840, he moved to Marion as a practicing attorney. Elected to the territorial legislature in the fall
of that year, he held office until 1842, when he moved to Dubuque.

In that bustling river town he continued his law practice, published a local paper called the *Miner's Express*, and in 1847 became an associate justice of the Iowa Supreme Court. He left the bench in 1854 to resume practice in various parts of the state. For a time he lived in Chicago but in 1865
returned to Linn County. In Cedar Rapids his interests proliferated at an
amazing rate. As a lawyer, judge, banker, publisher, mayor, churchman,

nurseryman, manufacturer, railroad president, opera house owner, edu-cator, and public-spirited citizen, his life was full, active, and meaningful. From that time on Judge Greene remained in his beloved Cedar Rapids, which he helped to found and of which he was a pioneer mayor.

Judge Greene aided in organizing the city's first bank and later headed the Union Bank. He published the first newspaper, owned the largest hotel (Greene's Hotel), and opened the town's earliest legitimate theater (Greene's Opera House). His Cedar Valley Variety Steam Works, which manufactured a wide range of farm implements, aided in bringing diver-sified industry to the community. But this is not nearly all: he helped or-ganize a score of institutions, including a water works, a hospital, and a cemetery.

A lifelong communicant, Judge Greene aided in building the Grace Episcopal Church, of which he was its first Sunday school superintendent. He also found time to head the Cedar Rapids Collegiate Institute, the fore-runner of Coe College. Best of all, however, he liked overseeing his Mound Farm, probably the first nursery in that locality. How the grand old man enjoyed showing his friends some of the 150,000 trees represented therein. Indeed, he had over a hundred varieties of apple trees alone, and a cata-log of the Mound Farm nurseries filled twenty pages.

If Greene can be said to have had one dominant interest, it was rail-roading. He was a rail enthusiast of the first order. Many and varied were the "paper" lines, surveyed, sometimes graded, but never operated, which he backed. Among them was the Dubuque & Keokuk, of which he was president. Dubbed the "Ram's Horn" because of its curious shape, the road was to go from Dubuque to Keokuk by way of Cedar Rapids and Iowa City. However, when Cedar Rapids saw its first railroad in 1856, Greene was a director and a zealous supporter. That line was the Chicago, Iowa & Ne-braska, now part of the North Western system. He was president of at least a half-dozen operating railroads and actively associated in even more rail-road construction companies and railroad manufacturing concerns.

While heading the Burlington, Cedar Rapids & Minnesota, he made many trips east to finance construction, secure rolling stock, and solicit traffic. Of these business activities he kept a diary which bubbled over with his various hobbies.

One of Greene's right-hand men was Dr. John F. Ely, vice president of the railroad. He came to Cedar Rapids in 1848 shortly after getting his "MD" from the College of Physicians and Surgeons in New York. John's trip was occasioned by the death of his brother, Alexander, who was a prominent Cedar Rapids businessman. John, in helping his brother's widow manage the estate, found his sister-in-law and the town to his liking. He subsequently married the lady and made Cedar Rapids his home.

Closely associated with John Ely was S. L. Dows, and both were active in organizing railroad construction companies. Dows, like the doctor, was a director of the BCR&M. Finally, there was William Greene, one of the two brothers of Judge Greene, who became general superintendent of the road. In later years William headed the Cedar Rapids & Marion City Railway, which went by the Coe College campus. In fact, all these men played an important part in launching the school.

Unfortunately, the BCR&M suffered reverses after the panic of 1873, which resulted in a change of management and receivership. The ubiquitous John I. Blair saw his chance to get control of the road, and for a time Blair interests dominated its management. Nevertheless, the company defaulted on its bonds, and in May 1875 W. W. Walker was appointed provisional receiver. Two months later General Edward F. Winslow superseded him as permanent receiver. This was the first and only receivership in the road's history.

An interesting sidelight on that trying period is that the bankrupt railroad paid its shipment not in cash but by checks, which might be delayed in payment for an extended time. While not a legal tender, these checks were generally accepted by local merchants. The vendors got into the habit of calling the men "Time-checkers" and the area in which they lived the "Time Check" district. To his day some of the older residents still refer to the northern end of the west side, where the railroaders resided, as the "Time Check" section.

The property was reorganized in 1876 as the Burlington, Cedar Rapids & Northern Railroad and became one of the best-managed lines in Iowa.

BCR&N

The Burlington, Cedar Rapids & Northern (incorporated in Iowa on June 27, 1876) had as its heritage a strategic 368-mile railroad—all in Iowa. When the property was purchased outright by the Rock Island in 1903, it had grown to be a 1,310-mile system, located in three states. Its main stem ran from Burlington through Cedar Rapids and Waterloo to Albert Lea, Minnesota. Another line ran northwest through Emmetsburg and Sibley, thence crossing the corner of Minnesota to Watertown, South Dakota. Branches veered off the main line at various points, serving Iowa City and Montezuma on the south, Clinton on the east, Decorah up in the northeast corner, and Estherville in northwestern Iowa.

First president of the road was Fred Taylor of New York, who represented eastern financial interests. But the man "on location" who ran the
railroad was General Edward F. Winslow, who had formerly been appointed
receiver of the old BCR&M when he was only thirty-eight. Irked when he
was not made president of the new company, the Civil War veteran gave up
his post as vice president and general superintendent to head the expanding St. Louis–San Francisco Railroad in 1880. That year, too, Judge Joshua
Tracy of Burlington, general solicitor of the BCR&N, replaced Taylor as
chief executive. The people of Cedar Rapids breathed a sigh of relief when
their home road was once again run by Iowans.

It was Charles J. Ives, however, who provided the continuity of leadership and sound business judgment which made "The Iowa Route" an outstanding railroad in the Midwest. From 1884 to its sale in 1903, Ives shaped
the destiny of the carrier as its president and general superintendent. A
strict disciplinarian with a somewhat austere exterior, he was highly respected for his honesty and fairness. Reared a New Englander, there was
always a trace of Green Mountain reserve in his makeup.

Born in Rutland County, Vermont, October 4, 1831, Ives came west and
entered railroad service as a clerk on what is now the Burlington Railroad.
After working in stations at Mount Pleasant and Ottumwa, he was sent to
Burlington. There he saw the rapid progress being made on Judge Greene's
new railroad and sensed greater opportunities for advancement in that
company. In July 1870 Ives was clerking for Greene. Ives's knowledge of
traffic and station accounting led to steady promotion. He soon became
general freight agent, then general passenger and freight agent, and in
1875 superintendent. By 1879 he was general superintendent; five years
later, president.

While Ives elected to remain with the BCR&N, others found the road a
valuable training school leading to railroad advancement elsewhere. Most
notable was A. L. Mohler, whose background in clerking on the North
Western and the Burlington closely resembled that of Ives. Mohler likewise
changed from the Burlington to the old BCR&M, being with the latter from
1871 to 1882. He rose from traveling auditor to general freight agent, when
he left to go with a forerunner of the Great Northern. Other roads followed, including a stint as general manager of the Minneapolis & St. Louis,
until he changed to the Union Pacific and subsequently became its president. To have worked on the Burlington, Cedar Rapids & Northern was
generally considered to be the hallmark of a good railroader.

The late 1870s saw new construction, although it was not until the next
decade that vigorous expansion ensued. The most important item on the

earlier agenda was the opening of the famous Albert Lea Route in 1877. By building a five-mile extension from Plymouth Junction to Manly Junction, the BCR&N hooked up with the Iowa Central Railway. From Manly, trackage rights were had over the latter road to Northwood; and from Northwood the BCR&N built its own track to the Minnesota border, where it connected with the Minneapolis & St. Louis Railroad for Albert Lea and the Twin Cities.

Here was the beginning of a new through line from the Twin Cities, via Albert Lea, Cedar Rapids, and Burlington, to St. Louis. South of Burlington the train ran over the present Chicago, Burlington & Quincy Railroad to the Missouri metropolis. For years the St. Louis Special was a popular train, having Pullmans, dining cars, and coaches on the 587-mile run. Another Limited, known as the Cannon Ball, ran between the Twin Cities and Chicago, operating over the Rock Island from West Liberty to the Windy City. Despite its circuitous route, it competed with five other railroads, all having more direct lines between the same destinations.

Travelers and the connecting roads could depend on the Burlington, Cedar Rapids & Northern to keep its trains on time. Punctuality was a fetish with the Old Man in Cedar Rapids. It was not by chance that Charles Ives had the dual position of president and general superintendent. He was as well posted on train operation as he was on finance.

Whereas the Burlington–Albert Lea line was distinctly "high iron" and the pride of the BCR&N, the branch from Clinton through Elmira to Iowa City was "hojack," shabby as a poor relation. It had little economic importance, probably never earned its keep, and was abandoned in sections between 1928 and 1943. The Elmira–Iowa City segment was opened in 1877 and the remainder of the route to Clinton in 1883. The road, like many other branches, was constructed by separate companies later absorbed by the BCR&N.

Another secondary line, built by the Iowa City & Western, ran south from Iowa City to Iowa Junction, thence west to Montezuma. A short branch from Thornburg to What Cheer was also part of the road. It was on the IC&W that a young man of nineteen, fresh out of the State University of Iowa, got his first railroad job as a rodman. He was John M. Brown, who later surveyed many more miles of the BCR&N before retiring after fifty years of service in 1929. Brown afterward became division engineer of the system, and after it was purchased by the Rock Island, he was made assistant to the president of the latter company.

The bulk of new construction in the 1880s was done under the auspices of the Cedar Rapids, Iowa Falls & Northwestern Railway, incorporated in Iowa on June 4, 1880. It was affiliated with the BCR&N, although not absorbed by the bigger company until 1902. We have seen that the BCR&N had a branch from Vinton to Traer, which was extended to Holland in 1877. From Holland the CRIF&NW took over and built in a general northwesterly direction through Iowa Falls to Clarion in 1880. The next year rails led to Emmetsburg, and by 1882 trains were running through Livermore, Estherville, and Lake Park to Worthington, Minnesota.

In 1884 the biggest jump of all was made when a 174-mile extension was opened from Lake Park through Sibley to Watertown, South Dakota. A branch was also built from Worthington to connect with the Watertown line at Hardwick, Minnesota. To tap the packing center of Sioux Falls, a road was run eastward from that city through Rock Rapids, Iowa, thence to Ellsworth, Minnesota, on the Watertown line. It was completed in 1886.

Meanwhile, in central Iowa a branch was slowly extending up from the Watertown line at Dows through Belmond, Garner, and Forest City to Armstrong. An extension was built by an affiliated road from Garner to Titonka (in Kossuth County), crossing the Des Moines & Fort Dodge Railroad at Hayfield. For a time trains ran over the DM&FTD until the Garner–Forest City segment was completed in 1895. Service from Dows to Armstrong (including running rights over the DM&FTD) was in operation by 1892.

Incidentally, the last track built by the BCR&N was the branch from Albert Lea to Estherville. This line went westward to Lakota, then over the already constructed road to Armstrong, from whence it was extended to Estherville in 1900.

To round out the picture, mention should be made of the Postville Junction–Decorah branch completed in 1884; the six-mile stub from Waverly Junction to Waverly, opened in 1886; and the ill-fated Davenport-Bennett line finished in 1890. The last-mentioned road was built by the Davenport, Iowa & Dakota Railroad, long in name and short in expectation. About half of the twenty-eight-mile diagonal route was abandoned in 1925; and the remainder, which was mostly in Cedar County, was scrapped in 1943. The only other abandonments associated with the BCR&N are the Muscatine-Riverside branch, which ceased operation (except for the short Nichols–Lone Tree sector) in 1938, and the little Thornburg–What Cheer feeder, which gave up in 1957. By 1958 the Nichols–Lone Tree segment had passed into history.

In reviewing the extensive expansion between 1880 and 1890, the Watertown line stands out as a somewhat incongruous extension for a basic

Iowa railroad. It seemed out of character, and in many ways it was. What is the explanation? The answer is found in the Rock Island, and especially in the ownership of its aggressive president, Ransom R. Cable.

Since the late 1870s the Rock Island had had a substantial interest in the Burlington, Cedar Rapids & Northern. This was increased until by 1885 it had a majority of the BCR&N's outstanding capital stock and, accordingly, dictated the road's policies. Cable, in the meantime, had embarked on a bold policy of expanding the Rock Island and its associated roads. During this period the Rock Island also controlled the Minneapolis & St. Louis, and for several years Cable headed the Mill City road. Cable had the M&StL built westward to Watertown. Cable strengthened the Albert Lea Route by closely integrating the BCR&N with the M&StL. In short, Cable wanted to make the M&StL a strong arm of his growing Rock Island. By extending the BCR&N into Watertown, it would further coordinate the M&StL with the Rock Island and give the latter a shortcut to the grain country of the Northwest. The M&StL later went bankrupt, and Cable's aim to bring it into the Rock Island fold never materialized.

Notwithstanding this sortie into Dakota, the BCR&N was primarily an Iowa railroad; and few had more affection for it than the people of its home state. Herbert Hoover had fond memories of that road as a boy in West Branch. He says in his *Memoirs*:

> I have mentioned the Burlington track. It was an inspiring place. It was ballasted with glacial gravels where, by hard search, you discovered gems of agate and fossil coral which could, with infinite backaches, be polished on the grindstone.

When Hoover's reminiscences appeared in the *Saturday Evening Post*, one reader took exception to the name "Burlington," averring that the distinguished ex-president had confused the local line with the Chicago, Burlington & Quincy, generally referred to as the Burlington Railroad. Since the CB&Q did not go anywhere near West Branch, Hoover seemingly was in error. Then along came another letter from a railway mail clerk who had serviced West Branch on his run. He said that Hoover was right and his critic wrong. The Burlington, Cedar Rapids & Northern was, indeed, locally referred to as the "Burlington."

An almost forgotten phase of BCR&N history is the role it played in making the Lake Okoboji–Spirit Lake region a popular vacation resort. It built to the lake area in 1882, and the Milwaukee Road came the following year. While the promotional activities of the two roads overlapped, the

BCR&N stressed Spirit Lake because it followed that body of water for several miles. The Milwaukee, on the other hand, confined its efforts more to
Okoboji on the south, which its line bisected.

Hardly had the cars arrived at Orleans, located near the isthmus between the two lakes, when the BCR&N began to exploit the region. It
brought the steamboat *Alpha* up from Burlington and promptly put it in
service on Spirit Lake. Having a capacity of forty passengers, the boat
soon did a thriving business. On hot summer days excursionists came from
all along the line to disembark at Orleans, where they boarded the *Alpha*
for a refreshing cruise on the big lake.

So successful was the undertaking that the railroad built an ornate three-
story hotel to accommodate the tourists. Called the Orleans, it had two
hundred guest rooms with one door leading to the corridor and another
door opening onto the spacious veranda. The latter afforded "a grand
promenade three thousand feet long and sixteen feet wide." The hotel
had nine towers, in keeping with the "gingerbread" architecture of the
period. It was opened with an elaborate ceremony on June 16, 1883, over
which S. L. Dows was the presiding officer.

To provide lake cruises in keeping with the luxurious hotel, the BCR&N
launched a new boat in 1884. Appropriately named the *Queen*, it was built
by Iowa Iron Works in Dubuque and sent to Orleans for assembly. Much
of the woodwork was milled in the road's own passenger-car shops in Cedar Rapids. The *Queen* was the first steel-hulled vessel on the lakes. She was
a beautiful smooth-running craft, equaled (but not excelled) by the Milwaukee's *Ben Lennox*, launched the same year on Lake Okoboji. Both boats
had a capacity of about 250 passengers.

The commodious hotel, however, proved to be too expensive for most
tourists; and the steamboats had difficulty in navigating the isthmus between the lakes, due to water receding nearly every year. By 1898 the lakes
were about eight feet lower than the high-water mark of 1882. As the water
dropped so did the patronage of the hotel and the boats. Other factors,
such as the depression of 1893, militated against costly vacations and fashionable hotels.

The day of special trains to the state's most exclusive watering place had
run its course. The hotel was razed in 1899, and the *Queen* was sold to outside interests two years afterward. The *Queen*, however, has continued to
blow her whistle for over sixty years, a pleasant reminder of a glorious era
that was and can never be again.

Time was running out also on the Burlington, Cedar Rapids & Northern as a separate entity. In 1902 the Rock Island leased the road and the next year purchased it. Charles Ives, who had been with the railroad almost from its inception, signed the papers conveying the entire property to the Rock Island. Now in his seventies, alert of mind and able of body, he presented a commanding appearance. A trim, close-cropped beard added dignity to the occasion as he laid down his pen, ending his long career on Iowa's last major independent railroad.

DISASTER AND ITS AFTERMATH

At the turn of the century the Rock Island was recognized as a profitable, well-run railroad. Its management was stable, its credit good. It continued to pay modest dividends all through the panic of 1893. The road had a favorable rating on the Big Board and a good reputation in Iowa and in the fourteen states it served. Unlike the Burlington, its stock was not closely held. In fact, the setting was just right for a group of speculators to get control, inflate the capitalization, and reap quick, unwarranted profits. That is exactly what took place.

In 1901 a group of promoters, which *Fortune* calls "The Big Four from the Prairies," bought heavily into the road. The quartet—also known as the Reid-Moore Syndicate—was composed of Daniel G. Reid; William H. Moore; his brother, J. Hobart Moore; and W. B. Leeds. William Moore, leader of the syndicate, made a fortune in organizing the National Biscuit and Diamond Match companies. The four had been active in organizing independent steel companies and having them absorbed into United States Steel. Thus, with the necessary means, they soon had firm control of the Rock Island.

It is not necessary to go into the financial picture painted by the new operators except to state they formed a pyramid of holding companies. In the words of Stuart Daggett, in his *Railroad Reorganization*, they had "three companies, of which one was to operate the railroad, one was to hold the stock of the operating company, and one was to hold the stock of the company which held the stock of the operating company!"

Never a compact system, the Rock Island soon became a hodgepodge of newly built merged and controlled roads without pattern and seemingly without plan. The system leaped from 7,123 miles of line in 1903 to 14,270 miles in 1907. Into the patchwork came the Chicago & Alton, the St. Louis–San Francisco, and the Chicago & Eastern Illinois. In an effort to make the sprawled-out Rock Island a transcontinental, the Moores bought into the Lehigh Valley and the Lake Erie & Western through an affiliated syndicate.

The top-heavy, overcapitalized, overexpanded road finally went into receivership in 1915. Two years later it emerged from court control with its debts scaled hardly at all. Then it struggled along for another sixteen years until it sought protection of the courts again in 1933. The Big Four from the Prairies had left the Rock Island in such a financial state as to haunt it for nearly three decades.

During the Reid-Moore administration, however, there were some extensions made which became valuable assets to the Rock Island. One was the building of a short, direct line from the Twin Cities to Kansas City. This later became a new route, cutting through mid-America all the way from Minneapolis–St. Paul to the Gulf of Mexico.

The first item of improvement was the extension of the Rock Island over its own rails and by trackage rights from Albert Lea to the Twin Cities. In comparison with the Minneapolis & St. Louis route, the new line had fewer curves and easier grades, which made for faster and more economical operation. When the extension was completed in 1902, through trains between St. Louis and the Twin Cities, operated jointly by the Rock Island and the Burlington, no longer used the M&STL from the Iowa-Minnesota border to Minneapolis.

This was fine for trips to St. Louis, but what about Kansas City? To reach the latter metropolis from principal cities in Minnesota, all passengers and freight routed over the Rock Island had to make a V-shaped detour in southeastern Iowa, thence southwest to Kansas City. Such a routing was costly, inconvenient, and time consuming. To eliminate the roundabout passage, a shortcut through Des Moines was commenced in 1901 and completed by 1913. It was the last significant railroad extension in Iowa.

The segment north of Des Moines was built by two companies. The Des Moines, Iowa Falls & Northern Railway constructed the seventy-mile line from the capital to Iowa Falls in 1903. Another firm called the St. Paul & Des Moines Railroad completed the line from Iowa Falls to Clear Lake Junction in 1909. The remainder of the route to Manly was secured by trackage rights over the Great Western.

South of Des Moines, the track from Carlisle to Allerton was largely built by the Rock Island's own construction crews. Work was started in 1911 and finished two years afterward. All the above-mentioned lines were acquired by the St. Paul & Kansas City Short Line Railroad, incorporated in Iowa on February 18, 1911. Also included in the purchase was the pioneer Des Moines Western Railway's line from Des Moines to West Des Moines (then called Valley Junction).

Although operated as an integral part of the Rock Island, the "Short

Line," as it was called, was not formally purchased by the railroad until 1922. The name was perpetuated by the Short Line Express, which ran between the Twin Cities and Kansas City until March of 1958.

In 1922, when the Rock Island reached its seventieth birthday, it decided to commemorate the occasion by a systemwide series of celebrations. Moreover, all the ceremonies were to be held the same day— October 10th. Each one followed the same pattern: a tree was planted and a stone marker dedicated to a loyal employee, living or dead, or one who had been killed in the line of duty. Altogether over one hundred trees and monuments were used for this purpose, of which thirty-three of each were singled out for Iowa. Never in the history of American railroading has there been such a far-flung, coordinated effort made to commemorate an anniversary.

The men so honored run the gamut from section hands to presidents, with superintendents predominating, of which there are nine in Iowa. The presidents represented are James Grant of the pioneer Chicago & Rock Island Rail Road and George Greene and Charles J. Ives of the Burlington, Cedar Rapids & Northern or its predecessor company. Markers in Davenport, Cedar Rapids, and Burlington, respectively, are inscribed to these executives. Two of the road's great engineers, Grenville M. Dodge and Peter A. Dey, are remembered by stone markers in Council Bluffs and in Iowa City. Also in Iowa City is a tree and stone for Chief Surgeon William D. Middleton, whose Iowa-born grandson of the same name has carried on the railroad tradition by writing a beautifully illustrated volume entitled *The Interurban Era*.

THE GREAT ROCK ISLAND ROUTE

Throughout the years the Rock Island has had (and still has) more through passenger trains going in more directions in Iowa than any other railroad. With Des Moines as the hub, trains radiate in all directions. "The Great Rock Island Route," as the road was called, meant just that to Iowans.

A glance at the timetable during the palmy days of 1927, when America was riding the crest of prosperity, reveals a profusion of named trains. Going east and west through Des Moines was the Rocky Mountain Limited. Linking Chicago with Denver and Colorado Springs, it carried a full complement of Pullman accommodations along with "Barber and Valet Service." For passengers going from the Windy City to San Francisco there was the Colorado Express, with through sleepers in conjunction with the Denver & Rio Grande–Southern Pacific route beyond Denver.

North and south, the Mid Continent Special backed into the busy Des Moines station just before midnight on its way north and shortly after midnight on the trip south. While the city slumbered, the red brick depot was agog with activity. The Mid Continent carried sleepers between the Twin Cities and Dallas and a twelve-section drawing-room and compartment car from Minneapolis to Los Angeles via Kansas City. There were also set-out Pullmans for Des Moines and Kansas City. In addition, the Firefly and the Short Line Express were likewise popular coach and Pullman trains shuttling between Minneapolis and Kansas City via Des Moines.

The pride of the road, however, was the much-publicized Golden State Limited, which cut across Iowa from Davenport to Allerton on its way between Chicago and Los Angeles. Operated over the famed "Golden State Route" in conjunction with the Southern Pacific west of Santa Rosa, New Mexico, the crack train was advertised as "extra fare, extra fine." It featured the plushest and most luxurious Pullman accommodations from Chicago to Los Angeles, along with sleepers for San Diego and Santa Barbara. For folks of modest means there was the Apache, a secondary train to Los Angeles, consisting of standard and tourist sleepers and coaches.

The Rock Island spelled travel and romance to many a boy, but to none more so than to James Norman Hall. The man who coauthored *Mutiny on the Bounty* and other adventures of the high seas found as much enchantment down at the Colfax depot in his teens as he did in later years while living in Tahiti. Hall, who was an airplane pilot in World War I yet never drove an automobile, loved trains. In his autobiography, *My Island Home*, he tells about his nocturnal escapades in riding to Grinnell:

Number Six was due at Colfax at 10:45 P.M., but a good five minutes before that time it appeared around the curve westward, at the top of the Mitchellville grade, six miles away. The headlight proclaimed the glory of its coming, and the first faraway whistle was like a call to adventure in the summer night, sending shivers of delight up and down the spines of three of us more than ready to respond to it—Buller Sharpe, "Preacher" Stahl, son of the Methodist minister, and myself. Number Six took water at Colfax, and we waited beneath the water tank about fifty yards past the end of the station. We would hear the fireman climb onto the tender and pull down the iron spout with the canvas nozzle attached; then silence, save for the splash of water pouring in and the gentle yet powerful breathing of the engine. Presently up went the spout, spilling the water remaining in it onto the ground just beyond where we were concealed. Then came the "highball"—the most stirring of signals—two short sharp blasts of the whistle. Peering out from behind the post supporting the water tank we would see the conductor swinging his lantern from the station platform. The fireman gave a pull at the bell rope; the great wheels began to move, and at the first mighty "hough!" of the engine we skipped out, leaped on the pilot—or "cowcatcher" as it is called by the uninitiated—and vanished into the pool of darkness just beneath the headlight.

A letter from a Rock Island official to "The Mayor, Colfax, Iowa," informing him of the "confirmed pilot jumpers," put an end "to those wonderful journeys." But Hall to the end of his life never ceased to have a fondness for railroads, especially the Rock Island. In his book *Under a Thatched Roof* he has a fine essay on "Trains," with nostalgic references to his boyhood on the Rock Island's main line. Again, from an earlier volume, *On the Stream of Travel*, one learns of his informal education imparted by wandering vagrants, traveling hoboes, and other "itinerant professors" as they sojourned at Colfax between trains.

The Rock Island has been celebrated in story, song, motion picture, and drama until it has become an institution in Iowa. Phil Stong's homespun novel, *Village Tale*, has its setting along the Keokuk and Des Moines Division. A little local train, called the "Kaydee," runs through the story as a quaint fixture in the life of the rural community. Who has not heard "Rock Island Line" ("is a mighty good road"), an old Negro work song, in its spirited recordings?

In the realm of motion pictures, *Rock Island Trail* recounts the building of the railroad westward. It was released by Republic Pictures in 1950 and is based on the historical novel *A Yankee Dared*, by Frank J. Nevins. Far more popular, however, is the motion picture *The Music Man*, starring Robert Preston and Shirley Jones. It will be recalled the inimitable "music man" came to River City (Mason City) on a Rock Island train to peddle his "seventy-six trombones" and to organize a town band. The Warner Brothers picture was the outgrowth of a Broadway hit of the same name written by Meredith Willson, who was born in Mason City. Great pains were taken in filming the picture to make the "River City" depot look like its prototype in Mason City as it appeared around the turn of the century.

Many people in Iowa remember the excursion trains which the Rock Island ran for various public functions. On the "Pea Vine," as the Decorah branch was locally known, there were special trains to the horse races at Independence. Racing enthusiasts came on excursions from many parts of the Midwest to Charley Williams's kite-shaped track in Rush Park. Here some of the nation's swiftest pacers and trotters raced on the "Fastest Track on Earth." Conductor R. C. Hubler recalls the exciting days when trainloads of passengers came up the branch to see the world-famous harness horses vie for rich prizes.

Excursions are rare today, with the exception of football extras, which still bring record crowds to Iowa City. When Iowa beat Wisconsin in 1960, the Rock Island ran four long specials carrying a total of 3,516 people. They came from Des Moines, Manly, and the Quad Cities, handling the mass movement smoothly and without strain. Going to and from the game by train is still a tradition for three generations of football fans and old grads.

LINE RELOCATION AND MODERNIZATION

During the depression of the 1930s the Rock Island deteriorated physically, its morale was low, and its finances precarious. Unfavorable economic conditions together with a heritage of burdensome fixed charges brought on the road's trusteeship in 1933. Things could hardly have been worse when John Dow Farrington left his post as general manager of the Burlington's lines in Texas to become chief operating officer of the Rock Island in 1936. Farrington, together with William H. Hillis, whom he brought in from the Burlington to become his assistant, set out to rebuild and modernize the run-down railroad. Rehabilitation began on all fronts, but the coming of the streamlined Rockets did more to usher in a new era in the public's mind than did any other single item.

When the Des Moines Rocket first came to Iowa City in 1937 (carrying the present *Palimpsest* editor and his bride home from their honeymoon), there were literally thousands of people lined along the track to see the silvery new streamliner. Two years later the Rocky Mountain Rocket was in service on an accelerated schedule between Chicago and Denver. In 1945 the road put the Twin Star Rocket in operation on the 1,363-mile run from Minneapolis to Houston. Serving Des Moines on its long course through the middle of America, the Twin Star attracted new passengers; and even today it is consistently well filled regardless of the season.

The last of the modernized fleet of passenger trains was the Golden State, which the road completely streamlined and placed on a forty-five-hour schedule between Chicago and Los Angeles on January 4, 1948. It superseded the somewhat shabby Golden State and clipped over four hours from the running time. Diesel streamliners first came to replace steam in passenger service. Then the road gradually dieselized its freights, thereby speeding up all trains. For example, in 1946, when the new

"Rocket Freight" was instituted between the Twin Cities and Texas Gulf points via Des Moines and Kansas City, it cut twenty-four hours from existing schedules.

Hand in hand with speeding up trains came extensive relocation on a systemwide basis. In Iowa both the main stem to Omaha and the southwestern route to Kansas City and New Mexico abounded in troublesome curves and uneconomical grades.

Work began initially on the southwestern route, of which some 82 miles of new line was built. This was done in seven sections, reducing the total length by 11 miles. In the particularly bad section between a point east of Paris westward to Centerville, a new 22-mile line shortened the route by 3.87 miles and reduced the grades from 1 percent by 0.5 percent. Relocation of the entire line, including the Ainsworth to Brighton segment, was completed on August 15, 1947.

The next big relocation project was the Atlantic Cutoff, finished in 1953. When completed, the new line resembled the string of a bow and the old line the bow itself. From Council Bluffs to Atlantic the old route went north through Shelby, Avoca, and Walnut, whereas the relocated line went through Hancock, shortening the run by ten miles. The Cutoff utilized eleven miles of the Great Western from a point just beyond Council Bluffs to Peter. The original line was subsequently abandoned except for the section between Shelby and Walnut, which is operated as a branch.

In 1954 six miles of new road were constructed near Adair, eliminating considerable curvature and complementing the Atlantic Cutoff. Again, on the other side of Des Moines about one and one-half miles of new line eliminated a stretch of difficult curves and grades near Colfax. All in all, the relocation projects in Iowa and elsewhere were of such magnitude that *Fortune* magazine sent Gilbert Burck, its top railroad authority, to do a comprehensive article on the Rock Island's rehabilitation in its December 1944 issue.

Another aspect of the rejuvenated railroad concerned pruning branches which were unremunerative and a drain on the company's finances. Foremost of these was the old Cedar Rapids & Clinton Railway, once a part of the BCR&N. This branch was totally abandoned, but the Rock Island did not pull out of Clinton. Instead, it secured trackage rights over the Davenport, Rock Island & Northwestern Railway between Davenport and Clinton.

In 1948 the Rock Island emerged from trusteeship "with a wide-open throttle and signal lights all green," as William E. Hayes put it in his *Iron Road to Empire.* John Farrington headed the reorganized company.

The Rock Island is now prosperous, efficient, and modern. Much of its major lines in Iowa are protected by Centralized Traffic Control and automatic block signals. Although the significant relocation projects had been completed, the road built a new eleven-mile branch from Earlham to Winterset in 1958. This took the place of the former Winterset-Summerset line, which was scrapped the same year. The relocated branch is shorter and has fewer grades and curves than the line it supplanted.

Current president of the Rock Island is R. Ellis Johnson, who started railroading as a file clerk on the Missouri Pacific at Osawatomie, Kansas, at fifteen. Eleven years later he switched to the Rock Island and has been with it ever since. He has held nearly every job in the operating department, which included being assistant general manager and later general manager with headquarters in Des Moines from 1950 to 1953.

Unlike some other Iowa railroads, the Rock Island is very much in the passenger business, and the "Rockets" continue to crisscross the state. With its major line relocations and up-to-date plant, no road in Iowa has done more to re-equip itself for today's requirements and tomorrow's needs. The state's first railroad is still pioneering to maintain its enviable role in hauling freight and passengers with economy and dispatch.

Today, in 1963, the Rock Island Line continues to keep abreast of modern Iowa by providing efficient freight and passenger service. For example, in addition to its regular Rocket Freight service, piggyback—the carrying of highway trailers on railroad flatcars—is growing more muscular at a steady pace. The Rock Island offers this service to shippers to and from Iowa City, Des Moines, Cedar Rapids, Davenport, and Council Bluffs on a daily basis.

The Rocky Mountain Rocket to Denver and Colorado Springs operates through Davenport, Iowa City, Grinnell, Newton, Des Moines, Atlantic, and Council Bluffs. Another fine train, the Des Moines Rocket, is an all-Iowa special and provides daily service between Chicago and Des Moines. Other passenger trains popular with Iowans are the Corn Belt Rocket to Omaha and the Twin Star Rocket which ties Iowa to Minneapolis–St. Paul on the north and to Dallas, Fort Worth, and Houston on the south.

Throughout its history, the Rock Island Line, like so many other pioneer railroads, has seen the face of America change many times. It not only has witnessed great events in history but has been an inseparable partner in the development of the thousands of communities it serves in Iowa and in thirteen other states along nearly eight thousand miles of railroad.

Significant technological advancements have been made by the Rock Island during its 111 years of operation. A long list of railroading "firsts" can rightfully be claimed by the company through the years. Among the more notable are the first use of microwave in its vast communications network and introduction of especially adapted electronic computers in its automated yards at Silvis, Illinois, and Armourdale, Kansas, and in its administrative functions. Says R. Ellis Johnson, president:

> In 1963 we are convinced that the Rock Island is a 111-year-old youngster capable of accommodating on its own system, and through its multi-interchange arrangements with other railroads, the transportation needs of all its customers.
>
> We are proud of our high-speed Rocket freights, piggyback hotshots and our fleet of Rocket passenger trains. Our railroad is imbued with a progressive spirit and it is our proud boast that no finer employees can be found anywhere.

Palimpsest 44 (September 1963)

Chicago, Rock Island & Pacific Railway.

Office of General Superintendent.

Chicago, Ill., May 20th, 1889.

NOTICE.

On date hereof, the station name of Clifton, in Louisa County, Iowa, will be changed to Cotter, and the station name of Marion, in Mercer County, Missouri, will be changed to Mercer.

H H Royce
GEN'L SUPT.

APPROVED:

GENERAL MANAGER.

The power of any railroad in establishing and naming communities is graphically revealed in this 1889 circular from the Rock Island. A village in Louisa County experienced a name change: Clifton became Cotter. H. Roger Grant Collection.

Early in the twentieth century, a passenger train steams into the Rock Island station in Indianola. Situated at the end of a branch to Des Moines, this thriving county seat and college community generated considerable traffic. At one time track extended west of the depot to the front entrance of the Simpson College campus. H. Roger Grant Collection.

A classic Burlington, Cedar Rapids & Northern depot (after 1903 part of the Rock Island) serves the county seat community of Montezuma, located at the end of a branch from Muscatine. Within two decades of this photograph a motor train will replace steam on the daily passenger run. H. Roger Grant Collection.

When steam ruled the rails, the Rock Island dispatched powerful locomotives for its "red ball" or fast freight service. In the 1940s, No. 2680 gallops through the central Iowa cornfields. George Niles photograph.

By the early 1950s, diesel-electric power propelled more and more Rock Island freight movements. A switcher (RS 1) approaches Short Line Junction near Des Moines. George Niles photograph.

Another early switcher pushes a cut of freight cars in front of the Rock Island's sprawling passenger station in downtown Des Moines. George Niles photograph.

About 1950 a glamorous Rocket, pulled by Electro-Motive E-8 diesels, nears Short Line Junction. George Niles photograph.

MCGREGOR GETS A RAILROAD

The Milwaukee Road first came to Iowa when it cut across the northeastern part of the state to complete its pioneer line between Milwaukee and the Twin Cities. It also had aspirations to cross Iowa, but these did not materialize until after other railroads had achieved that end. When it really got under way, however, the Milwaukee built two horizontal routes across Iowa; and it remains today the only railroad having dual lines. Although a latecomer to Omaha, it soon played a major role in handling freight through that gateway. Then, in 1955, when the Milwaukee took over the operation of transcontinental passenger trains in conjunction with the Union Pacific, the main line across Iowa became much more important.

The orange passenger trains and reddish yellow cabooses have long been a distinguishing feature of the railroad. While the color has since been changed to yellow, the Milwaukee is still distinctive in livery and in service as a dominant line in the Hawkeye State. The story of the Milwaukee Road in Iowa begins at McGregor, where it originally came into the state.

In the late 1850s McGregor was a thriving Mississippi port opposite Prairie du Chien, Wisconsin. When the Milwaukee & Mississippi Rail Road arrived in Prairie du Chien in 1857, it caused an influx of settlers to McGregor by ferry. Soon McGregor became the marketing entrepôt for northeast Iowa and a logical place from which to extend the new railroad to the Twin Cities. Moreover, the incentive to push due west was enhanced by the prospects of land grants in Iowa.

Like many alert communities in eastern Iowa, McGregor was agog with railroad plans. Projected roads were organized to go in all directions, one of which was to be a horse-propelled line to Fort Atkinson! The earliest company to operate trains, however, was the McGregor Western, which was incorporated February 12, 1863. Its first locomotive reached McGregor in October; and by March 1864 the cars were running into Monona, fifteen miles westward.

Among the prominent men active in promoting the little road were William B. Ogden, the "Father of the North Western System"; George Greene, the versatile Cedar Rapids jurist, railroad builder, and public-spirited citizen; and William Larrabee, later governor of Iowa. It was Larrabee who did much to secure land grants and to expedite railroad construction across the northern part of the state. Afterward, he was instrumental in fostering Granger legislation to check the abuses associated with some of the grants and to insure more adequate regulation of the railroads within the state.

Almost from the start, the McGregor Western appears to have been associated with the Milwaukee & Mississippi interests in Wisconsin. It was designed to be an extension westward from Prairie du Chien and a part of a unified through line from Milwaukee.

A contract was let with the Iowa Railway Construction Company to build the road through Conover and Cresco to the Minnesota state line. When the rails reached Conover, a new contract was signed with Russell Sage's Iowa & Minnesota Railroad Construction Company to push the rails on to Owatonna, Minnesota. In 1866 the road was completed to Cresco, and the following year trains were running through Owatonna to the Twin Cities. By this time, the struggling McGregor Western had been purchased by the Milwaukee & St. Paul Railway, which had already acquired the M&M and other roads, forming a pioneer through route from Milwaukee to the Twin Cities.

Heretofore, several of the important lines which had reached Iowa from the East affiliated themselves with steamboat companies operating from St. Louis to St. Paul. But the newly formed Milwaukee & St. Paul was the first road to provide the Twin Cities with an all-rail link with the East. What had formerly been a loosely knit assortment of individual railroads was shaping up into a strong trunk line. Under the leadership of Alexander Mitchell, ably assisted by S. S. Merrill, his general manager, railroads had been purchased and consolidated at an amazing rate.

PONTOON BRIDGE

One of the most interesting sidelights of Milwaukee railroad history was the manner in which it crossed the Mississippi River. It was the enterprising John Lawler of Prairie du Chien who, mindful of increased railroad traffic, began operating a line of barges between Prairie du Chien and Mc-

Gregor. Lawler contracted with the railroads to ferry cars of livestock across the Mississippi for $6 each, receiving up to $8 for loaded cars.

At first the cars were taken on barges and guided by a steamboat around the big island in the middle of the river. Then the resourceful Lawler had rails laid on the island so that the railroad cars could be moved more rapidly from shore to shore. Barges were loaded with the cars on one bank and pulled across to the island by a cable which was powered by a steam rig from another barge on the island's shore. A switch engine took the cars across the island. Then they were ferried a second time by cable-operated barges for the last lap of the journey to the opposite bank of the river.

Going across the island was less hazardous than going around it. Still, the possibility of losing a car in getting it on and off a barge was very imminent. Then, too, whenever a freight car plunged to the bottom of the Mississippi, Lawler did not get his toll charge, to say nothing of the threat of a lawsuit. Fortunately, he had in his employ a Bavarian shipbuilder, Michael Spettel, who came to his aid. Spettel advocated a pontoon bridge to solve the problem. He did more: he whittled out a model of the proposed structure and turned it over to his employer. Lawler subsequently financed the strange bridge, which was completed in 1874.

Essentially, the bridge in the east channel was three 131-foot barges lashed together by an immense strap-iron hinge to keep the span properly aligned yet flexible enough for vertical movement. The pontoon in the west, or Iowa, channel was a specially constructed single-deck scow, 408 long, 28 feet beam, and 6 feet depth. The pontoon in each channel, when in position in line with the piling, stood at an angle with the general direction of the current of about fifty-five degrees. At one end, the floating span was hinged to a permanent trestle. At the free end, a steam-operated powerhouse was installed along with a cable drum. A cable was run from the stationary approach to the drum, and from there it was anchored to a piling downstream and at right angles to the crossing. Whenever a riverboat whistled for the channel, the cable was wound around the drum, pulling the free end of the span toward the heavy piling and thereby opening the bridge.

Inasmuch as Lawler took out patent rights for the pontoon bridge in his own name, this action precipitated a long-standing controversy which was sparked by Spettel's dismissal in 1887. The bridge itself was Lawler's, but it would appear the patent belonged to Spettel, who failed to file a claim or take action until years after the rights had been appropriated by his employer.

The bridge continued to be controlled by the Lawler interests until John Lawler's death in 1891. It is estimated that nearly a million railroad cars crossed the floating tracks at a fee of a dollar a car. After the passing of its owner, the Milwaukee Road took over the operation of the structure.

In 1914 the east channel bridge was replaced by a stronger pontoon structure. Two years later a new 276-foot span was installed across the west channel. At the time of construction it was said to have been the largest bridge of its type in the world.

On the new bridge, the track was cradled between two upright structures which rested on the long bargelike pontoon. By an ingenious system of cables and pulleys the track could be raised or lowered as much as eighteen feet and blocked at the desired level. Variations in track elevation were desirable because the level of the Mississippi in this vicinity could vary as much as twenty-two and one-half feet.

The Prairie du Chien–McGregor pontoon bridges carried multitudes of immigrants on their way to homestead in Iowa, Minnesota, and the Dakotas and trainloads of grain and other commodities to the East. They gave reliable service except when the wind was unusually high or when, in the spring, the spans had to be kept open for several days to prevent floating ice from crushing them.

In recent years, however, with longer and heavier trains, it has become more economical to use the Milwaukee's orthodox bridges across the Mississippi at La Crosse, Wisconsin, and Savanna, Illinois, rather than the somewhat cumbersome pontoon crossing. Furthermore, the high cost of operation and repair of the historic floating structures was not warranted in light of declining traffic. The last train crept over the quaint span at the customary four-mile-an-hour speed limit on October 31, 1961. Shortly thereafter the bridges were dismantled.

CROSSING NORTHERN IOWA

The McGregor Western Railway originally intended building across northern Iowa along or near the 43rd parallel and thereby secure valuable land grants. But progress was so slow the road never received any of the government land.

A new company called the McGregor & Sioux City Railway (incorporated January 23, 1868) entered the picture to resume construction and get the grant. It built from Calmar to Nora Springs, a distance of sixty-four miles, by 1869. The carrier was renamed the McGregor & Missouri River Railway; and, by 1870, when it reached Algona, its mileage had about doubled. It received land grants up to that point only to have further progress halted by adverse business conditions and the panic of 1873. To qualify for the entire grant, the road had to reach the line of the St. Paul & Sioux City Railroad in O'Brien County. But when the land grant expired in December 1875, the track was scarcely more than halfway across the state.

Meanwhile, the McGregor & Missouri River had been absorbed by the expanding Milwaukee & St. Paul system, with which it was associated from the start. Naturally the Milwaukee wanted to have the land grant transferred to it as an incentive to build the rest of the line in Iowa and on to Dakota. At this juncture there was strong political pressure against extending the grant. Equally significant was the fact that Iowa's home railroad, the energetic Burlington, Cedar Rapids & Northern, was pushing its line through the northwestern part of the state to Dakota. Its hat was in the ring for the forfeited lands. The battle was long and bitter, but in the end the Milwaukee won.

Since the Milwaukee & St. Paul became the Chicago, Milwaukee & St. Paul Railway in 1874, it was the latter company which actually completed the extension westward. The segment from Algona through Sheldon (where it crossed the St. Paul & Sioux City Railroad) to Hull was in operation by 1878. The next year saw trains crossing the Big Sioux River into Canton, Dakota Territory.

While the Milwaukee completed its line in time to qualify for the land grant, a change in route of the St. Paul & Sioux City (now the North Western) resulted in overlapping grants. This in turn gave rise to years of litigation in which the federal government, the state, the two railroads, and the Grangers took part.

Because of the sparsely settled nature of northern Iowa, comparatively few branches were built by Milwaukee interests. The trans-Iowa line was, in truth, more of a gateway to the Dakota Territory than anything else. The Milwaukee and the North Western vied with each other in opening up to settlers what is now South Dakota. Indeed, Frank H. Spearman in his *The Strategy of Great Railroads* pointed out that the Milwaukee "has exploited South Dakota so long and so earnestly that it has come to be looked on by the State administration as a sort of advertising adjunct to its own and is accorded, after a manner, official recognition."

There were, however, some branches, the oldest of which was built from Conover to Decorah by the Milwaukee & St. Paul in 1869. The next year the Mason City & Minnesota Railway built a twenty-eight-mile line from the city in its title to the Minnesota border. An affiliated road continued the rails to Austin, Minnesota, where they met the trunk line linking the Twin Cities with the East.

In 1882 the Milwaukee acquired the picturesque little Iowa Eastern Railroad, connecting Beulah with Elkader. The nineteen-mile road, chartered in 1872, was of three-foot gauge. For many years William Larrabee was active in its management. Its two beautiful Mogul (2-6-0) locomotives, the Pathfinder and Diamond Joe, are said to have been the first of that wheel arrangement west of the Mississippi River. The line was also unusual in that it had iron-plated wooden rails, commonly called "strap rails," on about four miles of route in the vicinity of Elkader. These composite rails caused trouble, especially in very cold weather when the iron straps would curl up and derail trains.

Operating in rugged, hilly country, the short line was subject to bad washouts, one of which ripped out the track between Elkader and Stulta, causing that end of the line to be abandoned. After purchase by the Milwaukee, the road was widened to standard gauge, and the four-mile Elkader-Stulta section was rebuilt.

At the western end of the state, the Milwaukee built the nine-mile Rock Valley–Hudson (South Dakota) cutoff in 1880. This reduced the time of trains running from Sioux City to the East when the railroad entered the latter city only from the north.

Since the Canton and Sioux City line weaves in and out of Iowa and South Dakota, a brief history of it is in order. The stretch from Sioux City to Elk Point, South Dakota, was built by the Dakota Southern Railroad in 1872. The road from the latter community north along the Big Sioux River was the responsibility of the Sioux City & Pembina Railway. It built from Elk Point to Calliope in 1876 and to Canton in 1878. After a series of consolidations, all these lines became the property of the Milwaukee by 1881.

The rivalry between the Burlington, Cedar Rapids & Northern and the Milwaukee in northwestern Iowa was intense and led to classic right-of-way fights and to the construction of one ill-fated branch. When the BCR&N wanted to cross the Milwaukee's main line at Emmetsburg in building up to Estherville, it had to do so by force. The road waited until Sunday, when injunctions could not be issued, and with a crew of men ripped up the Milwaukee track and put in its own crossing frogs. Mustering up its own force a few days later, the Milwaukee tore out the crossing and kept a string of freight cars on the disputed territory. When a train appeared, the cars were sidetracked to let it pass and then quickly returned to the crossing. The inevitable court battle followed in which the BCR&N won the right to cross.

Alarmed by this incursion and still trying to keep what it regarded as an intruder out of its territory, the Milwaukee, under S. S. Merrill's supervision, commenced its own line to Estherville. Merrill, it is said, aspired to extend the road through Jackson and Crookston, Minnesota, and thence to Winnipeg.

Soon the two roads were building side by side northward from Emmetsburg. At the town of Osgood, the BCR&N was to cross to the east side of the Milwaukee's line. When they got there, they found their rival on the spot with an engine blocking the track where they had to cross. The steam bulwark remained there until removed by a court injunction. Both roads then resumed the race, which ended with the Milwaukee reaching Estherville a day or two before its competitor. But the winner in 1882 proved to be the loser in 1889, for the Milwaukee, after operating the line at a heavy loss, abandoned it. Today one can still see the old grade to the east of the present Rock Island line—a mute reminder of crossing fights and unfulfilled dreams.

The Milwaukee fared better when it built from Spencer to Okoboji to tap the largest lakes in Iowa and share that resort area with the Burlington, Cedar Rapids & Northern. The seventeen-mile branch was opened in 1882, and the following year it was extended another three miles to Spirit Lake. Shortly afterward both roads had hotels beside the lakes and boats with cruising vacationists on their waters. The two railroads soon made the Okoboji–Spirit Lake area a popular watering place for Iowans, a role which is largely forgotten in this day when the automobile has put the locale within a few hours' drive for everyone in the state.

WESTWARD TO OMAHA

The Milwaukee's second trans-Iowa line, which went through the central part of the state, was late in reaching Omaha. The North Western, the Burlington, and the Rock Island had already preceded it. Perhaps it never would have been built had it not been for the management team of Alexander Mitchell and S. S. Merrill. They were not content to see the Milwaukee play a minor role in the Hawkeye State.

The Omaha–Council Bluffs gateway had been the acknowledged entrance to the West ever since the first transcontinental railroad was completed in 1869. True, the Milwaukee dominated the Twin City portal to the Pacific Northwest, but in an expanding economy this was not enough. With only one significant western gateway, it made the Milwaukee second best to the North Western, which through affiliated lines reached *both* Omaha and the Twin Cities. To Mitchell and Merrill such a role was unthinkable. The Milwaukee, under their aggressive leadership, recognized no superior. They would see to it their railroad would dominate the central West as it did the Northwest. They would go to Omaha!

The first lap of the route across mid-Iowa was under the banner of the Sabula, Ackley & Dakota Rail Road, which was organized in 1870. As a matter of fact, the road was built with the helping hand of the Western Union Railroad, which had reached Savanna, Illinois, opposite Sabula. The Western Union (no relation to the well-known telegraph company of the same name) was in turn controlled by Milwaukee interests. To the uninitiated it looked like a haphazard assortment of strange railroads, but under the shrewd maneuvering of Alexander Mitchell it was the making of a new trunk line.

Western Union agreed to advance $3,000 a mile for the Sabula road so it could reach Marion. A contract was let to the Sabula & Marion Railway Construction Company; and by December 1870 the trains were running to Preston, 20 miles westward. Less than two years afterward the whistle of locomotives was heard in Marion. In the meantime, the "Sabula" was purchased by the Milwaukee, and through service was instituted over affiliated roads to the city of Milwaukee. Money troubles, accentuated by the panic of 1873, however, checked westward progress for a decade. But when work was resumed on the 260-mile stretch across the prairie from Marion to Council Bluffs, track was laid within a year's time! This long section of line, built by the Chicago, Milwaukee & St. Paul itself, was in operation by the end of 1882.

There is no question that the new line was a good investment. The Milwaukee, according to one authority quoted by the *Railway Gazette* of February 22, 1884, had "from the very beginning captured one-fourth of the Chicago–Council Bluffs through freight and almost ruined the value of the passenger business."

On the other hand, the road had great difficulty in getting the trains into Omaha over the Union Pacific. At one time, the Milwaukee teamed up with the Rock Island in an attempt to build a separate bridge over the Missouri River before wresting trackage rights over the UP's structure.

During the late 1870s and through the 1880s numerous independent railroads built in Iowa. Aware of this, the Milwaukee management took steps to control and purchase those they considered desirable feeders. Then, too, there was always the likelihood a competing trunk line would purchase the "independents" and muscle in on Milwaukee preserves.

The oldest of the independents which came into the Milwaukee fold was the meandering Dubuque South Western Rail Road, which was leased in 1878 and purchased three years afterward. The "Dubuque" road began its existence as the Dubuque Western Railroad and was incorporated September 10, 1855. It started at Farley, a point on what is now the Illinois Central, twelve miles west of Dubuque. By 1859 the little road had reached Sand Springs, fourteen miles to the southwest. In 1860 trains were running into Amana, when financial difficulties led to its reorganization as the Dubuque, Marion & Western Rail Road. Once again the road became insolvent. It emerged as the Dubuque South Western, which managed to extend track to Marion by 1863. In another two years it had laid track into the much more important community of Cedar Rapids.

The "Dubuque" road for a time was headed by Captain J. P. Farley, who operated a line of steamboats on the Mississippi and was instrumental in running the first "steam cars" on the present-day Illinois Central in Iowa. Also associated with the enterprise were William B. Allison, Morris K. Jessup, Platt Smith, and others, all prominent men who later did much to get the Illinois Central started across Iowa. But unlike the IC, the line to the southwest was never a financial success and remained local in character. It was poorly built and had steep grades and inferior equipment. There was an especially severe grade on the nine-mile section between Sand Springs and Marion. Shortly after the road was controlled by the Milwaukee, this section was abandoned and a two-mile connection built from Sand Springs to Paralta. Thereafter trains ran on the Milwaukee tracks from the latter town to Marion.

A far longer railroad system was the Davenport & North Western Railway, which was acquired by the Milwaukee in 1879 and consisted of about 150 miles. Incorporated as the Davenport & St. Paul Rail Road, August 26, 1868, the road seems to have had as stormy a financial existence as that of the hectic Dubuque property. By 1872 it boasted of a main line running from Davenport to Delaware, a distance of 89 miles, and a 38-mile branch from Eldridge to Maquoketa. When a scant year later tracks were laid between Delaware and Fayette, the railroad was only 48 miles short of the Minnesota state line. Indeed, it had graded most of the way from Fayette to Cresco, the latter being on the Milwaukee's line to the Twin Cities. Here was a serious threat of competition, especially if the newcomer would be picked up by one of the larger systems in Iowa.

When the Davenport & St. Paul Rail Road defaulted on its $6 million mortgage held by J. Edgar Thomson, head of the powerful Pennsylvania Railroad, William Dennison of Ohio, and others, the company was reorganized as the Davenport & North Western. Still in a precarious financial state, the Milwaukee had little trouble in getting control. The line was extended from Fayette to Jackson Junction by its new owners in 1880. Here it linked up with the Milwaukee's Iowa & Dakota Division and was soon integrated into the bigger system.

With the Omaha gateway in their hands, Mitchell and Merrill had out-generaled the North Western, which had vigorously tried to defeat them. The Milwaukee had eclipsed the North Western, more than held its own with the Rock Island, and ably competed with the powerful Burlington. In the cutthroat competition of the 1880s, the Milwaukee was a stormy petrel, getting new lines under its wings each year.

THE RIVER ROAD

We have traced two Milwaukee routes across Iowa, leaving only one significant part of the system unmentioned. This is the line hugging the west bank of the Mississippi, formerly known as the "River Road," and stretching from the Minnesota border through Dubuque to Clinton. Up until its purchase by the Milwaukee in 1880, the route was more or less independently operated.

The initiative for a north-south line along the Father of Waters stemmed from the desire of Dubuque to get more river trade, particularly during the winter months, when ice halted navigation. Moreover, McGregor, its principal Iowa rival on the north, boasted of being on the new railroad to the Twin Cities.

One of the chief promoters of the River Road was Platt Smith,.who was active in railroad building in eastern Iowa, especially around Dubuque. A big, robust man, Smith had migrated from New York State to the Territory of Iowa, where he engaged in lumbering. Possessing only a meager education but determined to be a lawyer, Smith studied in log cabins, in sawmills, and on steamboats whenever he had the chance. After passing the bar examination, he practiced law and later opened an office in Dubuque. A man of great versatility and keen intellect, he was associated with many of the city's business enterprises, particularly the new industry of railroading. It was Platt Smith, for example, who helped bring the Illinois Central to Dunleith, better known as East Dubuque, Illinois. It was Smith, too, who aided its course westward from Dubuque.

Platt Smith was a leading spirit in organizing the Dubuque & McGregor Railway, which was incorporated March 20, 1868. It was chartered to connect the two cities in its title. The following year the name was changed to the Dubuque & Minnesota Railway and the articles amended so it could extend to Winona, Minnesota. A branch up the Turkey River and beyond to Mankato, Minnesota, was also authorized. Smith, as head of the Dubuque & Minnesota, started construction northward along the Mississippi. In 1871, when the road was renamed the Chicago, Dubuque & Minnesota, it already had a 117-mile route carved out of the river bluffs from Dubuque to La Crescent, Minnesota. By this time, however, James F. Joy and his Burlington associates were dominating the road. In 1872 it completed its 13-mile Turkey River Junction–Garber branch.

Meanwhile, a separate corporation called the Dubuque, Bellevue & Mississippi Rail Way, organized January 21, 1870, commenced building southward from Dubuque. It was affiliated with the road to the north, and many of the officers held identical positions in the two companies. In view of the fact that the "south" River Road was also interested in making connection with Lake Michigan, it was retitled the Chicago, Clinton & Dubuque Railroad in 1871. That year its rails reached Sabula Junction, forty-four miles to the south. From the Junction, running rights were had over the Sabula, Ackley & Dakota for about five miles. Beyond that point, an additional two miles were constructed, bringing it to the "Midland Railroad" (now the North Western), over which it operated into Clinton.

To service and to repair equipment, the two River Roads built extensive shops in Dubuque which, until the time of their purchase by the Milwaukee, employed about a hundred men. Dubuque, likewise, served as headquarters for the two lines, and later, under the Milwaukee's jurisdiction, it became the operating base for the Dubuque Division.

The panic of 1873, together with high construction costs and other factors, put the River Roads into receivership. After a merry round of reorganizations, name changes, and consolidations, the River Roads were combined to form the Chicago, Clinton, Dubuque & Minnesota Rail Road in 1878.

In the meantime, branches were being built into the hinterlands. By 1877 the narrow-gauge Waukon & Mississippi (organized April 15, 1875) finished its twenty-three-mile line between Waukon Junction on the Mississippi and Waukon. Its first train, pulled by a neat American-type locomotive coupled to five flatcars filled with excursionists, arrived in Waukon on October 27, 1877, amid much rejoicing. The road soon came under the Joy interests, and plans were made to extend it to Decorah and into Minnesota. Considerable grading was done, and tracks were laid several miles beyond Waukon. Then the Chicago, Clinton, Dubuque & Minnesota acquired it, and all building ceased. It was converted to standard gauge shortly thereafter.

Farther south, the Turkey River branch had been extended to Wadena in 1878. Still farther to the south another road, long in name and narrow in gauge, ended its little rails at Cascade. This was the bucolic Chicago, Bellevue, Cascade & Western Railway, whose line started in Bellevue. It was likewise taken over by the Chicago, Clinton, Dubuque & Minnesota in 1880. Because the Cascade road was the oldest narrow gauge in Iowa, and the last to survive in the state, a separate chapter is devoted to it.

The River Road with all its branches was now a three-hundred-mile entity which connected with the main line of the North Western at Clinton. On the north it hooked up with the Milwaukee's Iowa & Dakota Division at McGregor and at La Crescent, Minnesota, both with its lines running to Madison, South Dakota, and its Milwaukee–Twin Cities main line.

The River Road, while associated with J. F. Joy, was still independently operated and never made a part of the Burlington Railroad, which the Joy interests dominated. As a consequence, the North Western and the Milwaukee looked with envy at the River Road. A clash soon resulted between the two trunk lines when both sought control. The North Western officials, a contemporary account records, were riding over the line in their business car and were getting ready to buy the River Road. Unfortunately for them, the Milwaukee officials got wind of the negotiations. While the North Western car was tied up for the evening at Lansing, the Milwaukee beat them to it by purchasing the road that night! At any rate, the Milwaukee took title to the Chicago, Clinton, Dubuque & Minnesota on October 19, 1880.

Shortly after the purchase, the new owners extended the rails into Clinton, but only after a spirited crossing fight with the "Midland" to get into the city. Trackage rights over the North Western were then quickly terminated.

In securing the River Road, the Milwaukee had matched its wits against the North Western and won. It had purchased the road from under the nose of the Burlington (Joy) interests and entrenched itself along the Mississippi. The loss to the Burlington, however, was not great, for it later built a fine new road on the east side of the river. But if the North Western had succeeded in picking up the property, it would have seriously affected the growth of the Milwaukee system. In short, the River Road was not so valuable in itself as it was a competitive threat in the hands of a rival!

THE GOLDEN AGE OF THE MILWAUKEE

August Derleth, in his history of the Milwaukee, calls the Mitchell-Merrill era "The Golden Age of the Milwaukee Road." With the exception of the

Des Moines–Spencer line, the Kansas City Cutoff, and a few unimportant branches, the system in Iowa had been completed when Mitchell died suddenly in 1887.

Too much credit can scarcely be given these two railroad statesmen. They complemented each other as few rail executives have ever done. Alexander Mitchell was a shrewd judge of men, deliberate, calculating, but not afraid to take a chance although weighing each move carefully. He had a sturdy, stocky figure, a commanding face, and luxurious whiskers. Immaculate in dress, courteous in manner, he looked and acted like a dynamic executive. In contrast, Sherburn S. Merrill was tall and angular, often careless in dress, nervous in manner, and ever on the move. A man of direct action, Merrill was markedly aggressive and always on the offensive.

Each man might well have succeeded in his own right, but when teamed together they were well-nigh invincible. They had great respect for each other's abilities. When Mitchell became president in 1865 (Merrill became general manager about the same time), the Milwaukee had about 850 miles of track. When Mitchell died trackage had risen to over 5,000 miles. Moreover, Iowa in 1887 accounted for 1,573 miles—or more of the Milwaukee's mileage than any other state.

In his *Transcontinental Railway Strategy*, Julius Grodinsky declares the "punch and drive that characterized the management early in 1879 was largely the work of Merrill, although Mitchell uniformly supported his program." This view is supported by Albert Keep, head of the North Western, who averred the Milwaukee's policy was dictated by Merrill in all things "as absolutely as if he were the sole owner of the property." Under Merrill's general managership the Milwaukee invaded the North Western territory at every opportunity.

Along with the North Western, the Milwaukee did battle with the Rock Island and the Burlington in maintaining its position in the Midwest. When the latter built its own line into the Twin Cities in the 1880s, the Milwaukee retaliated by entering Kansas City. The first part of the "KC" extension was made from Cedar Rapids to Ottumwa and finished in 1884. From Ottumwa the line ran in a southwesterly direction to Kansas City, which it reached in 1887.

Another important and logical extension was the branch constructed southeast from Sioux City through Rodney to Manilla, where it connected with the Chicago-Omaha line. The section north of Rodney was in service by 1886; the section south of that point was in operation the next year. This gave the Milwaukee an alternative route to the East from Iowa's packing center which was better and shorter than over the Iowa & Dakota Division.

Among the secondary items of construction during this period was the continuation of the Turkey River branch to West Union in 1882. Seven years later the Maquoketa branch reached Hurstville by a two-mile extension. It was incorporated in 1888 and built under the name of the Maquoketa, Hurstville & Dubuque Rail Road.

The Milwaukee's mileage in Iowa remained static until President Roswell Miller brought the system into the state capital. This was effected by the purchase of the 146-mile Des Moines, Northern & Western Railroad in 1899. At the time of the acquisition, the road had a line running in a northwesterly direction from Des Moines to Fonda and a branch from Clive 7 miles west of Des Moines to Boone.

The 178-mile route connecting the capital of Iowa with the state's chief lake area began with the ill-fated Des Moines Western Railway, which was incorporated in 1871. With high spirits and slender resources, the road planned to build from Des Moines through Waukee, Adel, and Panora to the Mississippi River. It did some grading between Adel and Waukee and faded out of the picture. Meanwhile, the populace of Adel, seat of Dallas County, was fearful that the county seat would be removed to some other locale already on a railroad. They took the initiative of reorganizing the dormant road in 1875 as the Des Moines, Adel & Western Rail Road. Most of the officers were from Adel, with T. R. Foster as president, who was shortly to be succeeded by J. Y. Caldwell. The pip-squeak short line was poorly graded, narrow in gauge, and merely connected Adel with Waukee, a seven-mile link. As Ora Williams recalled:

> The locomotive was much like a mine engine, with the water tank slung saddle fashion over the boiler. There were one or two freight boxcars in which wood benches had been set up for the guests. The two or three flatcars had boards across for seats for the youngsters. . . . There was no turntable, so the locomotive that pulled the train from the county seat, pushed the cars back, most of the way down hill, to the temporary platform across the river from the town [Adel]. There had not been enough money with which to build over the Raccoon River.

Passenger service was inaugurated in 1878 soon after the initial train, loaded with excursionists, returned to Adel by moonlight. Tom Ashton, the liveryman, served as general manager, conductor, and ticket agent; Sam Ward, the one blacksmith, filled the post of engineer; and Wes Howe, a local boy, shoveled coal into the locomotive.

Of limited importance, the narrow gauge did, nevertheless, succeed in keeping the county seat permanently in Adel. In 1879 the little rails reached Panora. Under the name of the Des Moines North Western Railway, the struggling company built through Rockwell City into Fonda, seventy miles from Panora. This was in 1881, when the Wabash leased the road and underwrote most of the cost of the extension. For a time, access to Des Moines from Waukee was had over the Des Moines and Fort Dodge Railroad (now the North Western), which added an extra rail to accommodate the narrow-gauge rolling stock.

Although surveys were made into the Okoboji and Spirit Lake country and considerable grading was done, the road never built beyond Fonda. The Wabash went into receivership in 1884, and not long afterward the narrow gauge was returned to its owners. But the three-foot system was enlarged when it consolidated with the Des Moines & Northern Railway in 1891. The latter had a narrow-gauge line from Des Moines westward to Waukee, where it connected with the road to Fonda. But that part which stood for "Northern" in its name ran in that direction from Clive—midway between Des Moines and Waukee—to Madrid and Boone. The road started its existence under the highly pretentious name of the St. Louis, Des Moines & Northern and was incorporated May 21, 1881. It was completed in 1882.

For many years Grenville M. Dodge, Civil War general, railroad builder, statesman, and one of Iowa's foremost citizens, headed the company. It was leased to the Wabash in 1881, and the lessee aided in its building. When the Gould lines later went bankrupt, the narrow gauge was left to shift for itself.

Since the "Dodge" line went to Des Moines, it was only logical that the Fonda road should secure trackage rights over it from Waukee to Iowa's capital. Indeed, the two companies were more or less under the same interests. With the amalgamation of the two roads to form the Des Moines, Northern & Western Railway, F. M. Hubbell became president and Dodge vice president. By 1891 the entire system was broadened to standard gauge. After numerous reorganizations and name changes, the Milwaukee got controlling interest in 1894 and purchased the "Des Moines" company from F. M. and F. C. Hubbell five years later, making it the Des Moines Division.

To integrate the property with the Iowa & Dakota Division, the Milwaukee extended the road from Fonda to Spencer, a distance of forty-three miles, in 1899. At Spencer it also hooked up with the Spirit Lake branch, thereby opening up a direct route from Des Moines to the popular resort and vacation area. At the same time, a thirty-eight-mile branch was completed from Rockwell City to Storm Lake.

As independent roads, the lines from Des Moines to Boone and to Fonda were often at sixes and sevens. But when absorbed into the Milwaukee system, they were rebuilt to receive heavier traffic from the main line connection at Herndon and Madrid. Thus the Milwaukee, rather late to be sure, got a firm toehold in the capital city, where it competed with the Rock Island, the Burlington, the North Western, the Great Western, and the Wabash.

The last major railroad extension of the Milwaukee in Iowa came with the building of the Kansas City Cutoff. Heretofore all trains from Chicago, Milwaukee, and other points in the Midwest to Kansas City were obliged to go over the long, circuitous, and hilly line between Marion and Ottumwa. As a result, the Milwaukee could never compete very successfully for passengers or freight to the great southwestern gateway of Kansas City. To rectify this shortcoming, the railroad quietly began buying land in southeastern Iowa for a low-grade, direct line to Kansas City. George M. Titus, who later became state senator, was instrumental in purchasing much of the right-of-way. The Milwaukee had the new line in operation between Muscatine and Rutledge by 1903.

Much of the remainder of the route between Muscatine and Clinton was had by a curious bit of trading. Inasmuch as the Rock Island desired a better line from Albert Lea, Minnesota, to the Twin Cities and the Milwaukee needed access between Muscatine and Davenport, a reciprocal agreement was reached. The Milwaukee agreed to give the Rock Island trackage rights over its line to St. Paul and Minneapolis. In return, the Rock Island allowed the Milwaukee to use its rails between Muscatine and Davenport.

But there was still a hiatus of some thirty-three miles between Davenport and Clinton. Here the Milwaukee teamed up with the Burlington in operating the jointly owned Davenport, Rock Island & Northwestern Railway. This joint facility started out as the Davenport, Rock Island & Railway Bridge Company in 1884. It subsequently linked Clinton and Davenport with a bridge across the Mississippi to East Moline, Illinois.

With the inauguration of the shortcut, running time of the Southwest Limited was cut and freight service accelerated to and from Kansas City. The cutoff has paid for its original investment many times over in economical operation.

Another line change of more modest proportions occurred when a low-grade alternate route was constructed on the main line between Green Island on the Mississippi and Browns—twelve miles inland. In the course of time, the old main stem between Browns and Elk River Junction, via Preston, reverted to local freight service, and in 1953 the nine-mile sector from the Junction to Miles was retired.

It should be pointed out that while the Milwaukee's expansion program in Iowa had run its course, such was not the case on the other parts of the system. For some years the road had looked longingly at the Pacific Coast as it extended its lines westward into the Dakotas. But it was not until November 1905 that the route to the West Coast was authorized. This was a bold step, for approximately 1,400 miles of new construction were involved. Furthermore, it meant crossing five mountain ranges—the Big Belt Mountains and the Rockies in Montana, the Bitter Root Mountains in Montana and Idaho, and the Saddle Mountains and the Cascades in Washington.

In the spring of 1906 construction was started, and on July 4, 1909, the entire line was opened for freight service and shortly thereafter for passengers. But the extension to Seattle and Tacoma proved a heavy financial burden. Then, too, the completion of the Panama Canal in 1914 and adverse economic conditions in the Northwest further weakened the road. The company went into receivership in 1925, which continued until it was reorganized on January 13, 1928. On that date the Chicago, Milwaukee, St. Paul & Pacific Railroad assumed control of the property. With the addition of "& Pacific" to the name, the line became known as the "Milwaukee Road" rather than the "St. Paul," by which it was previously called. For clarity, however, the Milwaukee Road has been uniformly used throughout this history and is so known by railroad men and the public generally today.

Shortly after the extension westward had been completed, the company decided to double-track its Omaha line. Work was started at Sabula in 1912, and by 1914 it was completed to Manilla. The sixty-mile gap to Council Bluffs was never double-tracked. Ironically, the increased traffic which was expected failed to materialize. The Milwaukee was now in a position to compete for Pacific Coast freight over its own rails, and the Union Pacific looked coolly at its new rival.

THE SLIM PRINCESS

In 1936 the last narrow-gauge railroad in Iowa ceased operation. This was the Milwaukee's 35-mile Bellevue and Cascade branch. Of the dozen slim-gauge lines in the state, the Cascade road lived to be the oldest and the best known. The "narrow-gauge fever" which spread across the country in the 1870s led to the construction of about 565 miles of three-foot gauge in Iowa. But in nearly every case, these three-footers were purchased by large railroads, widened, and continued operating. Several branches of the Burlington, one of the North Western, and the now-abandoned Lehigh spur of the Fort Dodge, Des Moines & Southern were originally three feet wide.

We have seen how the Milwaukee's Waukon Junction–Waukon, Beulah-Elkader, Clive-Boone branches and the Des Moines–Fonda segment of the Spirit Lake line were built to narrow gauge and later widened. This left the Cascade branch as not only the sole narrow gauge in the Hawkeye State but the last on the entire Milwaukee system. Because of its historic and sentimental importance, we will dwell on it at some length.

The little road came into existence because the people of Cascade feared their inland town would be more or less doomed if it did not have a railroad connection to the outside world. One by one plans for railroads going through the community failed to materialize. If its citizens were to be on a railroad, it was evident they would have to build one themselves. Finally, on October 13, 1876, Dr. W. H. Francis of Cascade wrote to Captain M. R. Brown of Bellevue concerning the feasibility of constructing a narrow-gauge road from Bellevue to Cascade. The idea met a favorable response in Bellevue. So with high courage they incorporated the Chicago, Bellevue, Cascade & Western Railway on January 30, 1878. Ground was broken in Cascade on September 19, and the route was partly graded to Washington Mills. Little, however, was done beyond that point to reach the eastern terminus at Bellevue on the River Road. Early in 1879 J. W. Tripp resigned from the presidency, and his place was taken by James Hill, who was formerly vice president.

The road had exhausted its finances when George Runkel, acting on behalf of the Joy interests, came along to refinance the line and complete it. By the end of 1879 he had the entire railroad in operation, and the following year it was taken over by the Chicago, Clinton, Dubuque & Minnesota Rail Road. A few months later the Milwaukee purchased the latter company, which included the "Cascade" narrow gauge.

Probably because of the prevailing interest in narrow-gauge railroads and on account of the rugged topography of Jackson and Dubuque counties through which the road ran, a three-foot width was selected. At any rate, the line abounded in steep grades and sharp curves. About six miles west of Bellevue there was a five-mile grade, much of which was at 2.8 percent. Once the trains reached the summit, they careened for a little over a mile downhill into La Motte. Other roller-coaster grades appeared east of Zwingle, near Washington Mills, and midway between Fillmore and Cascade. In fact, there was only one section nearly level, this being the four-mile stretch east of Fillmore.

On account of the long, steep grades, trains frequently had to "double" the hills. In this operation a train is divided on a siding at the bottom of a hill so the engineer can take one part up at a time. After the head-end is safely up-grade and set out, the engineer returns for the remainder of his train. Upon surmounting the hill again, the two parts are coupled together, and the whole train highballs down the line.

The Bellevue & Cascade Railroad had an interesting and characteristic assortment of motive power. It began business with two trim, straight-stacked 4-4-0s, outshopped by Pittsburgh Locomotive Works. Later, as trains became heavier, a secondhand Brooks Mogul, or 2-6-0 type, was purchased. A still more powerful Consolidation was acquired, which had seen service on the storied South Park line in Colorado. Two more secondhand Moguls, both constructed by Baldwin, were later put on the roster.

At first the line operated regular passenger service; but as riders decreased with the coming of the automobile, mixed trains prevailed. In February 1907 one of the latter came rollicking down-grade across the curved trestle near Washington Mills and derailed. Several freight cars, along with the passenger coach, fell about forty feet, killing two riders and a crewman. This was the only fatal accident to passengers in the history of the road.

In the early period cattle proved to be a lucrative source of revenue, and the branch had thirty-eight stock cars to haul this type of traffic. Since all freight had to be transshipped at Bellevue due to the break in gauge, livestock and other commodities were delayed in transit. Because of this drawback and the fact that the narrow-gauge rolling stock was limited in number and in carrying capacity, many and varied were the complaints of service and equipment.

Finally, shippers sought to have the Board of Railroad Commissioners compel the Milwaukee to widen the track to the standard four feet, eight-and-one-half-inch gauge. The commission had power to broaden the gauge of any railroad if it appeared to be "reasonable and just."

When hearings were held in 1915, the Milwaukee took the stand that it would not be feasible to build a standard-gauge railroad on the slim-gauge right-of-way. Furthermore, to relocate the branch where necessary and to reduce the grade to a maximum of 1.5 percent would cost about $2 million. In view of the losses sustained in operating the line, the Milwaukee contended it could not afford to widen, rebuild, or relocate the branch.

Speaking on behalf of shippers, I. W. Troxel, a civil engineer, argued that the cost of relocation would be slightly under a million dollars. To broaden the gauge on the present alignment, he put the figure at $451,115, which was about $100,000 less than the railroad's estimate for the same project.

At the hearing travelers and shippers had the opportunity to voice their complaints, which ranged all the way from the "*fear* of accident" and the allegation that narrow gauge detracted from the value of land to such tangible items as crippling of hogs and inadequate bedding of livestock in the transfer at Bellevue.

After pondering over the matter, the commission ruled out more than half of the complaints on the ground that they were not peculiar to narrow-gauge operation but more common to branch service as a whole. Moreover, it reminded the complainants that the act "does not contemplate that the location or route of the road shall be changed; authority is given the Commission to make orders only with reference to the gauge, and it cannot order a change of route or relocation of any part of the road."

The commission also had quite a time in trying to determine the amount of loss sustained by the branch. How much of the deficit should be assigned to the narrow gauge and how much to the rest of the railroad? There was a wide divergence of opinion on the matter, and no conclusion was reached.

Another furor resulted from the Milwaukee's arbitrarily limiting the grade to 1.5 percent. On this issue Commissioner Clifford Thorne vigorously dissented. He pointed out the twenty-one-mile Creston, Winterset & Des Moines Railway, which commenced operation between Creston and Macksburg in 1912, had an elevation of 5 percent. The commissioner, however, failed to add that the road with the toboggan-like grade was virtually insolvent, and, as a matter of fact, it was dismantled in 1918.

Weighing all the testimony on both sides, the commission concluded "that it was not feasible to standardize the Cascade Branch of the CM&stP Railroad upon its present alignment and grade." As a corollary it declared "that to require the Cascade Branch to be standardized would be in effect, a confiscation of the property of the branch line." That ended for all time the likelihood of Iowa's lingering narrow gauge being converted to standard; and the decision ultimately sealed the fate of the diminutive carrier.

The little trains continued to whistle through the hills and struggle up the grades, hauling fewer passengers and less tonnage as highways improved. It was a friendly, picturesque anachronism living on borrowed time. Operating on a marginal basis at best, the road rolled up alarming deficits during the early depression years. Finally, the Milwaukee, in poor financial health itself, petitioned to abandon the branch. The petition was granted and abandonment authorized in March 1933.

But in a last-ditch attempt to continue operation, a new company known as the Bellevue & Cascade Railroad was formed. The Milwaukee agreed to sell the line on easy, long-term payments, and service was resumed with rail motor units hauling mail and express. After a valiant attempt to make both ends meet, the new operators came out very much in the red. Regretfully they called it quits, and in January 1936 Iowa's narrow-gauge relic was sold for scrap.

THE ROAD OF ORANGE TRAINS

The harvest orange trains of the Milwaukee blended in well with the billowing fields of tall Iowa corn. Other roads, in sober contrast, had passenger equipment of an orthodox Pullman green service the state. But the Milwaukee was as distinctive in color as it was independent in management. For over a half century it operated its own sleepers, whereas nearly all the other lines contracted with the Pullman Company for such equipment. Apart from this, the Milwaukee built many of its own locomotives; and its Pacifics and Northerns are a legend to this day.

Excluding the North Western, the trains of the Milwaukee were the only ones crossing Iowa on double-track most of the way. The "high iron" between Chicago and Council Bluffs always commanded a goodly amount of freight going through the Omaha gateway. While for many years the North Western was the Union Pacific's preferred passenger connection, the Milwaukee had one or more trains with through equipment to the Pacific Coast for at least fifty years. There was a time, also, when the Union Pacific shifted its crack Overland Limited to the road with the orange trains east of Omaha.

During the heyday of passenger service the colorful Milwaukee cars blanketed Iowa. For a road which bypassed most of the larger cities in the state or served them by branch lines, the Milwaukee had an amazing lot of through coach and sleeper routes. In addition to the solid trains to the West Coast via Omaha, the once-popular line of the Southwest Limited accounted for many passengers through the Kansas City gateway. Up until the Milwaukee built the Kansas City Cutoff, all Chicago–Kansas City trains went via Cedar Rapids. With the advent of the cutoff, the shorter route through southeastern Iowa was used. Even so, for several years an Iowa section of the Southwest Limited carried a sleeper between Cedar Rapids and Kansas City.

Very popular around the turn of the century were the "Personally Conducted" Judson Tourist Cars, which were operated on Thursday and Saturday westward, and on Monday and Wednesday eastward, through Iowa.

They were through sleepers from Chicago via Kansas City to Los Angeles, Santa Barbara, and San Francisco over the Missouri Pacific, Rio Grande, and Southern Pacific railroads. The berth fare, Chicago to West Coast points, was only $7.

Among the standard through sleeping car runs, long since abandoned, was the Chicago–Twin City service via Savanna, Illinois, Dubuque, and Calmar. Dubuque, now without north-and-south passenger trains, was once an important center for rail service up and down the river on the Iowa side. The city was favored with a set-out sleeper from Chicago, along with a sleeper to Rapid City, South Dakota, via North McGregor (now Marquette) and the Iowa & Dakota Division.

The yellow-and-red timetable in 1909 indicates an equally strange "buffet sleeper" from Rapid City to Minneapolis via Calmar and another from Rapid City to Chicago via Dubuque and Savanna. For some reason through sleeper service from South Dakota points—as well as from the Twin Cities —to Chicago did not use the line by way of Prairie du Chien and Madison, Wisconsin, until the 1920s. But when the Madison line became an accepted route, Dubuque, as far as the Milwaukee was concerned, regressed to a community with infrequent branch-line coach service until all the road's passenger trains were removed.

Elsewhere in Iowa, sleepers rolled over the prairies on now-forgotten routes. One could get a berth at Union Station, Des Moines; and in the course of the night he would be taken up to the main line at Madrid, thence westward to Manilla, from whence he would travel the branch to Sioux City, arriving at the latter community in time for breakfast.

For day-coach riders there was through service between Minneapolis and Mason City via Austin, Minnesota. Although there were faster and more comfortable Limiteds on the Rock Island linking the Twin Cities with Cedar Rapids, the Milwaukee had a through coach between the two destinations. Leaving Minneapolis, the orange car went through Cresco and Calmar; and after a detour westward to Jackson Junction, it meandered southward on a circuitous course via Delaware and Monticello, finally arriving at Cedar Rapids twelve hours later.

On a humid summer day when it was sweltering in Des Moines, a relaxing ride in the observation-lounge or dinner in the buffet was a part of the fun in going up to the Okoboji–Spirit Lake region for a weekend. But long before through service was featured between the capital and Iowa's two great lakes, the Milwaukee sought to make Okoboji a fashionable and popular summer resort. Indeed, the Milwaukee and Rock Island pioneered in advertising the two lakes and in making them readily accessible to Io-wans. By low fares, frequent excursion trains, steamers on the lakes, and luxurious hotels, the railroads gave the initial impetus to the lovely region which later came to full fruition with widespread use of the automobile.

Since the Rock Island more or less preempted the Spirit Lake section, the Milwaukee concentrated its efforts on the Okoboji area. At a point known as Arnolds Park, where East Okoboji meets the waters of West Oko-boji, the road built a fifty-room inn. Called Hotel Okoboji, the imposing four-story structure stood beside the little depot. It had a restaurant and ballroom facing the lake, and it was regarded as a choice spot for dining and dancing in that vacation country.

Even before the Milwaukee financed the hotel, the road exploited the lakes with a palatial eighty-foot steamboat christened *Ben Lennox*, in honor of an official of the company. She was built in 1884 on the lakeside at a cost of between $6,000 and $7,000. With the possible exception of the Rock Island's S.S. *Queen*, the *Lennox* was the largest and finest boat on the lakes at that time. For years the two railroads sought to outdo each other in providing attractive rail service to the region, in maintaining the most luxurious steamers on the waters, and in the finest accommodations in company-sponsored hotels.

Besides the "railroad boats," smaller craft maintained scheduled sailings from points on the lakes to connect with the Milwaukee trains at Arnolds Park and those of the Rock Island at Orleans and West Okoboji. For sev-eral decades it was a common sight to see long lines of orange day coaches lined up in the Okoboji region as excursion trains, run in sections, puffed along the branch. Waiting boats were always on hand to take passengers to resorts, camps, and picnic grounds, for which the locale was famous.

Although Hotel Okoboji was burned in 1911, having been in use for about a decade, and the *Ben Lennox* was run by the railroad for only a few years, the Milwaukee continued to haul trainloads of vacationists until mo-tor vehicles became commonplace. Even then, parlor cars and buffet–drawing-room–observation units were still an added attraction on the branch when such vehicles had been removed from other secondary runs.

Without doubt, the strangest national convention for which the Mil-waukee unwittingly helped to provide transportation was that of "hoboes in Britt." The idea of a national assemblage of hoboes stemmed from the curiosity of T. A. Potter, a local businessman. He heard of a conclave of tramps in Illinois and wrote them, half seriously, that Britt would make an admirable locale for a national hobo convention. The idea gained momentum, and Potter was made Britt's first member of the "Order of the Honorary Sons of Rest," identified by a membership button for "Tourist Union No. 63." E. N. Bailey, editor of the *Britt Tribune*, joined Potter in promising a carload of beer and food to sustain up to five hundred tramps. It was pointed out that fast freight trains barreled through the town on the Milwaukee's main line from Chicago to Rapid City and that convenient north-and-south service was provided by the Minneapolis & St. Louis Railway.

The happy world of trampdom responded with enthusiasm at the prospect of free lodging, free "grub," and most of all free beer. Britt set August 22, 1900, as the date of the convention and waited to see what would happen. They soon found out, as tattered delegates alighted from boxcars of every train a day or two before the meeting. But the grand officers of the hobo association came in one of the Milwaukee's own orange sleepers, which was set out at Britt on the morning of the convention. Most of the conventioneers, however, came by "side-door Pullman," "riding the blinds" of passenger trains or the "rods" of freights.

It was estimated that 250 bona fide delegates, ranging from "society" tramps to genuine hoboes, attended the convention. Onlookers and town folk accounted for about five thousand more people. Ample lodging was provided at the fairgrounds, where the Weary Willies were housed in hog and cattle pens provided with clean, straw bedding. Chicago, St. Louis, and Twin City newspapers sent reporters to cover what is said to have been Iowa's first national convention.

The convention was well behaved, considering the nature of the guests, and it gave nationwide publicity to Britt. Very few delegates overstayed their welcome, for they promptly left town after the meeting. The next day saw Milwaukee freights carrying more than their usual quota of transients as police and trainmen graciously looked the other way. For one time, at least, they were acknowledged guests of the Milwaukee Road, as they had been of Britt the previous day.

To modernize its service through Iowa in the years preceding World War II, the Milwaukee added the Midwest Hiawatha to its growing fleet of streamliners in 1940. The sleek new train with its Tip Top Tap Dining Car and beaver tail observation-lounge created a sensation. It operated between Chicago, Sioux City, and Sioux Falls, with an Omaha section via Manilla.

Branch lines, on the other hand, often saw small, more economical motor units replacing steam trains where passenger service had not been already discontinued. Friendly "doodlebugs," as they were nicknamed, continued to link countryside and town. The late Robert S. Cooper, Sr., who for seventeen years was brakeman on the "motor train" between Cedar Rapids and Ottumwa, recalled the esteem in which railroaders were held by local people. His most poignant memory was the generosity of the thrifty Germans from the Amana Colonies at Christmas. They would appear at the rural depots with savory hams, delicious wines, and gifts for the crew. "If those folks took a liking to you," Cooper remarked, "there's nothing they wouldn't do for you."

The familiar orange trains, however, began to thin out as automobile, bus, and plane competition became more pronounced. Then, a few years after 1955, when the Milwaukee officially changed its color to yellow, only the main line to Omaha and the branch to Sioux City retained passenger service within the state.

THE BIG SWITCH

In the summer of 1955 Milwaukee track gangs began feverishly to resurface and lay new rail on the Iowa Division. Few people outside the Milwaukee Railroad, and not many in it, knew the reason for this sudden activity. It was not until almost the day of the "Big Switch" that all the nation became aware the Union Pacific would route its streamliners, operating through Omaha to and from Chicago, over Milwaukee rails effective October 30. The news weeklies and the country's leading papers heralded the fact that, with the termination of the Union Pacific's seventy-five-year-old agreement with the North Western, it would switch its passenger trains over to the Milwaukee.

The Milwaukee was so elated with the changeover it advertised the fact in some 138 newspapers, advertisements often occupying a full page. To expedite Union Pacific trains, it resolved to spend $7 million, of which $5.5 million was for new diesels and $1.5 million for improved signaling. What is even more striking, the road voluntarily changed its color from the traditional orange to the Union Pacific's yellow with red and gray trim.

On the day of the changeover the five crack Union Pacific streamliners, the City of Los Angeles, City of Denver, City of Portland, City of San Francisco (which is operated west of Ogden by Southern Pacific), and the Los Angeles Challenger began operating over Milwaukee rails east of Omaha. Despite some minor "bugs" in the new operation, the first week tallied a 98 percent on-time record. President J. P. Kiley was on hand in Chicago's Union Station to celebrate the Challenger–Midwest Hiawatha, first of the

trains to leave the Windy City. In Iowa people all along the line came out
to welcome the new service. A crowd of more than three hundred greeted
the Challenger at Perry, while at Marion Mayor L. A. Franke (who had
worked for the Milwaukee for thirty years) presided at a ribbon-cutting
ceremony honoring the new service with Union Pacific vice president
P. J. Lynch.

With the inauguration of the new trains, the main line to Omaha has
been constantly improved and Centralized Traffic Control extended over
virtually the entire route. Although the line in Iowa is now almost entirely
single track, its efficiency is nearly that of its former dual tracks, thanks to
CTC and long passing sidings.

In keeping with modern economical operation in which trains are consolidated whenever possible, numerous modifications have been made
since the changeover in 1955. Schedules have been altered and trains combined so that instead of five streamliners each way, there are now only two,
plus the Milwaukee's Arrow to Omaha, Sioux City, and Sioux Falls. The
Midwest Hiawatha had lost out in the shuffling, and it no longer appears
on the timecard, a fact that is much lamented by many Iowans.

By combining the Cities of Los Angeles and San Francisco and the Challenger, one train takes the place of three. Likewise, by consolidating the
Cities of Denver and Portland, another train has been eliminated. In times
of heavy seasonal traffic, particularly during the summer vacation period,
some streamliners may be run in sections or as separate trains.

It is a common sight to see trains of twenty or more cars on these luxurious streamliners. All the "Cities" trains stop at Marion and Perry in both
directions. From either of these Iowa towns, one can ride the finest trains
to Los Angeles, San Francisco, Portland, Salt Lake City, Denver, and intermediate points, stretching from Lake Michigan to the Pacific Coast.

What local service is required is performed by the Arrow. When the
Sioux was withdrawn from service between Chicago and Canton, South
Dakota, in 1960, thereby terminating passenger service across northern
Iowa, the Milwaukee concentrated its attention on its rehabilitated trans-
Iowa line to the south. Thus, while the Omaha line is the only route of the
Milwaukee's passenger trains across the state, it is more important than
ever before. There may not be the abundance of trains on this line as there
was when the orange Limited streaked over the rails, but the yellow streamliners are much longer, more significant, and much finer than their steam-
powered predecessors of yesteryears.

THE MILWAUKEE TODAY

Essentially, the Milwaukee looks the same on the map of Iowa as it did during the last century. But many branch lines which were so important to it fifty years ago have become of less significance today. Even at that, comparatively little pruning has taken place, considering the extensive mileage within the state.

Among the first of the early Iowa abandonments was the retiring of the little-used cutoff between Rock Valley and Hudson, South Dakota, in 1918. Next came the Farley-Worthington segment on the branch from Monticello. Indeed, the complex of branches from Monticello to Davenport, and from Eldridge Junction to Maquoketa, proved to be so light in traffic that substantial parts of them were removed. The section on the former, between Oxford Junction and Dixon, was scrapped in 1940 and between Monticello and Oxford Junction in 1957.

On the Maquoketa branch, the nine-mile section between De Witt and Long Grove was abandoned in 1931, and seven years later tracks were out of service from Long Grove to Eldridge Junction. The little two-mile extension from Maquoketa to Hurstville was retired in 1934.

The longest single abandonment, however, was the fifty-eight-mile Turkey River–West Union branch, which ceased operating in 1938. It was a victim of the depression, the motor truck, and possible overexpansion in the first place.

Line revision in the vicinity of Madrid in the Des Moines River valley has resulted in considerable revamping of operation. After the main line was shortened by the erection of the lofty new bridge across the river at Madrid, the old five-mile route through Phildia to the south was scrapped between 1918 and 1922.

Then, to eliminate the costly high bridge over the Des Moines River on the Boone-Clive branch, the section between Madrid and Granger was abandoned in 1943. By building a new road from Granger to Woodward Junction, where it connected with the main line, operation was continued. The historic High Bridge, which brought the original narrow gauge up from Des Moines, was subsequently dismantled.

The last addition to the Milwaukee in Iowa came when it purchased thirteen miles of the Minneapolis & St. Louis's Storm Lake branch in 1936. This line connects Storm Lake with Rembrandt, and it was slated for abandonment by the M&stL.

No, there are not many changes on the map, but there are far-reaching changes in methods of operation. Up until about the time of the depression, six Milwaukee division offices were located in Iowa. Five of these had much if not all their mileage within the state. In the south, Des Moines was headquarters of the Des Moines Division as was Marion for the Iowa Division. Down near the southern border, Ottumwa Junction had jurisdiction over the Kansas City Division. To the east, Dubuque supervised the Dubuque Division; and on the north, Mason City was the nerve center for the lengthy Iowa & Dakota Division. Finally, on the west, there was Sioux City, whose responsibility covered the Sioux City & Dakota Division, a territory largely outside of Iowa.

Today there are just three divisions in Iowa, and only one has its headquarters in the state. This is the Iowa Division with its central office in Perry. The other two divisions, the Dubuque & Illinois and the Iowa, Minnesota & Dakota, as their names would indicate, are not entirely confined to Iowa.

Modern diesel locomotives have eliminated delays incident to steam operation, such as stopping for coal and water, to say nothing of time lost in double-heading and frequent engine inspection. Longer and heavier trains on accelerated schedules to meet competition have tended to lengthen runs.

If the sleek "Cities" streamliners are the pride of the railroad, the "hot" time freights over the same track are the lifeblood of its existence. Currently, three scheduled fast freights shuttle across the state to and from Council Bluffs in each direction. They operate in close connection with the Union Pacific and account for considerable transcontinental tonnage going over the route.

They operate over a well-maintained, rock-ballasted track on 115-pound rails over a route protected by CTC and cab signaling. Radio communication between trainmen and enginemen is provided, along with communication to wayside points.

To expedite meat shipments and other high-grade commodities, a time freight highballs out of Sioux Falls, South Dakota, via Canton, and thence through meatpacking centers of Spencer, Mason City, and Dubuque to Savanna, Illinois. At Savanna, a connecting train rushes the meat to Chicago.

Another fast freight is carded between the Twin Cities and the Kansas City gateway via La Crescent, Minnesota, and Dubuque. In addition, going through southeastern Iowa the Milwaukee has two scheduled fast freights each way to and from Kansas City.

The Milwaukee has coordinated its service so that important branch line points, such as Sioux City and Des Moines, have time freights which connect with main line "hotshots." The road is also enthusiastically fostering trailer-on-flatcar service, Flexivan container traffic, and multilevel automobile shipments.

Confident of the fact that excellent passenger trains advertise a railroad as nothing else can and that such goodwill attracts freight, the Milwaukee is pleased with the increased importance of its main line across Iowa. The superiority of the "Cities" streamliners for passengers is being matched by the prompt dispatch of freight for shippers.

Palimpsest 45 (May 1964)

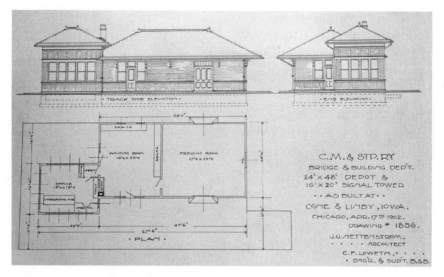

The Milwaukee Road contributed to the diversity of the Iowa railroad landscape. Although the majority of its depots were combination ones, with a section for passengers and freight and a central office, some were different. The Milwaukee erected unusual depot-signal towers at Cone and Limby on its Davenport–Ottumwa–Kansas City line. H. Roger Grant Collection.

Railroaders and townspeople gather at the Milwaukee Road depot in Lost Nation, a station on the company's main line across Iowa. Not long after this photograph was taken in 1918, automobile and truck competition lessened the importance of this local institution. H. Roger Grant Collection.

Less glamorous than main line trains were ones that consisted of gasoline or later diesel-electric motors that handled a passenger coach or two. In the late 1940s, Motor No. 5932 rolled over the 178-mile Des Moines–Spirit Lake branch. George Niles photograph.

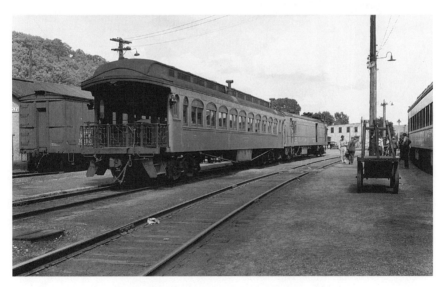

On August 4, 1940, Milwaukee Road Train No. 36, pulled by Motor No. 5928, stands in the Marquette station. A vintage wooden coach provides less-than-modern accommodations. John F. Humiston photograph.

Steam locomotive No. 30 heads Train No. 33, destined for Spirit Lake. The location is Des Moines Union Station, and the date is September 1, 1947. John Humiston photograph.

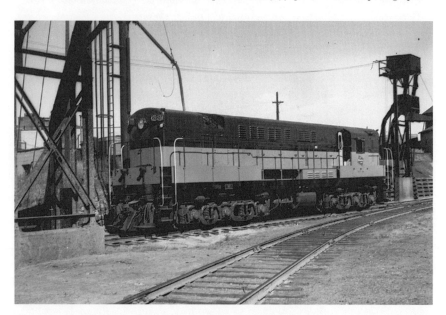

In 1953 a Milwaukee "Baby Trainmaster," built by Fairbanks-Morse, awaits an assignment in the yards of the Des Moines Union Railway. By this time steam was rapidly disappearing from the roster. George Niles photograph.

THE WABASH IN IOWA

BUILDING UP FROM MISSOURI

The Wabash Railroad is famous in song and story. In his book, *The Hobo's Hornbook*, George Milburn includes a colorful ballad entitled "The Wabash Cannonball."

> From the waves of the Atlantic to the wild Pacific shore;
> From the coast of California to ice-bound Labrador,
> There's a train of doozy layout that's well-known to us all—
> It's the "boes" accommodation, called the Wabash Cannonball.
>
> Great cities of importance we reach upon our way,
> Chicago and St. Louis, Rock Island—so they say—
> Then Springfield and Decatur, Peoria—above all—
> We reach them by no other but the Wabash Cannonball.
>
> Now listen to her rumble, now listen to her roar,
> As she echoes down the valley and tears along the shore.
> Now hear the engine's whistle and her mighty hoboes' call
> As we ride the rods and brakebeams on the Wabash Cannonball.

The legendary "Wabash Cannonball" of hobo fame stood for a mythical train which went far beyond the track of the railroad it made famous. As a folksong the "Cannonball" had another long run in jukeboxes throughout America. Either way, it is indicative of the sprawled-out Wabash system, which is the only major United States railroad with its mileage almost equally divided between the Eastern and Western Districts.

Operating from Buffalo to Omaha and Kansas City, the Wabash fell into the anomalous category of being both an "Eastern" and "Western" carrier, although technically it was grouped in the Eastern District. Furthermore, in the days of Jay Gould, the Wabash became the cornerstone of a railroad empire which very nearly reached from coast to coast.

Currently the Wabash has 209 miles of line in Iowa and serves such cities as Council Bluffs, Des Moines, Ottumwa, and Keokuk. During the zenith of Jay Gould's administration it operated about 565 miles of line in the state. Its history in Iowa and elsewhere is one of dramatic growth but followed by a series of receiverships and reorganizations. From a chaotic past, however, it has emerged to become a stable and prosperous railroad.

The beginning of the Wabash in Iowa goes back to the old North Missouri Railroad, which was building northward and westward from St. Louis. In the late 1860s the North Missouri extended to the Iowa state line at Coatesville, Missouri. It was anxious to build to Ottumwa and Cedar Rapids to connect with other rapidly building railroads in those communities. Ultimately, the North Missouri hoped to be a part of a new through line linking St. Louis with the upper Midwest.

Plans to extend into Iowa were broached at a preliminary meeting held in Cedar Rapids on September 27, 1865, at which A. W. Fagan of St. Louis presided. Delegates from Iowa and Missouri formed the St. Louis & Cedar Rapids Railway to build from the terminus of the North Missouri at Coatesville to Cedar Rapids. J. P. Farley, Dubuque County, and George Gillespie, Wapello County, were the prime movers in launching the new road.

On October 23, 1865, the company was duly incorporated with H. G. Angle of Cedar Rapids, president; C. C. Warden of Ottumwa, vice president; and E. L. Burton, also of Ottumwa, secretary. Very little progress was made, however, until H. H. Trimble of Bloomfield succeeded to the presidency in the fall of 1868. By December of that year the road built into Appanoose County and established the town of Moulton. Two years later the tracks reached Ottumwa amid wild rejoicing.

This called for an elaborate banquet at Taylor & Blake's Hall on July 26, 1870. After the festivities a special train took the celebrants over the newly constructed route to St. Louis. Contemporary accounts suggest the trip was a merry one with abundant refreshments for all.

The "Iowa extension" was operated under lease by the North Missouri; and, like the lessor, it was soon in financial straits. In 1871 Morris K. Jessup became trustee, and four years later it was reorganized as the St. Louis, Ottumwa & Cedar Rapids Railway. Meanwhile, the North Missouri had gone under the hammer to emerge as the St. Louis, Kansas City & Northern Railway, which continued to lease the Iowa road.

In spite of the "Cedar Rapids" in its name, the forty-three-mile road from the Missouri border to Ottumwa apparently gave up all hope of reaching the former city. Des Moines now became the objective of the St. Louis management. Then the notorious New York financier, Jay Gould, got control of the St. Louis, Kansas City & Northern, consolidated it with his other railroad holdings, and changed its name to the more embracive Wabash, St. Louis & Pacific Railway. Thereupon railway management in America, to say nothing of the public, was to witness some swift, unexpected, and far-reaching changes.

Gould wanted Des Moines in his orbit. He enlisted the support of influential people in Iowa's capital city to achieve this end. Prominent citizens, railroad builders, and businessmen of Des Moines joined the "Wabash syndicate" to expedite construction. They incorporated the Des Moines & St. Louis Railroad, January 27, 1881, which was to be built from the capital to Albia, a distance of sixty-eight miles. On November 6, 1882, the first passenger train steamed into Des Moines from St. Louis.

Ostensibly, the Des Moines & St. Louis was a local road. James S. Clarkson, who had been editor of the *Iowa State Register* and postmaster of the city, headed the enterprise. John S. Runnells, also of Des Moines, served as vice president. Secretary of the road was Frederick M. Hubbell, who was active in promoting narrow-gauge lines radiating from the city. Probably the best known of all was Jefferson S. Polk, treasurer of the company. He was a leading figure in building a three-foot gauge line to Adel and in later years fostered the construction of interurban electric lines as well as local trolley routes in Des Moines. But behind these men was the wily brain of Gould. From the time of its completion, the Des Moines line was operated under lease by the Wabash.

The Wabash now had an outlet to Des Moines over its own rails and in conjunction with affiliated roads. It was at best a patchwork of local lines haphazardly linked together. From Des Moines to Albia trains operated over the Des Moines & St. Louis, thence on Francis Drake's Centerville, Moravia & Albia Railway to Centerville, and from the latter point over the Missouri, Iowa & Nebraska Railway to Wabash rails at Glenwood Junction, Missouri, a few miles south of the Iowa-Missouri state line. The remainder of the way to St. Louis was, of course, over the Wabash.

In May 1883 Jay Gould with a party of Wabash executives visited Des Moines. One can visualize the shy, reticent financier coldly inspecting the railroad facilities. Not given to comment, his mind was always active as to ways and means of building up his railroad empire. Whatever may be thought of his business ethics, it was he who did much to bring the Wabash to Des Moines. He had plans for extensive expansion in Iowa, one of which was in southwestern Iowa, where the Wabash had been built into Council Bluffs.

THE WABASH REACHES OMAHA

Omaha loomed large as an objective for the Wabash since it was an important gateway after the first transcontinental railroad was completed in 1869. Previous to this event, a predecessor of the Wabash linked St. Louis with Kansas City. But it was not until the Council Bluffs & St. Louis Railway was incorporated, September 1, 1878, that the way was made clear to tap the Omaha gateway. This line was constructed from Council Bluffs to the Iowa-Missouri border between July 1878 and October 11, 1879. At the border it connected with a branch running through Pattonsburg, Missouri, to Brunswick, on the main stem between St. Louis and Kansas City.

The pattern of control was much the same as on the extensions to Ottumwa and Des Moines. The Council Bluffs & St. Louis was operated under lease by the St. Louis, Kansas City & Northern and afterward by its successor, the Wabash, St. Louis & Pacific. Also, according to pattern, the Council Bluffs road went into receivership, and it was reorganized as the Omaha & St. Louis Railway in 1887. It operated the line from Council Bluffs to Pattonsburg, Missouri, a distance of 143 miles.

Little is known about the early corporate history of the Council Bluffs road, for it was run by the Wabash as its "Omaha Division." With the reorganization of the company as the Omaha & St. Louis Railway, however, it issued a separate report to the Iowa Board of Railroad Commissioners. From this report it is noted that five townships in Page County, three in Mills County, and one in Fremont County voted an aggregate of $144,834 to aid in building the original line. Nevertheless, by 1889, out of the road's $ 4,500,000 capital stock, only one share was held in Iowa and that had a market price of $25. The lone shareholder was W. H. M. Pusey, a resident of Council Bluffs.

Most of the executives, along with an overwhelming majority of shareholders, lived in New York City. The only officers from Iowa during this time were General Manager F. M. Gault and Auditor W. L. Bedison, both of whom resided in Council Bluffs. All the directors were from New York City except the solitary Iowa stockholder—Pusey.

In 1889 the road had 144 employees in Iowa. Apart from officers, the best-paid men were locomotive engineers, who averaged $5.25 a day, and the lowest on the scale were sectionmen, whose average pay was $1.10. None of the rolling stock had automatic couplers, although such devices had made their appearance on many roads by this time. Gross earnings, from operation for the year ended June 30, 1889, were $455,509, of which approximately 29 percent came from passenger train operation.

At the time the road was being constructed to Council Bluffs, a feeder line was built from Roseberry, Missouri, to Clarinda under the auspices of the St. Louis, Kansas City & Northern. The twenty-one-mile short line, called the Clarinda & St. Louis Railway, was paralleled by a branch of the Burlington and had little economic justification. The little railroad struggled along for a dozen years, went into receivership in 1886, and was dismantled four years afterward.

By the time the Wabash reached Council Bluffs, Jay Gould had gained control of the system. Now he was in a position to shunt Wabash traffic from the East to connections at Omaha or at Kansas City. He made the most of this by cutting rates and making favorable traffic agreements through either gateway as it seemed expedient. As one who had controlled the Union Pacific and still had a heavy investment in that line, he was in a good position to bargain. By playing one gateway against the other, Gould jeopardized the rate structures in the Midwest. In having the only through line from the West to eastern points, such as Toledo and Detroit, he upset standard traffic patterns and wrought havoc in established rates and routings.

One never knew where Gould would strike next. Ruthless and calculating, he was a wizard in finance and a past master in getting control of railroads. He was equally adept in getting out from under, if they went bankrupt, and coming in by the back door again to regain control under more auspicious circumstances.

By the end of 1881, after a barrage of rate cutting, Gould had forced his way into the Iowa Pool. This association had been formed by all the other trunk lines entering Council Bluffs to stabilize rates. Once in the pool, the Wabash proceeded to cut rates as it had from outside the pool. Not content with his lines to Council Bluffs, Des Moines, and Ottumwa, Gould sought to invade the Burlington territory across southern Iowa.

EXPANSION UNDER GOULD

A glance at the map shows the Wabash's line between Council Bluffs and Chicago is long and circuitous, dipping down as it does into northern Missouri. The Burlington, North Western, and Rock Island railroads, on the contrary, had more direct lines between these points. Gould was as aware of this drawback to his company as he was that the Milwaukee was also pushing its rails across Iowa to Council Bluffs, which it completed in 1882.

Gould knew it would not be feasible to build an additional line all the way across Iowa in the face of well-entrenched competition. There was another alternative, however, which he often had recourse to elsewhere. That was to buy a secondary railroad and extend it to suit his purpose. Gould was an old hand in stringing railroads together by getting control and then merging, leasing, and building until he came up with a new through line. As often as not the "through" road would be hastily built and poorly maintained, but it served to harass its competitors and extend the "Wizard of Wall Street's" railroad dominion.

Gould had his eye on the 142-mile Missouri, Iowa & Nebraska Railway, which extended from Keokuk through the northeastern corner of Missouri to the Iowa communities of Centerville, Corydon, Humeston, and Van Wert. From Van Wert to Shenandoah, on the Wabash's line to Council Bluffs, it was only ninety-five miles. Thus, by extending the short line a little less than a hundred miles westward, the Wabash would have a shorter route from Council Bluffs to Chicago and other eastern points.

It should be noted that the Wabash also served Keokuk. It entered that river town in 1871 by a bridge across the Mississippi River, on which it had trackage rights. From Keokuk a branch extended down to the main line of the Wabash at Bluffs, Illinois, seventy-five miles to the southeast.

Meanwhile, the Burlington became alarmed over Gould's designs. It was generally understood that southern Iowa was strictly Burlington preserves. But there was no stopping the obstreperous Gould. The Burlington tried to get control of the Missouri, Iowa & Nebraska first but was outgeneraled by the quick-thinking, fast-acting Wabash president. Once having gained controlling interest in this short line, Gould had it leased to the Wabash. Then he set out to close the gap by extending the Missouri, Iowa & Nebraska westward to Shenandoah.

Here he was checkmated by Charles Perkins of the Burlington, who threatened reprisal by building into Wabash territory elsewhere. Gould then compromised by granting the Burlington a half interest in the extension. The connecting line, known as the Humeston & Shenandoah Railroad, was thereby completed as a joint enterprise in 1882. It reduced the Wabash's mileage from Council Bluffs to Chicago by nearly a hundred miles.

Another sidelight on these developments was that General Francis M. Drake, who headed the Missouri, Iowa & Nebraska, was also president of the little road linking Centerville with Albia. Known as the Centerville, Moravia & Albia Railroad, it was leased to the Missouri, Iowa & Nebraska and operated in conjunction with the latter company. In 1880, however, the

Wabash leased the Moravia line. In so doing it gave the Wabash a through route from Des Moines to St. Louis over affiliated roads, as we have previously seen.

During this period Gould sought to strengthen his hold in south-central Iowa by leasing the narrow-gauge line running from Waukee to Panora, a distance of twenty-eight miles. Jefferson S. Polk, who was active in extending the Wabash to Des Moines, headed the short line. The three-foot gauge carrier was leased to the Wabash in 1881. At that time it was known as the Des Moines North Western.

To bring the narrow gauge into Des Moines, a new company was formed in 1881 and partly financed by Gould interests. Under the impressive title of the St. Louis, Des Moines & Northern, it built from Des Moines to Waukee, with a branch from Clive to Boone. The forty-two-mile road was completed in 1882. For many years the great railroad builder and Civil War general Grenville M. Dodge headed the company. Dodge was also active in extending the Gould lines in the southwestern part of the country.

The new management planned to run the narrow gauge up into the Storm Lake region, and considerable grading was done in that area. But after extending the rails from Panora to Fonda, the Wabash went into receivership with a resounding crash in 1884. Thereafter, Gould's empire began to crumble.

The two narrow-gauge lines reverted to their owners, and, after a round of bankruptcy, they were merged into one company and widened to standard gauge. In 1894 the Milwaukee Road gained controlling interest and five years afterward purchased the short line. Today the ex-narrow-gauge lines perform the important function of bringing the Milwaukee into Des Moines over two separate routes.

Jay Gould's "shortcut across Iowa" never lived up to its expectation and even under Wabash management retained the status of a branch line. After the Wabash bankruptcy the Missouri, Iowa & Nebraska was reorganized and run independently as the Keokuk & Western Railroad. Later it was taken over by the Burlington and run as a secondary line. In recent years it has undergone piecemeal dismemberment until nothing remains west of Centerville except for a thirteen-mile stretch between Corydon and Humeston and a shorter stub connecting Clearfield and Merle.

As for the Albia and Centerville road, it eked out a precarious existence when cast adrift by the Wabash. General Drake, who later became governor of Iowa, continued to head the short line for many years. After his death it was electrified and operated as an interurban electric railroad. The line

north of Moravia was later abandoned, but the rest of the property operates today for freight service only as the Southern Iowa Railway.

With the shrinkage of mileage in Iowa occasioned by receivership, the
Wabash Railroad's Des Moines–Albia line no longer connected with the
rest of the system through affiliated roads. Fortunately, the Rock Island
had a connection between the Des Moines and Ottumwa branches of the
Wabash. Arrangements were made for running rights over the Rock Island from Harvey, on the Des Moines line, to Ottumwa via Givin, a distance
of thirty-seven miles. While a roundabout routing, it served to keep the
Wabash system in lower Iowa united. For many years afterward, however,
the track between Harvey and Albia remained unused because of light
traffic and competition from a parallel and better equipped line of the
Burlington.

Detouring Des Moines–St. Louis trains via Ottumwa, nevertheless,
turned out to be slow, cumbersome, and in many ways unsatisfactory. The
solution was, of course, to build a short, direct route between Albia and
Moulton. This was finally done by incorporating the Moulton, Albia & Des
Moines Railroad in 1899 to construct the desired link. The twenty-eight-
mile road was completed that year and promptly sold to the Wabash. The
new line closely followed the abandoned right-of-way of the Burlington
from Albia to Moravia; and from Hilton to Moravia it actually used the old
roadbed.

The region between Albia and Centerville is awash with memories of
mines and miners, for coal hauling was once a major source of revenue.
Extensive mine branches and spurs formerly dotted the area when mining was at its peak. The Wabash's once-flourishing coal trackage south and
west of Tracy was locally known as the "Pumpkin Vine." While much of the
mining is no longer profitable, the Tracy yard still has enough trackage to
handle 110 cars.

Perhaps there was no comparable area in Iowa that had such a welter of
partly built railroads paralleling each other. The region abounds in derelict branches, abandoned mine spurs, and defunct electric railways.

"FOLLOW THE FLAG"

For years the Wabash Railroad has had a banner with the inscription "Wabash" emblazoned on it and the catch line "Follow the Flag" written above
it. Passengers were urged to "Follow the Flag" when it came to traveling
in Wabash territory. The banner came to be regarded as a colophon for
speedy, dependable service.

In bygone days the Wabash featured luxurious name-trains from St. Louis through Council Bluffs and Omaha to West Coast points. Although Omaha never had the stature of Kansas City as the Wabash's western gateway, Omaha was still very important to the railroad.

During the latter part of Jay Gould's domination of the Union Pacific he had a merry time shunting passengers and freight to the Wabash at Council Bluffs. When engaged in his classic rate wars with the Union Pacific's other Omaha connections, Gould suddenly, and often without warning, shifted traffic to the all-Wabash route to Toledo and other eastern points. Being outside the Iowa Pool until the last few years of ineffective existence, Gould used the Wabash as a tool to outwit his federated rivals.

Since it originated less traffic than other roads of comparable size, the Wabash management aggressively sought interline traffic. From time to time it boasted of through sleepers to San Francisco on its Omaha line in conjunction with the Union Pacific and Southern Pacific. Then, too, when the old Wabash, St. Louis & Pacific had its first diner, this luxurious car was used exclusively on the fast train to and from St. Louis and run in and out of Council Bluffs.

In the late 1940s one could take the Omaha Limited, which carried a sleeper for San Francisco, from St. Louis at 7:50 P.M. The train arrived in Council Bluffs at 8:01 the next morning and twenty minutes later pulled into Omaha. Here the West Coast Pullman was set out and recoupled to the historic Overland Limited of the Union Pacific. Two mornings afterward the Overland Limited arrived at the Southern Pacific's Oakland pier, where an awaiting ferry took it to the foot of Market Street in San Francisco.

The Wabash train stopped at all stations in Iowa. A citizen of Strahan (population fifty), for example, could board the sleeper for the Golden Gate as readily as a passenger from a big city. Rural communities appreciated the Wabash's readiness to stop the Limited "on flag," whereas most other roads would not deign to call at such a tiny community.

Better known to Iowans, however, was the service to Des Moines. To reach the capital city from St. Louis was quite an undertaking. We have seen the Wabash line built from Des Moines to Albia in 1882. From the latter town the southbound train for St. Louis was shunted over the uncertain rails of the affiliated Centerville, Moravia & Albia to Centerville. Here it was again switched, this time to the Wabash-controlled Missouri, Iowa & Nebraska road for a twenty-one-mile run to Glenwood Junction, Missouri. At the Junction, the cars were finally returned to Wabash rails for the rest of the way to St. Louis.

The trip between Des Moines and St. Louis was something of an adventure, or an ordeal, depending on how one looked at it. By the time a passenger experienced traveling over the fifty-six-pound rails of the unballasted Centerville, Moravia & Albia road, he was conditioned to branch-line railroading at its worst.

When, at a later date, through trains were detoured via the Rock Island between Harvey and Ottumwa, this lengthened the mileage of the Des Moines–St. Louis route. Although the track may have been a shade better than the Albia route, no one boasted of the amenities of riding this line. When the Wabash completed its shortcut between Albia and Moulton, however, the new all-Wabash route became increasingly popular.

Passengerwise, the Des Moines branch reached its zenith after through coach and Pullman service was inaugurated between St. Louis and the Twin Cities in 1902. This was in connection with the Minneapolis & St. Louis–Iowa Central route by way of Albia and Albert Lea, Minnesota.

Always on the alert for more traffic, the Wabash was eager to join hands with the Minneapolis & St. Louis, which controlled the Iowa Central, in fostering joint through service. For its part, the Minneapolis & St. Louis wanted to continue its St. Louis service, and the road conducted a spirited contest for the best name for a new train to operate in conjunction with the Wabash. Out of about a thousand entries, L F. Day, vice president of the Minneapolis & St. Louis, and A. B. Cutts, its general passenger agent, selected the North Star Limited. For over three decades the North Star proved to be a popular train in the Midwest.

It proudly began operation with "electrically-lighted sleepers and chair cars" and high-caliber "dining car service" by way of Albia. As late as 1932 the dinner menu included a wide variety of selections at moderate cost. Passengers had the choice of chicken á la king, broiled steak, fried chicken, grilled lamp chops on toast, loin pork chops sauté with fried apple, omelette with bacon or chopped ham, and ham or bacon with eggs. Two fresh vegetables were included, along with a salad, bread and butter, a beverage; and for dessert, lemon cream pie, apple pie, or ice cream. The tab: $1.50.

To advertise the North Star as well as to provide a new insignia for the railroad, the Minneapolis & St. Louis had a caricature of a man running. His head, arms, and legs protruded from a large circle. Within the circle-bands was the name of the railroad, and serving as a spoke was a rectangular block on which was inscribed: "Albert Lea Route." Underneath the feet of the little fellow was the legend, "The Road that Runs." The comical insignia was designed by the well-known Minneapolis caricaturist Charles L.

Bartholomew, generally known as "Bart." It was widely used and served to identify the Minneapolis & St. Louis to the traveling public, as did the more orthodox flag of the Wabash.

The North Star Limited, in addition to its St. Louis–Twin Cities consist, provided sleepers and coaches between St. Louis and Des Moines. At one time it also had a Des Moines–Kansas City sleeper. The North Star was finally withdrawn in 1938, but Wabash continued its Des Moines sleeper until the late 1950s. Then, when the Wabash dropped its coach service on the branch September 30, 1959, it marked the final Wabash passenger train out of the Des Moines Union Station. Mr. R. E. Hughes, who called the first train from that station in 1898, came out of retirement to call the last.

The imposing block-long, two-story, stone-and-brick building was jointly owned by the Wabash and Milwaukee railroads. Besides the owning lines, it had the Burlington and the Great Western as tenants. In 1905 fifty trains used the station weekdays. One by one, however, its users gave up passenger service into Des Moines or moved their facilities elsewhere. The Great Western erected its own depot in the 1950s (and later abandoned passenger service), and around the same period the Milwaukee and the Burlington withdrew their branch-line passenger runs into the city.

With the closing of Union Station, only the nearby Rock Island depot was left to sell tickets on that road—the sole passenger line operating trains in or out of Des Moines. Incidentally, about two-thirds of the Union Station building has been razed. What is left is occupied by the local offices of the Wabash and Milwaukee railroads, Western Weighing & Inspection Bureau, and the headquarters of the Des Moines Union Railway.

It may be appropriate to add that the Wabash passenger trains which once served Ottumwa and Keokuk have long since made their final runs. They were early casualties of automobile and motor bus competition.

The Wabash, however, still continues to carry coaches on its fast freights between St. Louis and Council Bluffs. Equipped with reclining seats and air-conditioned, they are perhaps the fastest and most comfortable mixed trains in the country.

THE WABASH TODAY

Tall switch stands (about the height of a locomotive headlight), short freights, and a profusion of motive power ranging from American Standards, Ten Wheelers, Atlantics, and Pacifics to Moguls, Prairies, and Mikados once characterized Wabash operation. They have gone along with nearly all passenger trains in Iowa. But a heritage of fast running and highly competent dispatching is still a Wabash tradition. On the Wabash an operating man must know how to highball. This is just as true today for freights as for the more colorful Limiteds of yesteryear.

In Iowa on the road's fastest "Cannon Ball," freights are the "hotshots" to and from Council Bluffs. Carded as No. 211 westward and 214 eastward, they run at passenger-train speed. The former departs from St. Louis at 6:30 P.M. and arrives in Council Bluffs at 8:10 the next morning. Its eastern counterpart leaves the Bluffs at 8:45 at night and pulls into St. Louis at 8:55 A.M. There is also a tri-weekly time freight operating in each direction between Moberly, Missouri, and Council Bluffs. The light fifty-six-pound rails of the original line in Iowa have been replaced by ninety-pounders laid on gravel ballast.

The Des Moines line has always had time freights, even when trackage rights were over the Rock Island for part of the way. The road bravely advertised fast freights when they were routed via Harvey, Givin, and Ottumwa. The best time on this circuitous route from Moberly to Des Moines appears to have been about sixteen hours. When the Wabash built its shortcut from Moulton to Albia, the service was greatly accelerated. Today, with its modern diesel power, the Moberly–Des Moines "Red Ball" freights make the run in six and one-half hours. The branch has been upgraded to what the Wabash calls a "secondary main line."

The Ottumwa branch is serviced by way freights, as is the mile of track of the Keokuk line in Iowa. The latter comes into the state from Illinois on a bridge spanning the Mississippi River, over which it has trackage rights. It was built under the name of the Toledo, Wabash & Western Railroad.

In the preautomobile era numerous short lines funneled a modest amount of traffic to the Iowa lines of the Wabash. This was particularly true of the Council Bluffs branch. At Neoga, about five miles southeast of Council Bluffs, it interchanged with the Iowa & Omaha Short Line Railroad. This company built a twelve-mile road from Treynor, with trackage rights over the Wabash into Council Bluffs. The little carrier never showed a profit, and it quit in 1916 after operating only five years.

Another short-lived feeder was the Iowa & Southwestern Railway. It was built to connect Clarinda and College Springs with the Wabash at Blanchard, near the Missouri state line. Although Clarinda was on a branch of the Burlington, the town wanted another railroad. In the late 1870s it had hoped the Wabash's line to Council Bluffs would pass through Clarinda. Instead, the Wabash veered to the west through Shenandoah, whereupon the citizens of Clarinda helped finance the old Clarinda & St. Louis Railway, which was built from Roseberry, Missouri, under Wabash auspices. But after a decade of checkered existence the track was taken up in 1890.

Still hoping for an outlet on the Wabash, the people of Clarinda, aided by subscriptions from College Springs, financed the Iowa & Southwestern. The seventeen-mile line, opened in 1912, soon went bankrupt. Operation ceased in 1916, and the road was subsequently abandoned.

A shorter connection but one having a much longer life span was the Tabor & Northern Railway. It interchanged with the Wabash at Malvern and ran in a southwestern direction to Tabor, a distance of 8.79 miles. The road was organized late in 1887 and opened in 1889. Never a money-maker, the line managed to keep operating for some forty-five years. With the closing of Tabor College in 1927 and the completion of a paved high-way paralleling its line two years later, the handwriting was on the wall. When the short line sought permission to quit in 1934, no opposition was voiced, and the Interstate Commerce Commission promptly gave its ap-proval. Such is the doleful history of feeder lines which mushroomed along the Wabash in southwestern Iowa.

The Wabash proper has had only one short line abandoned but no cur-tailment of service in the state. This concerns the Des Moines branch and its peculiar relationship to a parallel line of the Burlington. Both the Wa-bash and the Burlington ran almost adjacent to each other for a score of miles on their Albia–Des Moines lines. The duplication vexed the United States Railroad Administration when it operated the roads during World War I. According to veteran employees, the United States Railroad Admin-istration ordered that the Wabash run its trains over the Burlington from Albia to the Monroe County line just north of Lovilia. The Burlington, on the other hand, shunted its trains over Wabash rails from the county line to Tracy.

After the conflict both roads returned to their respective lines. Then came the depression of 1929; and in the interest of economy, the two roads took a hard look at their parallel tracks. They decided to revert to the wartime practice of using parts of each other's lines to the best advantage. Thus, in a fifty-fifty changeover, the Wabash took up its eleven-mile seg-ment between Albia and the Monroe County line, and the Burlington dis-mantled its eleven miles of track north of the county line to Tracy.

Another change is imminent when the Red Rock Dam is slated to be completed about 1967 on the Des Moines River above Harvey. It is ex-pected the Wabash will use the Burlington rails between Harvey and Swan. At Swan a bridge is to be constructed across the Des Moines River, which will take the Burlington to the Wabash's current line on the east side of the waterway to a point below Runnells. Both the Wabash and the Burlington would use this partly relocated line as a joint route into Des Moines. The Wabash, of course, would then abandon that part of its branch between the new bridge and Harvey. The Burlington for its part would take out its line from Swan to Des Moines.

The Wabash has now purchased all its Iowa lines outright, and they have been completely integrated into its system. The parent company, like its components, has been in and out of receivership, emerging with a change of name each time. It is not necessary to go into details here except to say that the Wabash, St. Louis & Pacific was reorganized in 1889 as the Wabash Railroad. In a 1915 reorganization, the "Railroad" was changed to "Railway." Following insolvency during the Great Depression of the 1930s, the road came back on a firm financial footing in 1942 as the Wabash Railroad, which it is today.

The story of the Wabash in Iowa is not complete without some mention of the Des Moines Union Railway, which furnished terminal facilities in the capital city. The Union Railway is a joint facility of the Wabash and the Milwaukee railroads, and it has forty-two miles of valuable industry and terminal tracks. The Union was incorporated in 1884 by the railroads now embodied in the Wabash and the Milwaukee railroad systems which served Des Moines and vicinity. Frederick M. Hubbell, Jefferson S. Polk, and Grenville M. Dodge were the leading promoters of the enterprise. The Union purchased that portion of the Wabash's branch within the city to Chesterfield (also known as Wabash Junction), a distance of 2.4 miles.

The Union was part of a little railroad dynasty created by Fred Hubbell during this period. He likewise was instrumental in building the narrow-gauge lines from Des Moines to Boone and Des Moines to Panora which, as we have seen, were once a part of the Wabash system. He also helped build the three-foot gauge line from Des Moines to Ames and Jewell, which afterward became the Des Moines branch of the great North Western Railway.

In addition, Hubbell formed the Des Moines Terminal Company in 1902. This tiny carrier, which has ten miles of track in the factory district, is really a railroad within a railroad. It is operated by the Des Moines Union and is essentially a part of that line. For years the Tom Thumb road assessed a fee of $1 for every loaded car it interchanged with the Union. This and other factors led to protracted litigation, which lasted over a period of twenty-five years. In 1932, however, the Iowa Supreme Court ruled that the rate of compensation must be negotiated. Thus the long court fight between the Hubbell estate, representing the Terminal Company, and the Union Railway, backed by the Wabash and Milwaukee railroads, ended.

The Des Moines Union performs practically all the terminal work for the Wabash (as well as the Milwaukee) in Des Moines, and it is an important adjunct to the system. Its diesel switchers are constantly shunting freight cars to and from 160 industries in Iowa's largest city. Currently its motive power consists of a 660-h.p. Alco, which it owns, a 1,000-h.p. EMD leased from the Wabash, and a 1,000-h.p. Alco plus a 1,200-h.p. EMD leased from the Milwaukee.

In Council Bluffs the Wabash has its own freight house, whereas in Ottumwa it is a joint facility with the Milwaukee. South Ottumwa, however, is served exclusively by Wabash tracks. In Keokuk the road's traffic is handled at the Rock Island's freight house. But no matter what arrangement is made to expedite freight, the Wabash lines in Council Bluffs, Des Moines, Ottumwa, and Keokuk are as essential to the railroad as a whole as they are to the communities they service. Iowa shippers will continue to "Follow the Flag" in the future as they have in the past.

Palimpsest 45 (October 1964)

The Wabash selected standard plans for its depots in Shenandoah and Moravia. Since the former community sported a larger population, the building was longer, especially its freight section. By the time of the photograph of the Moravia depot in the 1960s, the Wabash had removed the decorative trim. This structure still stands, although it is a few hundred yards from its original trackside location. The former Moravia depot has been preserved by local residents. H. Roger Grant Collection.

*About 1920 a Wabash train crew and presumably other employees gather around a
Consolidation-type (2-8-0) locomotive in the Ottumwa rail yards.
H. Roger Grant Collection.*

*A diesel-powered freight is seen on October 14, 1956, headed through Albia on its way to Des
Moines. The steam-powered passenger train, which stands at the Albia station of the
Burlington, is a special excursion sponsored by the Iowa Chapter of the National Railway
Historical Society and is on its way to Indianola via the Chariton-Indianola branch.
John F. Humiston photograph.*

It is shortly after the "Follow the Flag" route has itself become a corporate fallen flag, losing its identity as result of union in 1964 with the Norfolk & Western Railway. A Moulton-bound freight blocks the South Main Street crossing in Albia. H. Roger Grant photograph.

GREAT NORTHERN– UNION PACIFIC– SANTA FE

THE GREAT NORTHERN IN IOWA

In the late 1880s Sioux City was well supplied with railroads which radiated in nearly every direction. But the packers and other industrialists wanted to have an independent and a more direct route to Duluth which would avoid the traffic congestion of the Twin Cities. They felt that better connections with the Lake Superior port would bring more manufactured goods to their city at lower cost. Again, a new railroad northward would cross the two transcontinentals serving the Pacific Northwest; and by so doing, Sioux City would get increased shipments of grain and livestock.

To achieve this end local businessmen formed the Sioux City & Northern Railroad, which was chartered October 23, 1887. It was projected from Sioux City northeastward to Duluth and from the Iowa line northwestward to Minot, North Dakota. Whether the incorporators ever seriously thought of reaching Minot is a matter of conjecture. If the plans were nebulous at the start, the backers soon faced reality by electing to build to the most convenient connection to form a through route to Duluth. This proved to be Garretson, South Dakota, on a railroad which James J. Hill headed.

Once the decision was made, management acted quickly. In June 1889 the project existed only on paper; six months later it was an operating railroad just short of one hundred miles long. On January 27, 1890, the ninety-six-mile route was opened for its entire length. Two factors did much to expedite its progress: ready capital and competent management.

From the start the line was a Sioux City enterprise locally owned and operated. At the outset it was headed by a veteran railroad builder, with a versatile and experienced Englishman as general manager. A third key officer was an enterprising financier who originally held the office of treasurer. These three officers served in chronological sequence as president of the thriving new railroad. Each had an interesting and varied background.

Thomas P. Gere, first president of the operating railroad, came from Wellsburg, New York, where he was born in 1842. When still a boy his parents moved to the Midwest, and his education was obtained in various communities where the family resided. At the outbreak of the Civil War he enlisted in the Fifth Regiment, Minnesota Volunteers. Mustered out a brigade adjutant, Gere was presented a medal of honor by Congress in 1865.

The next two decades he spent in railroad building. He helped survey what is now the River Division of the Milwaukee in Minnesota and later worked as a "leveler" on a predecessor line of the Omaha Road in Wisconsin. By 1867 he was assistant engineer of the Minnesota Valley and later of the St. Paul & Sioux City railroads, all of which were forerunners of the Omaha. With the formation of the Chicago, St. Paul, Minneapolis & Omaha Railway (the Omaha Road) in 1880, he became superintendent of the St. Paul Division. Two years later he was appointed assistant superintendent of the entire railroad.

Gere resigned from the Omaha in 1883 and subsequently formed a partnership with R. D. Hubbard of Mankato, Minnesota, in organizing the Sioux City Linseed Oil Works. For many years he managed that firm's Sioux City plant. But railroading was still in his blood. When the Milwaukee was built from Manilla to Sioux City, he had a hand in its construction. Gere, likewise, aided in bringing the North Western's Maple River branch into Onawa and in organizing the Pacific Short Line. All in all, he was a logical person to head and direct the building of the Sioux City & Northern.

Gere's general manager, Frederick C. Hills, was also a man of parts. He, likewise, was born in 1842, only he came from Bethersden, Kent, England. At the age of seven, young Frederick's parents emigrated to America and settled in Oneida County, New York. Frederick worked on his father's farm until he was fifteen. Then he became an apprentice in the carriage trimming trade. Eager for more education, he enrolled in a Rome business college, but upon the outbreak of the Civil War he enlisted in the army. Because of a physical disability his military career was cut short, and he went west to seek his fortune.

In the spring of 1864 Frederick Hills came to Sioux City from the railhead at Marshalltown with a yoke of cattle. Soon he was back in Marshalltown packing wood for what is now the North Western railroad. Then he had a stint at clerking farther west but returned to the railroad as local agent in Boone. When the road built farther westward, this ambitious Anglo-American lad was sent to open the station at Missouri Valley Junction in December 1866. Soon the carrier, then known as the Sioux City &

Pacific, reached Sioux City; and the young man became its local agent. He had risen on John I. Blair's road to the position of general traffic manager when he left its employ in 1881.

For the next seven years Hills was engaged in the hardware trade in Sioux City. In 1888, however, he sold his business to become assistant general manager of the Wyoming Pacific Improvement Company, builders of the Pacific Short Line.

The Short Line subsequently became the Sioux City, O'Neill & Western, which later was headed by his associate—Arthur S. Garretson. When the successor road went bankrupt following the panic of 1893, Hills was appointed receiver.

Prior to this Hills helped to promote the Sioux City & Northern, became its general manager, and was afterward its president. For many years the British-born executive with his great flowing beard was a prominent figure in Sioux City railroading. The town of Hills, Minnesota, on the road he operated, is named for him.

The third of the trio who headed the SC&N was Arthur S. Garretson. Banker, businessman, and rancher, he was another of the many-sided pioneers associated with the development of Sioux City. For several years he held the office of treasurer of the new railroad, until he succeeded Hills to the presidency in 1893.

Besides his railroad commitments, Garretson was cashier of the Sioux National Bank and owner of a three-thousand-acre cattle ranch in Grange Township near Luton. He also helped promote the city's widely publicized "elevated railroad" and served as treasurer of the newly organized University of the Northwest, now Morningside College. Garretson, South Dakota, honors his name.

The new railroad was constructed by the Sioux City & Northern Contracting Company and was controlled by Garretson and other local men. The contracting firm received the railroad's stocks and bonds at the rate of $15,000 and $20,000, respectively, per mile of road, an aggregate of $3,360,000.

The SC&N ran in a generally northward direction, paralleling the Illinois Central along the Floyd River to Merrill. From that town it continued northward into the more hilly country, through Struble, Sioux Center, and Doon to the state line south of Hills, Minnesota. The next 17 miles were divided between the southwestern corner of Rock County, Minnesota, and the eastern part of Minnehaha County, South Dakota. Its northern terminus was at Garretson, where it connected with the Willmar & Sioux

Falls Railway, which was headed by James J. Hill. The Hill road extended from Willmar, Minnesota, through Garretson and Sioux Falls to Yankton, South Dakota, a distance of 209 miles. The SC&N was laid with sixty-pound rails; and its shops and headquarters were located in Sioux City.

The company encountered no serious obstacles in building the line except at Maurice, where the North Western sought to prohibit it from crossing at the same grade. The North Western contended, before the Board of Railroad Commissioners, that the location in question was at the foot of a 1 percent grade in each direction, making it difficult to start and stop trains. Furthermore, it maintained that the curvature of its line was so great that the proposed grade crossing would be obscured in both directions. After hearing all arguments, the board directed the Sioux City & Northern to build a bridge across the North Western's line; and the latter road was ordered to lower its track under the proposed bridge. Both roads complied with the order, thereby making a grade crossing unnecessary.

By 1892 the tri-state railroad had twelve locomotives, nine passenger train cars, 470 freight cars, five cabooses, and two other cars. A tally of a hundred stock cars and fifty refrigerator cars would suggest cattle and packinghouse products were important items of revenue.

To strengthen its position in Sioux City's highly competitive packing district, an affiliated enterprise was chartered in 1889. Called the Sioux City Terminal & Warehouse Company, it soon had thirteen miles of track together with ample storage facilities and served as a valuable adjunct to its larger affiliate. It was leased to the Sioux City & Northern at an annual rental of $90,000. For many years Garretson headed the Terminal Company.

There was a curious affinity between the SC&N and the less successful Sioux City, O'Neill & Western Railway. As we have seen, both Frederick Hills and Arthur Garretson were associated with the latter road. Indeed, for a very brief period the two lines were jointly operated with identical officers for both carriers. The O'Neill line was subsequently operated separately from the Sioux City & Northern and then in an equally curious manner, as we will see later, it came back into the fold.

Through its decade of independent existence, the SC&N was rooted in the economy of Iowa's growing packing community. James E. Booge, who was a director and later vice president of the road, opened Sioux City's first packing plant in 1871. As his plant expanded so did the distribution of his products over the Sioux City & Northern. Then, too, D. T. Hedges, a very prosperous grocer and first president of the Union Stock Yards Company, was an influential director of the road and a heavy shipper. The SC&N had connections figuratively, literally, and physically. Small wonder that its high ratio of 5.06 cars for each mile of line was more than justified.

Shortly after the road reached Garretson a thirty-year traffic contract was made with the Hill road at that point. This apparently was so advantageous that no plans for further extensions were broached. Traffic flowed between the two roads in increasing amounts to the satisfaction of each. The Sioux City & Northern operated at a profit from the start.

The heady prosperity which characterized Sioux City's growth during the late 1880s and early 1890s, however, was not to last. The panic of 1893 wreaked havoc on the city and its industrial growth with greater toll than the periodic floods of the Missouri River ever did. Trouble came later to Sioux City than to many metropolitan centers of the East. But when it came, it was with devastating swiftness.

At 1 P.M. on April 25, 1893, Hedges, who was reputed to be the wealthiest man in town, assigned all his property to his creditors. Minutes later the Union Loan & Trust Company, which held the paper of many industries and railroads, declared itself insolvent. The Sioux City & Northern bravely held out until October, when Warwick Huge of St. Louis and Samuel J. Beals of Sioux City were made coreceivers.

The spectacular Corn Palace of 1890, to which Garretson is said to have underwritten the cost of a special train bringing prominent capitalists from Boston, would be rebuilt only once more. Likewise the city's famed elevated railway, which was backed by Garretson, Booge, and others and was proudly heralded as the third such facility in the world, now became a white elephant. It continued to go deeper into the red until 1897 when that "Wonder of the West" went the way of the corn palaces. Slowly and painfully the city recovered from the leveling depression. But the gusty, lusty boom times of the 1880s were never to be repeated.

While the sc&n floundered in receivership, new names appeared on the directorate. Local men were replaced by outsiders, principally from the Twin Cities. There was W. P. Clough of St. Paul, for example, who appeared in 1895 along with two others from the Twin Cities. To the average Sioux Citian these names meant nothing. But to financiers and railroad management they spelled out Great Northern, for Clough was vice president of that road. Jim Hill probably had an eye on the Sioux City gateway when he made an early traffic agreement with the sc&n. Apparently he did not show his hand until the railroad very conveniently went bankrupt. That made getting control a simple and relatively inexpensive matter.

In 1900 Hill garnered the Sioux City road into his rapidly expanding rail domain. He did this by having the Willmar & Sioux Falls Railway acquire the SC&N along with the Sioux City, O'Neill & Western. The latter road extended from South Sioux City (opposite Sioux City) to O'Neill, Nebraska, a distance of 129 miles. Doubtless it had trackage rights over the Omaha Road's bridge across the Missouri River, making a through route from Garretson via Sioux City to O'Neill.

The O'Neill line, however, never fitted very well into the Great Northern system. Hill preferred to keep his branch lines in the Dakotas all within the eastern boundary of the Missouri River. For this reason the Nebraska excrescence was later sold to the Burlington, and it is being operated by that road as a secondary line to this day.

Now that Hill had purchased the SC&N, he proceeded to integrate it into his far-flung system. Freight was speeded up by eliminating much of the interchange delay in Garretson and better coordinating through service to the Twin Cities and Duluth.

For passengers, through coaches were run between Willmar and Sioux City via Garretson. It is interesting to note that at one time there was through service from Duluth to Sioux Falls, calling at Willmar, Garretson, and other local points. Possibly a Sioux City car was included in the consist, although this has not been verified.

In 1907 the Willmar & Sioux Falls Railway was purchased outright by the Great Northern, and the former name disappeared from the rolling stock and letterheads. Meanwhile, the Sioux City branch had been upgraded over the years with heavier rail and better equipment. The once-popular American Standard had been replaced by the more powerful Pacific-type locomotive. A typical example of the latter engine has been preserved for posterity and is on permanent exhibit in Sioux City. This 4-6-2-type locomotive, No. 1355, was donated to the city by the railway and stands beside the tracks in a fenced enclosure.

Up until displacement by diesels, time freights were powered by well-kept Mikados, some of which had capacious Vanderbilt tenders riding on six-wheel trucks. By 1951 steam had practically disappeared from the Sioux City line, although the faithful old Mikes were again called into service during the floods of June 1953. They could operate with a foot of water on the tracks, whereas diesels were out of service if it reached a few inches over the rails.

The mainstays of passenger service between Sioux City and Willmar were trains 31 and 32 for day operation and Nos. 51 and 52 for overnight runs. No. 31 whistled for Sioux City late in the evening, whereas its eastward counterpart, No. 32, highballed out of town early in the morning. The "night trains" ran in the daylight hours on the Iowa segment of the run, arriving around noon and departing about suppertime. Mail was especially heavy on the night run, and much of it was posted to or from the Twin Cities. All passenger trains used Sioux City Union Station, which was owned and operated by the Great Northern Railway.

Diesel power was introduced relatively early on the night trains. In November 1939 an EMD-type NW-3 unit bearing road number 5400 was assigned to operation of Nos. 51 and 52, replacing 4-6-2- and 4-4-2-type steam power. This stalwart diesel (later renumbered 175) chalked up over two million miles before it was relegated to local freight service from Minneapolis in 1952.

When passenger traffic dwindled as the use of automobiles increased, gas-electric motor cars were periodically used on the day runs. During the depression years of the 1930s trains 31 and 32 disappeared from the timecard. Thanks to a healthy head-end revenue, principally from United States mail, overnight service continued until February 18, 1960. On that day Engineer David Munro of Sioux City pulled the last scheduled GN passenger train out of that community.

Freight service, on the other hand, continues to be heavy, and four- and five-unit diesels are regularly run during peak movements. A daily time freight is carded in each direction, and extras are run as traffic demands. Today, the 90- and 110-pound rail has replaced the original 60-pound steel, and facilities for trailer-on-flatcar and multilevel rack automobile loading are available in Sioux City.

We have seen that the Sioux City & Northern, predecessor of the Great Northern in Iowa, was a hometown road run by Hawkeye management. Although the Sioux City line can no longer be regarded as a local enterprise, two Great Northern presidents, under whom it operated or now operates, came from Iowa.

The first Iowan to head the GN was the late Ralph Budd. He was born on a farm near Washburn on August 20, 1879, and was one of six children. When Ralph was thirteen, the Budd family moved to Des Moines, where he was educated at North High School and Highland Park College. After getting his degree he went with the Chicago Great Western ballasting track and relaying rail between Des Moines and Oelwein. In 1902 young Budd shifted to the Rock Island and soon became first division engineer on the new line being built between St. Louis and Kansas City.

Ralph Budd's engineering genius came to the attention of John Stevens, then vice president of the Rock Island and soon to be appointed chief engineer of the Panama Canal. Shortly after Stevens went to Panama he sent for Budd to rebuild the railroad paralleling the canal. Later, when Stevens was in the Pacific Northwest constructing railroads for James J. Hill, Budd was again summoned to be his right-hand man. The Iowan acquitted himself well and rose to be chief engineer of the Oregon Trunk and later the Spokane, Portland, and Seattle railroads.

Meanwhile, Budd met James J. Hill, who although in his seventies, still dominated the policies of the GN. The "Empire Builder" was impressed by Budd, and the latter, at the age of thirty-three, was invited to become chief engineer and assistant to the president of Hill's prosperous transcontinental railroad. Ralph Budd rose rapidly on the GN and was elected president in 1919 when he was only forty. He held that post until 1932, then he became president of the Burlington. On this road, he had an equally distinguished career. Upon his retirement in 1949, the Burlington was said to be "principally the 'lengthened shadow' of Ralph Budd."

The current and second Iowan to become president of the GN is John M. Budd, son of Ralph Budd. John Budd was born in Des Moines, November 2, 1907, and was educated at the St. Paul and Phillips Exeter academies before entering Yale. The summer vacations of 1926 and 1927 found him working on the GN as chainman with the engineering party on the Cascade Tunnel and Chumstick line changes. After receiving his B.S. degree in 1930, he returned to the GN engineering department as assistant to the electrical engineer.

From 1933 to 1940 John Budd was assistant trainmaster and later trainmaster at various points on the extensive system. Sioux City was among the locales where he was stationed. Later he was made superintendent at Klamath Falls, Oregon, and afterward at Whitefish, Montana. His Great Northern employment was interrupted by World War II, but not his work at railroading, for he was a major and later lieutenant colonel in the Military Railway Service. After seeing active duty in Algiers, Italy, France, and Germany, he returned to the GN as assistant general manager of lines east of Williston, North Dakota.

John Budd left the GN to head the Chicago & Eastern Illinois Railroad in 1947. Then forty-one, he was at that time the youngest president of any Class I railroad. In 1949 John Budd came back to the GN as vice president of operation and held that position until elected president in 1951.

Thus the Sioux City line, the southernmost part of the Great Northern System, still retains a measure of its Iowa heritage and background.

THE UNION PACIFIC IN IOWA

A tall, gangling visitor was introduced to Grenville M. Dodge at the Pacific House in Council Bluffs in the summer of 1859. Dodge, who resided in that growing river town, had surveyed the route of a projected railroad across Iowa and on into the Platte Valley. The caller showed great interest in the young surveyor's knowledge of the country and his enthusiasm for a transcontinental line passing through Council Bluffs. When the two had finished talking, Dodge declared, in an expression of the period, "He shelled my woods."

The visitor had very adroitly drawn out nearly all Dodge knew about a route to the Pacific. Nine months afterward, the inquisitive visitor was nominated president of the United States. His name was Abraham Lincoln. Lincoln never forgot his meeting with Dodge on the veranda of the Pacific House. In later years, before President Lincoln specifically named Council Bluffs as the eastern terminus of the "Pacific Railroad," he again conferred with Dodge. It is very likely that Dodge's counsel and knowledge greatly influenced Lincoln's decision. Indeed, Dodge had the measure of zeal necessary to promote the Union Pacific that Theodore Judah had for the Central Pacific.

On July 1, 1862, President Lincoln signed the Pacific Railroad Act under which the Union Pacific was chartered. Unfortunately, it did not clearly spell out the eastern terminus of the line other than it was to be built westward from the Missouri River. Aware of this shortcoming, Lincoln called in Dodge, who was now a brigadier general in the federal army, to discuss the matter. Later an executive order of November 17, 1863, was issued establishing the terminus at "the western boundary of the State of Iowa, east of and opposite to the east line of section 10, in township 15 north, of range 13, east of the sixth principal meridian, in the Territory of Nebraska." A subsequent order in 1864 spelled this out clearly.

Ground was first broken for the UP on the west side of the Missouri River near Omaha on December 2, 1863. Since Council Bluffs was without a railroad connection from the East until the arrival of the North Western on January 22, 1867, construction material came up the river from St. Joseph by boat. The first locomotives came by rail to St. Joseph, thence upstream to Omaha. As railroads built westward across Iowa, some supplies were carted from the advancing railheads to Council Bluffs and ferried across the river to Omaha.

During this early period the UP had a fleet of steamboats known as the "Railroad Packet Line." Among them were the *Metamora, Colorado,* and *Den-*

ver, plus scows and ferries operating between Council Bluffs and Omaha. The expedient of constructing a temporary trestle across the Missouri was resorted to during the winter of 1867–1868. But as soon as navigation opened up in the spring, the bridge was dismantled.

Iowa's role in the UP would not be complete without further reference to Grenville M. Dodge, Council Bluff's most distinguished resident. After a valiant Civil War career, General Dodge was appointed chief engineer in 1866. He succeeded his friend, former employer, and fellow Iowan Peter A. Dey, who resigned because of differences in policies. During Dodge's leadership the UP was pushed to completion. In one year under his command 568 miles of line were located, built, and made ready for operation.

Following the junction of the Union Pacific and Central Pacific at Promontory, Utah, on May 10, 1869, Dodge left the UP and subsequently became chief engineer of the Texas & Pacific. Later he was associated with the Gould roads in the Southwest and assisted in the building and consolidation of nearly nine thousand miles of railroad. All told, he is said to have surveyed sixty thousand miles of right-of-way and is regarded as one of the nation's greatest railroad builders.

Dodge remained loyal to the UP the rest of his life. As a director during many of the years between 1870 and 1897, he continued to take an active interest in the road. Born on a farm in Massachusetts in 1831, the renowned railroad builder, civil engineer, army officer, and statesman made his home in Council Bluffs during the mid-1850s. From that time until his death in 1916, the eastern terminus of the UP was "home." It is fitting that his three-story brick home with a mansard roof and large French windows is preserved as a local shrine. In 1964 the site received greater recognition when it was made a registered National Historic Landmark, the second to be so favored in Iowa.

Coming back to the early development of the UP, it was not until 1872, or two years after Dodge resigned as chief engineer, that the first permanent railroad bridge spanned the Missouri River. The original single-track structure was begun in 1869 under the direction of Theopilus E. Sickels. It was 2,750 feet long and consisted of eleven spans of 250 feet each. The approach on the east was by solid embankment and on the west by a cottonwood trestle, which was shortly replaced by a fill. The substructure consisted of eleven iron piers and one stone pier. Each pier was made of two cylinders braced together by cast-iron struts and diagonal ties. When a storm blew down the two easterly spans in 1877, they were replaced by a timber trestle.

As tonnage increased and as newer lines built across Iowa to funnel more freight and passengers to the UP, the bridge soon became inadequate and congested. A double-track structure was the only solution to the problem. Work began on reconstructing the pioneer span in the summer of 1885, and it was opened as a two-track thoroughfare on October 1, 1887. The rebuilt bridge had five piers founded on pneumatic caissons. They were of limestone and granite. The roadbed rested on four through spans and three deck-truss spans at each end. The location remained the same.

A novel addition on each side of the structure was cantilever arms which supported roadways for highway vehicles. A toll was charged for wagons and carriages crossing the bridge.

Perhaps the most interesting features to passengers on transcontinental trains were the symbolic figures at each end of the superstructure. At the east end, a colossal bronze buffalo head representing the wilderness of the Great Plains was placed high above the tracks. On the west, there was a lofty bronze bas-relief showing a plow, anchor, and steam hammer, which stood for the agriculture, commerce, and manufacturing of the East.

The third and final rebuilding of the strategic bridge took place in 1916. It was found that the superstructure of the 1887 bridge was not strong enough for the demands of heavier trains, although the substructure remained in almost perfect condition. The piers were accordingly left intact, but all of the spans were removed. In the center part of the bridge, four new pin-connected Pratt truss spans were placed on the five sturdy masonry piers. On the east approach, an assortment of spans, including three deck-girders, one tower, and one riveted Pratt truss, characterized the rebuilt structure. The west approach was rebuilt with one deck-girder, a tower, and two Pratt truss spans.

By an ingenious system of shifting the old spans northward and easing the new structure into its place on permanent piers, traffic was held up for only ten hours. Indeed, the actual movement of the individual spans required hardly longer than fifteen minutes. The bridge was closed shortly after 11 A.M. on December 23, and by 9:40 P.M. the first train whistled over the rebuilt structure.

The spanning of the Missouri River by the UP has been emphasized because it was the first railroad to bridge that waterway in Iowa. With the exception of the Illinois Central, which crossed the Missouri in 1904, there is to this day no other railroad bridging the Big Muddy between Council Bluffs and Omaha.

Until the pioneer bridge was built, passengers were obliged to ride a shuttle train from connecting lines to the riverbank, where they alighted to go by ferry to Omaha. This double transfer was necessary because the three railroads which entered Council Bluffs from the east terminated several blocks from the bank of the Missouri.

After the UP spanned the river, it ran "dummy trains" from Council Bluffs directly to Omaha. For a time these "bridge trains" consisted of flatcars covered with awnings. The railroad also bought a controlling interest in horsecar lines serving the two cities and had them connect with the "dummies." By 1887 the UP had hourly "bridge service" from Ninth and Broadway in Council Bluffs to South Omaha, with several stops in Omaha.

The problem of a permanent depot in Council Bluffs was not resolved until the road's eastern terminus was definitely established. The railroad and the City of Omaha went to court in endeavoring to make the Nebraska metropolis the terminal. But a Supreme Court ruling in 1875 confirmed Lincoln's decision that Council Bluffs was to be the legal terminus.

Thereafter, the UP outdid itself in making its eastern gateway a terminal befitting the stature and importance of the nation's first transcontinental route. It erected a commodious two-story brick building with walls twenty-four inches thick. An unusual feature was a truncated cupola in the center of the structure.

Inside, passengers were awed by a twenty-foot-high ceiling and a spacious corridor, which had at its threshold the inscription "Where the West Begins." A grand ballroom or banquet room, two large parlors, and thirty-six palatial sleeping rooms furnished in attractive black walnut suites helped to make it a showpiece and the pride of everyone in Council Bluffs.

In the "first-class" dining room occupying the north wing, sumptuous meals were served for seventy-five cents. Special Sunday dinners proved very popular with townsfolk and travelers alike. There was also a barroom, serving mostly "mixed" drinks, and a barbershop. The usual complement of waiting rooms and baggage rooms along with a newsstand and lunch counter were provided. Five express companies were also housed in the building, which was opened in 1879.

For "foreigners" of limited means, there was the "Emigrant House"—a fifty-room frame building west of the terminal. A bakery, laundry, land office, and cold storage facility were housed in the wooden structure. Although the accommodations were Spartan in contrast with the luxurious quarters in the main building, they provided low-cost housing for thousands of immigrants who poured into the West.

The new terminal fostered business expansion and home building in the vicinity of the "transfer." The giant station, however, soon began to lose much of its importance as connecting lines acquired running rights to Omaha over the Union Pacific's bridge.

Trackagewise the UP hardly enters Iowa at all. The original single-track main line ran from what is now Union Avenue and South 12th Street, Council Bluffs, to the western border of the state, a distance of about 3 miles. The current double-track "high iron" extends from the eastern end of the Missouri River bridge to Union Station Transfer — a distance of 2.08 miles. But it is only by taking cognizance of *track miles* that the role of the company is apparent. Industry spurs and yard tracks tally an additional 82.14 miles.

The bulk of the trackage is in the Union Pacific's yard, where freight trains arrive from and depart for the West Coast and intermediate points. Thus Council Bluffs is still a busy and vital terminal as the eastern end of the giant system. The terminal area embraces about 725 acres. Included in the facilities are the yardmaster's and master mechanic's office, diesel house where locomotive running repairs are made, and a coach yard.

As a passenger terminal, however, Council Bluffs has largely been superseded by Omaha. None of the UP's crack "Cities" streamliners stop on the east bank of the Missouri River, and only a few passenger trains of other roads use this once-busy station. The historic structure was partly torn down in 1938 to make way for a mail terminal built that year. Only the north wing of the old building remains, and this has been revamped for today's modest traffic. In 1951 the mail terminal was remodeled and a conveyor system installed to expedite operation. From fifty to fifty-five cars of mail are worked here daily for western points and about fifteen eastern destinations. It is said that at one time Council Bluffs was the third largest terminal railway post office in America based on the volume of mail handled.

Currently all railroads entering Council Bluffs, with the exception of the Illinois Central, use the UP for freight or passenger service, or both, in reaching Omaha. Day and night luxurious streamliners, local passenger trains, long freights, and incessant switching keep the bridge athrob with activity. True, the Union Pacific's main line extends only a couple of miles into Iowa, but it is the nation's busiest and most strategic railroad gateway to half a continent.

THE SANTA FE IN IOWA

The reason for the Santa Fe's coming to Iowa is explained in the road's annual report of 1886. It stated in part: ". . . your Directors unanimously came to the conclusion that the interests of this Company required that it should have under its control an independent line to Chicago." Had the Missouri River remained the western terminus of its connecting lines to the Windy City, the Santa Fe would not have considered building into Chicago at that time. But the Burlington and the Rock Island had extended into Santa Fe territory west of the Missouri; and the Gould lines had their own rails from Lake Michigan to the Southwest.

While the Santa Fe boasted of a 6,500-mile system of owned or controlled lines extending from Kansas City to Los Angeles and San Diego, it was never sure of its eastern connections. All too often its Chicago links would expand beyond the Missouri, and overnight a new competitor would be born. Such a situation jeopardized the continued growth and stability of the far-flung railroad.

To gain entry into Chicago, the Atchison, Topeka & Santa Fe had three alternatives: it could buy the Chicago & Alton; build its own direct line; or purchase the ailing Chicago & St. Louis, use about a hundred miles of that Illinois railroad, and construct its own line the remainder of the way. The latter plan was adopted as the most feasible.

It is said that in planning the eastern extension Chief Engineer Albert A. Robinson took a ruler and drew a straight line between Kansas City and Chicago. Such an airline would cut across the southeastern corner of Iowa. While the road actually constructed is not entirely ruler-straight, there are few curves and none of a degree to impede fast running.

At first the Santa Fe considered crossing the Mississippi River at Keokuk; and, with great secrecy, a crew of surveyors made their headquarters in that town. Later, when Fort Madison learned of the surveys, its citizens agreed to furnish some eighty acres of land for railroad purposes. They also proposed to pay one-fourth of the right-of-way costs through Lee County. Because of these inducements and other factors, the Santa Fe agreed to go through Fort Madison rather than Keokuk in making the Mississippi River crossing. Subsequent events show that Fort Madison profited a great deal from the transaction because of increased property values due to the coming of the Santa Fe.

To build the new line, a company called the Chicago, Santa Fe & California Railway was incorporated in Illinois on December 3, 1886. A separate Iowa charter was obtained for construction in Iowa and Missouri. Early in 1887 construction was begun, and by the end of the year the entire line was completed from Chicago to Kansas City except for a bridge across the Missouri River. Also, because of settling track, through service was not begun until the following year. The new extension was about forty miles shorter than any other route linking Chicago and Kansas City. It was single track laid with steel rails, ranging from sixty-seven to seventy-one pounds, on good ballast. Designed for high-speed operation, it soon saw crack transcontinental trains highballing from Chicago to the West Coast.

One of the most expensive parts of the new road proved to be the bridge across the Mississippi River. The Mississippi River Railroad & Toll Bridge Company was chartered October 23, 1886. This firm was empowered to cross the waterway at Fort Madison. The bridge consisted of seven truss spans and an east approach of about 350 yards. A drawspan four hundred feet long permitted boats to pass through the structure. As its corporate name suggested, highway traffic was accommodated by a roadway on either side of the truss spans. The bridge, which was started in March 1887, was ready for traffic on December 7 of that year. The bridge company was soon absorbed by the Santa Fe, as was the Chicago, Santa Fe & California, although the latter was not officially merged until 1900.

The old wrought-iron structure was superseded by a $5 million double-track bridge in 1927. Like its predecessor, it has a highway component. The bridge has deck-girders at either end, with four large through truss spans in the central portion. About halfway up between the tracks and the top of the truss was the highway. On the Illinois side motor vehicles descended to the south of the right-of-way, on the Iowa side to the north. At the time the bridge was built, its 525-foot drawspan near the Iowa shore was said to be the longest in the world.

Although the Santa Fe has only nineteen miles of line in Iowa, the state is of singular importance to the railroad because it has been headquarters of the Illinois Division since 1956. Company records also indicate that division headquarters were likewise located there from 1901 to 1903. The first division superintendent was Frank T. Dolan, whose jurisdiction was then known as the Chicago Division. He later became general superintendent, Southwestern District, of the Chicago, Rock Island & Pacific Railway.

Today, as in the past, all passenger trains make two stops in Iowa. One is at Fort Madison, and the other is at Shopton, 1.7 miles westward. The latter stop is so named because it was the locale for extensive shop facilities. Trains crews change here, and freight engines are refueled.

Shop construction started in 1888 along with the erection of a hospital for railroad employees. A planing mill and bridge and building maintenance facilities were the chief features of the shops. Later a blacksmith shop was included and the roundhouse quarters greatly enlarged for bigger steam locomotives. In 1917 a new power plant was built. The same year saw the completion of a two-story brick structure providing dormitory facilities and a well-stocked reading room for employees. Heretofore crude bunkhouses and cheap hotels often characterized lodging quarters available at division points.

Throughout the years, this railroader's "home away from home" has been modernized with radio and television to supplement books and periodicals. Pool tables, pianos, showers, and a lunch counter make Shopton a pleasant place for trainmen on their layovers in Iowa.

Modern railroading, especially the use of diesel power, has tended to consolidate shop facilities and to do away with many points formerly needed for car and engine repair. For this reason, the Fort Madison shops were closed in 1951. Similarly, the Santa Fe Hospital was discontinued and the building, together with five acres of land, given to Fort Madison to be administered by a trust fund.

Shoptown, nevertheless, continues to have a busy yard, whose tracks total thirty-nine miles. Passenger train icing facilities, stock pens, and a piggy-back ramp for trailer-on-flatcar equipment are some of the adjuncts in yard operation. Then, too, Fort Madison's industries, including a multimillion-dollar fertilizer plant, provide considerable freight for many points on the Santa Fe system.

Instead of a single-track railroad equipped with light rails, the Santa Fe's main line through Lee County is now double-track "high iron" of 131- and 132-pound rail protected by efficient Traffic Control Signaling. Every day a dozen crack passenger trains go through the southeastern tip of Iowa as they speed to and from the Southwest or Pacific Coast points and Chicago. Notwithstanding the fact that the Super Chief, the Chief, and other famous streamliners do not stay long in the state, they all stop at the historic town of Fort Madison—a site of the old fort on the Mississippi named after the fourth president of the United States.

Palimpsest 46 (April 1965)

A familiar sight for Iowans was a lash-up of well-maintained Great Northern diesel locomotives on long freights. In September 1969 a train rolls near Sioux City, and it is only a few months from the company's entry into the Burlington Northern.
Don L. Hofsommer photograph.

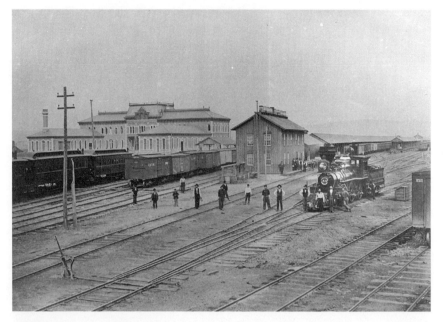

In 1877 the Union Pacific complex at Council Bluffs includes the impressive Transfer Hotel (on left). An American-type locomotive, No. 53, sports the era's common balloon smokestack. Union Pacific Museum Collection.

In the early 1970s a Santa Fe freight train roars out of Shopton near Fort Madison. Don L. Hofsommer photograph.

THE
BURLINGTON
IN IOWA

BURLINGTON AND MISSOURI RIVER

The Burlington was not the first railroad to build across Iowa, nor was it the last. But it was the only federal land-grant railroad to span the state that did not go bankrupt in the process. It came in third in the trans-Iowa race—and solvent. As a matter of fact, the Burlington is outstanding in that it is one of the very few roads in Iowa which has never been in receivership.

The story of the Chicago, Burlington & Quincy Railroad in Iowa begins with the river town on the Mississippi from which it derives its name. Burlington in the 1850s had no railroad. The people in that community, however, were clamoring for better transportation. To this end they formed the Burlington & Mount Pleasant Plank Road, which was completed in December 1851. But this was not enough—the town had developed "railroad fever."

Meanwhile, Davenport also was agog with plans for a line due west to the Missouri River. This was the forerunner of the Rock Island, which later crossed Iowa. Clearly, Burlington must look to the railroad or fall behind.

Mindful of this fact, two exponents of the plank road now turned their sights on an iron road. William F. Coolbaugh, a local merchant, and James W. Grimes, lawyer and businessman, along with other Burlingtonians incorporated the Burlington and Missouri River Rail Road on January 15, 1852. Coolbaugh headed the enterprise. Grimes, who was soon to be governor of Iowa, was sent to Washington to seek a land grant.

The astute Grimes, by a felicitous chain of events, got the so-called Boston Group, under the leadership of John Murray Forbes, interested in his "paper" railroad. This group, with Forbes furnishing the capital, James F. Joy the legal talent, and John W. Brooks the operational know-how, was pushing the Michigan Central on to its Chicago destination. They were also quietly acquiring a group of Illinois railroads, from which was to emerge the Chicago, Burlington & Quincy. Grimes found Forbes and his associates interested. On the other hand, they looked with greater favor on building across more populous Missouri to St. Joseph and Kansas City.

What clinched the matter for Grimes, however, was the discovery by the Boston Group that Rock Island Railroad interests had secured a charter to build across Iowa. The Rock Island, it may be added, was promoted by the Michigan Southern, which was racing its northern competitor, the Michigan Central, into Chicago! Messrs. Forbes, Joy, and Brooks saw the light. From that time on the Boston Group backed the Burlington and Missouri River project. In 1853 John Brooks became president of the B&M. On March 17, 1855, the Burlington reached the Mississippi, and the stage was set for construction across Iowa.

Brooks and Joy dispatched Hans Thielsen, a Danish-born civil engineer on the Michigan Central, to survey the Iowa line from Burlington to Ottumwa. They also sent Alfred Hebard, a Yale graduate, to select the best route from Ottumwa to Council Bluffs. Although born in Vermont, Hebard had lived in Iowa for sixteen years and knew the terrain well. Finally, Forbes persuaded his brother, Robert Bennet Forbes, to make a trip across Iowa and report his findings.

On New Years's Day, 1856, the citizens of Burlington cheered at the sight of a brass-trimmed wood-burner puffing along a few miles of track in town. Then, on May 15, President Franklin Pierce signed the Land Grant Act of 1856, giving aid to four east-west lines in Iowa. The B&M's share was about 300,000 acres.

The road was built to Mount Pleasant by July of 1856. Yet, by the end of the following summer, it had only reached the hamlet of Rome on the Skunk River, five miles beyond Mount Pleasant. The panic of 1857 stalled further construction.

Meanwhile, Forbes, desiring to have a man on the spot who could keep close tab on the finances, selected twenty-three-year-old Charles Russell Lowell for the job. Nephew of the poet, young Lowell was appointed assistant treasurer with headquarters in Burlington.

It was soon apparent that Lowell had too much work for one person. Besides his treasury duties he was responsible for managing the land department. In choosing a competent assistant, Forbes picked Charles Elliott Perkins, a mere boy of eighteen, who hailed from Cincinnati where he was clerking in a local wholesale fruit store. The lad was a second cousin of Forbes, at whose house Lowell had made his acquaintance.

Perkins eagerly took the job at $30 a month. Early in August 1859 he came to Burlington and gladly accepted Lowell's invitation to share his cottage. A brief sketch of this remarkable young man is in order, for he was to head the entire Burlington system by 1881; and for nearly two decades thereafter he shrewdly and conscientiously guided its phenomenal growth. Moreover, for the rest of his life he proudly regarded himself as an Iowan: a Burlington man from Burlington.

Charles E. Perkins was born in Cincinnati, November 24, 1840. The oldest of five sons of a Unitarian minister, Perkins learned to accept responsibility early, for his father committed suicide when he was nine. Finishing high school at sixteen, he set out to support the family by working in a Queen City wholesale fruit firm.

Having reached Iowa in time for the "Grand Railroad Celebration" in Ottumwa, Perkins no doubt thrilled to what the iron horse meant to the town and what it would mean to the growing West. The festivities to honor the arrival of the B&M were held on September 1. About 12,000 visitors swarmed the streets for the occasion. With all passenger coaches filled to capacity, the pioneer line resorted to flatcars fitted with benches to take care of the overflow. Not to be outdone by the bountiful spread Fairfield had put on with a 986-foot table to celebrate the B&M's coming the previous year, Ottumwa countered with eight tables of delectable food each 460 feet long.

Under the helping hand and friendly counsel of Lowell, Perkins learned railroading. The two became good friends. Lowell, who graduated from Harvard at the head of his class, would sometimes spend an evening reading the *Philosophy of Immanuel Kant* or the latest works of Charles Darwin. Perkins more than likely got a smattering of philosophy by osmosis, sitting nearby under a sperm-oil lamp. The perceptive and inquiring mind of Perkins nevertheless matched the cultured and scholarly intellect of Lowell. Both were hard workers, keen students, energetic railroaders. But late in 1860 Lowell decided to return to the iron business, in which he was earlier associated. Before resigning, however, he highly recommended Perkins for his job. And so, not yet twenty, Charles Perkins became assistant treasurer and land agent at a salary of $800 a year.

Much to the disappointment of Perkins, the railhead continued to remain at Ottumwa. While the B&M was marking time, its competitors were not. Ottumwa was also served by the Des Moines Valley Railroad. It had built up from Keokuk and passed through Ottumwa on its way to Des Moines. Ultimately to become a secondary branch of the Rock Island, the

Des Moines Valley was of considerable importance in its earlier days. Meanwhile, running parallel to the B&M on the north were the rapidly advancing extensions of the Rock Island and of the North Western. Each line had its own bridge spanning the Mississippi—the Rock Island completed in 1856 and the North Western in 1865. The B&M, on the other hand, still relied on ferries to make the crossing.

Would the Burlington & Missouri River be relegated to an inconsequential local line? No, insisted Perkins. Made superintendent in 1865, he now had more say in management. Although Brooks was replaced by the more energetic James F. Joy as president in 1866, it was Perkins who got action from Boston. Tactfully, yet persistently, the youthful executive outlined the dilemma of the road. Forbes understood but had trouble convincing his New England associates. But in the end he won them over to his point of view.

Spurred on by fresh capital, tracklaying went on with vigor following the Civil War. The Burlington reached Chariton in the summer of 1867 and Woodburn by the end of the year. It was now halfway across Iowa. Trains steamed into Osceola late in January 1868, and on November 12 the railroad was at Red Oak.

In the meantime, the Chicago, Burlington & Quincy board of directors had finally authorized a bridge across the Mississippi at Burlington. Completed in 1868, the iron span measured 2,237 feet, with a drawbridge in the center. It linked the rails of the CB&Q with those of the B&M.

The Mississippi bridge proved a boom to Burlington track construction in Iowa. Tracklaying redoubled as the company pushed eastward from East Plattsmouth. On November 26, 1869, the Burlington rails met at Hastings. There was no formal ceremony. Superintendent Perkins, on hand to witness the event, wrote in his notebook, "Last rail laid and spiked at noon today—went through with special train to Plattsmouth."

On January 3, 1870, regular service was established into Council Bluffs by the way of Pacific Junction over the rails of the St. Joseph & Council Bluffs Rail Road.

BRANCH LINE CONSTRUCTION

There was no marking time, once the dynamic Perkins was given free hand. When the B&M pushed westward beyond the Missouri River, Perkins went with it, soon becoming its vice president. The line was called the Burlington & Missouri River Rail Road Company in Nebraska, to distinguish it from its Iowa counterpart. It reached Kearney, a point on the Union Pacific, in 1872.

One reason for the westward course was that the B&M had expected, and hoped, Plattsmouth, Nebraska, would be the termination of the Union Pacific. Instead, the UP decided on Council Bluffs. Not to be daunted, the B&M continued its southern route as a shortcut to Kearney.

From the early 1870s and for nearly twenty years thereafter, the Missouri River was crossed by car ferry, the first transfer boat being the *Vice President*, built in Jeffersonville, Indiana. Later a railroad bridge replaced the ferry, and while Omaha–Council Bluffs became the favored passenger gateway, the Plattsmouth route loomed increasingly important in expediting freight.

Westward expansion or not, Charles Perkins had a warm spot in his heart for Burlington. Although he spent most of the time in Nebraska, his home and his family remained in Burlington, and his employers allowed him to keep his headquarters there. Moreover, he had a deep affection for the B&M and stood by Iowa and the railroad when other officials looked elsewhere. James F. Joy, for example, was a partisan of the Hannibal & St. Joseph, another Boston Group railroad, which crossed northern Missouri. Then, too, there was intense competition from the other east-west railroads in Iowa. And, finally, there was the sinister hand of Jay Gould!

Because of the above circumstances, the B&M's branch line building had no hard-and-fast pattern. One feeder might be constructed to fill an economic need, another to tap new territory, a third to fend off completion, or a fourth to acquire an independent railroad to keep a rival from gobbling it up first. Expansion was afoot, unbridled competition reigned, and there were no holds barred.

The first branch line left the main stem at Red Oak and went in a southwesterly direction to Hamburg, on the Missouri River. Completed in 1870, it measured thirty-nine miles. Three more feeders, all to the south, were completed by 1872. One veered southwest from Creston to Hopkins, Missouri, just over the state line. At the latter terminal it connected with a railroad which had been built up from Amazonia, Missouri, along the Big Muddy. Then there was a stub line from Villisca to Clarinda and a much longer mid-Iowa branch linking two county seats—Chariton and Leon.

By the end of 1872 the Chicago, Burlington & Quincy Railroad leased the B&M, and the Hawkeye road became an integral part of the larger system. The parent company now continued expanding with renewed zeal. Before the decade was over it had flung out a half-dozen feeders. Perhaps the most important branch was the northwesterly line from Albia to the state capital. Governor Samuel Merrill was president of the component companies of the line. This sixty-eight-mile property not only put the Burlington directly into the Rock Island preserves in Des Moines, but it also paralleled the latter's Des Moines Valley road. We have seen that the "Valley" had been a thorn in the side of the B&M—halting progress across Iowa in the late 1850s. Now the thorn changed hands—the Burlington did the pricking.

The Burlington's "branching out" of component roads from 1870 to 1880 is listed below. The town connected, the mileage, and the years of initial construction and completion are indicated.

Albia, Knoxville & Des Moines RR
    Albia-Knoxville, 32 mi.; 1871–1875
Brownville and Nodaway Valley Ry.
    Clarinda Jct. (Villisca)–Burlington Jct., Mo., 35 mi.; 1872–1879
Burlington & Missouri RR
    Chariton-Leon, 36 mi.; 1871–1872
Chariton, Des Moines and Southern RR
    Chariton-Indianola, 33 mi.; 1878–1879
Creston and Northern RR
    Creston-Fontanelle, 27 mi.; 1878–1879
Creston Branch of the Burlington & Missouri River RR
    Creston to Iowa state line near Hopkins, Mo., 42 mi.; 1871–1872
Des Moines & Knoxville Ry.
    Knoxville–Des Moines, 35 mi.; 1879–1880
Hastings and Avoca RR
    Hastings-Carson, 15 mi.; 1880
Leon, Mount Ayr and Southwestern RR
    Leon–Grant City, Mo., 78 mi.; 1879–1880
Nebraska City, Sidney and North Eastern Ry.
    Hastings-Sidney, 21 mi.; 1878
Red Oak & Atlantic RR
    Red Oak–Griswold, 18 mi.; 1879–1880

Considerable credit for the aggressive expansion of the "Q" must go to Perkins, who became vice president in 1876. To quote Richard Overton, distinguished Burlington Railroad historian: "From the time that Charles Elliott Perkins became vice president of the Chicago, Burlington & Quincy . . . until he resigned as president of the system in 1901, he *was* the Burlington."

Another facet of the Burlington's growth required getting control of roads already built. In western Iowa the Council Bluffs & St. Joseph Rail

Road, originally incorporated in 1858, had undergone little construction until after the Civil War. In 1867, however, this road had a line following the east bank of the Missouri River from Council Bluffs to the Missouri border. At that point it linked hands with affiliated roads continuing south to St. Joseph and Kansas City. In 1870 these roads were consolidated to form the Kansas City, St. Joseph & Council Bluffs Railroad.

The Boston Group had an interest in the above property which, at the end of the decade, had turned into virtual control. It will be recalled the B&M's pioneer line had used the road from Pacific Junction to Council Bluffs. In other hands this Council Bluffs–Kansas City line could retard the Burlington's growth by severe competition.

In eastern Iowa two roads came into the Burlington's domain. Both terminated in Keokuk. The Iowa portion of the St. Louis, Keokuk & Northwestern, which was completed in 1881, stretched some forty-eight tenuous miles to Mount Pleasant on the main line of the "Q." It had a checkered and precarious history, beginning life as the Iowa Northern Central chartered in 1866.

The other road, the Keokuk & St. Paul, never went beyond Burlington, a distance of forty-two miles. Completed in 1869, it formed a link in an important through route from St. Louis to the Twin Cities. It, too, had a hectic past, going back to the high-sounding Fort Madison, West Point, Keosauqua & Bloomfield Rail Road in 1853. John Edgar Thomson, president of the Pennsylvania Railroad, had an interest in the company. This line, along with the other Keokuk road, passed on to Burlington control upon completion.

An interesting sidelight during this decade was joint control, with the Rock Island, of the Burlington, Cedar Rapids & Northern in 1879. Going from Burlington to Albert Lea, Minnesota, it was part of the through line from St. Louis to St. Paul mentioned above. The Burlington later sold its interest in the BCR&N to the Rock Island.

Brief mention should be made of the so-called River Roads episode culminating in more unified Burlington management. The trouble arose from questionable construction contracts and irregular financing of two lines along the Mississippi River. Both were based in Dubuque. One went north to the Minnesota line; the other south to Clinton. They both were built by Joy and his associates with the financial support of the Burlington. The outcome was a disastrous receivership of the River Roads in 1875. Subsequently reorganized, they were bought by the Milwaukee Road in 1880.

Meanwhile, Joy had been dropped from the Burlington's directorate.

Forbes, determined to tighten the reins of management, headed the road for a three-year period. After that he had a man selected for his job, and that man was Perkins.

PERKINS — MAN FROM BURLINGTON

Prior to his becoming president, Perkins had been described as the Burlington's strongman of the West; Forbes the strongman of the East. After that, Charles Elliott Perkins alone was the road's strongman. Forbes, who gave up the presidency in favor of Perkins in 1881, was active, however, in the road's affairs, but his role was like that of an elder statesman. Perkins was at the helm, sure of himself, of his railroad, and of the road's future. In fact, he more than any other man made the Burlington one of the leading railroads in the West and in the nation.

The year 1881 was one of continued instability in Burlington territory. Jay Gould was at the height of his power. He has been aptly described by Julius Grodinsky, his biographer, as a "competitive bull thrown into the stabilized china shops." Always a trader, he "obtained results on one property by exploiting another."

The Burlington needed a strongman to do battle with the crafty, unprincipled, and piratical "Wizard of Wall Street." Physically a weakling, Gould was nevertheless a mental giant. Perkins complained bitterly that "Gould moves so rapidly it is impossible to keep up with him. . . ." And well might Perkins complain, for Gould tried to checkmate the Burlington at every turn.

During the mid-1870s Gould bought heavily into the Union Pacific and soon had working control. After that he used the UP to harass the Burlington at every opportunity. He tried to break up the Iowa Pool, formed by the Burlington, North Western, and Rock Island railroads to stabilize trans-Iowa rate-making. Failing in this, he sought to control the Council Bluffs–Kansas City road and shunt traffic to and from the UP across Missouri instead of Iowa. Thwarted again, the quick-acting Gould turned to the Hannibal & St. Joseph. He had been buying into that road and now had enough stock to control its policies. In the meantime he had corralled the much larger Wabash and Missouri Pacific systems. The upshot was new and cutthroat competition for the Burlington, not only across Missouri but over much of the Midwest.

Gould's getting the "St. Joe" hurt Perkins the most because it severed the Burlington's best route to St. Joseph and Kansas City. It infuriated Perkins, for he long regarded the H&StJ as basic to the Burlington system.

Worse still, Gould planned forthwith to invade the Burlington's territory in Iowa. He achieved this end in purchasing the Missouri, Iowa & Nebraska Railway from under the nose of Perkins. The MI&N, headed by General Francis M. Drake, ran from Alexandria, Missouri, west and northwest to the Iowa border near Sedan, thence through Centerville and Humeston to Van Wert. Chartered in Missouri in 1857 as the Alexandria & Bloomfield, it had a succession of names and mishaps before it became the MI&N. By 1880 the entire 142-mile line was in operation.

Gould now proceeded to extend the MI&N toward Council Bluffs. If completed to that destination, it would make a through line, in conjunction with the Wabash and affiliated properties, from Toledo and Chicago to the Council Bluffs–Omaha gateway. Perkins countered by organizing his own company to parallel that of Gould's. Both parties bought right-of-way and did considerable grading. Finally, an agreement was reached for a jointly owned road which would terminate at Shenandoah. The line was completed in 1882 under the name of the Humeston & Shenandoah Railroad.

The inroads of Gould also prompted Perkins to lease the Chicago, Burlington & Kansas City Railway in 1881. At that time the road went from Viele, on the Mississippi River, west and southwest through Bloomfield and Moulton to the Missouri state line near Cincinnati, Iowa. From the latter hamlet it continued south into Missouri through Unionville to Laclede. The two-state property totaled 146 miles, not including trackage rights over the Wabash between Bloomfield and Moulton and over a Burlington affiliate from Viele to Burlington. Generally known as the Burlington & Southwestern, its antecedents went back to the Iowa & Missouri State Line Railroad in 1859. Perkins intended to extend the line on to Kansas City to compete with the Gould roads. With Burlington money, the company had reached Carrollton, Missouri, in 1885, when the collapse of the Gould empire made further construction unnecessary.

Gould's invasions of the "Q" territory had much to do with the plethora of branches jutting from the main line in Iowa down to points on the Council Bluffs–Kansas City road. All these provided alternative Chicago–Kansas City routings now that the "St. Joe" was in enemy hands. Excluding the Red Oak–Hamburg line, completed before Gould came on the scene, most of the branches seem to have been built to ward off the "Railroad Wrecker" or other competition.

The first (going eastward) was from Villisca to Corning, Missouri, via Northboro. When the Iowa segment was finished in 1882, its Missouri counterpart had come up the Tarkio Valley to meet it.

A little farther to the east the same situation obtained. Here a branch went from Clarinda down to Bigelow, Missouri, through Burlington Junction, Missouri. That part north from Burlington Junction opened for traffic in 1879. Next year the southern section was constructed up through the Nodaway Valley to make it a through line.

A third route, connecting Creston with Amazonia, Missouri, via Hopkins, Missouri, was an earlier pre-Gould undertaking, being spiked down in 1872.

Finally, the last branch in the category began halfway across Iowa at Chariton. It went in a southwesterly course through Leon, thence down to the Missouri towns of Bethany and Albany, reaching the latter in 1881. Here it met an independent narrow-gauge road which had been built up from St. Joseph in 1879. Probably to strengthen its position against Gould encroachments, the Burlington leased the slim-gauge property in 1885 and widened it to standard the same year.

With the exception of the narrow gauge, it should be noted that all these extensions from the south were built under the auspices of the Council Bluffs–Kansas City road, controlled by the Burlington. Had it not been for the obstreperous Gould, probably two-fifths of these branches would never have been completed to their ultimate destination.

During Perkins's tenure as president, from 1881 to 1901, the following branch lines were completed by the Burlington in Iowa:

Clarinda, College Springs and South Western RR
    Clarinda-Northboro, 15 mi.; 1881–1882
Humeston and Shenandoah RR
    Van Wert–Shenandoah, 95 mi.; 1881–1882
Leon, Mount Ayr and Southwestern RR
    Bethany Junction (Togo)–Albany, Mo., 46 mi.; 1880–1881
Western Iowa RR
    Fontanelle-Cumberland, 20 mi.; 1884–1885

Under Perkins's steadying hand the Burlington moved forward in many directions. Rather than temporize with Gould any longer, Perkins ordered the "Q's" rails westward to Denver. In 1882, after less than a year in building, the road entered the mile-high city.

During Perkins's administration Postmaster General Walter Gresham queried several western roads about putting on a special mail train between Chicago and Council Bluffs. He wanted a connection for mail arriving from New York so that it could be hurried to Council Bluffs in time for early evening departure for California. The first road Gresham contacted turned him down flat; the second wanted a substantial bonus; and the third—well, that was the Burlington. Vice President Thomas Potter agreed to the proposition with no strings, no subsidy—just an exclusive mail contract. When asked when such a train would be ready, Potter promptly replied, "Tomorrow morning, General."

Thus began the first run of the famed Fast Mail on March 11, 1884. It pulled out of Chicago at 3 A.M. with a car of mail from New York, a baggage car filled with local papers, and a special coach for the postmaster and his party and Tom Potter. It reached Burlington at 7:40 A.M., having made the 205-mile run, including five stops, at an average speed of nearly forty-four miles an hour. Then like a jackrabbit it sped across Iowa, arriving in Council Bluffs on time!

Charles Perkins for some time eyed the rapidly growing Twin Cities, generally regarded as Milwaukee Road territory. He prodded John Murray Forbes and was given the nod from Boston to build up to St. Paul. A separate company was formed with the backing of the Burlington, and the road reached the Twin Cities in 1886. An important by-product for Iowa resulted; it put the "Q" back in Dubuque for keeps. With trackage rights over the Illinois Central from East Dubuque, Illinois, to Dubuque, that thriving city was reached under more auspicious circumstances. The River Roads fiasco had irked Perkins. He made sure while he headed the railroad that it had no direct or indirect association with off-color financing. A man of great personal integrity, that policy carried over into all his business dealings.

Putting the "Q" into the Twin Cities, however, angered the Milwaukee. They in turn retaliated by building to Kansas City. Fortunately, Perkins had regained the Hannibal & St. Joseph from the Gould interests, and the Burlington was in a better position to meet the new competition.

During the summers of 1886 and 1887 the road aided in the technology of railroading by fostering air-brake tests on its West Burlington hill. George Westinghouse had already invented the remarkable "triple-value," which sets the brakes by releasing the air. Hence, if a train parted, the brakes would automatically be applied. This device, while satisfactory for passenger trains, was not well adapted for heavy freights. So exhaustive tests were made; and in the fullness of time an improved heavy-duty triple-value evolved, thanks largely to the testing in Iowa.

The year 1888 was memorable because of the great Burlington strike. The conflict, among other things, stemmed from the fact that enginemen were paid on a trip basis, the main line runs being more lucrative than the branches. This practice the men deemed unfair, and they pressed for uniform mileage pay. One thing led to another. The fact that Vice President Thomas J. Potter, who was highly respected by men and management, resigned to go with the Union Pacific did not help matters. His place was taken by Henry B. Stone, an able and honest man but unfortunately more aloof and impersonal than the genial Potter. As a consequence, the men struck all over the system.

At the height of the walkout Governor William Larrabee of Iowa urged Perkins to arbitrate. Perkins, however, was against arbitration on principle and backed Stone on management's position. Pinkerton detectives were called in to protect company property and nonstrikers hired to operate trains. After much violence and some bloodshed the strike finally petered out. In the end the railroad "won," but it caused hard feelings and bitterness for a long time thereafter.

Also in 1888 the road completed its high bridge across the Missouri River between Payne and Nebraska City, Nebraska, at a cost of half a million dollars. Prior to that the Plattsmouth bridge, built in 1880, was the Burlington's only structure crossing the Big Muddy. Incidentally, the Plattsmouth span had the distinction of being the second steel railway bridge in America, the steel employed being made by the Hay process, an invention of Abram Tuston Hay of the Burlington.

The last major extension made by Perkins was northwest to Billings, Montana, which the Burlington reached in 1894. Here the "Q" met the Northern Pacific and in conjunction with it formed a new transcontinental line.

During Perkins's administration three relatively unimportant Iowa roads were leased or controlled, all of which curiously enough began as narrow-gauge lines. The earliest to come under the Burlington's protective wing began in the city of Burlington itself. This was the Burlington & Western, which left town by trackage rights (and another rail for it was of three-foot gauge) over the standard-gauge Burlington, Cedar Rapids & Northern to Mediapolis. From the latter point it ran over its own iron through Winfield to Washington, a distance of thirty-seven miles. At the time of completion in 1880 it operated under the name of the Burlington & Northwestern.

Probably to keep rival lines from picking it up, the Chicago, Burlington & Quincy got control and extended the road from Winfield to Oskaloosa by the end of 1883. In going to "Osky" it met the Iowa Central's construction crews at Brighton. Both roads raced each other to the crossing, and a pitched battled ensued in the classic tradition of early-day railroading. In the end, after pulling up each other's crossing frogs, a truce was signed and the crossing permitted to stand. The Oskaloosa extension went under the label of the Burlington & Western, which absorbed its predecessor.

The second slim-gauger was the Chicago, Ft. Madison & Des Moines Railroad. Organized in 1871 as the Fort Madison, Oskaloosa & Northeastern, it underwent another name-change before constructing from Fort Madison to Collett in 1884. Under the banner of the CFtM&DM, it was widened to standard gauge in 1891. The next year the road was extended through Batavia to Ottumwa. In 1900 the seventy-one-mile property was leased by the Burlington. Shortly thereafter the Batavia-Ottumwa segment, which paralleled the main line of the "Q," was abandoned.

Finally, the last three-foot-gauge carrier to be acquired under Perkins went from the state capital to Osceola. Appropriately called the Des Moines, Osceola & Southern, it began life in 1879 and was completed three years afterward. An extension from Osceola via Leon to coal mines in Cainsville, Missouri, brought the total length to 111 miles by 1884. Following a foreclosure, a name-change, and a gauge-change, the road emerged as the Des Moines & Kansas City Railroad, four feet, eight and one-half inches wide. It was known as the "Blue Grass Route of Iowa."

More financial legerdemain ensued; and that road, along with Gould's earlier Missouri, Iowa & Nebraska, came under the umbrella of the Keokuk & Western. (When the Gould empire collapsed in 1884, the MI&N went down with it. Out of the chaos emerged the Keokuk & Western.) Then at long last the Burlington in 1900 leased the K&W, making for order and stability.

Under Perkins's presidency the Burlington grew from a 2,924-mile road to a major western trunk line embracing 7,992 miles. He became a symbol of the railroad. Whereas most of his predecessors had other interests not associated with their executive responsibilities, Perkins was first, last, and always a professional railroader. His life was the Burlington, and the Burlington was his life. He frowned upon divided responsibilities. Then, again, as we have seen, he was scrupulously honest in all his dealings. He despised the policies of Jay Gould and the way the Union Pacific was run during Gould's overlordship. In this connection he disdainfully observed: ". . . two generations of speculators have grown rich out of it [UP]—one out of the construction and another out of the profits of operating the Road."

Aggressive and a tireless fighter if provoked, Perkins was above all a strategist. As the writer Frank H. Spearman put it:

> The Burlington management has always been characterized by astuteness, and its people have cultivated the art of making friends.

Mr. Perkins, who made that wonderful road what it is, never liked to have enemies or trouble. His motto was, briefly, "eighty per cent of the business and peace. . . ."

On the other hand, Perkins was extremely modest as a person and shunned publicity. He, from all available accounts, never made a speech. If it were not for his voluminous correspondence, many of these policies and ideas would have been lost to posterity. Fortunately, he left about fifty thousand letters and some fifty copies of memoranda outlining his managerial policies, objectives, and philosophy. One finds, for example, a thirty-page text on railroad administration directed to Vice President Thomas J. Potter and files of letters probably averaging two a week to John Murray Forbes. Nearly all of them were addressed to the Boston financier as "Mr.," very rarely as "Cousin John."

Basically conservative in his views on labor, legislation, and welfare, he differed little from the average executive of his day. While he adjudged the Interstate Commerce Act as "wrong in principle" and feared regulation would be a step toward government operation, which would be "the sum of all folly not to say wickedness," he could also postulate, "It is well to bear in mind that most of the improvements to which the world largely owes its progress have been opposed in the beginning by the most level headed men, level headed men being naturally conservative."

In railroad stewardship Perkins showed great courage, never avoiding responsibility and occasionally advocating bold policies far in advance of his time. During one of his bouts with Gould he advised taking over the Santa Fe to strengthen the Burlington's position. But "Cousin John" reneged. Perhaps if Perkins had gotten the financial backing from Boston it might have drastically altered the course of western railroad development.

The grand old man of the Burlington resigned from the presidency in 1901. All during his term as chief executive he had put "Burlington, Iowa," opposite his name in the annual reports, and to that city he retired. He died in 1907. An appropriate monument to him stands alongside the tracks today on West Burlington hill.

THE HILL REGIME

In the late 1890s James J. Hill, seeking a Chicago outlet for his St. Paul–based Great Northern, determined to acquire the Burlington. The "Empire Builder" had the GN and the Hill-controlled Northern Pacific secretly buy into the "Q." Meanwhile, E. H. Harriman wanted the Burlington to achieve the same purpose for his Union Pacific. In order to do this Harriman tried to buy the NP and thereby get half interest in the Burlington. The outcome was a titanic struggle between the two giants of American railroading. Northern Pacific stock zoomed upward, and on May 9, 1901, during the peak of the battle, it reached $1,000 a share. In the end, Hill won.

Now firmly in control, Jim Hill dictated the Burlington's policies. Apart from being a director or on the executive committee, Hill never held an office on the CB&Q. But whatever he controlled he managed. So for the rest of his life the ex-Canadian was "boss." Top management was accountable to him at all times, and not infrequently Hill brought in the men he wanted for key positions.

With the resignation of Charles E. Perkins as president, George B. Harris, his right-hand man, took over that post in 1901. Harris ably held that office for a decade. When he in turn retired, Jim Hill saw to it that Darius Miller was made president in 1910. It was Hill who had brought Miller from the Michigan Central to the Great Northern as vice president and later had shifted him to the same post on the Burlington in 1902. Known as Darius the Silent, Miller generally listened quietly in conferences before giving his opinion.

After Miller's sudden death in 1914, Hale Holden, formerly vice president and head of the road's legal department, took his place.

During Hill's regime the Burlington was known for its galaxy of managerial talent. Indeed, the road became widely acknowledged as a training school for railway executives. On the Hill team was a series of vice presidents who went on to achieve fame elsewhere. The first was Howard Elliott, vice president under Harris, who left the road in 1904 to assume the presidency of the Northern Pacific and still later the New Haven.

James J. Hill thereupon brought in Daniel Willard from the vice presidency of the Erie to a similar post on the "Q." Willard is remembered for having advocated the use of the Prairie-type locomotive (2-6-2) and track modernization. "Uncle Dan," as he was later affectionately called, left the Burlington after a six-year stint to rehabilitate the Baltimore & Ohio. Since Hill was not the easiest man to work for, Willard no doubt reasoned he would have more freedom on the B&O. Willard's job then went to Harry E. Byram; and the latter in turn, a few years afterward, departed for the top position on the Milwaukee.

Even before Hill's stewardship of the Burlington, the road's alumni had been impressive. Robert Harris, president in the late 1870s, subsequently held a like post on the Northern Pacific. More than any other road, however, the Santa Fe recruited its top echelon from the Burlington. In this category fell William B. Strong and Edward P. Ripley. Before "graduating" from the "Q," Strong had been general superintendent in the 1870s and Ripley vice president late in the next decade. To this list may be added the name of W. C. Brown, superintendent of the Iowa lines in the 1880s. He, several decades later, became president of the New York Central.

The Hill years of the Burlington were years of great expansion, although almost entirely outside of Iowa. An exception was the building of the Iowa & St. Louis Railway from 1901 to 1903. This fifty-two-mile feeder went from Sedan to Elmer, Missouri, where it tapped coal mines. Upon completion in 1903, it was leased by the Burlington. (The road also had a short branch from Centerville to Sedan, which was abandoned in 1903.)

That same year the Burlington & Western was extended from Oskaloosa to Tracy—thirteen miles. Built to standard gauge, it met the Albia–Des Moines branch at Tracy. Meanwhile, the entire B&W had been widened from narrow to standard gauge, and it was bought by the Burlington in 1903.

Apart from construction, the "Q" in collaboration with the Milwaukee Road jointly leased the Davenport, Rock Island & Northwestern in 1901. The forty-one-mile short line had its own bridge crossing the Mississippi between Rock Island and Davenport, with tracks extending along the Iowa bank of the river up to Clinton. It gave access to many industries in the area not hitherto accessible to the Burlington.

Outside of Iowa important developments were afoot, for Hill was desirous of promoting a new short route from Billings to the Gulf of Mexico. He unceasingly strove for a better traffic balance. With such a line he could ship goods from the Orient and lumber from the Northwest directly to the Gulf. From there it would go on to eastern cities by water. In the reverse direction, manufactured goods from the East and the Gulf area would flow readily to the Pacific Northwest.

To implement this plan he had the Burlington construct a new line from western Nebraska to Billings by way of Casper and the Wind River Canyon. In conjunction with this project, the Burlington acquired the Colorado & Southern in 1908. With some additional construction and trackage rights, the "Q" now had a new direct route from Billings to Houston via Casper, Denver, and Fort Worth.

Meantime, the Burlington, as always, was intent on developing the territory it served. One aspect of this purpose in Iowa was the operation of a Silo Train, calling at forty-two towns in the state during 1913. Agents on the train made talks concerning the proper storage of corn and distributed thousands of pamphlets urging construction of silos. A "Dairy Special" was likewise run during February 1914, visiting twenty-four Iowa locales in the interest of better dairying.

The Hill regime gave employment to Harry Bedwell, a young man from Kellerton, near Mount Ayr in southwestern Iowa. He lived on the longer line of the loop connecting Giles with Albany Junction, Missouri. (The loop was in the middle of the extensive Chariton–St. Joseph branch.) When the little local trains paused at his village, they spelled adventure and romance to country-bred Harry. He was soon helping around the depot in return for being taught "Morse" by the friendly agent. Upon mastering "the key," he fudged his age a bit and got a job as operator at Andover, Missouri, a tiny station on the other side of the loop. Later he pounded brass as re-lief operator on branch lines in Iowa and Missouri as well as on the "high iron" between St. Joseph and Council Bluffs. Having gotten a "good going over" on the Burlington, the young "lightning slinger" lit out for the West to become an "op" on the Rio Grande, Southern Pacific, and Pacific Electric railroads.

All this time the itinerant railroader was committing to paper his experiences and those of his fellows. Bedwell's first significant article, an autobiographical account of "The Mistakes of a Young Railroad Telegraph Operator," ran as a two-part serial in the *American Magazine* for November–December 1909. Throughout the years he wrote thirty-five stories for *Railroad Magazine* and its predecessors and had fictional tales in ten issues of the *Saturday Evening Post* as well. Some of these yarns were woven into a novel called *The Boomer* (1942). He died in 1955, but his remarkable and authentic short stories continue to appear in anthologies. Harry Bedwell, last of the great railroad storytellers, was at his best in portraying the colorful "boomer" of yesterday, when steam was king and railroading more of an adventure than a science.

WAR AND THE POSTWAR ERA

James J. Hill died in 1916, and his place on the Burlington directorate was filled by the "Empire Builder's" understudy—Ralph Budd. This Iowa-born railroader later carried out many of Hill's policies, and he in due time would head the "Q." In the meantime, war clouds were on the horizon. Then, on that fateful Good Friday, April 6, 1917, the United States declared war on the Central Powers. Just before the end of the year the nation took over the railroads.

In the shake-up during federal control, Hale Holden was called upon to be a regional director. Thereupon Charles E. Perkins, Jr., became president of the corporation for the duration. Son of the former president, thirty-seven-year-old Perkins was born in Burlington. Educated at Harvard, he had been a director of the "Q" since 1914 and was familiar with its policies.

Fortunately, during 1917 the West Burlington locomotive repair and machine shops were rebuilt. Completed in 1883, these facilities had become inadequate to meet the demands of the larger engines rapidly coming into use. After modernization, however, they were able to cope with newer motive power, already hard-pressed to expedite the greatly expanding wartime railroad traffic.

With the armistice signed on November 11, 1918, and the subsequent return of the railroads to their owners, Holden resumed his role as chief executive of the Burlington. During this time the old Adams Express was replaced by the American Railway Express Company.

The postwar years again brought up the plan envisioned by Hill to consolidate the Burlington, Great Northern, and Northern Pacific into one unified, compact system. This giant corporation would be called the Great Northern Pacific. Hearings were held over the years. Finally, early in 1930 the ICC gave its official approval for the two Northerns to merge. But in doing so the commission specified that the Burlington be divorced from control by the Northerns. It meant, in effect, the cornerstone of the new "house" would be left out. Management felt that such a plan without the strategic Burlington would not be desirable, and the matter was reluctantly dropped.

For the most part traffic held up fairly well during the postbellum decade, except for passengers. Better highways, more automobiles, and the rise of the motor bus took their toll, especially of short-haul riders. To combat this declining patronage and still provide passenger service, the Burlington made widespread use of rail motor cars. At first they were of mechanical transmission, but with the perfection of gasoline-electric propulsion the latter soon predominated. In 1928, for example, the road acquired thirty-one "gas-electrics," principally for branch-line use, in a valiant effort to reduce expenses. With the traditional steam power, a minimum of five men was required; whereas the "doodlebugs," as the motor units were dubbed, needed only a three-man crew.

On the twenty branch lines in Iowa, some of which spilled over into Missouri, ten made use of the motor units by 1929. Usually supplanting steam passenger trains, they in some instances merely supplemented the steamers. Occasionally mixed trains and even freights provided an additional service of sorts.

On the Shenandoah branch a motor unit traversed the 244-mile run in slightly under ten hours, making thirty-seven stops en route. The little train, which left Keokuk and thence dipped down to Alexandria, Missouri, went west by northwest through Missouri and Iowa to its Shenandoah destination. It made a twenty-minute lunch stop at Sedan. Its counterpart, leaving Shenandoah on the eastward run, took a little longer, due in part to a half-hour meal stop at Clarinda.

A few lightly traveled branches, such as between Keokuk and Mount Pleasant, the two stub lines out of Hastings, and the nineteen-mile Red Oak–Griswold feeder, had by this time degenerated to mixed-train service only.

The year 1929, better remembered for the stock market crash, saw a new man at the helm. Hale Holden had left the road, in the traditional Burlington manner, to become chairman of the executive committee of the Southern Pacific. His place was filled by Frederick E. Williamson, formerly vice president, who came to the "Q" from a similar position on the Northern Pacific.

After the Wall Street debacle traffic began to decline, and a sharp falling off continued for the duration of the depression. That tragic year, too, marked a relatively high point in passenger miles, although not in riders. It forms a suitable benchmark from which to take a look at the overall picture of Burlington passenger service.

The road's "candy" train was its Overland Express, with through sleepers from Chicago to San Francisco (Oakland) via Omaha, Denver, and Salt Lake City. Also between its headlight and markers were an observation-lounge, a diner, plus a full assortment of chair cars and coaches. It operated over the Rio Grande west of Denver and the Western Pacific beyond Salt Lake City. This was in the days before the Rio Grande went "through the Rockies, not around them" with its Dotsero Cutoff. As a result, the Overland had to detour south from Denver to Pueblo before heading west. Scenicwise the ride was "tops," but in elapsed time it could not compete with the much shorter Union Pacific–Southern Pacific route.

On the Burlington one left Chicago at 11:30 P.M.; and, what with an hour layover in Denver plus a nearly two-hour rendezvous in Salt Lake City, the train pulled into the Oakland Mole at 4:20 P.M., four days later. Actually the scenic sojourn took three full days plus the better part of a fourth. Commercial travelers in particular would fortify themselves for the long jaunt. It was waggishly observed that when one found four drummers in the cars one usually found "a fifth."

In comparison with the Overland's figurative "dogtrot" across Iowa, the schedules of the Colorado Limited and the Chicago Nebraska Limited were more of a sprint. The former train linked Chicago and Denver and the latter Chicago and Lincoln. Both trains, of course, went across Iowa from Burlington to Council Bluffs. They had the usual make-up of Pullmans, diners, coaches, and chair cars, plus an observation-lounge unit, the latter being described as "a palatial rear car." The Nebraska train also trundled a Peoria-Lincoln sleeper, which it picked up from a connecting local at Galesburg.

The 1929 timecard shows only one through train using the Plattsmouth, Nebraska, bridge in crossing the Missouri River. This was No. 4, a plodding accommodation, leaving Omaha at 9:35 A.M. and stopping everywhere before pulling into the Windy City's Union Station at 10:55 A.M. the next day. In crossing Iowa it made exactly forty-nine stops, only a few of which were on flag! Leaving the state, it gained more stature with a Chicago sleeper picked up in Burlington. The sleeper had come up on a connecting train from Keokuk.

The Burlington, in addition, had fairly good trains north and south through Iowa. Best of the lot was the Twin Cities Limited northbound and its southern counterpart, the St. Louis Limited. They shuttled between St. Louis and St. Paul–Minneapolis via Keokuk, Fort Madison, and Burlington. North of Burlington was the responsibility of the Rock Island.

In the western part of the state there were more and better trains on the line running south from Council Bluffs to St. Joseph. Over this route came sections of the Overland Express and the Colorado Limited from St. Louis with cars designed for sleeping, eating, lounging, and just "sitting up."

To make the record complete, the "Q" had shuttle service from Dubuque to East Dubuque, Illinois, connecting with all Chicago–Twin City limiteds. On the western border the Burlington came in from Nebraska to Sioux City over trackage rights on the North Western.

The depression was in full swing when Frederick Williamson resigned at the end of 1931 to head the New York Central, where his railroad career had started. Thereupon Ralph Budd was given a dual title: director and president.

BUDD — MASTER RAILROADER

Ralph Budd was born on a farm near Waterloo on August 20, 1879. He was one of six children, three boys and three girls. Being patient and gentle by nature, Budd was usually given the chore of coaxing the young cows into being milked. When he was thirteen the Budds moved to Des Moines, and it was there he went to high school. Meanwhile, his older brother, John, had graduated from Highland Park College in Des Moines as a civil engineer.

Ralph often helped John in surveying locally, and he regularly attended lectures at Highland Park College while still in high school. An aptitude for mathematics plus a strong interest in engineering aided him in combining high school and college in six years. Even before graduating he was enthralled by his older brother's tales of railroad building in Iowa, Nebraska, and Wyoming.

Upon getting a degree in civil engineering, Ralph persuaded the Chicago Great Western to take him on as a draftsman. Later he went out on the line and helped ballast track and relay rail between Des Moines and Oelwein. Rapid advancement on the CGW led to an even better job with the Rock Island. By 1903 he became the first division engineer of the latter road, then building between St. Louis and Kansas City. On the Rock Island he met Vice President John F. Stevens, an outstanding engineer of his time. Stevens took a liking to young Budd and observed how competently he worked. As a result, when Stevens was later appointed chief engineer of the Panama Canal, he sent for Budd to help rehabilitate the railway across the isthmus. Thereupon Budd went from Iowa to Panama to "railroad" in the tropics. When Stevens left, Budd continued under his successor, Major George W. Goethals.

In the interim Stevens was back in the States working for James J. Hill. The "Empire Builder" was projecting his Oregon Trunk Line into central Oregon to give the Hill roads access to that area. Stevens needed a capable assistant, and he again sought Ralph Budd. Heeding his former chief's call, the Hawkeye engineer left Panama to take up reconnaissance work in Oregon. He subsequently became chief engineer of the Oregon Trunk and soon afterward of the Hill-controlled Spokane, Portland & Seattle.

In the course of his work Budd met the shaggy-bearded Hill, then past seventy but as alert and domineering as ever. Jim Hill, likewise, was much impressed by Budd's ability, not to say his amiable disposition and modesty. The result was that late in 1912 Hill called Budd to St. Paul as assistant to the president of the Great Northern. Thereafter the rail magnate took a personal interest in his thirty-three-year-old appointee. Soon Budd became chief engineer of the GN and a confidant of the man who dominated its management.

James J. Hill was a hard taskmaster, yet Budd met his exacting requirements and pleased the old man. Hill could be severe, arbitrary, and almost ruthless at times, but there was also a lighter, more human side of his nature.

A former GN employee tells of an occasion when Budd, then chief engineer of the road, was discussing a matter of policy with Hill. The engineer held one point of view, the railroad tycoon another. Lunchtime came, and an attendant brought in some sandwiches, milk, and beer. In observing the latter, Hill remarked with a twinkle in his one good eye, "Ah, Anheuser-Busch to make Budd wiser."

But Hill never seriously doubted the wisdom of his talented protégé. In fact, he was all the time grooming Ralph Budd for the top job. Moreover, he ordained that when a new president was needed the opening would go to Budd. The time came in 1919, three years after Hill's death. Then, as Richard Overton expressed it, "Budd inherited the office and responsibilities of the Empire Builder."

When Budd came to the Burlington in 1932 after his Great Northern stewardship, he came to head a road which was bigger, hauled vastly more tonnage, and earned substantially more revenue than the "Big G." The CB&Q, with its affiliated Colorado and Southern and Fort Worth and Denver City lines, had a combined mileage of 11,314.

All during the depression the Burlington had made a better showing than its two "parents," the Great Northern and the Northern Pacific. In fact, the parents' "interest" in the "Q" had helped the two Northerns remain solvent during the lean years of bank closings, business failures, and mortgage foreclosures. In Iowa nearly all of its railroads sought the protection of the courts. Among them were the Milwaukee, Rock Island, North Western, Great Western—but never the Burlington. Even so, things were far from rosy on the big Granger Road. In the month that Budd took office (January 1932) the net railway operating income had slipped 72 percent in comparison with the same month of the previous year.

Budd trimmed costs by reducing the operating divisions from seventeen to eleven. On the positive side, he sought more traffic. For one thing, he felt the Burlington was not getting its share of transcontinental tonnage. True, the "Q" interchanged with the friendly Rio Grande at Denver, which in turn connected with both the Western Pacific and the Southern Pacific at Salt Lake City for the West Coast. But the Rio Grande, as we have seen, went south to Colorado Springs and Pueblo before it headed west. It interchanged with the Rock Island at the Springs and the Missouri Pacific at Pueblo. Inasmuch as the Rio Grande received the same rate for through traffic from all these gateways, it naturally favored Pueblo first, Colorado Springs second, and Denver last. The reasoning behind this was, of course, to reduce the length of haul for the same rate of pay. So, in the eyes of the Rio Grande's traffic men, the "Mopac" was their fair-haired connection, with the Rock Island second in favor, and the Burlington a poor third.

Budd studied the matter. He looked at the map. Yes, there was a way out. A railroad called the Denver and Salt Lake had completed the remarkable 6-mile Moffat Tunnel through the Rockies on its line going west from Denver. It terminated at a small community named Craig but on the way went only 40 miles from the Rio Grande's main line. By building a cutoff one could, as if by magic, shorten the Rio Grande's main stem from Denver to the west by 175 miles. Furthermore, the proposed line would have better grades than the roundabout route through Pueblo.

The Iowa railroader carefully planned his strategy. He discussed the matter with his friend Arthur Curtiss James, the power behind the Western Pacific and a Burlington director of long standing. James was amenable. On the other hand, James thought the Rio Grande was doing a fairly good job in keeping up its main line and was reluctant to intercede. Budd clinched his support when he said, "I've learned that one party in such a deal can stop improvement work, but it takes two of them to go ahead and do it."

James quickly grasped the idea. Work soon began on the project, and in 1934 the Dotsero Cutoff was completed. In a few years the "Q" quadrupled its transcontinental tonnage through Denver. Formerly that gateway ranked only sixth as an interchange point on the system, but within a decade it moved up to third, being exceeded only by Chicago and Kansas City. Later the cutoff was of tremendous importance in handling unprecedented traffic occasioned by World War II.

Even before America entered the conflict Ralph Budd was active in expediting defense traffic on a national scale. Appointed commissioner of transportation by President Franklin D. Roosevelt in May 1940, he was soon shuttling between Chicago and Washington.

From the date of Pearl Harbor, December 7, 1941, until the end of 1946, the Burlington hauled 3,526,151 military personnel in 11,591 special trains. Another 1,667,176 servicemen were handled on special cars on regular trains. Overton in his *Burlington Route* summed this feat up by saying, ". . . every type of rail transportation smashed records." Budd himself pragmatically declared, "During the war years we at the Burlington did twice as much as we thought we could."

Both the pre- and postwar years were noteworthy for the role the Bur-

lington played in developing the streamlined train and in inaugurating diesel power. Another significant improvement envisioned by Budd was the
construction of a cutoff to shorten the Burlington's route to Kansas City.

Being seventy in 1949, Budd retired from the Burlington, as he himself
had advocated that retirement age for the road's officers. But he continued
on the directorate for another five years. Meanwhile, John M. Budd, president of the Great Northern, was made a director. So it was that father and
son sat on the board.

Apart from railroading, Ralph Budd was a man of many interests and
every inch a scholar. All his life he was an avid reader. It was only natural
for him to serve on the boards of such institutions as St. Paul's James Jerome Hill Reference Library, Chicago's Newberry Library, and its Museum
of Science and Industry. After his "retirement" he was asked to lecture at
Northwestern University. Another invitation came to become chairman
of the Chicago Transit Authority. He chose the latter. During the next five
years he did much to modernize and consolidate the Windy City's urban
transportation facilities. In 1954 Budd moved to Santa Barbara, where he
died in 1962.

WAY OF THE ZEPHYRS

The Zephyr saga goes back to 1933. Its principal actors were a railroad
president, a manufacturer, and an inventor. Ralph Budd sought a fleet of
lightweight internal-combustion trains to reduce expenses and win back
passengers from the highways. (Budd had experience with diesel-electric
power units in building the Cascade Tunnel when he was with the Great
Northern.) He gave Edward G. Budd (no relation) of Philadelphia's Budd
Manufacturing Company carte blanche to build such a unit. And he left it
up to Charles W. ("Boss Ket") Kettering, General Motors vice president of
research, to design the engine. Thus it came about that the two Budds and
Boss Ket evolved America's first diesel-powered streamlined train. It was
outshopped on April 7, 1934, and two days later made a shakedown run
over the Reading Company rails from Philadelphia to Perkiomen Junction, about twenty-five miles.

In the words of David P. Morgan, editor of *Trains*, the creation "was like
nothing else on rails." From slanted nose to rounded solarium-lounge, the
bantamweight, snakelike train tipped the scales at ninety-seven and one-
half tons. The three-unit job was articulated, thereby having only four
trucks instead of the normal six. The lead car, powered by a 600-h.p. diesel generator set, was the "working unit." It also had a Railway Post Office and mail storage compartment. Next came a combination baggage-

express, buffet-grill, and coach unit. Finally, there was the coach and observation-lounge car at the end of the silvery streamliner.

Indirect lighting, pastel shades of pleasing gray and green, silk drapes, air conditioning, carpeted floors, radio reception, and trays for meals while seated made it so far removed from the orthodox day coach or Pullman as to seem almost preposterous on any railroad. Apart from this, it was the first stainless steel train. Unorthodox, new, daring, little wonder Boss Ket characterized Budd, who sparked the idea, as "a very nervy railroad president."

The little streamliner was called Zephyr, the Greek personification of the west wind. Much to the amazement of a Chicago columnist, Budd explained the derivation of the word and nonchalantly quoted a passage from Chaucer's *Canterbury Tales* which he deemed especially appropriate. The Zephyr soon took off on a five-week barnstorming tour of the East before the acid test: a 1,000-mile nonstop run on the "Q."

Budd, for all his modesty and engineering exactness, had a bit of showmanship in his makeup. He and his associates set out to really dramatize the new train. The Zephyr would make a dawn-to-dusk run without a stop from Denver to Chicago where, as a grand climax, it would be on hand for the reopening of the Century of Progress.

Once committed to the idea, Budd never faltered. The day before the run an inspector discovered a cracked armature bearing in one of the Zephyr's traction motors. Mounting tension was temporarily released by an unusual phone call from a Denver newspaper editor. He asked Vice President Edward E. Flynn if he could bring along a Rocky Mountain canary as a gift to the Century of Progress.

"What's a Rocky Mountain canary?" queried Flynn.

"A burro."

"A what?"

"A donkey, a small one."

Flynn was nonplussed. He contacted Budd and received the now-classic reply.

"Why not? One more jackass on the trip won't make any difference!"

That evening Ralph Budd went on the air before a nationwide radio audience and announced, "Tomorrow at dawn we'll be on our way!"

By this time a new armature had been discovered in the UP's Omaha shops, and it was being flown by chartered plane to Denver. It was, however, en route when Budd was at the "mike." In fact, it did not arrive until after midnight.

Scheduled to leave at 4:00 A.M. on May 26, the Zephyr did not get under way until 5:05 A.M. Ahead lay a 1,015.4-mile route. This was less than the regular run, for a shortcut into Iowa was made by using the Plattsmouth bridge instead of going via Omaha and Council Bluffs. As a precaution against accidents, a flagman was stationed at each of the 619 private roads and two men at each of the 1,070 grade crossings. In switch-shanty lingo, "The Zephyr was given the railroad."

Speed was moderate at first so the new bearing would not run hot. Later on the train averaged 90 miles an hour. Then it was revved up to 106.2. Top speed was 112.5 m.p.h. Budd was exultant, as were all the other road's officials on the epoch-making ride, not to say members of the press. But their hopes were soon dashed. A short circuit, caused by a slammed steel door, burned out the engine starter cable. The train slowed down to a mere 15 m.p.h. At this point a courageous mechanic grabbed and held the ends of the wires together, and with a flash the engine started up. The man's hands were burned, but the streamliner did not stop.

Later the prolonged blowing of the horn for crossings reduced the air pressure to where the brakes were automatically set. Again the train was about to halt. A quick-thinking technician, however, jammed the throttle wide open. The motors pulled against the brakes and speeded up the air pumps fast enough to supply more air. The brakes finally released as the streamliner zoomed ahead.

The train dashed across Iowa, going through Burlington like a flash. At 7:10 P.M. the Zephyr broke the timing clock tape at Halstead Street, Chicago, making the run in thirteen hours, four minutes, and fifty-eight seconds. It was a world's record for a nonstop run. Soon afterward the party, including the donkey, rolled onto the stage of the "Wings of a Century" at the Century of Progress Exposition.

The pioneer Zephyr went into revenue service between Kansas City, St. Joseph, Council Bluffs, Omaha, and Lincoln on Armistice Day, 1934. By this time the Union Pacific had two aluminum nondiesel streamliners on the rails. But they were still on tour, thereby making the Burlington's tri-state run the nation's first streamliner in revenue operation.

After that came a rash of lightweight streamliners gliding over the Burlington. The next train of this type in Iowa was the Mark Twain Zephyr. As its name would suggest, the train ran through Samuel Clemens's hometown of Hannibal, Missouri, on its 217-mile run between St. Louis and Burlington. The four-car articulated unit began operation October 28, 1935.

Meanwhile, management was thinking of a genuine long-distance streamliner with full Pullman, dining, and coach facilities. The remarkable

Hudson-type steam locomotive at the head-end of the Aristocrat did a splendid job. With coal and water stops, the Aristocrat took twenty-eight hours and forty minutes to make the Chicago-Denver trip. Could the run be sliced to sixteen hours? Budd and his colleagues thought so. The goal became a reality with the inauguration of the Denver Zephyr on November 8, 1936. Actually, there were two ten-car trains having nonarticulated locomotives, with up to five times the horsepower of the original Zephyr. And they ran the gamut of accommodations, from reclining coach seats to open-berth and private-room sleeping accommodations. (For the record, it may be added that while the deluxe long-distance streamliner was in the process of construction, the original Zephyr equipment was run on the sixteen-hour schedule as a forerunner of what was to come, as well as to protect the mail contract.) Four years after the Denver streamliner went into service, the road put in operation its Ak-Sar-Ben Zephyr between Lincoln and Chicago.

The first north-and-south stream-style train to go from border to border in Iowa was the Zephyr-Rocket, a joint Burlington–Rock Island creation. It entered service between St. Louis and the Twin Cities on January 7, 1941. That part of the run north of Burlington was over the Rock Island.

Iowa had to wait until the end of World War II for more "Q" streamliners. During the summer of 1947 the road put in effect what was a form of commuter Zephyr. Leaving Hannibal, Missouri, at 5:50 A.M. and calling at Quincy, Keokuk, Fort Madison, and Burlington, it gave patrons of the river communities a chance to reach Chicago before noon. Returning, the mini-"lightweight" departed from Union Station at 6:15 P.M. and finished up at Hannibal by 12:40 A.M. Later that year saw the Nebraska Zephyrs gliding across Iowa on their daylight runs between Chicago and Lincoln.

But the road's flagship, "America's most talked about train," was in the works. First, however, some background history. With the formation of a shorter route through the Rockies via the Moffat Tunnel and the opening of San Francisco's Golden Gate International Exposition in 1939, a new travel market beckoned. The one through sleeper on the old Overland, jogging along on its eighty-hour schedule from Chicago to the West Coast, was pitifully inadequate. So the collective heads of the three interested roads, the Burlington, Rio Grande, and Western Pacific, decided to "do something." They came up with the Exposition Flyer on a sixty-hour "transcontinental schedule." Mostly steam powered, it had standard equipment, was air-conditioned, and featured economy meals as low as ninety cents a day. It was popular in peacetime and infinitely more so during the war years. Later on, after the conflict, it boasted of coast-to-coast sleepers. East of Chicago, transcontinental Pullmans were handled to and from Gotham on alternate days via the New York Central's Commodore Vanderbilt and the Pennsylvania's General.

Success of the "Expo" convinced management that the time was ripe for the grandest, most luxurious streamliner to polish the rails of the three component roads. The tab was approximately $15 million. For that money the roads got six eleven-car streamliners. Each train was amply supplied with five of the new Vista Domes. Meals of culinary splendor were made by reservation—no waiting. A pretty and efficient hostess, known as a "Zephyrette," was on beck and call to minster to the travelers' needs. Called the California Zephyr, the train was a success from the start. Time and again the "cz" established new highs in occupancy, and for the first ten-year period it operated at 89.4 percent of capacity.

MIDCENTURY AND AFTER

Ralph Budd's successor was his associate, Harry C. Murphy. Murphy worked closely with Budd in Chicago from the time the latter first came with the Burlington. It made for continuity in management and, incidentally, brought together two men reared in small Iowa towns.

Born in Canton, Illinois, August 27, 1892, Murphy as a child moved with his family to Eldora. He spoke of his youth in that town with affection and found the people much to his liking. Not afraid of work, young Murphy had a variety of part-time jobs while in grade and secondary schools. He also gravitated to the depot, as did many boys, to watch the old Iowa Central trains steam by. Sometimes a friendly engineer would let him ride in the cab of a little American Standard locomotive. Later he worked for the Iowa Central as a laborer and station helper in Eldora.

After graduating from high school, Murphy went to Iowa State College in Ames, where he took up civil and mechanical engineering. Finishing college and still interested in railroading, he got a job as a clerk in the Burlington's Chicago accounting office. Later he switched to the engineering department as a rod and instrument man.

During World War I Murphy served as a pilot in the air force. Upon his discharge from the army in 1919, he returned to the Burlington as assistant engineer at Centralia, Illinois. The next few years found him at various points as division engineer, engineer of maintenance of way, assistant superintendent, and division superintendent. In 1933 he was promoted to executive assistant to the president. Six years later found him assistant vice president of operations, and by 1945 he became operating vice president. With Budd's retirement in 1949, Murphy succeeded to the presidency.

As a line officer prior to becoming chief executive, Harry Murphy had assisted Budd in replacing conventional passenger trains with Zephyrs, in switching from steam to diesel motive power, and in extending Centralized Traffic Control. Murphy's place, by the way, as operating vice president was taken by Samuel L. Fee, who had started his Burlington career as a station helper in Knoxville, Iowa, where he was born.

In 1952 the Kansas City Cutoff was completed, reducing the distance of the Chicago-"KC" line by twenty-two miles. This bit of "super railroad" meant completely rebuilding almost thirty miles of the Carrollton branch. In addition, it called for an entirely new forty-two-mile line to Missouri Junction, where trackage rights on the Wabash were held jointly, to Birmingham, thence over the Burlington rails to Kansas City. Besides being much shorter than the old line, it had far less curvature and only half the ruling grade of the former route. So rugged was the terrain that the track went through a mile-long cut ninety-five feet deep at one point.

Murphy, being very passenger-minded, chalked up another "first" for the Burlington when he put slumber coaches on the new Denver Zephyr in 1956. These cars provided the coach rider with a small room by day and a roomette-type bed for the night, including a built-in toilet. Passengers paid only coach fare plus a nominal charge for the room. Four years later the road reported the highest passenger revenues since 1946.

Freight service perhaps showed even more improvement. In 1962, for example, the road inaugurated a meat train from Omaha to Chicago that took less than ten hours for the 488-mile run. This carding was comparable to the schedule of the Nebraska Zephyr. The train handled a complete line of specialized equipment including standard refrigerator cars, refrigerated trucks, and containers on flatcars. Fresh meat from Omaha reached the East twelve to twenty-four hours earlier.

Murphy, while he was thoroughly committed to diesel power, had a nostalgic fondness for steam. In his wood-paneled office there was a color painting of a powerful Baldwin-built 2-10-4-type locomotive steaming through Thayer, Iowa, along with a signed photo of Ralph Budd and an oil painting of James J. Hill. Furthermore, he endeared himself to railroad buffs by donating a majestic Hudson-type engine (4-6-4) to the City of Burlington along with other cities.

The railroad has always favored its namesake community. When Burlington's depot burned in 1943, a modern fieldstone structure replaced it. The new station was dedicated by Governor Bourke B. Hickenlooper, Mayor Max A. Conrad, and Ralph Budd on March 28, 1944. During the ceremony a large panel on the west wall was featured honoring Charles E. Perkins.

It is significant that the busy West Burlington Shops still give employment to many local people. Originally built on a thousand-acre tract, the facility was opened in 1883. At its peak it employed about sixteen hundred men. The shops had facilities for building freight and passenger cars, along with locomotive repair. Some of the road's finest steam engines were also constructed at West Burlington.

The shops are now considerably smaller due to fewer men needed for diesel repair. While construction and repair of rolling stock, other than locomotive, is currently done elsewhere, West Burlington is the sole facility for heavy diesel repair, with five hundred employees on the payroll.

When Harry Murphy retired in 1965 after fifty-one years of railroading, West Burlington had seen its last steam locomotive. He, next to Budd, had done most to effect this transition.

PRUNING THE BRANCHES

When the Burlington built its branches in Iowa, there were no motor vehicles and modern highways. During the horse-and-buggy era it was desirable to have a plentiful supply of feeders so that any point had a railroad within a day's wagon drive. The automobile and truck changed this. What was formerly an all-day trip for Old Dobbin now took hardly an hour by car. Furthermore, the flexibility and convenience of the motor car made such inroads into branch-line travel that all Iowa passenger trains in this category were discontinued by 1959. The final run of this type was the little motor train shuttling between Creston and St. Joseph.

It was inevitable that some branches faced partial or total abandonment due to changing conditions. A few should never have been built, and others had outlived their usefulness. Again, some sections of a line faced retirement because of track relocation to provide better grades and more efficient operation. Occasionally, floods made rehabilitation of marginal branches unfeasible.

Iowa's first abandonment came in 1889 when the eleven-mile Albia-Moravia stub line quit. It had been constructed as the Albia & Moulton Railway in 1880 to forestall Jay Gould's extending a line from southern Iowa to Des Moines. It served no purpose, for Gould completed his extension anyway, and the Burlington-backed companies died.

The influence of Gould, as we have seen, also led to the extension of the Alexandria, Missouri–Van Wert line another ninety-five miles farther westward to Shenandoah. The addition was never profitable, and most of it was abandoned by 1945. In 1958 the twenty-eight-mile stretch of original line between Centerville and Corydon was likewise scrapped.

Main line relocation between Fairfield and Batavia, nine miles, and between Murray and Creston, twenty-one miles, rendered the pioneer routes in these segments unnecessary, and they were abandoned in 1900 and 1901, respectively. On the Albia–Des Moines branch, completion of the Red Rock Dam made relocation imperative. The Burlington's rails between Swan and Des Moines accordingly were pulled up in 1967, and trackage rights were arranged over the Norfolk & Western from Swan.

Probably the branches most vulnerable to highway competition were the marginal lines originally built to narrow gauge. They were the old Burlington & Western, the Fort Madison–Batavia branch, and the Des Moines–Cainsville, Missouri, line. Most of what was the B&W took the count when the Winfield-Oskaloosa line folded in 1934.

That portion, however, between Coppock and Martinsburg was sold to the Minneapolis & St. Louis, which then bought the thirteen-mile Oskaloosa-Tracy section but later abandoned it.

Thin traffic brought about the retirement of the upper end of the Fort Madison–Batavia branch. First the Batavia-Birmingham section was lopped off, and by 1956 the line was cut back to Stockport. Insufficient tonnage also accounted for the abandonment of most of the Keokuk–Mount Pleasant line in 1932, save the Salem-Hamill portion.

Scrapping of the Des Moines–Cainsville route was due to several factors. To begin with, the entire line was built with curves and grades acceptable for narrow-gauge running but quite unsuitable for modern railroading. Then, coal mines at the Missouri end of the line were worked out. This prompted abandonment of the road south of Osceola in the 1930s. A bad flood in June 1947 severely damaged the road north of Osceola, dooming that section, too. Piecemeal curtailment of service resulted in the whole Des Moines–Osceola portion becoming a memory in 1957. To protect freight service from the state capital to the West, trackage rights were secured over the Chicago Great Western from Des Moines to Talmage on the "Q's" main line.

Other total abandonments included the Sedan–Elmer, Missouri, line in 1936 and the Indianola branch by 1961. The former's demise resulted from unprofitable coal mines in northern Missouri, the latter because of meager traffic. Indianola, however, is still served by the Rock Island road.

Turning again to southeastern Iowa, one finds the long branch extending from Viele to Carrollton, Missouri, partly dismembered. First the Unionville, Missouri–Moulton segment was abandoned early in the 1950s, and by 1969 the remainder of the line in Iowa ceased operation.

Railroad competition, which prompted building of most of the five lines running in a southwesterly direction from the main stem to points on the Missouri River, became economically redundant by the mid-1960s. One by one, parts of four of these failed to earn their keep and were subsequently abandoned. The lower end of the Red Oak–Hamburg branch was cut back to Riverton in 1961 after a washout. The Clarinda–Corning, Missouri, and the Clarinda–Bigelow, Missouri, branches were likewise severed. The former abandonment between Clarinda and Westboro, Missouri, was effective partly in 1958 and the remainder in 1961; the latter, from Clarinda to Skidmore, Missouri, was authorized piecemeal in 1941 and 1961. Finally, the "long side" of the loop of the Chariton–St. Joseph, Missouri, line was separated between Mount Ayr and Grant City, Missouri. This resulted in the "Burlington Formula" of 1944 protecting an employee, in the event of abandonment, from reduction in pay by the use of a displacement allowance.

THE GREATER BURLINGTON

The mid-1960s and thereafter was one of change in top management and in traffic characteristics. Louis W. Menk succeeded Murphy to the presidency in October 1965. Menk, who had headed the St. Louis–San Francisco, remained with the Burlington for only one year when he left to become chief executive of the Northern Pacific. The Burlington's top post then went to William J. Quinn, formerly Milwaukee Road president.

It was evident that the Burlington, along with most of the other railroads in the United States, found passenger trains becoming increasingly unprofitable. What precipitated a crisis, however, was the Postal Department's policy of shifting mail from train to truck and plane. Heretofore many passenger trains just about paid their out-of-pocket costs, thanks to income from carrying first-class mail. The annual report for 1967, for example, laments that in dropping twenty-two Railway Post Office cars, the Burlington suffered a revenue loss of $900,000. The grim fact is that unless it is subsidized, passenger service cannot meet its out-of-pocket costs, much less operate at a profit.

A casualty of the trend from rail to airway and highway was withdrawal of the famed Fast Mail in 1967. This eighty-three-year-old train, renowned in story and song, was a Burlington institution.

One by one the road's proud streamliners operating through Iowa were discontinued, until only the Denver Zephyr, the California Zephyr, the Ak-Sar-Ben Zephyr, and the Nebraska Zephyr remained. The "cz," up for abandonment in 1968, was given a year's reprieve by the ICC, and its future is very much at stake. Similarly, the Burlington has petitioned the ICC for permission to end its Nebraska Zephyr.

From the days when the first trains steamed across Iowa on the old Burlington & Missouri River until the present, however, freight was and is the backbone of the railroad and its main source of income and reason for being. The future of the big Granger Road lies in carload tonnage by the trainload. Time freights now speed across the state on passenger-train carding. Specialized equipment, such as piggybacks hauling trailer trucks on "flats" and tri-level cars toting a dozen automobiles in one unit, bring new traffic formerly considered lost to the highway. Unit trains of one commodity and use of "jumbo" freight cars reduce the unit cost and keep the railroad competitive with truck and barge competition.

Indeed, the road's main stem linking Burlington and Council Bluffs is admirably suited to heavy mass-movement of tonnage. Virtually double-tracked with rail mostly in the 129 to 136 pound (per yard) category, the line has few curves and limited grades. Moreover, the "high iron" is fully protected by either Centralized Traffic Control or automatic block signals.

In concluding the story of the modern Burlington, mention should be made of the proposed merger with the Great Northern, Northern Pacific, and lease of the Spokane, Portland & Seattle. As we have seen, James J. Hill tried to bring the two Northerns into the fold with the Burlington. Again in the late 1920s another attempt was made to consolidate the roads. Finally, during the 1960s the matter was brought up with renewed vigor.

In 1967 the ICC lent its support to the long-sought merger only to have the Justice Department bring it before the Supreme Court, where it should be decided in 1969. In light of several major consolidations already consummated, some of which have similar characteristics to the "greater" Burlington, there is every indication the Northerns and the "Q" will be in one family in 1970.

At first it was decided to call the new twenty-five-thousand-mile railroad the Great Northern Pacific & Burlington. This cumbersome title was later given up in favor of the shorter Burlington Northern. But Iowans, and probably most of the nation, will strive for further brevity. They will call it Burlington. Charles Perkins would have like that, too.

Palimpsest 50 (September 1969)

During the first decade of the twentieth century the Burlington not only installed double track along much of its main line in Iowa, but it also erected several county seat—style brick depots, including this one in Red Oak. H. Roger Grant Collection.

A turning point in intercity railroad service occurred in 1934 with the debut of the Burlington Zephyr. This pamphlet promotes the soon-to-be famous streamline motor train. H. Roger Grant Collection.

While Zephyrs, "America's Distinctive Trains," sped across Iowa, the Burlington was retiring unneeded and unprofitable appendages, including most of its ninety-two-mile Humeston-Clarinda branch line. In 1946 a work crew removes rails in front of the depot at Weldon. H. Roger Grant Collection.

On September 1, 1947, Burlington Train No. 178 heads eastward from Albia on its daily run to Ottumwa from Des Moines. The ninety-two-mile trip was scheduled to take nearly three hours. John Humiston photograph.

In the late 1940s, a first-generation diesel freight set idles in the Burlington's Des Moines yards. George Niles photograph.

SELECTED BIBLIOGRAPHY

Bryant, Keith L. *History of the Atchison, Topeka and Santa Fe Railway.* New York: Macmillian, 1975.

Butts, Albert Parks. *Walter Willson and His Crooked Creek Railroad.* Webster City, Iowa: Fred Hahne Printing Company, 1976.

Carlson, Norman, ed. *Iowa Trolleys.* Chicago: Central Electric Railfans Association, 1975.

Casey, Robert J., and W. A. S. Douglas. *Pioneer Railroad: The Story of the Chicago and North Western System.* New York: Whittlesey House, 1948.

Corliss, Carlton J. *Main Line of Mid America.* New York: Creative Age Press, 1950.

Derleth, August. *The Milwaukee Road: Its First Hundred Years.* New York: Creative Age Press, 1948.

Donovan, Frank P., Jr. *Mileposts on the Prairie: The Story of the Minneapolis & St. Louis Railway.* New York: Simmons-Boardman, 1950.

Grant, H. Roger. *The Corn Belt Route: A History of the Chicago Great Western Railroad Company.* DeKalb: Northern Illinois University Press, 1984.

———. *The North Western: A History of the Chicago & North Western Railway System.* DeKalb: Northern Illinois University Press, 1996.

———. *Railroads in the Heartland: Steam and Traction in the Golden Age of Postcards.* Iowa City: University of Iowa Press, 1997.

Grodinsky, Julius. *The Iowa Pool: A Study in Railroad Competition, 1870–1884.* Chicago: University of Chicago Press, 1950.

———. *Jay Gould: His Business Career, 1867–1892.* Philadelphia: University of Pennsylvania Press, 1957.

Hayes, William Edward. *Iron Road to Empire: The History of 100 Years of the Progress and Achievements of the Rock Island Lines.* New York: Simmons-Boardman, 1953.

Hidy, Ralph W., Muriel E. Hidy, and Roy V. Scott, with Don L. Hofsommer. *The Great Northern Railway: A History.* Cambridge: Harvard Business School, 1988.

Hilton, George W., and John F. Due. *The Electric Interurban Railways in America.* Stanford, Calif.: Stanford University Press, 1960.

Hirshon, Stanley P. *Grenville M. Dodge, Soldier, Politician, Railroad Pioneer.* Bloomington: Indiana University Press, 1967.

Hofsommer, Donovan L. "A Chronology of Iowa Railroads." *Railroad History* (September 1975):70–88.

Johnson, Arthur M., and Barry E. Supple. *Boston Capitalists and Western Railroads: A Study in the Nineteenth-Century Railroad Investment Process.* Cambridge: Harvard University Press, 1967.

Kerr, Duncan J. *The Story of the Great Northern Railway Company—and James J. Hill*. Princeton, N.J.: Princeton University Press, 1939.

Klein, Maury. *The Life and Legend of Jay Gould*. Baltimore: The Johns Hopkins University Press, 1986.

———. *Union Pacific: The Birth of a Railroad, 1862–1893*. Garden City, N.Y.: Doubleday, 1987.

———. *Union Pacific: The Rebirth, 1894–1969*. New York: Doubleday, 1989.

Larson, John Lauritz. *Bonds of Enterprise: John Murray Forbes and Western Development in America's Railway Age*. Cambridge: Harvard Business School, 1984.

Lindsay, Bill, and Brent Maxwell. *The History of the Muscatine North and South Railroad Co.* Burlington, Iowa: privately printed, 1996.

Malone, Michael P. *James J. Hill: Empire Builder of the Northwest*. Norman: University of Oklahoma Press, 1996.

Marshall, James. *Santa Fe: The Railroad That Built an Empire*. New York: Random House, 1945.

Martin, Albro. *James J. Hill and the Opening of the Northwest*. New York: Oxford University Press, 1976.

McMurray, Donald L. *The Great Burlington Strike of 1888: A Case History in Labor Relations*. Cambridge: Harvard University Press, 1956.

Morgan, David P. *Diesels West: The Evolution of Power on the Burlington*. Milwaukee: Kalmbach Publishing, 1963.

Overton, Richard C. *Burlington West: A Colonization History of the Burlington Railroad*. Cambridge: Harvard University Press, 1941.

———. *Burlington Route: A History of the Burlington Lines*. New York: Knopf, 1965.

———. *Perkins/Budd: Railway Statesmen of the Burlington*. Westport, Conn.: Greenwood Press, 1982.

Sage, Leland L. *A History of Iowa*. Ames: Iowa State University Press, 1974.

Saunders, Richard L. *Railroad Mergers and the Coming of Conrail*. Westport, Conn.: Greenwood, 1978.

Scribbins, Jim. *The Hiawatha Story*. Milwaukee: Kalmbach Publishing Company, 1970.

———. *The 400 Story*. Park Forest, Ill.: PTJ Publishing, 1982.

Stover, John F. *History of the Illinois Central Railroad*. New York: Macmillian, 1975.

Stromquist, Shelton. *A Generation of Boomers: The Pattern of Railroad Conflict in Nineteenth-Century America*. Urbana: University of Illinois Press, 1987.

Thompson, William H. *Transportation in Iowa: A Historical Summary*. Ames: Iowa Department of Transportation, 1989.

Tigges, John, and Jon Jacobson. *Milwaukee Road Narrow Gauge*. Boulder, Colo.: Pruett, 1985.

INDEX